China's Industrial Reform

A World Bank Research Publication

[redacted]

China's Industrial Reform

Gene Tidrick and Chen Jiyuan
Editors

Published for The World Bank
Oxford University Press

Oxford University Press

NEW YORK OXFORD LONDON GLASGOW
TORONTO MELBOURNE WELLINGTON HONG KONG
TOKYO KUALA LUMPUR SINGAPORE JAKARTA
DELHI BOMBAY CALCUTTA MADRAS KARACHI
NAIROBI DAR ES SALAAM CAPE TOWN

Manufactured in the United States of America
First printing June 1987

The findings, interpretations, and conclusions
expressed in this study are the results of research supported
by the World Bank, but they are entirely those of the
authors and should not be attributed in any manner to
the World Bank, to its affiliated organizations,
or to members of its Board of Executive Directors
or the countries they represent.

Library of Congress Cataloging-in-Publication Data
China's industrial reform.
"Published for the World Bank."
Includes index.
Bibliography: p.
1. Industry and state—China. 2. Industrial
management—China. I. Tidrick, Gene, 1942–
II. Chen, Jiyuan. III. International Bank for
Reconstruction and Development.
HD3616.C63C495 1987 338.951 87-5616
ISBN 0-19-520592-8

Contents

Contributors vii

Preface ix

1 *The Essence of the Industrial Reforms* 1
Gene Tidrick and Chen Jiyuan

2 *Characteristics of the Twenty Firms* 11
Gene Tidrick and Chen Jiyuan

Part One. The Broad Issues 39

3 *Increasing the Vitality of Enterprises* 44
Dong Fureng

4 *Factor Allocation and Enterprise Incentives* 60
William Byrd and Gene Tidrick

5 *The Industrial Environment in China and the CMEA Countries* 103
David Granick

6 *The Reform of China's Industrial System* 132
Gao Shangquan

Part Two. Planning, Supply, and Marketing 143

7 *The Planning System* 148
Chen Jiyuan

8 *Planning and Supply* 175
Gene Tidrick

9 *Supply and Marketing* 210
Tang Zongkun

10 *The Role and Impact of Markets* 237
William Byrd

Part Three. Enterprise Organization 277

11 *Industrial Corporations* 281
Xu Lu

12 *The Leadership System* 297
Zheng Guangliang

Part Four. State Enterprise Management in Other Countries 313

13 *The Dual Dependence of the State-Owned Firm in Hungary* 317
Janos Kornai

14 *The Self-Managed Firm in Yugoslavia* 339
Martin Schrenk

Index 371

Contributors

William Byrd is an economist in the China Division of the World Bank.

Chen Jiyuan is senior research fellow and deputy director of the Institute of Rural Development and former researcher at the Institute of Economics, both of the Chinese Academy of Social Sciences.

Dong Fureng is director of the Institute of Economics of the Chinese Academy of Social Sciences and professor of economics at Beijing University.

Gao Shangquan is vice chairman of China's State Commission for Restructuring the Economic System and chairman of the Editorial Board of the journal *China's Economic System Reform.*

David Granick is professor of economics at the University of Wisconsin–Madison.

Janos Kornai is director of the Institute of Economics of the Hungarian Academy of Sciences and concurrently professor of economics at the Karl Marx University of Economics in Budapest and at Harvard University.

Martin Schrenk is a senior economist in the Country Policy Department of the World Bank.

Tang Zongkun is managing deputy editor-in-chief of the journal *Economic Research* and senior research fellow at the Institute of Economics of the Chinese Academy of Social Sciences.

Gene Tidrick is the policy adviser in the Country Policy Department of the World Bank and former senior economist in the China Division of the Bank.

Xu Lu is a research fellow at the Economic Management Research Center in the State Economic Commission, adviser to China Cost Research Association, and adviser to the journal *Enterprise Management.*

Zheng Guangliang is chief economist at the Enterprise Management Bureau of the State Economic Commission.

Preface

CHINA HAS HAD ONE of the world's highest sustained rates of industrial growth during the past thirty-five years. It has broadened its industrial base to encompass an increasingly full range of production, and it has expanded its industrial employment to provide 63 million jobs, equal to the industrial employment in all of North America and Western Europe. China has done this while being isolated from the rest of the world for long periods and while undergoing frequent and often radical changes in the organization of industry. Since the 1950s it has continually adapted the Soviet central-planning model to develop unique forms of organization, such as locally controlled small-scale industry, in line with the strategy of "walking on two legs." And since 1979 it has introduced industrial reforms that in some ways are more far-reaching than anything undertaken in the socialist countries of Eastern Europe.

Despite these achievements, little was known about how the Chinese industrial system worked—mainly because almost no systematic research could be done on the Chinese economy by either Chinese or foreign scholars from 1966 to 1978. In early 1983, to study China's systems for guiding industrial enterprises and find out how reforms were affecting China's economic development, the World Bank and the Institute of Economics of the Chinese Academy of Social Sciences (CASS) agreed to collaborate in conducting research on Chinese systems of industrial enterprise management. The State Economic Commission supported this collaboration, and enterprises and their superior organizations cooperated. It was agreed to base the research on in-depth interviews with twenty state-owned enterprises and their supervisory organizations. The study covered internal management, relations among enterprises, and relations between enterprises and the state. The main emphasis was on relations between enterprises and the state, particularly the response of enterprises to incentives and planning directives set by the state.

We chose the methods of interviews and case studies for three main reasons. First, in-depth interviews are the best way to understand underlying motives and behavior and to integrate qualitative with quantitative information. The interview technique had been successfully applied in other socialist economies. A study by David Granick (1975) provided a methodological model and a basis for comparison with several East European economies. Second, Chinese and foreign scholars had also used interviews and case studies successfully in China during the 1960s. Ma Hong and others (1980) wrote a detailed report of a case study of the Beijing No. 1 Machine Tool Plant in 1961 (though it was not published until 1980), and many other investigators have published enterprise reports in China in recent years. A Western scholar (Richman 1969) also published a major study based on interviews in thirty-eight enterprises just before the Cultural Revolution began in 1966. Third, the quantitative information for a broader empirical study was inadequate in China. Statistical services were weakened during the Cultural Revolution, and it was difficult to obtain data that were consistent across enterprises or over time for the same enterprise.

The CASS and World Bank teams conducted interviews with key personnel in the enterprises and in supervisory organizations and other enterprises or organizations with close supply, marketing, or other links. Each enterprise provided basic quantitative information on its operations and performance, but the interviews focused mainly on nonquantifiable aspects of enterprise management. The interview questionnaire was a checklist of issues and hypotheses rather than a set of questions common to all enterprises. First we examined how the enterprise reacted to a problem (such as the loss of a market) or opportunity (such as the introduction of profit retention), next we cross-checked the facts, and then we explored the implications for enterprise performance and government policy. Interviews with each enterprise and its associated organizations took a week or longer.

The teams began by conducting pilot interviews in two enterprises in the first half of 1983: Chongqing Clock and Watch Company and Qingdao Forging Machinery Plant. They prepared a detailed interview report so that researchers who did not participate directly could understand what went on in the interviews. The two teams then jointly reinterviewed each enterprise and wrote case studies of the enterprises (Byrd and Tidrick 1984; Chen and others 1984). Based on experience in the two pilot enterprises, the two teams formulated a new set of hypotheses to guide the remainder of the research. They also revised the quantitative questionnaire and the checklist of issues.

From mid-1983 through mid-1984 the CASS team interviewed the remaining eighteen enterprises and wrote a detailed report on each set of interviews. In October and November 1984 the CASS and World Bank teams jointly reinterviewed five enterprises: Anshan Iron and Steel Corporation, Shenyang Smelting Plant, No. 2 Automobile Plant, Nanning Silk and Linen Textile Mill, and Mindong Electrical Machinery Corporation. Supplementary questionnaires were sent to the remaining thirteen enterprises to help clarify some issues arising from the interviews; all but two of the enterprises responded. These interviews, some 750,000 words of reports based on them, and the quantitative information obtained were the basis for most of this book.

Members of the research team (Chen Jiyuan, Xu Lu, Tang Zongkun, Zheng Guangliang, Gene Tidrick, William Byrd, and David Granick) wrote eight papers analyzing various aspects of enterprise management based mainly on information collected from the twenty enterprises. They presented their papers—chapters 4, 5, and 7 through 12—at the International Symposium on State Industrial Enterprise Management Systems in Beijing in August 1985. Several distinguished economists from China and abroad were also invited to present papers on broader aspects of China's reform and the experience of other countries. Two papers (chapter 3 by Dong Fureng and chapter 6 by Gao Shangquan) summarize the official agenda of projected reforms and reflect the state of debate in China on the direction of reforms over the longer term. In addition, two papers, by Janos Kornai and Martin Schrenk (chapters 13 and 14), assess enterprise management in Hungary and in Yugoslavia—the two socialist economies that have gone furthest in reforming the Soviet model of central planning. Their papers were intended to put the discussion of Chinese industrial reform into an international perspective. Introductions to the papers are at the beginning of each part of the book. Two other papers on public enterprise management in nonsocialist countries were presented at the conference by Leroy Jones and Prem Shanker Jha, but we have not included them in this volume because we wished to retain its focus on reform of state enterprise management in socialist countries.

The results of this joint study by CASS and the World Bank show that it was a success. Through it the Bank has gained a more systematic and comprehensive understanding of China's system for managing state industrial enterprises. Researchers at CASS learned much about the experience with industrial reform in their country and about some research methods applicable to China. Both sides have gained experience in collaborative academic study. We believe that this book will provide materials and thoughtful questions for people interested in China's industrial reforms. It will promote further collaborative studies between the World Bank and the Chinese Academy of Social Sciences on questions of China's economy. It will also promote collaborative studies in still wider fields between Chinese scholars and those in other academic groups and international organizations.

Acknowledgments

This study would not have been possible without the help of many people and organizations. We especially want to thank the enterprises and their supervisory organizations for their cooperation and the State Economic Commission of China for its support of the research project. The main source of funds for the research was a World Bank research grant. This was supplemented by support from the Institute of Economics of the CASS and the China Division of the World Bank.

Dong Fureng and Edwin Lim promoted the idea of collaborative research and were involved with the project from the beginning. The members of the CASS research team were Chen Jiyuan (team leader), Xu Lu, Tang Zongkun, Zheng Guangliang, and Chen Lantong. The World Bank team consisted of Gene Tidrick (team leader), William Byrd, David Granick, and Josephine Woo. Other staff from the CASS and the World Bank participated in some interviews. Margaret Cassidy coordinated typing and administrative arrangements for the World Bank team. Betty Ting supervised most of the translation. Bruce Ross-Larson edited the English version of the manuscript. Finally, we are grateful to many readers and to conference participants for helpful comments on the papers.

References

Byrd, William, and Gene Tidrick. 1984. "Adjustment and Reform in the Chongqing Clock and Watch Company." In *Recent Chinese Economic Reforms: Studies of Two Industrial Enterprises.* World Bank Staff Working Paper 652. Washington, D.C.

Chen Jiyuan, Xu Lu, Tang Zongkun, and Chen Lantong. 1984. "Management and Reform in the Qingdao Forging Machinery Plant." In *Recent Chinese Economic Reforms: Studies of Two Industrial Enterprises.* World Bank Staff Working Paper 652. Washington, D.C.

Granick, David. 1975. *Enterprise Guidance in Eastern Europe.* Princeton, N.J.: Princeton University Press.

Ma Hong and others. 1980. *Beijing Diyi Jichuang Chang* (Beijing No. 1 Machine Tool Plant). Edited by Cai Xiaoyu. Beijing: China Social Sciences Publisher.

Richman, Barry. 1969. *Industrial Society in Communist China.* New York: Random House.

1

The Essence of the Industrial Reforms

Gene Tidrick and Chen Jiyuan

AFTER THE END OF THE CULTURAL REVOLUTION in 1976, the main concern of China's leadership was to overcome the disruption of the previous ten years, to resume rapid growth, and gradually to modernize the economy. It quickly became clear, however, that the ambitious investment plan and modernization program adopted in 1977 would strain China's resources. They would also fail to correct the underlying inefficiencies and structural imbalances in China's economy. So in December 1978, the Third Plenary Session of the Eleventh Party Congress adopted a new program of "adjustment and reform." (For general discussions of Chinese reforms, see World Bank 1983, 1985; Perry and Wong 1985.)

The fundamental weaknesses of China's economy had been inefficient use of labor, capital, energy, and raw materials and a mismatch between the composition and quality of production and demand. Adjustment was to achieve five main objectives. First, it would reverse the traditional order of priority given to heavy industry, light industry, and agriculture. Second, it would increase the share of consumption in national income. Third, it would reduce the consumption of energy. Fourth, it would increase exports, especially of manufactured goods. Fifth, it would emphasize plant modernization and improved efficiency in existing enterprises rather than economic development through new capital construction. But reform, particularly reform of incentives to link rewards to performance, was viewed as the key to raising efficiency. This increased efficiency would in turn permit consumption to rise and investment to fall without sacrificing growth. Improved incentives would thus pay for themselves by raising productivity. Two other guiding principles of reform were to decentralize decisionmaking and to place more reliance on market mechanisms rather than administrative controls. These principles, like the improved incentives, were intended to invigorate enterprises and other producers.

Table 1-1. *Selected Indicators of the Chinese Economy, 1970–84*

Indicator	*1970–77*	*1978*	*1979*	*1980*	*1981*	*1982*	*1983*	*1984*[a]
				Annual growth in constant prices (percent)				
NMP[b]	5.3	12.3	7.0	6.4	4.9	8.3	9.8	12.1
Gross value of output								
Agriculture[c]	3.8	9.0	8.6	3.9	6.6	11.0	9.6	17.1
Industry	11.3	13.5	8.5	8.7	4.1	7.7	10.5	14.0
Heavy	12.3	15.6	7.7	1.4	−4.7	9.8	12.4	14.2
Light	10.0	10.8	9.6	18.4	14.1	5.7	8.7	13.9
				Annual growth in current prices (percent)				
Exports[d]	33.7	28.5	40.1	33.7	14.3	4.5	1.7	9.9
				As a percentage of NMP				
Consumption[e]	67.4	63.5	65.4	68.4	71.5	71.0	70.0	68.8

a. Preliminary figures.
b. Net material product.
c. Includes brigade and team-run industry.
d. On the basis of data in U.S. dollars from the Ministry of Foreign Economic Relations and Trade.
e. On the basis of NMP available in current prices. (NMP available differs from NMP because of differences between imports and exports and because of statistical discrepancies.)
Sources: State Statistical Bureau 1984 and 1985.

China fulfilled the main objectives of adjustment during 1979–81 (see table 1-1). Agricultural growth accelerated sharply in response to improved producer prices and radical reforms, including a system of household production responsibility and more flexible pricing and marketing arrangements. A stabilization program in 1980–81 helped to reduce the shares of heavy industry and investment, exports grew rapidly despite a slowdown in the growth of world trade, and the progress in energy conservation was considerable.

Some of the achievements of adjustment, however, have been temporary, and others have been affected by the incompleteness of reform. Agricultural growth has been very high, largely because of effective reform measures. But the shift toward light industry appears to have been at most a once-and-for-all increase in its share, and aggregate demand has grown faster than desired. Consumption has been difficult to control because of unauthorized bonus payments. Investment has proven even more difficult to control because the reforms decentralized many investment decisions before prices were reformed and before effective instruments of macroeconomic control were developed.

After the stabilization program of 1980–81, the economy began to grow more rapidly. The Central Committee of the Chinese Communist party put forth a long-term goal of quadrupling gross output of agriculture and industry between 1980 and 2000 (with an implied annual average growth of 7.2 percent), but even these growth targets were consistently exceeded. By mid-1985 the economy was growing so rapidly that new controls on investment and imports were introduced to reduce inflation and a large balance of payments deficit.

There was no comprehensive blueprint for the reforms, which have been piecemeal and uncoordinated, with much experimentation and modification to cope with unforeseen problems. Yet the direction of reform has broadly followed the principles set in December 1978. Moreover, while reforms in industry have been less sweeping than those in agriculture, the changes have been substantial. Reforms in enterprise management can be grouped in five main areas: profit retention; wages and employment; investment finance; planning, pricing, and marketing; and industrial organization.

Profit Retention

The key objective of industrial reform was to improve incentives. The main instruments were profit retention for enterprises and bonuses for workers. On the basis of earlier local experiments, notably in Sichuan Province, a profit-retention scheme was introduced in mid-1979. A few enterprises were allowed to retain a fixed part of profits: some experimented with profits within quota, others with profits above quota. Although profit retention was intended to be only a limited experiment, it spread rapidly and by mid-1980 included 6,600 enterprises producing 60 percent of output and 70 percent of profits under the state plan. This rapid expansion reduced state revenue and was one of the reasons for the 1980–81 stabilization program.

In 1981 a new contract system of profit retention was introduced under which enterprises contracted to hand over only a certain percentage or fixed amount of incremental profits. In 1983 the government—still faced with uncertain profit remittances, previously a prime source of revenue—introduced a scheme that substituted tax payments for profit remittances. State enterprises paid a progressive profit tax of up to 55 percent. Since profit retention had been introduced without comprehensive price restructuring or capital charges, not all enterprises were receiving equal treatment. Therefore, an adjustment tax supplemented the profit tax. The imposition and the amount of the adjustment tax depend on whether an enterprise with a favorable price structure or other special circumstances has been able to capture excess profits and to what extent. The discretion inherent in the adjustment tax meant that different industries and even individual enterprises in an industry often faced different rates. In addition, there were restrictions on the uses of retained profits, and these also varied by enterprise.

Although profit retention increased the incentives to enterprises, it also created problems, as some of the chapters in this volume make clear. Since the price structure is still distorted, allocative decisions of enterprises pursuing greater profits may also be distorted (chapter 3). Different rates of tax or profit retention have led to considerable bargaining between enterprises and higher authorities, which has thus weakened the incentives that profit retention provides (chapter 8). Moreover, since enterprise managers and workers have complex objectives, profit retention may induce enterprises to behave in ways inconsistent with the needs and interests of society (chapter 4).

Wages and Employment

Bonuses, which had been abolished during the Cultural Revolution, were reintroduced to provide incentives to individual workers. As with profit retention, there were changes over time, and the system was not unified. Most enterprises now pay bonuses out of retained profits, thereby providing a link with overall economic performance. Average bonus payments initially were subject to limits, generally 25 percent of basic wages. This limitation was replaced in 1984 by a progressive bonus tax to control bonus payments, but enterprises have found ways to evade both the limits and the taxes. Individual bonuses are supposed to be differentiated by productivity, but egalitarian distribution still prevails. Egalitarianism has also limited the use of piece rates, floating wages, and other payment-by-result schemes. And although there are new forms of hiring practices, such as contract labor and dependents' collectives, the wage and employment system in state enterprises remains the least reformed aspect of China's industrial management—surprising in a system that has always been more restrictive than that of other socialist economies (chapters 4 and 5).

Investment Finance

Chinese reformers recognized early that capital charges are a precondition for the financial autonomy of enterprises. Before the reforms, state industrial enterprises received most circulating capital and all investment funds as budgetary grants. They then remitted all profits and a large share of depreciation allowances to the government. Capital was thus costless to the enterprise, but the state retained control over its allocation. Reforms increased the financial autonomy of enterprises through profit-retention schemes and increased retention of depreciation funds. At the same time, capital ceased to be entirely costless.

Taxes on fixed assets were introduced on an experimental basis in 1979 along with loans for a part of fixed investment and circulating capital. Since then, loans have increasingly replaced budgetary grants, and interest charges have gradually increased. But capital charges have been introduced slowly and partially. Fees on fixed assets varied by province and were never applied to all enterprises with the right to retain profits. With the introduction of the new income tax system in 1983, these fees were no longer imposed. The impact of the shift from grants to loans was mitigated by permitting enterprises to deduct principal as well as interest repayments from tax liability.

The net effect of this complex system is difficult to calculate, but it generally makes loans less costly to the enterprise than they would be under a conventional tax and accounting system in the West. In general, the increases in financial autonomy have outpaced the increases in the cost of capital. Thus, the financial reforms may have weakened rather than strengthened some areas of financial discipline (chapter 4).

Planning, Pricing, and Marketing

The Chinese system of planning and material allocation has always been in some respects more decentralized than that in Eastern Europe and the U.S.S.R. (chapters 5, 7, and 9).[1] Even such key products as coal and steel are produced in enterprises at both central and lower levels of control and are allocated through largely separate and self-contained channels. Furthermore, prices are also multitiered, with the same product selling at widely different prices, depending on the level of administration that controls production and pricing. To this multitiered planning and pricing system inherited from the past, the period of adjustment and reform has added a new dimension—allocation through the market, often at flexible prices.

Adjustment and reform have brought about greater changes in marketing industrial products than in any other aspect of enterprise management. Adjustment was perhaps more important than reform in this case. Changes in market conditions—a shift from sellers' to buyers' markets—prompted marketing reforms. Self-marketing was introduced on a large scale during the stabilization of 1980–81, when commercial agencies experienced difficulties selling many goods. By 1981 factories were directly selling about 20 percent of industrial consumer goods and, more remarkably, up to 100 percent of some types of machinery and other producer goods. With the expansion of demand and the resumption of heavy industry's growth after 1981, some buyers' markets have again reverted to sellers' markets.

Self-marketing has tended to fluctuate with market conditions, but the trend has been toward greater reliance on market than on planned allocation. The evidence here suggests that changes in marketing have had a large and beneficial impact on enterprise behavior, with the shift to buyers' markets being more important than self-marketing (chapters 9 and 10).

Reforms of marketing and changes in market conditions have also brought about some reforms in planning and pricing. An increasing part of production (usually, but not always, self-marketed production) is no longer subject to mandatory planning. Numerous quasi-market mechanisms of obtaining supplies have been sanctioned or newly developed (chapters 8 and 9). China has not had a comprehensive price restructuring like those periodically undertaken in some East European countries, but a few individual industrial prices have been adjusted. There was a major restructuring of textile prices in 1983, for example. Changes in the price-setting mechanism have also been introduced. Prices of some minor industrial products have been decontrolled, and since 1984, all above-quota output could be sold at floating prices of up to 20 percent above or below the administered price. Thus, a new tier has gradually been added to the previous multitiered system, and only partly as a result of conscious policy. A large but shrinking share of the supply of most important goods is still subject to mandatory plan allocation and administratively set prices. But at the margin, the market mechanism allocates a substantial and growing share, largely at flexible prices.

Industrial Organization

China has experimented extensively with new forms of industrial organization since 1978. First, in line with the new open door policy of recent years, it has encouraged the inflow of foreign capital and technology through joint ventures, compensation trade, and (to a limited extent) wholly owned direct foreign investment. In the Special Economic Zones established early in the reform, foreign investors have greater autonomy in matters of labor relations, supply contracts, and foreign trade than domestic enterprises elsewhere in the economy. In 1984 some of these same privileges were extended to joint ventures in several coastal cities. A second major reform has been to encourage expansion of the collective sector and to permit the establishment of individual enterprises with several employees and apprentices. With the number of their workers increasing from 12 million in 1978 to 16 million in 1984, collective industrial enterprises have grown twice as fast as state industrial enterprises, and employment in individual enterprises in cities and townships rose from 150,000 in 1978 to 3.4 million in 1984.

There have also been organizational innovations in the state enterprise sector (chapters 4 and 11). Many industrial corporations have been formed with authority over a group of enterprises that have supply links or produce similar products. Most of these corporations have been promoted by administrative decree to help attain economies of scale or to upgrade technology by linking backward with more progressive enterprises. Voluntary associations between enterprises have also been permitted, including mergers and joint ventures across administrative boundaries and even between state and collective enterprises. The motives for these associations have usually been to gain captive supply sources or to overcome constraints on expansion imposed by rigid administrative allocation of land, labor, or capital or by regional protectionism. Organizational changes have thus substituted for reforms that would create genuine factor and product markets. One final, uniquely

Chinese innovation has been to encourage or permit state enterprises to set up collectives to employ dependents of state workers. The practice varies enormously from province to province, and no national figures are available. But in 1982 the Anshan Iron and Steel Corporation employed 180,000 people in collective enterprises set up for this purpose.

The rules that govern organizational changes, such as the formation of joint ventures or the creation of subordinate collectives, greatly affect the way enterprises respond to incentives that the higher authorities establish (chapter 4), as do internal organizational changes (chapter 12). Reforms in the leadership systems of enterprises have strengthened the orientation toward production. Factory managers chosen for their technical competence have largely replaced managers who were also the party secretaries immediately before the reforms. But factory managers have less authority than in the 1950s, when China's one-man director system was modeled on that of the U.S.S.R.

How far has China come in reforming industrial enterprise management? Clearly, Chinese industrial reforms are not comparable in extent or form with those in Yugoslavia (chapter 14), but they can fairly be compared with those in Hungary (chapter 13). China has not undertaken comprehensive price adjustments or completely abolished mandatory planning as Hungary has done, but marketing reforms are more advanced in China (chapters 8, 9, and 10), and enterprises appear to be more profit oriented (chapter 4). Moreover, although Hungary's initial comprehensive reform package of 1968 was more dramatic than China's first steps, the cumulative effects of China's less-structured reform have been substantial and are still unfolding in their breadth and depth.

China has had problems, including some loss of macroeconomic control, because the reforms have been uneven and uncoordinated. The critical missing elements are price reform to give better signals for decentralized decisionmaking, greater accountability for performance to ensure responsibility for losses and profits, and increased competition to promote buyers' markets. China's leaders recognize the need to move in these directions. In October 1984 a major party document on the reform of the economic structure called for rational prices, increased enterprise accountability, reduced mandatory planning, and new instruments of macroeconomic regulation.[2] The rationale of these proposals for future reform is set out in chapter 6. In September 1985 a national party conference adopted guidelines for drafting the seventh five-year plan, that for 1986–90. These guidelines stress the need for reforms to adjust prices, to make greater use of markets, and to develop indirect levels of control. They also emphasize the need for mutually reinforcing reforms in planning, pricing, banking, fiscal management, and the labor and wage systems. The reforms put into effect during 1979–85 are thus only the first stage of an ongoing process.

Common Themes and Unresolved Issues

At the Beijing conference where the papers in this volume were first presented, most participants broadly agreed with the main principles of reform as outlined in recent official documents and as summarized by Gao Shangquan in chapter 6. First, price reform is the key to other reforms. Second, the scope of mandatory planning should be decreased and the role of the market increased. Third, the reforms have to be coordinated or carefully sequenced on several fronts (prices, wages, welfare, the fiscal system, and so on). Fourth, new macroeconomic tools will have to be developed so that the government can focus on macroeconomic management rather than on microeconomic administrative intervention. Despite this consensus, there were differences of opinion or unresolved questions on several important issues.

What Kind of Price Reform?

There was more agreement on the importance of price reform than on which of two kinds of price reform should be undertaken: price adjustment (restructuring administratively controlled prices) or price relaxation (changing the price-setting mechanism from administrative control to determination through the market). There were also differences of opinion about the implications of China's unusual multiple-pricing system for the efficiency of resource allocation.

Should Mandatory Planning Be Abolished?

Some conference participants felt that the experience of Hungary and Yugoslavia showed that mandatory planning could be eliminated. Other participants were unwilling to go that far, however, even though they favored reducing the scope of mandatory planning. Some felt that the Yugoslav experience showed the dangers of abolishing mandatory planning. Others felt that China's size precluded the abolition of planning. On one point there was near unanimity: price reform—at a minimum, price restructuring—would have to precede or accompany the abolition of mandatory planning.

Should Reform Be Comprehensive or Gradual?

Most participants favored the official strategy of "growing out of the plan"—that is, of gradually narrowing the scope of mandatory planning, gradually adjusting administered prices, and gradually relaxing price controls. The arguments were that gradual reform, particularly of prices, would be less inflationary and less disruptive of income distribution and would provoke less political resistance. The counterargument was that Hungary shows that comprehensive reform can work—that such reform can eliminate difficult problems of sequencing and command greater political support than piecemeal change. As Janos Kornai put it, people may tolerate major surgery better than repeated small amputations.

Should Enterprises Have Autonomy over Investment?

On the issue of investment autonomy, there also were wide differences of opinion. Arguments against it stressed three things: the limited investment autonomy permitted in divisions of large capitalist firms, the bias toward excessive risk taking because of the difficulty of ensuring enterprise accountability for losses, and the need to maintain central control over allocation of capital. Arguments for autonomy stressed the incentives it would provide for expansion of efficient enterprises and the elimination of delays caused by the cumbersome procedures for gaining central approval. There was wider agreement that price restructuring, stronger financial intermediation, and improved financial discipline should precede increased enterprise autonomy in investment decisionmaking.

How Can a Buyers' Market Be Created?

The importance of creating buyers' markets was widely accepted, but there were no clear-cut answers on how to do so. Can tight aggregate demand policies sustain buyers' markets? If so, is the cost in growth too high? Is it possible to create a buyers' market, or to equilibrate supply and demand, simply by letting prices rise? David Granick argued that sellers' markets have been virtually eliminated where dual pricing exists (though dual pricing raises interesting questions about how sellers' and buyers' markets are defined). Other participants felt that buyers' markets could not be created without greater financial discipline (a harder budget constraint) than exists in China. There was general agreement that improved financial discipline and accountability are essential for increasing price responsiveness.

What Should Be the Structure of Ownership?

The issue of financial discipline and accountability leads to the issue of ownership, which Dong Fureng raised. Is it possible to harden the budget constraint of enterprises without altering in some way the structure of ownership? Some participants argued that Western corporations, where management is often separate from ownership, and efficient public enterprises in some nonsocialist countries show that ownership is not the issue. Generally, however, it was felt that China's system of ministerial or regional control of enterprises weakened enterprise accountability and financial discipline. Conference participants had many suggestions for changing the structure of ownership in a socialist framework.

Notes

1. The Chinese economist Liu Guoguang and others, however, hold that China's original economic structure was "basically of the traditional central planning model with elements of a military communist payment-in-kind system; it had gone farther than other socialist countries with respect to centralization, payments in kind, being closed off to outside forces, and equalitarianization" (Liu 1984).

2. "Decision of the Central Committee of the Communist Party of China on Reform of the Economic Structure," published in English in *China Daily*, October 23, 1984.

References

Liu Guoguang. 1984. "Guangu woguo Jingji tizhi gaige de mubiao moshi wenti." *Zhongguo Jingji Kexue* ("Questions on the Target Model of China's Economic Structural Reform." *China's Social Sciences*) 5 (May):37–54.

Perry, Elizabeth J., and Christine Wong, eds. 1985. *The Political Economy of Reform in Post-Mao China.* Cambridge, Mass.: Harvard University Press.

State Statistical Bureau. 1984. *Statistical Yearbook of China, 1984.* Hong Kong: Economic Information Agency.

———. 1985. *China: A Statistics Survey in 1985.* Beijing: New World Press and China Statistical Information and Consultancy Service Center.

World Bank. 1983. *China: Socialist Economic Development.* 3 vols. Washington, D.C.

———. 1985. *China: Long-Term Issues and Options.* Baltimore, Md.: Johns Hopkins University Press.

2

Characteristics of the Twenty Firms

Gene Tidrick and Chen Jiyuan

TWENTY ENTERPRISES and their associated organizations made up the sample for this study. Because the aim of the research was to gain an overview of management systems in China's state industrial enterprises, much care was given to selecting them. All are state enterprises, since the state sector accounted for nearly 80 percent of gross industrial output in 1982. There are large, medium-size, and small enterprises. Some are in big cities, and some are in remote areas. Some make producer goods; some, consumer goods. Some are experimental enterprises in which the reforms were more advanced, and some retained the original systems. The sample was also weighted toward large and medium-size experimental enterprises, probably desirable, given the focus of the research.

The enterprises in the sample cover many dimensions (tables 2-1 and 2-2). The twenty enterprises are in fifteen provinces. Five enterprises are in cities with over 3 million nonagricultural residents, three are in cities of 1 million to 3 million, one is in a city of a half million, and eleven are in smaller urban or rural areas. Their products range from candy to trucks. In size, they range from the Shanghai High-Pressure Oil Pump Factory, with 437 workers and gross output of Y5.8 million ($3.1 million) in 1982, to the Anshan Iron and Steel Corporation, with 195,000 workers and gross output of Y3.5 billion ($1.9 billion) in the same year (these figures exclude the 180,000 employees and the output of Anshan's dependent collectives).[1]

Perhaps the most remarkable feature of the twenty enterprises is that they made up only 0.02 percent of the 86,000 enterprises in the state industrial sector in 1982, but they accounted for 2.1 percent of gross industrial output, 2.5 percent of net output, 1.2 percent of employment, 2.8 percent of gross fixed assets, and 3.9 percent of profits of all state industrial enterprises. Five enterprises in the sample were under central government administration in

Table 2-1. *Location and Products of Sample Enterprises*

Enterprise	*Full name*	*Location*	*Main product*
Anshan	Anshan Iron and Steel Corporation	Liaoning	Steel
Baoji	Baoji Nitrogen Fertilizer Plant	Shaanxi	Fertilizer
Chengdu	Chengdu Locomotive and Rolling Stock Factory	Sichuan	Locomotive overhaul
Chongqing	Chongqing Clock and Watch Company	Sichuan	Clocks and watches
Jiangmen	Jiangmen Nanfang Foodstuff Factory	Guangdong	Candy and soft drinks
Jinling	Jinling Petrochemical General Corporation	Jiangsu	Petrochemicals
Mindong	Mindong Electrical Machinery Plant (Corporation)	Fujian	Small electrical machinery
Nanning	Nanning Silk and Linen Textile Mill	Guangxi	Ramie textiles
North China Petroleum	North China Petroleum Administration	Hebei	Crude petroleum
Northwest Cotton	Northwest No. 1 Cotton Mill	Shaanxi	Cotton gray cloth
No. 2 Auto	No. 2 Automobile Plant	Hubei	Trucks
Qingdao	Qingdao Forging Machinery Plant	Shandong	Twin-disc friction presses
Qinghe	Qinghe Woolen Textile Mill	Beijing	Woolen textiles
Qingyuan	Qingyuan County Economic Commission	Guangdong	General[a]
Sanchazi	Sanchazi Forestry Bureau	Jilin	Timber
Shanghai Cotton	Shanghai No. 17 Cottom Mill	Shanghai	Cotton and blended textiles
Shanghai Oil Pump	Shanghai High-Pressure Oil Pump Factory	Shanghai	Oil pumps
Shenyang	Shenyang Smelting Plant	Liaoning	Nonferrous metals
Tianjin	Tianjin Color Textile Corporation	Tianjin	Textile finishing
Xiangxiang	Xiangxiang Cement Plant	Hunan	Cement

a. Comprises seventeen factories, with products including agricultural machinery, fertilizer, cement, matches, and food processing.

Source: Unless otherwise stated, all tables are based on enterprise interviews and questionnaires.

Table 2-2. *Size and Administrative Level of Sample Enterprises, 1982*

Enterprise	*Level of subordination*[a]	*Gross output (yuan)*	*Employment*	*Total gross fixed assets (yuan)*
Anshan	I, II, III	3,765,370	194,638	6,696,530
Baoji	II	29,680	1,984	50,090
Chengdu	I	51,650	4,744	59,130
Chongqing	III	64,894	4,287	63,703
Jiangmen	III	15,270	638	28,940
Jinling	I	1,350,922	23,716	937,088
Mindong	II	36,351	3,335	19,089
Nanning	III	42,680	3,159	26,167
North China Petroleum	I	1,218,860	79,053	2,105,540
Northwest Cotton	II	91,189	6,452	45,513
No. 2 Auto	I	1,084,197	53,062	1,596,691
Qingdao	III	16,184	1,561	20,890
Qinghe	II	78,470	3,320	30,804
Qingyuan	III	51,260	6,218	43,236
Sanchazi	II	62,297	10,029	107,615
Shanghai Cotton	II	251,192	9,805	55,432
Shanghai Oil Pump	II	5,789	437	3,280
Shenyang	III, I[b]	684,390	6,770	177,770
Tianjin	II	282,448	12,612	54,893
Xiangxiang	II	57,880	2,320	86,658

a. I = First level of administration, directly under the central government. II = Second level of administration, directly under provincial, municipal, or regional (autonomous region) government. III = Third level of administration, directly under city or county government.

b. Under Shenyang municipal government (level III) from 1971 to May 1983; under China Metal General Corporation (level I) since December 1983.

1985, nine were under provincial control, five were under municipal or county administration, and one (Anshan Iron and Steel) was under the joint administration of all three levels. Anshan's status is a legacy of cycles in which the administration of even large enterprises was first decentralized and then partly recentralized when it became apparent that local authorities could not handle the sales, supplies, and technical problems of such enterprises. Because of its national importance and nationwide contacts, Anshan is controlled at the center. Subordination is less clear for several of the other enterprises that are nominally under one level of administration but that suffer from "multiheaded leadership," in which production plans, financial targets, and managerial appointments may be handled by different agencies, frequently at different levels (chapters 8 and 11). (See also Chen and others 1984 for a discussion of multiheaded leadership at the Qingdao Forging Machinery Plant.)

Several enterprises in the sample have been reorganized or placed under a different level of administration in recent years. Jinling Petrochemical

Table 2-3. *Capital, Labor, and Output Ratios: National Average and Sample Enterprises, 1982*

Item	*National average*	*Sample enterprises*	*Sample as percentage of national average*
Gross output per worker[a]	12.1	21.6	179
Gross output per gross fixed assets	1.0	0.8	79
Net output per worker[a]	4.0	8.0	197
Net output per total fund	0.3	0.4	115
Gross fixed assets per worker[a]	12.8	28.5	223
Total fund per worker[a]	12.1	21.1	174
Profit rate on gross fixed assets[b]	13.7	18.9	138
Profit plus tax rate on gross fixed assets[b]	22.2	25.1	113
Profit plus tax rate on total fund[b]	23.4	33.9	145

Note: Gross fixed assets = original value of fixed assets. Total fund = net fixed assets plus quota circulating assets. National average = average for state-owned independent accounting units.

a. Thousands of yuan per worker.

b. Percent.

Sources: State Statistical Bureau 1984 and sample data.

General Corporation was formed from separate enterprises at different levels of administration in 1982, Mindong Electrical Machinery Corporation moved from local to provincial administration in 1981, No. 2 Automobile Plant was transferred from provincial to central authority in 1981 and was then placed under different administrative authority at the central level in 1984, and Shenyang Smelting Plant was moved from municipal to central control in 1983.

Compared with the national average, the enterprises in the sample are larger, more capital-intensive, generally more productive, and more profitable (table 2-3). Capital per worker and output per worker are both about twice as large in the sample as the national average, both gross and net. Net output per unit of total funds (net fixed assets plus quota circulating assets) is slightly higher in the sample enterprises, but gross output per unit of gross fixed assets is lower. If equal weights are given to capital and labor inputs, total factor productivity is more than 50 percent higher (gross and net) in the sample enterprises than in all state industrial enterprises. The profit rate is also higher.

Comparison with the national average of profitability and other indicators may be misleading because the sample has a different sectoral composition and a smaller share of small enterprises than the national average. Moreover, there are no loss-making enterprises in the sample, perhaps its greatest weakness. Data are not available for comparisons by size of enterprise, but it is possible to compare profitability with sectoral averages for 1982 (table 2-4).

Table 2-4. *Profitability by Industry, 1982*

Enterprise	Ratio of profit + taxes to gross total fixed assets: Sample	Ratio of profit + taxes to gross total fixed assets: National average	Ratio of profit + taxes to net fixed + quota circulating assets: Sample	Ratio of profit + taxes to net fixed + quota circulating assets: National average	Comparator
Anshan	0.234	0.166	0.358	0.184	Ferrous metals
Baoji	0.146	0.080	0.182	0.088	Chemical fertilizer
Chengdu	0.304	0.100	0.333	0.089	Transport equipment
Chongqing	0.440	n.a.	0.341	n.a.	
Jiangmen	0.604	0.317	0.376	0.345	Food and oil
Jinling	0.428	0.216	0.452	0.260	Basic chemicals
Mindong	0.165	0.164	0.069	0.138	Other machinery
Nanning	0.423	0.551	0.308	0.435	Textile industry
North China Petroleum	0.195	0.241	0.321	0.393	Petroleum extraction
Northwest Cotton	0.598	0.625	0.719	0.525	Cotton textiles
No. 2 Auto	0.175	0.100	0.170	0.089	Transport equipment
Qingdao	0.116	0.111	0.089	0.102	Industrial machinery
Qinghe	0.953	0.551	0.718	0.435	Textile industry
Qingyuan	0.267	0.222	0.250	0.235	All branches
Sanchazi	0.196	0.162	0.250	0.169	Forest industry
Shanghai Cotton	1.623	0.625	2.458	0.525	Cotton textiles
Shanghai Oil Pump	0.926	0.164	0.721	0.138	Other machinery
Shenyang	0.476	0.156	0.460	0.178	Metallurgical industry
Tianjin	0.751	0.551	0.610	0.435	Textile industry
Xiangxiang	0.320	0.136	0.394	0.154	Cement
Average	0.251	0.222	0.337	0.235	All branches

n.a. = not available.

Sources: State Statistical Bureau 1983 and sample data.

Not all sectors correspond exactly to the sample enterprises, but the general pattern is clear. Most sample enterprises are much more profitable than the average for their sectors. But the sample also contains a fair number of average and below-average enterprises. Four enterprises are close to the average (Mindong, Northwest No. 1 Cotton Mill, Qingdao, and Qingyuan County Economic Commission), and two have below-average profitability (Nanning Silk and Linen Textile Mill and North China Petroleum Administration). No sectoral data are available for the Chongqing Clock and Watch Company, but cost data for 1980 show that Chongqing had higher costs, and probably lower profits, than the industry averages (Byrd and Tidrick 1984).

Several of the enterprises are key enterprises: that is, enterprises of national importance. In this rather select group, the enterprises in the sample may be regarded as typical. Table 2-5 shows that, in the seven cases for which comparisons are possible, the enterprises in the sample are neither consis-

Table 2-5. *Key Enterprises in Sample Compared with Other Key Enterprises, 1983*

Enterprise	*Number of key enterprises compared*	*Rank in size (employment)*	*Rank in profit + taxes as a percentage of gross fixed assets*
Anshan	15	1	8
Nanjing Refinery (part of Jinling)	10	8	4
North China Petroleum	5	4	3
No. 2 Auto	10	1	5
Sanchazi	10	5	4
Shanghai Cotton	15	5	1
Xiangxiang	10	9	1

Source: State Statistical Bureau 1985.

tently larger nor consistently more profitable than other key enterprises in their sectors.

The sample has a bias toward success, but it by no means includes only showcase enterprises. In 1983, of the ten enterprises that received a national award for distinction in management, three were in the sample: Anshan, No. 2 Auto, and the Shanghai No. 17 Cotton Mill. During 1984, seven of the sample enterprises won ten national prizes for quality control or product quality—about 1 percent of the prizes awarded, a percentage not much different from the sample's share in state industrial employment. Many other enterprises won prizes in other years, but the sample also contains some technologically backward enterprises (some of which are also prizewinners). Two of the five engineering enterprises in the sample concentrate their main production entirely within families of products that are clearly obsolete by Chinese standards.

The sample contains a number of pilot reform enterprises, some of which are nationally known pacesetters in reform. Chongqing, Jiangmen Nanfang Foodstuff Factory, No. 2 Auto, and Qinghe Woolen Textile Mill were designated as pilots for profit-retention schemes, while Qingyuan and Tianjin Color Textile Corporation were pilots for organizational change. The sample also contains several average and unreformed enterprises. Chengdu Locomotive and Rolling Stock Factory and North China Petroleum are controlled much more tightly than most state enterprises in the sense that their production plans remain completely mandatory (chapter 8). Still, all twenty enterprises participate in some form of profit-retention scheme, and most have been granted some other common form of increased autonomy.

Chongqing and Jiangmen were among the handful of experimental enterprises that substituted taxes for profit retention before this change was instituted on a national scale. (See Byrd and Tidrick 1984 for a detailed analysis of Chongqing.) No. 2 Auto was an early pilot in adopting the system

Table 2-6. *Profit Retention*

Enterprise	Ratio of retained profits to total profits						Ratio of retained profits to total employment, average, 1980–82
	1978	1979	1980	1981	1982	Average, 1980–82	
Anshan	0.007	0.012	0.052	0.074	0.162	0.094	0.658
Baoji	0.019	0.166	0.164	0.146	0.324	0.220	0.650
Chengdu	n.a.	0.058	0.075	0.103	0.126	0.100	0.329
Chongqing	0.022	0.131	0.419	0.391	0.203	0.343	1.103
Jiangmen	n.a.	0.183	0.629	0.728	0.695	0.701	0.941
Jinling	n.a.	n.a.	n.a.	0.069	0.109	0.090[a]	0.965[a]
Mindong	n.a.	0.237	0.160	0.238	0.461	0.256	0.292
Nanning	0.014	0.145	0.137	0.128	0.199	0.145	0.527
North China Petroleum	0.008	0.008	0.002	0.013	0.020	0.009	0.060
Northwest Cotton	0.010	0.186	0.129	0.134	0.107	0.126	0.542
No. 2 Auto	n.a.	0.209	0.218	0.271	0.236	0.239	0.799
Qingdao	n.a.	0.100	0.030	0.184	0.077	0.080	0.092
Qinghe	0.006	0.082	0.179	0.170	0.166	0.171	0.920
Qingyuan	0.260	0.184	0.273	0.305	0.200	0.266	0.307
Sanchazi	0.060	0.260	0.270	0.279	0.225	0.256	0.397
Shanghai Cotton	0.009	0.033	0.068	0.076	0.083	0.075	0.428
Shanghai Oil Pump	n.a.	0.081	0.092	0.092	0.087	0.090	0.605
Shenyang	0.015	0.070	0.080	0.072	0.077	0.077	0.621
Tianjin	0.013	0.112	0.122	0.110	0.149	0.124	0.522
Xiangxiang	0.006	0.064	0.085	0.087	0.069	0.079	0.674
Sample average	n.a.	n.a.	n.a.	0.184	0.189	0.177	0.535
National average[b]	0.021	0.067	0.096	0.118	0.170	n.a.	n.a.

n.a. = not available.
a. Average for 1981–82.
b. Average for state-owned enterprises from Naughton 1985, p. 237.

of contracts for increasing profit made famous by Capital Iron and Steel (which is not in the sample). Under this system the enterprise contracted to hand over an increasing amount of profit each year but could retain all profits above that amount. Other enterprises participated in a variety of profit-retention schemes, usually with a retention rate negotiated annually by the enterprise and its supervisory organization. Table 2-6 shows that this rate varied widely and fluctuated substantially from year to year. (The determinants of profit retention are discussed in chapter 8.)

Several enterprises in the sample gained greater flexibility in wage payments. Chongqing and Jiangmen, in substituting tax payments for profit remittances, calculated both profit and wages as a residual, leaving open the possibility that wages could either be very high or negative, depending on overall profitability. In practice, the two enterprises were restricted in the wages and bonuses they could pay in highly profitable years, and the issue of

Table 2-7. *Average Bonus as Number of Months' Average Basic Wages*

Enterprise	*1978*	*1979*	*1980*	*1981*	*1982*	*Average, 1980–82*
Anshan	n.a.	3.1	2.6	2.9	3.1	2.9
Baoji	0.6	1.5	2.1	4.1	3.9	3.3
Chengdu	0.8	1.5	3.1	3.6	3.9	3.5
Chongqing	2.0	2.3	3.0	3.4	2.3	2.9[a]
Jiangmen	0.3	3.0	3.6	6.7	5.7	5.3
Jinling	n.a.	n.a.	n.a.	3.3	3.8	3.5
Mindong	n.a.	1.5	2.0	1.8	2.0	1.9
Nanning	n.a.	3.5	5.0	4.2	3.4	4.2
North China Petroleum	n.a.	2.3	2.4	2.4	4.9	3.3
Northwest Cotton	0.6	3.0	3.5	2.8	3.0	3.1
No. 2 Auto	0.1	2.4	2.8	2.7	3.0	2.8
Qingdao	n.a.	3.1	3.2	2.9	1.9	2.7[a]
Qinghe	1.4	3.2	3.7	3.9	3.9	3.8
Qingyuan	0.4	3.6	4.4	6.5	4.4	5.1
Sanchazi	0.9	1.7	2.0	2.7	2.6	2.5[b]
Shanghai Cotton	0.2	1.7	2.0	n.a.	2.4	n.a.[b]
Shanghai Oil Pump	n.a.	2.0	4.9	5.3	5.1	5.1
Shenyang	0.6	2.5	2.9	4.6	4.3	3.9
Tianjin	0.2	3.1	3.6	2.7	2.7	3.0
Xiangxiang	0.8	2.8	3.8	4.0	4.2	4.0

n.a. = not available.

Note: Unless otherwise noted, figures in this table are derived by dividing average total bonus by average basic wages and multiplying by twelve.

a. For Chongqing and Qingdao, the figures are derived by dividing the sum of average bonus from retained profits and average bonus charged to production cost by average basic wages and multiplying by twelve.

b. For Sanchazi and Shanghai Cotton, the figures are derived by dividing total bonuses by total number of staff and workers and then by average basic wages and multiplying by twelve.

losses did not arise. Both enterprises were also permitted to experiment with a floating wage scheme that tied promotions and overall wage increases to profitability. This differs from another, more prevalent floating wage scheme in which some basic wages can be held back and placed in the pool of bonuses available for payment on the basis of results.

Flexibility in hiring practices (apart from setting up collectives to employ dependents of workers) was less common in the sample. But Nanning has started hiring all new workers on a fixed-term contract, and Jiangmen has the more unusual authority to lay off redundant workers. All twenty enterprises gained the right to give bonuses to workers. What is remarkable is the extent to which average bonus payments exceeded the nominal limits of three months of basic wages (table 2-7). This excess is partly due to special performance bonuses—such as those for winning national prizes—but not entirely (see chapter 4).

In several other areas of reform, the twenty enterprises largely followed national trends. Most began to self-market some output, though not all faced buyers' markets (chapters 8 and 9). For most, the scope of guidance planning and price flexibility increased (chapters 7 and 8), and for many, bank loans and capital charges also increased. For six of the enterprises, however, the share of government grants in total enterprise investment increased, in contrast to the national trend (chapter 4).

Several of the enterprises initiated major organizational changes. Chongqing, Jinling, Mindong, No. 2 Auto, Qingyuan, and Tianjin all became corporations with greater autonomy, including the right in some cases to form joint ventures and other types of association. Not all these associations worked well. The experiment in which the Qingyuan County Economic Commission took over economic (not just administrative) responsibility for several county-level state enterprises was not carried through, nor has Jinling lived up to expectations. (See chapters 3, 7, and 10.)

Only a few of the twenty enterprises are model reformed enterprises, but nearly all have greater autonomy in some field. This increase in autonomy often follows a principle of compensation. In the steel industry, for example, the Capital Iron and Steel Company was put on an increasing profit contract system and given substantial self-marketing rights. Anshan was denied similar rights but was given autonomy in foreign trade. Similarly, Shenyang was compensated for its lack of reform in other areas by being given greater flexibility in the use of its wage fund and by being chosen to participate in an experimental democratic election of managers (chapter 12). The twenty enterprises are thus generally typical of Chinese state enterprises in that they are only partly reformed.

Table 2-8. *Gross Value of Output, Constant Prices*
(thousands of yuan)

Enterprise	*1975*	*1976*	*1977*	*1978*	*1979*	*1980*	*1981*	*1982*	*Average, 1980–82*
Anshan	2,597,770	2,821,610	2,863,040	3,350,230	3,565,120	3,537,970	3,374,910	3,518,910	3,477,263
Baoji	16,050	8,820	11,520	21,760	24,450	25,710	28,460	29,680	27,950
Chengdu	44,150	48,380	53,560	66,250	69,270	69,290	75,240	77,950	74,160
Chongqing	6,194	6,450	13,140	23,589	30,886	53,277	85,228	88,543	75,683
Jiangmen	12,700	11,830	13,820	13,110	13,630	17,000	19,350	14,110	16,820
Jinling	n.a.	n.a.	n.a.	n.a.	n.a.	n.a.	1,223,857	1,288,532	1,256,195[a]
Mindong	5,634	4,887	6,599	8,041	12,063	20,185	30,307	35,818	28,770
Nanning	28,927	31,514	36,190	37,830	41,326	50,541	62,060	66,525	59,709
North China Petroleum	n.a.	465,640	949,570	1,351,780	1,351,770	1,255,500	956,330	886,840	1,032,890
Northwest Cotton	51,591	54,160	56,000	67,244	74,929	91,055	103,622	98,628	97,768
No. 2 Auto	52,883	63,821	43,505	170,838	426,952	895,115	1,076,471	1,449,052	1,140,213
Qingdao	17,087	22,800	25,732	18,903	21,093	20,884	16,555	17,357	18,265
Qinghe	48,751	53,737	57,626	60,792	52,445	53,519	71,742	76,956	67,406
Qingyuan	28,360	25,890	28,250	34,940	37,920	37,010	42,730	46,300	42,013
Sanchazi	26,721	28,071	28,485	30,336	31,210	34,307	33,320	36,419	34,682
Shanghai Cotton	159,883	157,997	166,691	179,713	209,191	241,249	264,516	265,617	257,127
Shanghai Oil Pump	2,564	3,394	4,167	5,274	7,123	9,519	11,766	13,101	11,462
Shenyang	460,490	471,160	405,020	478,660	503,760	553,420	538,250	528,470	540,047
Tianjin	n.a.	n.a.	n.a.	174,566	220,438	288,000	n.a.	n.a.	n.a.
Xiangxiang	24,082	30,548	31,762	34,620	36,812	46,693	49,688	51,430	49,270

n.a. = not available.
a. Average, 1981–82.

Table 2-9. *Gross Value of Output, Current Prices*
(thousands of yuan)

Enterprise	*1975*	*1976*	*1977*	*1978*	*1979*	*1980*	*1981*	*1982*	*Average, 1980–82*
Anshan	n.a.	n.a.	2,860,340	3,332,460	3,581,940	3,576,180	3,608,680	3,765,370	3,650,077
Baoji	14,450	8,060	11,520	21,760	24,450	25,710	28,460	29,680	27,950
Chengdu	32,990	35,320	39,080	48,930	52,080	51,120	50,090	51,650	50,953
Chongqing	5,418	5,699	10,750	20,488	27,430	45,858	73,642	64,894	61,465
Jiangmen	13,180	12,310	14,380	13,640	14,180	17,700	20,330	15,270	17,767
Jinling	n.a.	n.a.	n.a.	n.a.	n.a.	n.a.	1,246,419	1,350,922	1,298,671[a]
Mindong	n.a.	n.a.	n.a.	n.a.	12,268	20,320	30,422	36,351	29,031
Nanning	24,450	25,980	28,070	25,890	28,410	36,630	49,830	42,680	43,047
North China Petroleum	n.a.	583,520	1,189,950	1,689,730	1,680,280	1,568,900	1,235,880	1,218,860	1,341,213
Northwest Cotton	54,745	56,231	58,445	68,334	76,819	98,795	99,593	91,139	96,509
No. 2 Auto	52,883	63,821	43,505	170,838	426,952	848,605	920,193	1,084,197	950,998
Qingdao	16,796	21,751	23,367	18,254	18,993	19,147	16,020	16,184	17,117
Qinghe	49,765	54,855	52,813	63,401	55,367	55,020	71,220	78,470	68,237
Qingyuan	31,040	27,080	29,200	36,210	40,830	40,460	48,600	51,260	46,773
Sanchazi	28,374	30,227	29,827	31,710	34,154	45,318	52,253	62,297	53,289
Shanghai Cotton	166,308	164,066	171,917	186,071	211,187	246,903	262,967	251,192	253,687
Shanghai Oil Pump	2,231	1,535	1,906	2,211	2,994	4,365	5,499	5,789	5,218
Shenyang	n.a.	471,160	430,240	506,900	538,940	662,510	697,280	684,390	681,393
Tianjin	n.a.	n.a.	n.a.	191,251	239,397	309,567	360,563	282,448	317,526
Xiangxiang	30,380	33,188	34,491	31,816	40,163	51,585	55,008	57,880	54,824
Total	n.a.	n.a.	n.a.	n.a.	n.a.	n.a.	8,932,949	9,240,923	9,065,745

n.a. = not available.
a. Average, 1981–82.

Table 2-10. *Net Value of Output, Current Prices*
(thousands of yuan)

Enterprise	*1975*	*1976*	*1977*	*1978*	*1979*	*1980*	*1981*	*1982*	*Average, 1980–82*
Anshan	n.a.	1,274,910	1,358,570	1,827,490	1,547,260	1,673,190	1,612,290	1,670,620	1,652,033
Baoji	3,150	1,930	2,760	5,130	5,190	6,510	7,380	8,730	7,540
Chengdu	n.a.	n.a.	26,780	26,560	27,810	24,870	20,650	21,840	22,453
Chongqing	n.a	n.a.	5,002	11,206	15,591	27,637	42,135	40,000	36,591
Jiangmen	1,590	1,550	1,530	1,470	1,960	1,870	3,060	2,820	2,583
Jinling	n.a.	n.a.	n.a.	n.a.	n.a.	n.a.	384,769	422,371	403,570[a]
Mindong	n.a.	n.a.	n.a.	n.a.	4,262	5,928	7,936	8,976	7,613
Nanning	10,510	10,652	10,719	11,304	14,610	21,880	24,000	16,310	20,730
North China Petroleum	n.a.	266,760	513,070	787,120	901,020	888,870	544,320	500,380	644,523
Northwest Cotton	n.a.	n.a.	26,675	30,679	35,807	46,452	47,818	34,290	42,853
No. 2 Auto	n.a.	n.a.	−1,749	54,897	128,056	250,739	271,279	312,639	278,219
Qingdao	n.a.	n.a.	4,842	4,745	5,280	5,234	4,428	4,353	4,672
Qinghe	21,700	23,922	25,898	26,937	23,890	23,800	31,230	34,530	29,853
Qingyuan	8,800	6,670	6,720	11,230	5,880	15,570	19,060	18,840	17,823
Sanchazi	18,248	19,735	16,979	20,533	20,681	29,842	36,709	40,463	35,671
Shanghai Cotton	n.a.	n.a.	71,799	76,375	86,318	101,530	106,806	96,673	101,670
Shanghai Oil Pump	n.a.	n.a.	n.a.	1,821	1,914	2,954	3,524	3,662	3,380
Shenyang	n.a.	68,430	56,520	68,170	83,870	96,840	96,470	93,900	95,737
Tianjin	n.a.	n.a.	n.a.	42,228	51,820	66,798	75,828	55,376	66,001
Xiangxiang	n.a.	n.a.	12,307	14,176	16,833	25,386	27,644	27,651	26,894
Total	n.a.	n.a.	n.a.	n.a.	n.a.	n.a.	3,367,336	3,414,424	3,500,410

n.a. = not available.
a. Average, 1981–82.

Table 2-11. *Wage Bill*
(thousands of yuan)

Enterprise	*1975*	*1976*	*1977*	*1978*	*1979*	*1980*	*1981*	*1982*	*Average, 1980–82*
Anshan	163,986	164,613	166,400	177,030	212,980	195,480	190,290	197,290	194,353
Baoji	809	864	893	1,137	1,255	1,466	1,677	1,788	1,644
Chengdu	2,625	2,668	2,738	3,019	3,343	4,297	4,352	4,614	4,421
Chongqing	810	887	978	1,342	1,837	2,950	3,174	3,335	3,153
Jiangmen	322	333	321	348	444	583	740	675	666
Jinling	n.a.	n.a.	n.a.	n.a.	n.a.	n.a.	18,312	20,901	19,607[a]
Mindong	355	345	338	390	578	1,167	1,337	2,627	1,710
Nanning	1,147	1,131	1,176	1,343	1,683	2,229	2,314	2,403	2,315
North China Petroleum	n.a.	23,618	32,320	38,958	54,044	65,629	70,763	86,898	74,430
Northwest Cotton	2,592	2,633	2,607	3,041	3,791	4,494	4,481	5,114	4,696
No. 2 Auto	23,409	24,061	24,534	27,194	34,837	39,073	41,327	45,243	41,881
Qingdao	546	545	602	788	999	1,123	1,307	1,159	1,196
Qinghe	1,680	1,686	1,679	1,865	2,201	2,731	2,901	3,043	2,891
Qingyuan	2,507	2,569	2,572	3,241	3,567	3,872	4,110	4,438	4,140
Sanchazi	7,264	7,232	7,134	7,537	8,189	9,718	10,115	10,557	10,130
Shanghai Cotton	6,574	6,309	6,200	6,575	6,906	8,188	8,775	8,728	8,564
Shanghai Oil Pump	137	147	160	186	215	302	373	407	361
Shenyang	5,026	5,069	5,111	5,656	6,581	7,335	7,949	7,511	7,598
Tianjin	n.a.	n.a.	n.a.	6,787	8,351	9,262	9,435	10,287	9,661
Xiangxiang	947	918	954	1,130	1,468	1,898	1,985	2,026	1,970
Total	n.a.	n.a.	n.a.	n.a.	n.a.	n.a.	385,717	419,044	395,388

n.a. = not available.
a. Average, 1981–82.

Table 2-12. *Workers and Staff*
(number of persons)

Enterprise	*1975*	*1976*	*1977*	*1978*	*1979*	*1980*	*1981*	*1982*	*Average, 1980–82*
Anshan	208,148	211,202	216,380	214,983	214,438	187,237	188,241	194,638	190,039
Baoji	1,373	1,493	1,478	1,678	1,701	1,738	1,822	1,984	1,848
Chengdu	3,730	3,849	4,014	4,051	4,235	4,458	4,592	4,744	4,598
Chongqing	1,515	1,746	1,948	2,501	2,654	3,787	3,978	4,287	4,017
Jiangmen	625	623	620	614	620	615	643	638	632
Jinling	n.a.	n.a.	n.a.	n.a.	n.a.	n.a.	22,129	23,716	22,923[a]
Mindong	612	599	588	593	919	1,406	1,882	3,335	2,208
Nanning	2,364	2,355	2,338	2,371	2,349	2,642	2,828	3,159	2,876
North China Petroleum	n.a.	33,102	45,556	49,988	62,497	68,555	73,965	79,053	73,858
Northwest Cotton	3,592	3,827	3,937	4,103	4,175	4,678	5,119	6,452	5,416
No. 2 Auto	39,664	40,719	41,595	42,503	44,536	47,885	50,875	53,062	50,607
Qingdao	1,008	1,030	1,089	1,467	1,502	1,709	1,616	1,561	1,629
Qinghe	2,364	2,399	2,467	2,514	2,438	2,723	3,114	3,322	3,053
Qingyuan	4,608	4,710	4,455	5,498	5,534	5,663	5,969	6,218	5,950
Sanchazi	8,744	8,689	8,668	8,490	8,912	9,114	9,677	10,029	9,607
Shanghai Cotton	8,125	8,039	7,948	7,995	7,681	9,357	9,933	9,805	9,698
Shanghai Oil Pump	205	213	235	257	284	325	397	437	386
Shenyang	5,924	6,100	6,208	6,301	6,255	6,250	6,441	6,770	6,487
Tianjin	n.a.	n.a.	n.a.	8,841	8,873	9,188	10,745	12,612	10,848
Xiangxiang	1,678	1,656	1,687	1,699	1,805	2,171	2,274	2,320	2,255
Total	n.a.	n.a.	n.a.	n.a.	n.a.	n.a.	406,240	428,142	408,935

n.a. = not available.
a. Average, 1981–82.

Table 2-13. *Average Basic Wages*
(yuan per month per person)

Enterprise	*1975*	*1976*	*1977*	*1978*	*1979*	*1980*	*1981*	*1982*	*Average, 1980–82*
Anshan	51.2	50.8	50.3	55.7	54.6	57.4	54.8	54.2	55.5
Baoji	49.0	48.2	50.3	53.9	55.3	60.8	58.4	58.0	59.1
Chengdu	51.1	50.3	48.9	50.4	48.9	49.7	49.8	49.9	49.8
Chongqing	45.3	42.8	42.4	49.6	58.8	74.5	77.4	73.7	75.2
Jiangmen	38.5	41.9	41.3	41.9	42.8	46.4	46.0	50.3	47.6[a]
Jinling	n.a.	n.a.	n.a.	n.a.	n.a.	n.a.	45.2	48.7	46.9[b]
Mindong	48.3	48.0	47.9	54.8	52.4	69.2	59.2	65.6	64.7
Nanning	40.4	40.0	41.9	40.0	40.1	41.9	40.6	39.2	40.6
North China Petroleum	n.a.	40.5	40.3	42.8	44.7	47.7	47.4	48.7	47.9
Northwest Cotton	54.1	51.9	50.0	51.2	55.2	51.8	48.4	47.6	49.3
No. 2 Auto	45.1	43.9	44.3	47.0	47.5	49.4	49.6	49.5	49.5
Qingdao	45.1	44.1	46.1	44.8	55.4	54.8	67.4	61.8	61.3
Qinghe	51.4	50.3	48.4	51.5	50.1	47.9	45.3	46.0	46.4
Qingyuan	45.3	45.3	47.9	48.1	49.3	52.6	52.8	55.0	53.4
Sanchazi	52.9	52.6	50.5	53.2	52.0	50.0	50.2	51.6	50.6
Shanghai Cotton	67.4	65.1	65.0	67.6	65.7	61.8	n.a.	62.6	n.a.
Shanghai Oil Pump	55.8	57.5	56.6	60.3	53.8	55.0	54.3	54.4	54.6
Shenyang	60.2	58.6	58.0	60.6	59.3	61.3	60.0	58.0	59.8
Tianjin	n.a.	n.a.	n.a.	55.7	52.8	53.4	49.9	46.0	49.8
Xiangxiang	47.0	46.2	47.1	46.6	48.2	46.7	46.5	46.4	46.5

n.a. = not available.

a. For 1975–77, from quantitative tables provided by the enterprise in January 1984; for 1978–82, calculated from revised data on basic wages provided by the enterprise in December 1985.

b. Average, 1981–82.

Table 2-14. *Gross Fixed Assets*
(thousands of yuan)

Enterprise	1975	1976	1977	1978	1979	1980	1981	1982	*Average, 1980–82*	*Average, 1975–77*
Anshan	5,004,980	5,220,220	5,623,750	6,061,210	6,360,240	6,185,930	6,512,900	6,696,530	6,465,120	5,282,983
Baoji	40,080	41,110	42,020	43,200	42,410	43,000	50,400	50,090	47.830	41,070
Chengdu	42,150	42,550	45,600	47,190	47,440	52,760	56,360	59,130	56,083	43,433
Chongqing	13,774	16,793	21,603	22,432	27,236	31,892	39,813	63,703	45,136	17,390
Jiangmen	1,072	1,285	1,600	1,571	1,796	1,814	1,987	2,894	2,232	1,319
Jinling	n.a.	n.a.	n.a.	n.a.	n.a.	n.a.	379,513	937,088	658,301[a]	n.a.
Mindong	3,408	3,610	3,768	4,200	4,621	7,463	9,153	19,089	11,902	3,595
Nanning	15,119	15,601	15,851	16,012	16,128	16,540	23,978	26,167	22,228	15,524
North China Petroleum	n.a.	533,190	917,760	1,205,790	1,485,490	1,652,030	1,859,000	2,105,540	1,872,190	725,475[b]
Northwest Cotton	31,076	33,000	35,498	36,198	36,656	37,362	37,263	45,413	40,013	33,191
No. 2 Auto	721,065	855,066	969,297	1,146,464	1,268,836	1,439,396	1,528,850	1,596,691	1,521,646	848,476
Qingdao	12,682	13,838	14,778	16,080	17,524	19,253	20,627	20,890	20,257	13,766
Qinghe	14,194	14,572	14,570	15,221	14,242	15,189	30,427	30,804	25,473	14,445
Qingyuan	22,253	23,464	28,883	32,238	33,321	33,099	38,369	43,236	38,235	24,867
Sanchazi	63,411	68,382	72,675	75,331	76,498	84,867	98,650	107,615	97,044	68,156
Shanghai Cotton	49,292	49,563	50,760	50,760	52,501	53,583	53,574	55,432	54,196	49,872
Shanghai Oil Pump	1,871	2,048	2,216	2,626	2,758	2,977	3,193	3,280	3,150	2,045
Shenyang	108,620	113,690	138,780	159,950	156,150	170,180	174,520	177,770	174,157	120,363
Tianjin	n.a.	n.a.	n.a.	34,219	35,068	39,346	46,089	54,893	46,776	n.a.
Xiangxiang	51,729	53,555	56,069	56,323	56,809	55,035	85,222	86,658	75,638	53,784
Total	n.a.	n.a.	n.a.	n.a.	n.a.	n.a.	11,049,888	12,182,913	11,277,606	n.a.

n.a. = not available.
a. Average, 1981–82.
b. Average, 1976–77.

Table 2-15. *Productive Fixed Assets*
(thousands of yuan)

Enterprise	*1975*	*1976*	*1977*	*1978*	*1979*	*1980*	*1981*	*1982*	*Average, 1980–82*
Anshan	4,626,600	4,808,520	5,183,970	5,529,270	5,755,420	5,533,640	5,747,900	5,876,660	5,719,400
Baoji	35,700	35,880	36,480	37,850	37,340	37,830	38,830	38,840	38,500
Chengdu	32,849	33,085	35,226	36,496	35,954	38,959	43,998	45,173	42,710
Chongqing	n.a.	n.a.	n.a.	n.a.	25,397	28,790	34,747	55,268	39,598
Jiangmen	1,068	1,281	1,596	1,552	1,684	1,543	1,716	2,197	1,819
Jinling	n.a.	n.a.	n.a.	n.a.	n.a.	n.a.	342,011	656,371	499,191[a]
Mindong	3,029	3,230	3,388	3,735	3,475	6,475	7,388	14,447	9,437
Nanning	13,518	13,959	14,154	14,222	14,338	14,775	21,365	23,215	19,785
North China Petroleum	n.a.	507,220	830,520	1,110,940	1,352,690	1,462,620	1,595,340	1,787,820	1,615,260
Northwest Cotton	26,759	28,028	30,326	31,137	31,168	31,295	31,649	33,524	32,156
No. 2 Auto	102,076	775,879	875,034	926,023	1,024,982	1,272,364	1,354,572	1,395,912	1,340,949
Qingdao	12,194	13,307	13,888	15,184	15,935	17,763	18,632	18,273	18,223
Qinghe	13,055	12,880	12,892	13,540	12,408	13,031	27,520	27,260	22,604
Qingyuan	20,991	22,135	27,114	30,179	30,952	30,336	34,673	37,891	34,300
Sanchazi	46,871	50,679	54,039	57,282	61,438	58,930	67,776	76,561	67,756
Shanghai Cotton	44,184	44,443	44,941	45,383	46,665	48,208	48,256	49,895	48,786
Shanghai Oil Pump	1,508	2,028	2,196	2,324	2,175	2,538	2,884	2,972	2,798
Shenyang	90,010	95,720	120,720	136,060	127,800	134,990	134,610	136,150	135,250
Tianjin	n.a.	n.a.	n.a.	29,846	31,807	36,126	42,317	48,496	42,313
Xiangxiang	50,098	51,914	54,428	54,573	45,110	45,539	73,412	73,880	64,277
Total	n.a.	n.a.	n.a.	n.a.	n.a.	n.a.	9,669,586	10,400,805	9,795,111

n.a. = not available.
a. Average, 1981–82.

Table 2-16. *Net Fixed Assets*
(thousands of yuan)

Enterprise	*1975*	*1976*	*1977*	*1978*	*1979*	*1980*	*1981*	*1982*	*Average, 1980–82*
Anshan	2,744,680	2,834,790	3,117,760	3,383,880	3,548,650	3,415,490	3,555,810	3,586,250	3,519,183
Baoji	31,530	31,060	30,720	30,370	29,510	27,490	33,290	31,650	30,810
Chengdu	27,307	26,523	28,298	28,727	28,242	32,209	34,305	35,777	34,097
Chongqing	12,149	14,604	18,803	18,689	21,162	24,771	31,563	54,447	36,927
Jiangmen	674	798	1,010	951	706	699	787	2,048	1,178
Jinling	n.a.	n.a.	n.a.	n.a.	n.a.	n.a.	179,723	691,412	435,568[a]
Mindong	2,022	2,066	2,056	2,409	2,797	5,207	6,097	12,734	8,013
Nanning	12,408	12,431	12,217	11,904	11,657	11,554	18,434	19,784	16,591
North China Petroleum	n.a.	403,070	679,240	854,520	966,910	967,820	1,006,940	1,051,500	1,008,753
Northwest Cotton	10,082	11,028	12,502	12,624	12,038	11,741	11,227	18,313	13,760
No. 2 Auto	710,097	835,296	945,156	1,111,670	1,211,266	1,334,911	1,368,893	1,380,352	1,361,385
Qingdao	9,307	9,891	10,234	10,894	11,338	12,964	13,536	13,060	13,187
Qinghe	6,325	6,308	5,856	6,183	5,744	6,183	21,318	20,724	16,075
Qingyuan	14,693	15,047	19,498	22,169	22,436	21,749	25,703	29,217	25,556
Sanchazi	49,182	54,098	58,388	61,042	65,144	59,763	70,921	75,900	68,861
Shanghai Cotton	15,418	15,307	15,568	15,485	15,901	17,071	16,922	16,085	16,693
Shanghai Oil Pump	1,411	1,595	1,712	2,070	2,116	2,311	2,497	2,497	2,435
Shenyang	29,010	28,620	47,950	62,400	62,590	68,420	70,870	71,740	70,343
Tianjin	n.a.	n.a.	n.a.	16,276	17,098	20,100	25,123	31,648	25,624
Xiangxiang	41,985	41,993	42,702	41,147	39,860	37,042	65,043	63,413	55,166
Total	n.a.	n.a.	n.a.	n.a.	n.a.	n.a.	6,559,002	7,208,551	6,760,205

n.a. = not available.
a. Average, 1981–82.

Table 2-17. *Input Inventory*
(thousands of yuan)

Enterprise	*1975*	*1976*	*1977*	*1978*	*1979*	*1980*	*1981*	*1982*	*Average, 1980–82*
Anshan	739,990	753,870	777,640	823,250	611,580	593,170	599,570	605,180	599,307
Baoji	9,410	8,520	6,980	8,410	8,350	6,960	7,800	7,800	7,520
Chengdu	8,628	9,028	8,731	8,979	11,023	7,825	10,970	11,028	9,941
Chongqing	3,548	4,359	5,229	6,507	7,969	10,018	11,523	14,683	12,075
Jiangmen	1,420	1,669	2,275	2,084	1,678	1,534	2,308	1,911	1,918
Jinling	n.a.	n.a.	n.a.	n.a.	n.a.	n.a.	113,939	129,193	121,566[a]
Mindong	n.a.	n.a.	n.a.	n.a.	n.a.	n.a.	6,045	9,890	7,968[a]
Nanning	5,894	7,097	6,132	6,355	5,465	6,328	9,336	8,226	7,963
North China Petroleum	n.a.	134,560	179,450	210,660	201,860	202,470	199,570	176,580	192,873
Northwest Cotton	3,626	7,573	8,777	7,774	10,714	7,987	15,468	12,769	12,075
No. 2 Auto	130,942	174,270	177,329	149,487	197,348	237,387	230,588	208,871	225,615
Qingdao	7,374	8,514	10,579	13,651	10,845	10,137	7,165	6,983	8,095
Qinghe	16,115	15,059	16,071	14,185	8,062	8,026	8,676	7,976	8,226
Qingyuan	5,628	7,265	7,805	8,328	8,801	7,823	8,699	11,913	9,478
Sanchazi	3,524	3,608	3,455	3,667	3,530	4,246	4,159	4,059	4,155
Shanghai Cotton	9,321	9,359	10,093	15,002	11,502	17,168	14,734	15,046	15,649
Shanghai Oil Pump	700	755	728	820	902	847	804	962	871
Shenyang	82,340	62,120	47,650	42,350	58,570	79,520	71,260	63,300	71,360
Tianjin	n.a.	n.a.	n.a.	13,093	14,646	15,770	20,510	16,930	17,737
Xiangxiang	6,790	8,255	6,294	5,564	4,449	4,232	5,043	5,535	4,937
Total	n.a.	n.a.	n.a.	n.a.	n.a.	n.a.	1,348,167	1,318,835	1,339,328

n.a. = not available.
a. Average, 1981–82.

Table 2-18. *Final Products Circulating Assets*
(thousands of yuan)

Enterprise	*1975*	*1976*	*1977*	*1978*	*1979*	*1980*	*1981*	*1982*	*Average, 1980–82*
Anshan	14,270	21,680	14,410	13,080	15,000	43,880	44,860	29,040	39,260
Baoji	140	160	80	50	90	570	410	420	467
Chengdu	134	86	55	39	4	60	232	117	136
Chongqing	253	214	613	583	1,459	1,586	3,852	4,244	3,227
Jiangmen	423	102	649	405	1,079	1,111	922	684	906
Jinling	n.a.	n.a.	n.a.	n.a.	n.a.	n.a.	9,365	19,582	14,474[a]
Mindong	1,587	1,597	1,686	1,696	2,422	3,617	10,214	16,081	9,971
Nanning	60	133	44	681	1,043	565	2,211	5,333	2,703
North China Petroleum	n.a.	6,970	14,820	44,150	38,930	40,070	34,020	45,390	39,827
Northwest Cotton	62	74	96	483	194	969	1,171	4,312	2,151
No. 2 Auto	29,188	12,057	27,148	23,561	17,679	22,773	44,950	14,560	27,428
Qingdao	823	1,479	2,874	1,493	1,250	2,003	879	904	1,262
Qinghe	194	81	77	190	199	315	292	1,712	773
Qingyuan	977	894	1,356	1,233	2,179	2,225	2,334	2,689	2,416
Sanchazi	718	386	549	389	237	550	1,914	1,969	1,478
Shanghai Cotton	272	294	257	185	188	328	192	1,510	677
Shanghai Oil Pump	2	2	12	51	18	26	89	56	57
Shenyang	3,290	6,250	4,020	5,050	4,800	4,000	4,980	3,050	4,010
Tianjin	n.a.	n.a.	n.a.	346	437	1,062	5,186	8,208	4,819
Xiangxiang	727	705	569	775	525	679	1,000	593	757
Total	n.a.	n.a.	n.a.	n.a.	n.a.	n.a.	169,073	160,454	156,797

n.a. = not available.
a. Average, 1981–82.

Table 2-19. *Total Quota Circulating Assets*
(thousands of yuan)

Enterprise	*1975*	*1976*	*1977*	*1978*	*1979*	*1980*	*1981*	*1982*	*Average, 1980–82*
Anshan	1,012,670	980,330	970,430	998,720	951,200	841,300	849,610	782,500	824,470
Baoji	10,000	9,020	7,130	8,510	8,490	7,550	8,430	8,420	8,133
Chengdu	14,100	16,577	16,424	15,432	19,948	17,512	15,996	18,164	17,224
Chongqing	4,908	6,357	7,758	8,856	12,976	15,733	21,169	27,691	21,531
Jiangmen	1,843	1,771	2,924	2,429	2,854	2,677	3,230	2,595	2,834
Jinling	n.a.	n.a.	n.a.	n.a.	n.a.	n.a.	153,204	195,879	174,542[a]
Mindong	3,573	4,245	4,202	4,854	7,406	11,612	16,988	32,740	20,447
Nanning	7,014	9,153	8,083	9,302	9,157	9,363	14,274	16,236	13,291
North China Petroleum	n.a.	143,380	195,470	255,730	242,300	245,740	236,430	226,020	236,063
Northwest Cotton	4,892	8,871	9,946	9,613	12,168	10,596	18,779	19,444	16,273
No. 2 Auto	213,687	253,942	265,887	226,899	255,074	290,289	309,264	261,473	287,009
Qingdao	11,881	15,823	18,241	23,656	17,887	18,771	15,322	14,007	16,033
Qinghe	21,027	20,402	21,209	20,475	13,611	17,377	18,891	20,147	18,805
Qingyuan	7,725	9,493	10,450	11,080	12,249	11,880	13,028	17,042	13,983
Sanchazi	6,172	5,678	5,724	6,143	6,434	7,439	8,802	8,365	8,202
Shanghai Cotton	12,692	13,040	13,884	18,984	14,779	21,135	18,603	20,522	20,087
Shanghai Oil Pump	963	924	956	1,369	1,443	1,327	1,602	1,716	1,548
Shenyang	128,520	112,820	99,660	97,230	118,390	138,550	120,250	112,210	123,670
Tianjin	n.a.	n.a.	n.a.	23,934	27,304	29,457	38,265	35,952	34,558
Xiangxiang	8,070	9,558	7,385	8,446	7,234	5,978	6,925	7,050	6,651
Total	n.a.	n.a.	n.a.	n.a.	n.a.	n.a.	1,889,062	1,828,173	1,865,354

n.a. = not available.
a. Average, 1981–82.

Table 2-20. *Fixed Investment, 1975–77 and 1980–82*
(thousands of yuan)

Enterprise	*Total, 1975–77*	*Average, 1975–77*	*Total, 1980–82*	*Average, 1980–82*
Anshan	936,460	312,153	972,000	324,000
Baoji	3,347	1,116	18,310	6,103
Chengdu	6,330	2,110	9,788	3,263
Chongqing	11,020	3,673	38,500	12,833
Jiangmen	620	207	1,518	506
Jinling	n.a.	n.a.	72,043[a]	36,022[a]
Mindong	n.a.	n.a.	n.a.	n.a.
Nanning	909	303	10,156	3,385
North China Petroleum	676,680[b]	225,560[b]	651,690	217,230
Northwest Cotton	3,373	1,124	2,908	969
No. 2 Auto	419,950	139,983	214,486	71,495
Qingdao	6,442	2,147	3,427	1,142
Qinghe	1,577	526	18,675	6,225
Qingyuan	8,610	2,870	14,246	4,749
Sanchazi	15,897	5,299	29,726	9,909
Shanghai Cotton	6,290	2,097	14,232	4,744
Shanghai Oil Pump	380	127	775	258
Shenyang	27,420	9,140	78,920	26,307
Tianjin	n.a.	n.a.	58,176	19,392
Xiangxiang	n.a.	n.a.	23,298	7,766
Total	n.a.	n.a.	n.a.	n.a.

n.a. = not available.

a. Total and average, 1981–82.

b. Total and average, 1976–77.

Table 2-21. *Sales Revenue*
(thousands of yuan)

Enterprise	*1975*	*1976*	*1977*	*1978*	*1979*	*1980*	*1981*	*1982*	*Average, 1980–82*
Anshan	2,599,160	2,806,840	2,937,850	3,438,040	3,620,510	3,824,230	3,673,970	3,915,400	3,804,533
Baoji	15,440	8,704	11,351	22,437	24,525	25,818	27,712	30,389	27,973
Chengdu	35,689	29,317	45,400	49,100	51,991	48,904	47,864	53,439	50,069
Chongqing	5,571	5,605	10,431	20,477	28,087	42,570	66,641	56,414	55,208
Jiangmen	10,977	10,457	12,145	10,621	11,376	13,887	17,904	14,645	15,479
Jinling	n.a.	n.a.	n.a.	n.a.	n.a.	n.a.	1,172,209	1,333,097	1,252,653[a]
Mindong	4,931	4,718	6,369	8,234	11,194	19,438	19,834	27,356	22,209
Nanning	23,619	24,544	26,613	26,518	29,394	38,463	43,279	36,391	39,378
North China Petroleum	n.a.	506,450	1,140,730	1,553,640	1,663,620	1,581,310	1,235,880	1,121,940	1,313,043
Northwest Cotton	55,176	56,848	58,352	67,929	78,536	98,479	104,928	85,454	96,287
No. 2 Auto	49,720	78,422	40,180	163,727	410,225	835,069	683,063	1,167,692	895,275
Qingdao	13,177	12,387	18,524	18,844	20,477	19,654	15,363	16,744	17,254
Qinghe	49,389	52,925	52,820	62,812	54,049	54,791	70,931	75,123	66,948
Qingyuan	28,615	27,075	28,796	36,199	40,337	39,696	49,297	50,544	46,512
Sanchazi	36,858	36,481	38,965	43,437	44,515	51,723	63,787	68,483	61,331
Shanghai Cotton	221,971	216,249	227,248	248,941	211,528	246,536	261,889	250,355	252,927
Shanghai Oil Pump	1,218	1,535	1,911	2,105	3,015	4,352	5,079	5,662	5,031
Shenyang	436,620	458,900	394,580	467,240	495,650	537,930	570,800	602,620	570,450
Tianjin	n.a.	n.a.	n.a.	141,113	163,198	167,346	178,290	147,841	164,492
Xiangxiang	26,091	29,675	30,845	34,085	35,869	50,441	52,796	56,923	53,387
Total	n.a.	n.a.	n.a.	n.a.	n.a.	n.a.	8,361,516	9,116,512	8,810,439

a. Average, 1981–82.

Table 2-22. *Indirect Taxes*
(thousands of yuan)

Enterprise	*1975*	*1976*	*1977*	*1978*	*1979*	*1980*	*1981*	*1982*	*Average, 1980–82*
Anshan	204,970	221,500	232,270	272,040	241,650	244,940	241,960	305,400	264,100
Baoji	462	259	339	672	735	775	831	912	839
Chengdu	1,785	1,466	2,270	2,455	2,600	2,449	2,397	2,672	2,506
Chongqing	1,291	1,201	2,667	6,583	8,976	12,289	16,222	16,466	14,992
Jiangmen	549	523	615	542	574	699	902	802	801
Jinling	n.a.	n.a.	n.a.	n.a.	n.a.	n.a.	125,578	144,040	134,809[a]
Mindong	n.a.	n.a.	n.a.	n.a.	558	1,034	1,056	1,405	1,165
Nanning	2,755	2,996	3,766	4,315	4,881	6,333	6,884	4,799	6,005
North China Petroleum	n.a.	25,070	56,400	76,880	82,820	78,850	61,800	98,340	79,663
Northwest Cotton	9,873	10,149	10,451	11,379	12,274	15,460	16,221	11,721	14,467
No. 2 Auto	1,181	3,516	1,487	7,637	21,287	41,440	33,502	60,593	45,178
Qingdao	659	619	782	865	919	723	529	801	684
Qinghe	7,432	8,679	9,049	10,067	7,822	7,721	10,735	10,761	9,739
Qingyuan	4,596	3,555	4,171	5,084	5,235	4,306	4,512	5,440	4,753
Sanchazi	2,411	2,498	2,529	2,821	2,805	3,163	3,929	3,995	3,696
Shanghai Cotton	28,374	27,888	30,004	31,445	31,242	34,743	36,238	39,855	36,945
Shanghai Oil Pump	61	77	96	105	151	218	264	283	255
Shenyang	28,190	29,040	25,570	28,450	29,760	30,400	32,420	34,210	32,343
Tianjin	n.a.	n.a.	n.a.	6,751	8,022	8,215	8,792	7,390	8,132
Xiangxiang	3,914	4,451	4,627	5,113	5,380	7,566	7,919	5,724	7,070
Total	n.a.	n.a.	n.a.	n.a.	n.a.	n.a.	612,691	755,609	668,144

n.a. = not available.
a. Average, 1981–82.

Table 2-23. *Administrative Profits*
(thousands of yuan)

Enterprise	*1975*	*1976*	*1977*	*1978*	*1979*	*1980*	*1981*	*1982*	*Average, 1980–82*	*Average, 1975–77*
Anshan	770,970	867,810	945,560	1,300,610	1,336,570	1,449,650	1,299,460	1,258,510	1,335,873	861,447
Baoji	50	−2,963	19	2,764	3,465	4,420	5,539	6,395	5,451	−965
Chengdu	13,191	13,661	20,458	20,507	20,523	17,376	12,778	15,276	15,143	15,770
Chongqing	61	4	1,025	2,901	4,271	10,314	16,959	11,535	12,936	363
Jiangmen	361	251	356	103	153	383	1,218	946	849	323
Jinling	n.a.	n.a.	n.a.	n.a.	n.a.	n.a.	235,041	257,348	246,195	n.a.[a]
Mindong	958	957	1,633	2,487	2,517	3,226	2,582	1,749	2,519	1,183
Nanning	6,085	5,996	5,214	4,837	7,944	11,490	13,505	6,279	10,425	5,765
North China Petroleum	n.a.	144,240	418,670	675,480	770,220	716,830	454,710	312,300	494,613	281,455[b]
Northwest Cotton	12,033	13,066	12,191	15,528	24,510	27,818	26,509	15,416	23,248	12,430
No. 2 Auto	−25,443	−50,657	−37,498	1,309	73,243	161,469	126,775	219,131	169,125	−37,866
Qingdao	2,303	2,166	2,901	2,521	3,016	2,672	1,322	1,616	1,870	2,457
Qinghe	14,800	13,958	14,380	15,282	13,565	13,033	17,641	18,589	16,421	14,379
Qingyuan	1,305	109	−315	1,260	4,252	5,196	9,268	6,123	6,862	366
Sanchazi	3,508	5,133	5,708	6,508	8,314	12,128	15,563	17,084	14,925	4,783
Shanghai Cotton	28,945	29,966	32,621	35,369	43,841	56,347	58,779	50,110	55,079	30,511
Shanghai Oil Pump	488	555	842	1,053	1,471	2,318	2,682	2,754	2,585	628
Shenyang	32,170	31,500	22,700	18,760	43,050	53,320	54,160	50,350	52,610	28,790
Tianjin	n.a.	n.a.	n.a.	26,492	34,085	48,538	54,734	33,828	45,700	n.a.
Xiangxiang	5,070	6,161	6,600	8,858	11,167	16,619	18,708	22,017	19,115	5,944
Total	n.a.	n.a.	n.a.	n.a.	n.a.	n.a.	2,427,933	2,307,356	2,531,544	n.a.

n.a. = not available.
a. Average, 1981–82.
b. Average, 1976–77.

Table 2-24. *Retained Profits*
(thousands of yuan)

Enterprise	*1978*	*1979*	*1980*	*1981*	*1982*	*Average, 1980–82*
Anshan	8,850	15,390	75,330	95,850	203,910	125,030
Baoji	52	575	727	808	2,070	1,202
Chengdu	n.a.	1,189	1,311	1,311	1,921	1,514
Chongqing	65	561	4,320	6,627	2,347	4,431
Jiangmen	n.a.	28	241	887	657	595
Jinling	n.a.	n.a.	n.a.	16,267	27,978	22,123[a]
Mindong	n.a.	597	516	615	806	646[b]
Nanning	66	1,150	1,576	1,724	1,249	1,516
North China Petroleum	5,250	6,010	1,200	5,950	6,170	4,440
Northwest Cotton	152	4,550	3,599	3,563	1,642	2,935
No. 2 Auto	n.a.	15,321	35,261	34,411	51,654	40,442
Qingdao	n.a.	301	81	243	124	149
Qinghe	93	1,111	2,335	2,993	3,094	2,807
Qingyuan	327	781	1,419	2,830	1,227	1,825
Sanchazi	389	2,159	3,272	4,336	3,844	3,817
Shanghai Cotton	330	1,464	3,856	4,458	4,150	4,155
Shanghai Oil Pump	n.a.	119	214	248	239	234
Shenyang	280	3,000	4,280	3,910	3,900	4,030
Tianjin	335	3,828	5,923	6,039	5,036	5,666
Xiangxiang	56	715	1,406	1,636	1,516	1,519
Total	n.a.	n.a.	n.a.	194,706	323,534	229,077

n.a. = not available.

a. Average, 1981–82.

b. Retained profits used, rather than accrued, for the year.

Table 2-25. *Use of Retained Profits*

	Percentage share			
Enterprise	*Production development*	*Workers' welfare*	*Workers' bonus*	*Other*[a]
Anshan	53.6	23.6	20.7	2.1
Baoji	27.9 (6.4)	39.1 (16.3)	33.0 (25.4)	0 (51.9)[b]
Chengdu	26.4[c]	42.7	30.9	0.0
Chongqing	60.0 (35.0)	30.0 (60.0)	10.0 (5.0)	0.0
Jiangmen[d]	38.7	25.3	25.8	10.2[e]
Jinling[f]	61.0	13.3	13.1	12.6
Mindong	n.a. (23.4)	n.a. (34.2)	n.a. (42.4)	0.0
Nanning	25.2	35.7	39.1	0.0
North China Petroleum	n.a. (52.9)	n.a. (35.6)	n.a. (11.5)	0.0
Northwest Cotton	39.1	25.3	25.0	10.6[g]
No. 2 Auto	41.7	35.5	22.8	0.0
Qingdao	49.1	24.5	26.4	0.0
Qinghe	39.7	29.9	21.2	9.2[e]
Qingyuan	32.4	12.9	48.0	6.7[h]
Sanchazi	13.8	39.9	46.3	0.0
Shanghai Cotton	23.6	42.7	33.7	0.0
Shanghai Oil Pump	24.7	44.9	30.4	0.0
Shenyang	11.3	41.5	47.2	0.0
Tianjin	24.9	40.6	31.6	0.0
Xiangxiang	42.2	28.9	28.9	0.0

n.a. = not available.

Note: Figures are for 1980–82 unless otherwise indicated. Percentages are for retained profits put into the different funds, not necessarily those actually used for the purpose specified, unless otherwise indicated. Figures in parentheses indicate actual uses of retained profits.

a. Available information on precise use appears in footnotes.

b. Used for mandatory purchases of treasury bonds from the government and uncompleted construction.

c. Starting in 1982, no money was put into the production development fund.

d. Figures are for July 1, 1980 through June 30, 1983.

e. Reserve fund, apparently accumulated mainly so that the enterprise can provide bonuses in bad years.

f. 1981–82 only.

g. Funds turned over to the Shaanxi Provincial Textile Corporation.

h. Includes the transfer, made by the country's nitrogenous fertilizer plant, of Y500,000 to the local finance bureau, plus some small expenditures on education and family planning.

Note

1. "Billion" means "thousand million."

References

Byrd, William, and Gene Tidrick. 1984. "Adjustment and Reform in the Chongqing Clock and Watch Company." In *Recent Chinese Economic Reforms: Studies of Two Industrial Enterprises.* World Bank Staff Working Paper 652. Washington, D.C.

Chen Jiyuan, Xu Lu, Tang Zongkun, and Chen Lantong. 1984. "Management and Reform in the Qingdao Forging Machinery Plant." In *Recent Chinese Economic Reforms: Studies of Two Industrial Enterprises.* World Bank Staff Working Paper 652. Washington, D.C.

Naughton, Barry. 1985. "False Starts and Second Wind: Financial Reforms in China's Industrial System." In Elizabeth J. Perry and Christine Wong, eds., *The Political Economy of Reform in Post-Mao China.* Cambridge, Mass.: Harvard University Press.

State Statistical Bureau. 1983. *Statistical Yearbook of China, 1983.* Hong Kong: Economic Information Agency.

———. 1984. *Statistical Yearbook of China, 1984.* Hong Kong: Economic Information Agency.

———. 1985. *Industrial Development in China, 1949–1984: Statistical Data.* Beijing: Chinese Statistics Publications.

PART ONE

The Broad Issues

DONG FURENG, DIRECTOR of the Institute of Economics of the Chinese Academy of Social Sciences, discusses in chapter 3 some of the key issues with which Chinese theorists of economic reform are grappling. The issues show that the Chinese debate over reform has gone far beyond that in most socialist countries—and beyond the measures that have so far been implemented in China. For Dong, as for most reformers, the fundamental question is how to increase enterprise vitality: that is, how to induce enterprises to innovate, to increase their efficiency, and to behave in ways that promote intensive growth.

The issue of enterprise vitality raises a host of questions about enterprise autonomy. Should enterprises be allowed to pursue independent goals? Should they be allowed to pursue only the single goal of profits? How can profit seeking be harmonized with the broader interests of society? Should enterprises have autonomy to make investment decisions and to set prices? In answer to each of these questions, Dong argues for nearly complete autonomy. Enterprises should be encouraged to pursue profits because there is no conflict between profits and use value. This supposed conflict disappears when enterprises also have responsibility for marketing their output and, as a result, have to respond to market demand, which by definition reflects use value. Or the conflict can be made to disappear through pricing, tax, and other policies to influence profitability.

What about the recent problems of excessive and haphazard investment? They have arisen because of distorted prices and the lack of a mechanism for enterprise risk bearing. Dong argues that it is essential to create an environment in which enterprises have the autonomy to invest, for only in such an environment will they be able to innovate and meet market demand. He also argues that, except for a few key products, enterprises should have the autonomy to set prices. As the surreptitious price cutting by one of the sample enterprises shows, such autonomy promotes competition and helps expand the output of low-cost products.

Dong also asks what the driving force of enterprise behavior should be. It is commonly accepted in China today that enterprise incentives must be based on economic benefit rather than on administrative orders or moral incentives. But Dong argues that it is necessary to go beyond profit sharing and to come to grips with what Janos Kornai (in chapter 13) identifies as the most basic issue for the reform of a socialist system: getting rid of the soft budget constraint inherent in government bailouts and creating a hard budget constraint for the enterprise. Capital charges, closer bank supervision, and bankruptcy laws may mitigate the tendency to bail out loss-making state enterprises. Dong is skeptical, however, about whether such changes will address the fundamental problem of shifting risk and the responsibility for loss to the enterprise. He feels that it may be necessary to alter the structure of ownership of state enterprises, and he asks whether the sale of share capital in state enterprises might solve the problem. In chapter 3, he merely poses the question, noting that any alteration in the structure of ownership will have social and other consequences requiring further policy changes.

Dong concludes by outlining the changes needed in the external environment to enable enterprises to operate autonomously. These include a unified national market for products, capital, and labor; competition in all markets to keep enterprises under constant pressure to perform better; and price reform to create a reliable information system for decentralized decisionmaking. The implication of Dong's proposals is that traditional mandatory planning would be replaced by a market system in which the state would intervene only to influence the market rather than to make individual enterprise decisions. But Dong makes it clear that he would limit his proposals to small and medium-size state enterprises. The question of how to increase the vitality of large state enterprises remains.

William Byrd and Gene Tidrick take an empirical instead of a normative approach in chapter 4. They first ask what enterprise motivation is rather than what it should be. They analyze the effects of enterprise objectives and of the reform's incentives on factor allocation and use in the twenty enterprises. They conclude that enterprise objectives in China differ from those in capitalist countries and in other socialist countries.

Chinese enterprises have a hierarchy of motives based on the differing interests of workers, managers, and supervisory agencies. But because of the system of lifetime employment and enterprise responsibility for most aspects of worker welfare, the family motive is prominent in most enterprises. Minimum levels of worker welfare must be attained before managers can indulge other motives, such as an expansion drive. Although it is often argued that worker-managed enterprises will restrict employment more than profit-maximizing firms, China's abundant labor, tight wage control, and hiring rules (permitting or requiring enterprises to provide jobs for the children of workers) lead enterprises to expand employment. One policy implication of the analysis is that giving family-oriented enterprises greater autonomy over wage payments, although possibly beneficial for worker motivation and productivity, would also give enterprises an incentive to restrict employment.

Traditionally under tight but fragmented administrative control, factor allocation has been reformed much less than production planning and marketing. Byrd and Tidrick show in a review of land, labor, and investment allocation that enterprises have nevertheless found ways to circumvent controls. Joint ventures and other forms of enterprise associations, analyzed in chapters 4 and 11, have been important mechanisms for gaining access to scarce factors. Such reforms as profit retention and bank loans have given enterprises somewhat more autonomy in their use of funds, but enterprises have often preferred to use added funds for bonuses or worker housing rather than for investment.

Extensive bargaining and the manipulation of bonuses, loan repayment, and rates of profit retention show that there are ample grounds for concern about the soft budget constraint of enterprises. These features also suggest that the present enterprise-based welfare system reinforces the family motive and is thus an obstacle to giving enterprises more autonomy in the use of funds. At the same time, enterprise-based welfare inhibits the government from shifting responsibility for losses to enterprises. The implication is that in the sequence of reform the "socialization of welfare" should, like price reform, precede increased enterprise autonomy.

Byrd and Tidrick also conclude that changes in product markets have influenced enterprise incentives for factor use. The prevalence of buyers' markets in 1981 and 1982 influenced the type of investments and appears to have increased enterprise sensitivity to capital costs. The market constraint may thus have partly substituted for a hard budget constraint in curbing the investment hunger of enterprises. In addition, product competition has restricted the tendency of enterprises to expand employment through direct hiring or mergers.

In chapter 5 David Granick compares the environment for state-owned industrial enterprises in China and in the Council of Mutual Economic Assistance (CMEA) countries of Europe. He draws on the survey of twenty Chinese enterprises, his previous interview research in Eastern Europe, and the literature on the U.S.S.R. Focusing on differences between China and the U.S.S.R., Granick analyzes four main areas: trade among industrial enterprises, labor allocation and payment, the role of the plan, and the role of regional economic authorities.

Granick argues that the most distinctive feature of the Chinese system is the extent to which interenterprise trade is conducted in markets equilibrated by price. (In the CMEA countries other than Hungary most trade among industrial enterprises is conducted through a rationing system of physical allocation in disequilibrated sellers' markets.) Chinese enterprises normally receive supply allocations intended to cover only a part of their needs. They obtain, with little apparent difficulty, most of their additional supply needs through various barter mechanisms or by outright purchases at premium prices. Granick argues that the market is stronger in China than in any CMEA country, including Hungary. Markets remain segmented, however, by regional protectionism, and the multiple-price system has many disadvantages that make price reform necessary.

The market for labor is the opposite of that for products. In the CMEA countries there is a genuine labor market, with a high degree of labor mobility and productivity-based wage differentiation within the framework of a wage fund. In China there is little labor mobility, and wage differentiation is rarely based on differences in skill or effort. China's labor abundance also has a big impact. In both China and the U.S.S.R., worker dismissal is difficult, but in China this difficulty may impede development of an active labor market because of the shortage of employment opportunities in state enterprises.

Granick finds that formal plans are less important in China than in the U.S.S.R. Overfulfillment is easier in China, rewards are less closely linked to fulfillment, and neither supply allocations nor labor recruitment quotas are linked tightly enough to planned output targets to make plans a binding constraint. Retained profits drive Chinese enterprises more than do plan targets. Granick also concludes that the higher degree of localism in China—in contrast to the greater central control of Soviet industry—may reinforce the role of the market in the regulation of Chinese industry.

Gao Shangquan, vice-minister of the System Reform Commission under the State Council, provides insights in chapter 6 about the thinking behind two important official statements of plans for future reform. One statement is the "Reform of the Economic Structure," issued by the Central Committee of the Chinese Communist party on October 20, 1984. The other is the "Proposal of the Central Committee of the Chinese Communist Party for the Seventh Five-Year Plan," adopted by the party national conference on September 23, 1985.

Gao focuses on planning and pricing. The main defects of the planning system are that it is too centralized, that it sets planning in opposition to the law of value, that it relies too much on direct administrative intervention, and that it fails to hold enterprises responsible for performance. In the future the scope of mandatory planning will be drastically reduced, and even mandatory plans will follow the law of value (relying on rational prices). Planning will also be decentralized to lower levels of administration. Central planning will increasingly focus on achieving longer-run macroeconomic targets through indirect levers of control, such as the policies for wages, prices, taxes, credit, and the exchange rate.

Gao explains why official policy now holds that "reform of the pricing system is the key to the success or failure of the reform of the economic system." He also spells out the main principles of price reform. One is that price reform will be incremental to avoid inflation, protect living standards, and encourage users to absorb price increases through increased efficiency. In the dual-price systems, such as that for coal, the incremental approach implies that the share of production sold at market prices will gradually increase and that planned prices will also gradually be increased. But for important products whose prices have been deregulated, the state stands ready to intervene to avoid "wild fluctuations due to blind market forces."

3

Increasing the Vitality of Enterprises

Dong Fureng

CENTRAL TO THE REFORM of China's economic system is an increase in the vitality of enterprises. Enterprises—the cells that make up the national economy—must have vitality if the total organism is to be exuberant. Such vitality has three interconnected aspects.

- The enterprise must be capable of autonomous operation. If it is not, it cannot be fully vital.
- The enterprise must have an internal driving force for improving its operations, for self-transformation, and for self-development. If it does not, it cannot be fully vital.
- The enterprise must take advantage of the external environment and conditions of its vitality. If it does not, it cannot be fully vital, even if the first two conditions are met.

The Capability for Autonomous Operation

Whether enterprises under the system of ownership by the whole people should be capable of operating autonomously is one extraordinarily important question. How they should be given this capability is another. The questions involve three main issues: the independence of the enterprise's objectives, the enterprise's decisionmaking authority, and the unleashing of the enterprise from the state's administrative structures.

Issue 1: Should the Enterprise Have Independent Objectives?

An enterprise operates autonomously to achieve independent goals; without them its autonomous operation is unnecessary or inadvisable. The objective of a private enterprise is to earn more profit. But for enterprises under the system of ownership by the whole people, the state sets goals according to what is best for society. Aside from the goals set by the state, however, do or should such enterprises have their own independent goals?

According to traditional theory, the state represents the common interests of society and sets common goals for society in consideration of these common interests. This approach makes it possible to ensure that resources are allocated properly to achieve the objectives of society, that they are used optimally, and that the national economy develops proportionally. The aim of the enterprise, then, is to achieve that portion of society's common goals assigned to it. If the enterprise has other objectives as well, the goals become pluralistic—hindering the realization of society's common goals, creating an anarchic production situation, destroying the planned development of the national economy, and skewing the allocation of resources.

Under this theory, the enterprise does not and cannot have independent goals. The enterprise's sole mission is to implement the ordered plan targets, which express the interests of the state and serve as the common objectives of society. The more concrete and numerous the ordered targets set by the state for the enterprise, the more the enterprise's activity can be guided onto the path of the state's plans.

A control system of this sort undoubtedly has its advantages, but it carries with it three serious drawbacks. First, the enterprise's vitality is constrained, for the enterprise passively implements the ordered plans set down by the state. It cannot and does not need to operate autonomously.

Second, the state expects to achieve the planned goals by controlling targets and to set the enterprise's various activities on the path toward realizing common goals. Because of the wide variety of product types, however, the responsible agencies find it difficult to check on the enterprise's implementation of the plans. More often than not, the agencies concentrate on the targets for total output value, and the enterprises view meeting these targets as their primary task. They often do not care whether the other targets are met or not, and they may even sacrifice the other targets (such as profit, productivity, comparable cost, and product quality and variety). The results of such an approach are well known: the enterprise often chooses to make products with high output value and heavy material consumption; it is unwilling to replace products and does not consider whether the products correspond to demand. A target of higher total output value may be reached or even exceeded, but at the cost of excessive input and of warehouses stacked with products whose only significance lies in their calculated output value. Consequently, society's common goals are not completely and effectively realized.

Third, under the system just described, the state is always inclined to raise the targets year after year, thereby producing a so-called ratchet effect. Because the enterprise has no objectives of its own and only passively completes those set by the state, it often adopts two methods to complete the ordered assignment easily: it conceals its production capacity from the state or underreports it, and it asks the state for more inputs. As a result, either the state-set goals are met, but with added inputs, or the higher goals that originally could have been met now cannot be.

Strengthening the vitality of enterprises requires that the enterprise have independent goals and that it make an effort to realize them. Here, two issues must be studied: what are the enterprise's independent goals? what is the relationship between the enterprise's goals and the common goals of society? Both issues are complex, and I discuss them only briefly.

To be fully vital, an enterprise must be able to operate autonomously and must have an independent goal. Profit can be the goal, inasmuch as profit best reflects the enterprise's operating situation. To reap greater profits, the enterprise must use the least possible input to achieve the corresponding output. Its products must match the buyers' demands as closely as possible. It must make maximum use of new technology, improve product quality, develop new products, and so on. Furthermore, the total profit determines the amount of profit that the enterprise will be able to keep for itself, and the amount of retained profit, in turn, determines the enterprise's capability and prospects for self-transformation and self-development.

Should an enterprise have objectives other than increasing profit? In other words, should the enterprise's independent goals be unitary or multiple? In the view of some people, it should have at least one goal other than profit: meeting the demands of the people. Because this is the goal of socialist production, it should be the primary one. To achieve it, the enterprise should place most importance on the value of product use; otherwise, the enterprise may neglect the primary goal for the sake of pursuing a profit. The problem with this view is that it puts the two objectives in opposition to one another.

Autonomously operated enterprises must always be concerned with the use value of their products—with how their products correspond to people's demands. (Under a system using a market mechanism, use value is expressed as market demand.) The reason for such concern is that the enterprise's products will sell well only if they match people's demands, and only if the products sell well will the enterprise be able to earn a greater profit. Therefore, by making profit its goal, an enterprise has already included the premise of meeting people's demands.

Making the meeting of the people's demands (product use value) and profit the enterprise's goals and subordinating profit to product use value do not go beyond the framework of the original economic system. If the enterprise takes product use value as its primary goal, the state must set such material targets as output, variety, and specifications for all products, and the enterprise will still be without an autonomous operating capacity, as it was in the past. Will some contradiction arise, however, between the enterprise's behavior in earning more profit and the requirements of meeting the demands of the people?

Individual enterprises can consider only whether their products correspond to popular demand. The policies an enterprise sets to earn more profit may not tally with the demands of the people. For example, when market conditions are good for a product, the enterprise will increase the output of that product to earn more profit and will perhaps produce too much. Under the original system, the enterprise is concerned only with meeting plan targets, not with whether the product corresponds to the demands of the people. But under the effects of the market mechanism, the enterprise would react quickly to correct the problem.

The enterprise cannot take the entire national economy into account, and its actions to earn more profit cannot on their own correspond to common social goals. Therefore, the state must guide the actions of the enterprise according to society's wants. The state can use various measures (primarily such economic measures as prices, taxation, and credit) to influence increases and decreases in the enterprise's profits. As a result, the enterprise's goal of earning profit is coordinated with society's common goals, and the enterprise's efforts to realize its goals are channeled toward realizing society's common goals. Such a path is complex, but it is possible to follow it.

Issue 2: How Much Decisionmaking Authority Should the Enterprise Have?

If an enterprise should have independent goals and if it should be capable of operating autonomously, it should have decisionmaking authority. Decisionmaking authority is necessary not only for achieving goals but also for determining them (particularly their structure).

One key element of the reform of the economic system is that the enterprise must have everyday decisionmaking authority over its operations, so that it can operate autonomously. The problem is, exactly what decisionmaking authority should be handed over to the enterprise? The difficulty of drawing a clear boundary line between the economic decisionmaking authority of the state and that of the enterprise makes this question complex, and since many factors and changes determine its resolution, it cannot be settled once and for all.

The debate over whether enterprises should receive the authority to use fixed-asset basic depreciation funds has already been settled; the state has ceased drawing them. I shall discuss two other types of decisionmaking authority, both of which are still being debated.

First, should the enterprise enjoy partial authority for its investments? In a socialist economy, the state, by controlling investment decisionmaking, can achieve common social goals. It can also make adjustments in production sectors and local structures, overcome imbalances in the economy, and match production and demand. It can then regulate employment ratios and, to some extent, people's income (for example, by allocating investments in two large categories). At the same time, it can regulate and control the direction in which the enterprises develop.

In the last few years, however, enterprises have had some investment authority: in addition to using part of their withheld profits to constitute an enterprise fund, they have borrowed funds from banks to use as investments. Some economists—Sun Yefang, for instance—oppose such investment authority for enterprises, believing that it may create economic chaos and lead to haphazard investment. True, there has been some haphazard investment, and some enterprises have gone so far as to divert state allocations for technological transformation in order to expand their scale of operation—just what those opposed to enterprise investment authority worry about.

The way this situation arises must be analyzed. Without partial investment authority, an enterprise is not capable of self-transformation and self-development, so there is no way it can make significant technological advances, adapt to major changes in market demand, or open new markets. With this authority, however, the enterprise might proceed blindly, in which case the state must provide guidance and supervision. But partial investment authority may lead to cautious consideration by the enterprise of the risks of investment, which in turn may lead to better results.

Nevertheless, because the investments are insufficient, the blame for haphazard investment in the last few years should be placed on the partial investment authority of enterprises. Another cause of haphazard investments has been the erroneous information of distorted prices and the absence of mechanisms for enterprises to bear the risks of the investments. At the same time, the state has been unable to use a number of economic levers (credit, profit margins, taxation, prices, and so on) to guide enterprise investments according to society's wants. If these conditions can be changed, and if certain control and supervisory measures can be taken (such as bank control and supervision), this haphazardness can be easily rectified, either by the state or by the enterprise. The social economy will then benefit from the enterprise's having partial investment authority and the capability for autonomous operation.

Second, should enterprises have authority to set prices? This question is also hotly debated. Before the economic reforms, the state controlled prices very closely, except for some small commodities of no special importance.

Therefore, prices lost their function as economic regulators. Because prices did not reflect changes in labor productivity and supply-demand relationships, the enterprise might proceed according to the inaccurate price information, leading to imbalances in supply and demand. And if enterprises took profit as their goal, the results were even more serious.

Enterprise participation in price setting helps not only in price regulation of the supply-demand relationship. It also helps develop competition, encouraging enterprises through changes in prices to modernize their technology and improve their productivity. Therefore, except for a few product prices that the state should set to induce the enterprise to pursue state-selected goals, the market mechanism should regulate prices, and the various actors in enterprises and the market should participate in setting prices.

The demand by enterprises for price-setting authority is now intense because of the various problems caused by state-set price controls. For example, because of high prices, wristwatches are now unmarketable. Some enterprises have low production costs for wristwatches, however, and they could expand their outlets by lowering prices. But their lack of authority to lower prices by themselves causes production problems.

Recently, people have been stressing that the state should strengthen its price controls to rectify the unfavorable impact of fluctuating prices on living standards during the reform of the economic system. This attitude is understandable, but if we take as a goal the reform of the existing economic system and the establishment of a new one, we should give enterprises the authority to set prices. If the state sets all prices and if enterprises have no right to participate in setting them, prices will not act as economic regulators, and it will be impossible to overcome the ills of the original economic system.

Issue 3: Should Enterprises Be Made Independent of the Direct Jurisdiction of Administrative Structures?

One characteristic of the original economic system is that the state's administrative structures manage the enterprises directly. The enterprises belong to administrative structures at various levels and are subordinate units of those structures, which set and approve the activities of their enterprises. Administrative formalities, bureaucratic red tape, and inefficiency are necessary products of this type of system. Just to build a toilet, an enterprise may have to obtain ten or more stamps from various administrative agencies. This type of economic system, with its unity of government and enterprise, means that the enterprise has no capacity for autonomous management. Removing the enterprise from its position as an appendage of a government structure is an important reform for increasing enterprise vitality. But two difficulties arise in implementing a division of functions between government and enterprise, one from the state's administrative structures, one from the enterprise.

First, people are accustomed to having enterprises directly managed and controlled by the state's administrative structures. They do not understand how to use economic methods to control the economy and indirectly to regulate enterprise activities. Also, they are concerned that a division of functions between government and enterprise will cause the state to lose its economic management function and make it unable to control enterprise activities, which may deviate from state plans. Therefore they often think, consciously or unconsciously, that the original set of methods should be used to control enterprises.

For these reasons, a good many organizations called "administrative companies" have cropped up in recent years (they are disguised administrative structures). They present a "company" façade, but they still use the old methods of administrative structures to intervene directly in the enterprise's everyday operations and activities. Not only is there no separation between enterprise and administrative structure, but the "unity" is even tighter than it was under the old system. In addition to the same old procedures, such as requesting instructions and making reports, the enterprise must also ask the "company" for management costs and service costs.

The other difficulty comes from the enterprises, many of which operated for so long under the past system that they became dependent on the administrative structures. They asked for instructions in all matters and proceeded accordingly, never having to bear the risks in their own actions, never having to worry about administration. Thus, although the enterprises resent the fetters the various administrative structures impose on their activities, many of them are at a loss as to what to do when government and enterprise functions are separate. On the one hand, the enterprises do not believe that it is good to have many administrative structures controlling them. On the other hand, they do not believe that it is feasible to have no such control, and they hope for some administrative structure to come and take charge of them.

These two difficulties hinder attempts to make enterprises independent of their respective administrative structures. In a socialist economy, state management of the economy is important for planned, harmonious development and for achieving society's common goals. Nevertheless, the management must be made different from that of the past economic system in nature, procedures, and methods. State management should not intervene in the everyday operations and activities of the enterprise or be a superior structure that issues orders. Instead, it should set standards of behavior for the enterprise, providing direction and guidance to the enterprise's activities and intervening administratively only when necessary. Otherwise, there may be a return to direct management and administration of the enterprise by administrative structures, which would cause the enterprise to lose its capacity for autonomous operation.

The Internal Driving Froce

Should enterprises under the system of ownership by the whole people have their own internal driving force for improving operations, self-transformation, and self-development? If they should, how should this force be stimulated? The questions raise two issues: what the enterprises' driving force should be and whether a hard budget constraint can replace the present soft budget constraint.

Issue 1: What Should the Enterprise's Driving Force Be?

For private enterprises, the driving force is clear and precise: it is the pursuit of greater profit. For enterprises under the system of ownership by the whole people, the matter is not so clear or precise. Under the original economic system, an enterprise has not had independent goals. Its mission has been to achieve that part of the social goals assigned to it, and its driving force has been a sense of political mission and responsibility—that is, meeting and exceeding the plan targets sent down by the state. The state has relied on political mobilization to arouse this sense in the enterprise and in its staff and workers; it has regularly selected model workers, made presentations during major events and holidays, and initiated such political movements as the Increase Production Movement and the Practice Thrift Movement to arouse the political fervor of the enterprise and staff and workers.

Under the right conditions, such political movements can have an effect. But ultimately this type of driving force has limits. The political fervor thus aroused cannot be sustained for long, and when it subsides it has to be aroused again. For example, holding Quality Month activities may raise the enterprise's concern with product quality, but this concern cannot be continued indefinitely or made a part of regular activities, so a Quality Month has to be held every year.

In addition, the state relies on such administrative approaches as binding orders, directives, and decisions to propel the enterprise and the entire economy. Such approaches have a major shortcoming: they fail to mobilize the enterprise's internal enthusiasm, and as a result the enterprise often uses all sorts of methods to counter them. For example, to deal with high targets sent down by the planning agencies, the enterprise holds down its production capacity, limiting in various ways the year-end production it could reach. Or it produces products that consume large amounts of raw materials but that do not yet have markets—thus realizing the targets for total output value but paying no attention to economic results.

Practice has demonstrated that enterprises under the system of ownership by the whole people must have their own internal economic driving force. This driving force is economic benefit. Without it, or if it bears no relationship to the enterprise's operating circumstances, the economic benefit of the staff and workers cannot bear any relationship to that of the enterprise, and the enterprise will be unable to sustain enthusiasm for autonomous operation.

The state also sets profit targets for the enterprises, but profit cannot be the internal driving force for the enterprise, since this profit is turned over to the higher authorities. The enterprise obtains no real benefit from an increase in profit, nor do the staff and workers. Economic benefit can serve as the internal driving force for the enterprise's autonomous operations, and the enterprise and its staff and workers will be concerned with rational operation, only under two circumstances: when a direct relationship is established between profit and the income withheld by the enterprise, and when a direct relationship is also established between the income of staff and workers and the income withheld by the enterprise.

Is it possible under these circumstances for the enterprise's benefit to differ from the state's? It is possible. We have recently seen enterprises everywhere wildly issuing wage and bonus subsidies. The reason for this behavior is not that economic benefit is serving as the enterprises' internal driving force but that no mutually restricting and mutually promoting relationships have been established. For example, when an enterprise sacrifices the state's benefits and reduces the state's income to increase the wages, bonuses, and subsidies for staff and workers, and when there is no rigorous system of taxation to control this behavior, the taxation system remains loose, and the results are less than outstanding, even if there is a bonus tax. In addition, the starting point for individual income tax is too high, and the enterprise income tax is also incomplete, so that taxation cannot have its desired effects.

Establishing the various mutually restricting and mutually promoting economic relationships is indeed difficult. Only by resolving this question can the enterprise's internal driving force for autonomous operation be aroused and the various driving forces channeled in the proper direction. The experiences of two of the enterprises surveyed for this study can serve as examples of the importance of stimulating an enterprise's internal driving force.

The Chongqing Clock and Watch Company was one of the first enterprises in Sichuan to receive expanded enterprise autonomy. The company has the authority to market its products, and the trade agencies use a pick-and-choose system for the company's products instead of the controlled procurement contract system of the past. The company can market on its own what is left over from the picking and choosing of the trade agencies. The company also enjoys economic benefits and can withhold part of its profits. If it has a loss, it must find a way to make it up.

Under these circumstances, the old system of relying on plan targets to regulate production began to be ineffective, and Chongqing had to pay more attention to market changes and to profit and loss. In 1982, as the plans for

1983 were being set, the company, taking into account that alarm clocks were becoming unmarketable, reported to its administrative agency a cutback in production plans. Still, the ordered plan targets sent down by the agency remained very high. Alarm clocks had been subject to controlled procurement, with the state responsible for all enterprise profit and loss and the company producing according to the targets sent down by the agency. Therefore, even though too many alarm clocks were produced, the company suffered no direct losses.

Because of reforms, however, the enterprise and the staff and workers became concerned with their economic benefit. If too many alarm clocks were produced, the trade agencies would not purchase them, and the company might suffer losses. Therefore, even though the agency sent down ordered plan targets, the enterprise did not implement them. Instead, it produced according to its own plans. The results show the correctness of the enterprise's policy.

Another example is the Qingdao Forging Machinery Plant. This plant had always produced forging press machinery; production plans were always compulsory, and the supply of the product never met the demand. In 1980, because of adjustment in the national economy, the state cut back on the production of forging press machinery. No production targets were sent down to this plant, which suddenly was in an extraordinarily difficult situation. Unable even to pay its wages, the plant had to look for markets on its own. It discovered that several enterprises under the collective system of ownership were new customers for forging press machinery, enterprises that previously had been unable to obtain forging press machinery from the state because of short supply.

To produce the forging presses for these new customers, the plant also had to look for steel and fuel, means of production that had previously been distributed according to state plans. But with the state no longer giving production assignments to the plant, it no longer gave the plant these means of production. The plant overcame this difficulty, too. It continued to produce, and both the plant and its staff and workers benefited.

These two examples show that the enterprise and its staff and workers need to be concerned with the enterprise's production and operation from the standpoint of economic benefit. This concern stimulates the enterprise's internal driving force, and the enterprise can then actively overcome difficulties and strive for rational operation. When the state's policies are mistaken, the enterprise may do its part to correct them.

Issue 2: Can a Hard Budget Constraint Replace the Soft Budget Constraint?

For enterprises under the system of ownership by the whole people, economic benefit must be the internal driving force. This requirement presents one problem that is not easily resolved: turning the enterprise's soft budget constraint into a hard budget constraint. Since the means of production of enterprises under the original economic system have been owned by the whole people, most of the enterprise's income has had to be turned over to the state for social allocation and use. The enterprise bears no risks for losses: if losses occur, it can shift the burden of those losses to society by means of financial subsidies. With this kind of soft budget constraint, economic benefit cannot be the enterprise's internal driving force.

Reforming the economic system to make the enterprise responsible for its profit and loss is a necessary condition for making economic benefit the enterprise's internal driving force. But changing soft budgets to hard budgets and getting the enterprise to take genuine responsibility for profit and loss—without going so far as to have the economic benefit of the enterprise and of its staff and workers related only to enterprise benefit and not to enterprise losses—are problems that remain to be solved. These problems are complicated by the fact that enterprises under the system of ownership by the whole people are different from private enterprises and collectively owned enterprises.

Many small and mid-size enterprises under the system of ownership by the whole people are implementing trial reforms. For example, they are changing over to collective ownership and making operating contracts for staff and workers, or they are being run by staff and workers under leases. The experiments are helping to impose a hard budget constraint for these enterprises, but they cannot be extended to all enterprises.

Whether large enterprises—and small and mid-size enterprises not suited for the foregoing experiment—can impose a hard budget constraint by sharing capital is a question that can be answered only after the system is tried. Discussions surrounding the question of share capitalization for state-owned enterprises are now going on, and experiments are now under way in a few enterprises. Since making the state-owned enterprise responsible for its profit or loss is not possible by relying only on the strengthening of the management of funds, however, some other measures would be useful: for example, a system of user fees for capital, tight bank supervision over the enterprise, or even a bankruptcy law stipulating that enterprises whose liabilities exceed their assets should be forced to go bankrupt.

But these measures cannot completely solve the problem. Whenever a state-owned enterprise suffers financial losses because of inept operations, the state invariably shows meticulous care to help the enterprise out of trouble (some say maternal concern, others paternal). For instance, the state might reduce taxes and profits that should be remitted or allow a reduced interest payment; or it might permit a rescheduling of bank loans or totally forgive the loans, or pump in additional financial assistance—say, by providing new loans—or even allow the enterprise to raise the prices of its products. In some cases, the supervising department will set a deadline for the enterprise to change from a money loser to a profit maker, and during the interim the state will underwrite all losses, despite its declaration that it will no longer assume responsibility once the deadline has passed. All such stipulations are only a sort of reminder; they are not legally binding. If the enterprise still suffers losses after the deadline, the state can do nothing but go on giving subsidies and extending the deadline.

All these problems have prompted people to consider share capitalization for state-owned enterprises. The questions now being studied are how this change might be implemented and what the consequences might be.

The External Environment and Conditions

If enterprises under the system of ownership by the whole people are to achieve full vitality, they must have an external environment and conditions that enable them to operate autonomously. Most important, they must have a market environment and market conditions, for without them it will be impossible to stimulate their internal capacity for autonomous operation. The main factors in achieving a market environment and market conditions are having inputs and outputs circulate freely, creating normal competitive market conditions, and providing enough accurate economic information.

First, funds, materials, workers, and products must be able to circulate freely. The original economic system hinders the formation of this market environment, inasmuch as it manages the economy through sectoral and regional administrative systems. It divides the national economy, produces barriers between sectors and regions, and obstructs the flow of funds, materials, workers, and products. An enterprise is largely restricted to its sector and region. If an enterprise is to operate autonomously and develop its vitality, these barriers and obstructions must be removed. To this end, enterprises must be separated from administrative structures, and the system of managing the economy according to the administrative system must be reformed.

In the last few years, barriers and obstructions have been somewhat overcome. For example, the Chongqing Clock and Watch Company broke through regional restrictions and, cooperating with Yunnan Province, made a joint investment to build the Kunming Watch Plant in Kunming. The Chongqing Clock and Watch Company provides most of the watch parts to the Kunming plant, and the Kunming plant makes a few parts on its own and then assembles the watches. This type of movement of funds and materials from region to region has a favorable impact on increasing enterprise vitality. It also promotes development in backward regions. As another example, many plants are beginning to break through the sectoral boundaries, carrying out interindustry production. For example, some national defense plants, facing inadequate production assignments, are beginning to produce civilian products. Plants producing the means of production are beginning to produce the means of subsistence: the Qingdao Forging Machinery Plant is preparing to install a production line to produce beer cans.

The flow of labor between regions and sectors is also developing. Barriers and obstructions still exist, however, and the domestic market is not yet fully open and unified. In the last few years, local protectionism has flourished in some places. To protect their backward industries, some regions have blocked the inflow of products from other regions. Certain raw materials (such as tobacco) of a given region must first be used by enterprises in that region, with restrictions on their transfer to other regions, and so on. Enterprises encounter many obstructions of this sort in their operations, and they must be eliminated through reform.

If funds, materials, workers, and products are to flow freely, it is necessary to create markets for them. Today the quantities of means of production entering the market are very limited. More and more means of production must be brought to the market, so that, when the enterprise adapts to changes in the market by adjusting its production, it will be able to obtain the means of production quickly.

In the financial market, the horizontal movement of funds is expanding daily, and this is significant. But for loans between individuals in rural areas, there still is no free financial market. A trend toward pooled-capital enterprises—in which two or more individuals or collectives contribute capital and share profits in proportion to their contributions—has begun. If there is no corresponding financial market, it will be very difficult for the pooled-capital enterprises to develop. The development of the financial markets will certainly strengthen enterprise vitality, but in a socialist economy, problems may arise after a share-capital stock market is created. These problems—for example, speculation and dividend income—have yet to be studied.

The labor market is even more of a problem, one that has not been studied. Labor is not a commodity in a socialist economy, so how can there be a labor market? Yet if there is no labor market, how can labor supply and demand be regulated? Planned allocation of the labor force cannot become the universal mode of regulation; regulation of labor should include market regulation of labor supply and demand. Since the enterprise's operating autonomy requires that it be able to handle the labor force autonomously, there must be a corresponding labor market to supply the labor force and keep reserves for it. How is a socialist labor market to be organized? What differences will there be from a capitalist labor market? These questions must also be studied.

The second problem in achieving a market environment is creating normal competitive market conditions. Such conditions are significant for increasing enterprise vitality and autonomous operation for two main reasons: they provide the enterprise with a normal domain of activity that can stimulate the enterprise to operate rationally; they force the enterprise to move ahead constantly, never being complacent and never quitting. To create such conditions, the following problems must be solved during the reform:

• Special treatment must be eliminated from economic activity, for it hinders the development of normal competition. Under the original economic system, there was a distinction between enterprises directly under the central government and local enterprises, including provincial and county enterprises. There was also a distinction between key enterprises and nonkey enterprises. There even was a distinction between ministerial, departmental, and board categories. All these different enterprises were treated differently in regard to funds, materials, labor (including technical personnel), product marketing, foreign-directed economic activities, prices of raw materials, and so on.

If special treatment and "pull" are not eliminated from economic activity, the various enterprises will not be able to achieve equal footing in normal market competition. Some enterprises receiving special treatment have no need to be conscientious in improving their operations. Other enterprises, not receiving any special treatment, are in an unfavorable situation and find it difficult to compete. For example, enterprises that have to purchase their own raw materials may find that they have to pay several times more for the same raw materials than do enterprises receiving supplies under state plans.

• Monopolies must be prevented, an important condition for increasing enterprise vitality. During the reform of the economic system, many enterprises have combined to form a few companies in order to promote specialization and cooperation in production. This merging is necessary, but these few companies must be prevented from monopolizing the market. Monopolies are not conducive to technological progress or to encouraging enterprises to improve their operations. They may also give rise to price distortions.

• Markets must be opened on the one hand and guided on the other. If a market cannot be opened, several economic levers that have an effect on market mechanisms (prices, credit, taxation, and so on) cannot work normally in regulating the economy. Because market mechanisms cannot alone bring about the realization of common social goals, their effect on the market must be guided to lead to the realization of those goals. This guidance gives the enterprise vitality and enables it to operate autonomously. It also coordinates enterprise goals and common social goals with the necessary market conditions.

Because the market has not yet opened and forceful guidance has not yet been achieved, some enterprises cannot operate normally. For example, there are many different prices for the same type of steel—the difference sometimes being many times over. These differences cause extreme instability in the cost of an enterprise's products, making it difficult for the enterprise to operate rationally or to forecast its operating results. These differences also cause the favored enterprises not to devote effort to improving their operation but to rely on price differences to earn a profit.

The third problem in achieving a market environment is providing ample and accurate economic information. Such information is necessary if an enterprise is to develop its vitality and operate autonomously. Under the original economic system, information did not seem terribly important. Like the highly centralized systems for decisionmaking, regulation, and management, the systems for gathering, transmitting, storing, and processing information were essentially vertical and all carried out by the administrative system. The gathering and transmission of information were slow, and reactions to information were sluggish. Enterprises were not concerned with information.

Under the new economic system, with enterprises having the capacity for autonomous operation and an internal driving force, it has become extraordinarily important that they get ample, accurate, and timely economic information. To this end, it is necessary to reform the old information system, which means changing the primarily vertical system to a primarily horizontal one. Enterprises should get the necessary information from all quarters and, at the same time, from many information channels.

Prices are an important source of information for enterprises, but currently they are severely distorted and provide skewed information. Because enterprises must judge market trends and their operating situation according to the information that price changes provide, that information must be accurate. Price reform, however, has not been regarded as determining the success or failure of the reform of China's national economic system. In addition to domestic market information, it is becoming ever more important that enterprises—especially those producing export products and those involved in import-export trade—get ample, accurate, and timely information about international markets.

One final major problem is increasing the vitality of large enterprises under the system of ownership by the whole people. Large enterprises hold an important place and have a major impact on the national economy, but compared with small and mid-size enterprises, they have less capacity for autonomous operation. They must still proceed basically according to the principles of the original economic system. Only after they have met the state's ordered plans can they produce outside the stipulated plans according to market demand and their own excess production capacity. Under such circumstances, economic benefit cannot become an effective internal driving force.

Because they lack the capacity for autonomous operation, large enterprises cannot compete with the more flexible small and mid-size ones, despite their preferential treatment for funds, materials, labor, and prices. After some small and mid-size enterprises have begun hiring and have implemented operating contracts for staff and workers, the inability of the large enterprises to compete with them will be even more acute. The problems discussed here have basically not been solved for large enterprises, and it is therefore essential to concentrate on doing so.

In summary, if we are to increase the vitality of enterprises, we must proceed on many fronts. The problems I have discussed involve the entire economic system. Because of the scope of these problems, I have not been able to discuss each aspect and each problem in depth. Nor have I gone into the problem of how to take advantage of having the labor force as masters of the enterprise, though this too is an important aspect of increasing enterprise vitality. We can nevertheless see from the foregoing summary that the reform of the economic system must be centered on increasing the vitality of enterprises. By grasping this central link, we will have seized the entire chain of the economic system's reform.

4

Factor Allocation and Enterprise Incentives

William Byrd and Gene Tidrick

UNTIL ABOUT 1960 it was commonly accepted that the main source of economic growth is the growth of land, labor, and especially capital inputs. Then it was discovered that such growth could not account for a large part of growth in the industrial countries (see Denison 1967). This led to the new views that the allocation of factors, the incentives for using them efficiently, and technological change are frequently as important as the growth of factor inputs.

At about the same time, economic policymakers in the U.S.S.R. and the socialist countries of Eastern Europe concluded that their economic growth could be sustained only by shifting emphasis from extensive growth (which relies on the growth of factor inputs) to intensive growth (which concentrates on upgrading technology and improving total factor productivity). Since 1978 China, too, has adopted a strategy of intensive growth, stressing the growth of factor productivity rather than the accumulation of capital as the main source of output growth. The program of adjustment and reform launched that year was to be the means for attaining high living standards and greater efficiency.

Total factor productivity in Chinese industry has been essentially stagnant for twenty-five years. Although the failure to upgrade technology is partly to blame, the main fault apparently lies with inefficient factor use and the failure to diffuse best-practice techniques (Tidrick 1986). McKinnon (1973) has shown that one of the main obstacles to the efficient use of capital in developing countries is the fragmentation of capital markets. In China there is no market for capital—or for land or labor—and allocation of all factors is fragmented. The recent reforms have nevertheless changed enterprise incentives and provided more opportunities for enterprises to influence factor allocation and use. Equally important, the reforms have affected enterprise objectives, sometimes with paradoxical effects on incentives and factor allocation.

Enterprise Objectives

Policymakers in China often advocate reforms to "stir the enthusiasm" of enterprises and workers. Bonuses, retained profits, and enterprise autonomy have all been promoted for this reason. Too often, however, the assumptions about enterprise motivation that underlie these recommendations remain unexamined. It is important to understand what enterprises are enthusiastic about—to know, for example, whether enterprises would like to use their retained profits to expand production or to increase bonuses—before recommending how to stimulate their enthusiasm. This section examines the objectives of enterprises in our sample and analyzes what these objectives mean for enterprise behavior and public policy.

There are three main models of socialist enterprise objectives. The model of enterprise behavior in the U.S.S.R. and Eastern Europe has typically assumed that enterprise managers make enterprise decisions and that they maximize their (discounted) future earnings, including salaries, bonuses, and benefits from promotions. Managerial rewards, in turn, are based on fulfillment of plan targets, so that enterprises maximize some function of performance targets set by outside authorities (Granick 1975, chap. 4). A second model, proposed to predict the behavior of Yugoslav labor-managed enterprises, assumes that labor-managed firms will act on behalf of worker interests. They will therefore maximize average net product, or income per worker. The relevance of this model for Yugoslavia has been debated extensively (see chapter 14 in this volume). The third model of socialist enterprise behavior assumes that enterprises maximize output. This is stated most comprehensively in Kornai's theory of the "expansion drive." Enterprises exhibit the expansion drive or "investment hunger" even when there is no central plan with ambitious production and investment targets. Enterprises wish to expand because managers identify with the organization and believe it is important. They perceive a shortage of output and therefore an urgent need to expand—and they face no penalties if an investment fails. The expansion drive is thus a function of the shortage economy with its soft budget constraint (Kornai 1979, 1980).

How, if at all, do these models apply to China? The question is important because different enterprise objectives have different implications for enterprise behavior. Three examples of such implications can be cited. First, labor-managed firms will often strive to distribute their surplus, whereas a firm driven by investment hunger will reinvest its surplus. Second, an enterprise whose manager is mainly concerned with fulfilling plan targets will produce an unprofitable product if given a variety target, whereas a profit-maximizing firm will not, unless it is subject to profit deductions for failing to do so. Third, an enterprise maximizing average product will be more restrictive in hiring labor than either a profit-maximizing or an output-maximizing firm.

Several unusual features of the Chinese economy affect enterprise goals. First, the welfare of workers is closely tied to the enterprise they work in. Workers are typically employed in the same enterprise for life and receive housing, medical benefits, and a pension from the enterprise. For the enterprise, labor is virtually a fixed cost, because workers cannot be fired. The dependence of workers on the enterprise is thus more like that in large Japanese firms than that in other socialist economies.

Second, China's labor-abundant economy has many unemployed urban youths. As a result, it is accepted in many parts of China that enterprises should provide employment for the dependents of workers, either directly or by setting up separate collective enterprises.

Third, the rewards, authority, and career paths of Chinese managers are different from those of their counterparts in Eastern Europe and the U.S.S.R. Managerial salaries are fixed and not much higher than those of skilled workers. Bonuses are small and rarely vary much with enterprise or individual performance. Managerial authority, though strengthened in recent years, is more circumscribed by government regulation and party influence than in most other socialist countries. Moreover, turnover is low, and promotion from inside the enterprise is the most frequent route to a managerial position. Although some managers are appointed from outside, most spend long periods with one firm and are likely to identify closely with the long-term performance of the firm and the welfare of its workers.[1]

Fourth, most state enterprises can now retain profits and use them for investment, worker bonuses, and collective welfare, including housing. The amount retained is formally linked to plan fulfillment, but the use of retained profits is regulated, and there is much scope for bargaining with higher authorities over plan targets and rates of profit retention. (See "The Bargaining Economy" in chapter 8 in this volume.)

Motives of Chinese Enterprises

No single, or simple, objective function applies to all Chinese state-owned industrial enterprises. Enterprise objectives combine the motives of workers and managers and reflect the attitudes of supervisory and local government authorities. They also depend on the incentives and constraints that the enterprise faces. In this rubric, five main motives are distinguishable: family, expansion, engineering, compliance, and (more recently) profit.

Family. The dominant motive of workers in every Chinese enterprise is to maximize their family income and benefits. Although workers rarely have anything other than a nominal right to appoint managers, the identification of managers with the interests of workers means that maximizing worker benefits is frequently the dominant motive of enterprises. Many enterprises in the sample strongly prefer to use retained profits for worker benefits rather than productive investment. Some have diverted retained profits from the production development fund to worker benefits. Others have regularly paid bonuses equal to more than four months of basic wages, even though the legal limit is about three months, depending on locality and year. And after the imposition of a progressive bonus tax in 1984, many Chinese enterprises began to try to evade it by paying bonuses in kind or by paying extra subsidies—so many that the authorities recently instituted a major campaign to restrict such practices.

But the twenty enterprises in our sample generally have not tried to restrict employment, because workers (and local governments) have a strong interest in securing employment for their children.[2] If workers want to maximize family income rather than individual income, if alternative employment opportunities are limited, and if the enterprise can hire family members directly or subsidize their employment indirectly through enterprise-sponsored collectives, the likely objective will be to maximize total net product rather than average net product.[3] A worker-dominated enterprise maximizing total net product will be very expansionist in its employment, for it will want to employ more workers (family members) as long as their marginal product is greater than zero.

The expansionist tendency of some worker-oriented firms thus differs from the expansion drive of the shortage economy in that its underlying motive is family welfare. The tendency arises only when there are limited alternative employment opportunities for family members, and it is primarily a concern of workers rather than managers.

Expansion. Expansion drive of the Kornai variety also exists in China. The size and importance of an enterprise affect managerial prestige, and no ambitious manager would turn down an opportunity to expand his firm. In our sample a few enterprises were extremely expansionist at various stages of their development. The key ingredient appears to have been an exceptionally ambitious manager or a management team with the entrepreneurial talent to overcome most of the usual obstacles to expansion. If expansion through investment was thwarted, these firms turned to mergers. The three clearest examples of the drive to expand in our sample—the No. 2 Automobile Plant, the Chongqing Clock and Watch Company, and the Mindong Electrical Machinery Corporation—all expanded both through investment and through mergers. All had an explicit goal to increase their share of the national market, and all were able to do so.

A lack of concern about short-term profitability characterizes these expansionist enterprises. In their mergers and associations all three firms offered favorable transfer prices to their partners in return for the ability to expand production or penetrate new markets. Expansionist managers have also been able at times to override concerns about the welfare of workers and their families. Mindong's strategy involved breaking out of its isolated mountain location and expanding production in the coastal provincial capital of Fuzhou. But competing motives—or opposition from the many enemies it creates—can thwart the expansion drive. More important, adverse market conditions, such as those that Chongqing faced, can extinguish the drive.

Engineering. Another prominent managerial stimulant is the engineering or technological motive. Engineers often derive their greatest satisfaction from producing excellent products or using the most modern technique of production (Wells 1975), and Chinese managers are increasingly selected from the ranks of engineers. A system of prizes for high-quality products and recognition for "advanced enterprises" reinforces this motive. Almost all of the sample enterprises proudly recounted their achievements, ranging from winning gold prizes to being designated as a leak-free plant. The motto of the Shanghai High-Pressure Oil Pump Factory is "Win a gold medal, export, and be the best."

Gold or silver prizes for high-quality products sometimes mean an extra bonus for workers. Advanced enterprises may also receive favored treatment. Mindong wanted to break into the export market to enhance its reputation because, as one manager stated, "if an enterprise is well-known and well-managed, it may get more investment from the State." But the engineering motive is not always as ulterior as this. The Nanning Silk and Linen Textile Mill received only a television set for winning a silver medal, yet the enterprise lobbied hard to gain a tax exemption so that it could go on producing its famous silver-prize product after a price adjustment in 1983. The Xiangxiang Cement Plant has forgone easier bonus targets to maintain its "honored place as an advanced unit."

Emphasis on prizes for product quality may be of dubious benefit to product users. The Shenyang Smelting Plant's very pure refined copper exceeds customer needs, for example (Byrd 1985). And in the textile industry, mills have often been content to produce only a small quantity of prize-winning products. The shift to a buyers' market has been far more significant in giving customers what they want—especially when they want lower-quality, cheaper products (see chapters 8 and 10 in this volume).

Compliance. Another managerial motive, closely related but distinct, is compliance with the directives of superiors. This motive stems from a desire to be a good bureaucratic citizen rather than to produce a superior product and gain peer approval. And while it sometimes leads to a similar quest for recognition, it is more often associated with a desire for a quiet life and easy plan targets.[4] This interpretation is particularly likely for enterprises caught between conflicting demands of multiheaded leadership, such as Shenyang Smelting and the Qingdao Forging Machinery Plant.

The compliance motive was especially important when firms had less autonomy. The Nanning Textile Mill, for example, wasted much time and effort in establishing a farm in 1978 in order to unite industry and agriculture. The mill succeeded in becoming a Daqing-style enterprise,[5] but the farm was a failure and was abandoned after three years. Some workers complained that the mill had bought the Daqing-style banner for Y120,000.

The compliance motive still drives many managers. It is unlikely to be manifested in strenuous efforts to fulfill plan targets because of the weak link between managerial bonuses and plan fulfillment and because bargaining over targets is so prevalent. But managers clearly respond to general policy directives from the party and from the superior agencies that appoint them. One cannot even discount the possibility that some of the profit-oriented behavior of Chinese enterprises in recent years is the result of directives from above. But while compliance with plan directives and national campaigns may appear to simplify the task of planners, this motive leads to the fulfillment of the letter rather than the spirit of directives, sometimes distorting their intent.

Profit. The possibility of retaining profits has noticeably increased the profit-oriented behavior of Chinese enterprises. The link of profit retention with plan fulfillment and the use of retained profits for worker benefits or for investment means that enterprises will be profit oriented whatever their underlying objective—plan fulfillment, worker benefits, or expansion. But profits are only the immediate objective, and because of restrictions on the use of retained profits, enterprises will rarely wish to maximize profits. For example, an enterprise trying to increase the family income of workers will be interested in increasing retained profits, but only as long as these profits can be used to increase family benefits.

Even this partial increase in profit orientation causes problems, because profitability is a distorted measure of social and economic benefits. Profitability depends in part on arbitrary pricing and the historical accident of investment allocation. For this reason, individual profit-retention rates are set for each enterprise. But the search for complete equity or for full allowance for objective circumstances leads to extensive bargaining over these rates. As a result, they differ widely among enterprises and even for the same enterprise over time. Evidence from the sample shows that differing rates of profit retention have not succeeded in greatly reducing the variability of retained profits as compared with that of gross profits.[6] Authorities may try to reduce variability of after-tax profits, but because profit retention is subject to bargaining with many agencies and levels of government, retention rates are highly variable and only weakly correlated with profitability.

Objectives, Incentives, and Constraints

Enterprise motives interact in complex ways. When the expansionist tendency of the family motive and the expansion drive of a dynamic manager converged at the Chongqing Clock and Watch Company, the result was an extremely powerful drive to expand. More typically, however, the different motives diverge or conflict. Mindong was able to expand through mergers outside its original base, but it was also forced to expand production at the original factory to pacify the original core group of workers, even though this expansion probably was less profitable. The No. 2 Automobile Plant, on the other hand, earns and retains such a large amount of profits that it has been able to pay workers good bonuses and still have plenty of resources left for expansion.[7] The result is that expansion appears to be the dominant objective of the enterprise.

Even when managers have objectives that are different from the family motive of workers, they must ensure a minimum level of worker bonuses and welfare payments. Most enterprises thus have a hierarchy of motives. A threshold satisfaction of the family motive must be attained before other motives can come into play. But if the enterprise has enough resources to reach this threshold, managers can indulge their other aspirations.

The incentive system makes this hierarchy of motives possible. It changes the enterprise objective from simple maximization of family welfare to the satisfaction of multiple objectives.[8] Profit retention gives all firms an incentive to increase profits whatever their motive. If enterprises had full autonomy to use profits as they wished, many of them would choose to distribute all profits as bonuses or use up all profits in employing children of workers. But restrictions on the use of profits and limits on bonus payments ensure that the family motive is not completely dominant.

Such constraints as hiring rules also affect the fundamental objectives of the enterprise. If enterprises could not hire children of workers or set up collectives to employ dependents, they might cease to be expansionist and might restrict employment growth to maximize the incomes of existing workers. In other words, the underlying family motive would be to maximize average net product rather than total net product. Because of this strong family motive, the government must be very cautious about giving Chinese enterprises more autonomy in hiring or in setting wages under present conditions. Enterprises might otherwise raise wages and restrict employment to a favored few workers, adversely affecting employment generation and equity.

Market conditions and competition can also constrain the objectives of enterprises. Most Chinese managers can attempt to pursue their own motives only when there is a sellers' market or when profits are high. The managers may not be able to indulge the engineering motive, for example, if the enterprise is facing a buyers' market that threatens profits. Nanning was forced to suspend production of its silver-prize product because it was unprofitable and jeopardized a wage increase. Similarly, Chongqing could no longer afford to indulge the expansion motive once the market for clocks collapsed and that for watches became highly competitive. Competition forces enterprises to be more concerned with sales and profits if they are to survive.

Competition can also change the behavior, though not necessarily the objective, of an enterprise trying to maximize family incomes. The Northwest No. 1 Cotton Mill has reduced employment below its allowable quota despite unemployment among workers' children and pressure from the municipality to expand employment. Instead, it has hired extra temporary workers who can be laid off if the market deteriorates. The reason for this action is that it fears it would suffer losses (and a lower average net product per worker) if market conditions worsen and it cannot get rid of any workers. The Jiangmen Nanfang Foodstuff Factory has long had the flexibility to hire contract workers who could be terminated if there was a seasonal or cyclical drop in demand. Few of these contract workers are children of employees. This fact illustrates the tendency of labor-managed enterprises to hire wage workers from outside to bear the burden of adjustment to adverse conditions, leaving the "core" group of worker-members intact.

Labor

Labor is unique in being both a factor input and a participant in forming enterprise objectives. Workers' interests in their employment and payment are clear. They want secure employment for themselves, jobs for their children, and higher wages, bonuses, and other benefits. Managers' interests vary, depending on their motives, but in all cases they would like to have greater flexibility in hiring, firing, and rewarding labor. The desires of workers and managers sometimes coincide and sometimes conflict, but they are seldom decisive because the allocation and payment of labor is the most tightly controlled aspect of enterprise operations. Nevertheless, there are some ways to evade these controls, and recent reforms have increased the flexibility of the system somewhat.

The Present System of Allocation

The control of labor allocation is more far-reaching in China than in Eastern Europe and the U.S.S.R. because it extends to the assignment of individual workers to particular jobs. Neither workers nor enterprises have much say in job assignments, and most workers expect to spend their working lives in the enterprise they are assigned to when they leave school. Job swaps to allow families to be together or for other personal reasons are sometimes allowed, but permission is not assured. Workers have no right to quit their jobs. Residence permits and grain ration coupons have precluded migration to seek employment. And the local labor bureau usually has control over job assignments within an overall quota set by the Ministry of Labor.

This system is loosening up slightly. At Nanning, for example, youths are assigned to a trade (such as textiles), and there is some scope for choosing assignments through mutual agreement with interested enterprises in that trade. Similarly, technicians may now move from a job in a large city to a job offered in a smaller city or rural area. Enterprises also have some flexibility in hiring children of workers (see below under "Areas of Flexibility"). But the general system of allocation remains much as it has always been.

Dismissing workers is extremely difficult. Workers depend on the enterprise for housing, pensions, and many of their medical and educational benefits. Loss of employment is thus more serious for workers in China than in most other countries. As a result, workers feel they have a right to the job they have been assigned, almost a property right. Dismissal can therefore occur only for flagrant misbehavior after exhaustive administrative procedures. Even then dismissal may prove impossible. The Xiangxiang Cement Plant, for example, fired a worker and asked him to return to his village. But the village sent him back four times, so the plant eventually had to reinstate him.

Residence permits, grain rationing, and job-linked welfare benefits restrict labor mobility as well. Workers are reluctant to lose housing rights by changing jobs, and enterprises may be reluctant to hire older workers because of the huge unfunded pension liability thereby incurred. Transfer to another location, even in the same enterprise, is difficult because of residence permits and grain rationing. When Mindong expanded to the coast, for example, only a few leading cadres were allowed to move temporarily. The North China Petroleum Administration, which spans several provinces and has mobile drilling teams, has to ship grain from Hebei to 3,100 people working in Daqing. It also has to transport grain from Tianjin back to Hebei for 10,000 staff and workers registered in Tianjin.[9]

Labor quotas from the Ministry of Labor and its bureaus restrict the level and composition of employment. Quotas are generally linked to capacity expansion but are not related to variations in market conditions. More workers may be allocated to an enterprise because of a shift in national or local priorities, and quotas may lag far behind changes in output. At the Northwest No. 1 Cotton Mill, an extreme example, output fell 4.8 percent in 1982, but employment increased 26 percent. For many enterprises in the sample, output per worker has fluctuated substantially from year to year. Generally the allocation of labor, like that of materials, is badly coordinated with production planning.

Although Chinese factories are frequently overstaffed by international standards, neither workers nor managers would necessarily like to reduce employment. Few managers interviewed would admit to overstaffing; most said they had a shortage of good workers and a surplus of bad workers. Almost every enterprise manager or labor section chief complained that he had too many female workers, who were said to be generally unsuited for first-line work, even in textiles, where female workers predominate in most of the world. The manager of one textile mill, however, complained of having too many male workers.

The enterprise's objective function may contribute to overstaffing, which is tolerated mainly because there is little incentive to improve productivity. Workers like to have more employment opportunities for their children, and managers may wish to please workers or the local government by providing more jobs. Even enterprises wishing to maximize their market share may wish to get as much labor as possible in the short run for fear that future restrictions will constrain their growth. If the enterprise could use the savings from lower employment to increase the wages of its workers or its funds for investment, it would have an incentive to improve productivity. But few have this authority. The Shanghai No. 17 Cotton Mill, for example, hired fewer workers than its quota allowed and tried to use the savings to increase bonus payments (which were still below the ceiling). But the municipal financial office argued that the mill had used this money improperly and should return it.

Although enterprises have little to gain from improving labor productivity, they may have something to lose from not doing so when markets become more competitive. Both the Northwest No. 1 Cotton Mill and the Jiangmen Foodstuff Factory have tried to restrict employment and shift the burden of market fluctuations onto temporary employees for fear that losses would reduce benefits for permanent workers. If enterprises face a danger of becoming unprofitable and are responsible for losses, both their objective function and incentives will impel them to try to reduce overstaffing.

Areas of Flexibility

There are several ways for enterprises to get around controls on labor quotas and to expand (or, much less commonly, reduce) the labor force. Some enterprises have been able to hire contract or temporary workers outside the plan in cooperation with local governments, but this practice is by no means widespread. In the sample, the two enterprises with the highest proportion of temporary workers were the Qingyuan County Economic Commission (21.5 percent of total workers in 1982) and the Jiangmen Foodstuff Factory (40–53 percent, depending on the season). Moreover, government authorities periodically try to restrain the use of labor outside the plan. Qingdao, which had used rural contract workers in the 1970s to augment its labor force by 50 percent, is being forced to phase out all contract workers.

Contract labor outside the plan is distinct from contract labor introduced under a recent reform in which new workers allocated under quota are given a fixed-term contract rather than permanent employment. This new form of contract labor does not give enterprises flexibility over the number of workers, but it does give managers an added measure of disciplinary authority, if not always to the extent expected. In many cases it has proved nearly as difficult to avoid renewing contracts when they expire as it was to dismiss a permanent worker, because of worker and community views about job rights. The new contract system paradoxically may increase the flexibility of workers more than managers. The Nanning Textile Mill has complained that the best workers tend to learn a skill and then quit at the end of the contract, or even before, to go into business for themselves. But after having gained experience with the new system of contract labor and having given workers some choice of job assignment, managers have concluded that the new system has improved worker motivation and has somewhat increased the disciplinary authority of managers.

The most important area of enterprise flexibility over employment is in hiring children and other dependents of workers, an area in which the interests of managers and workers, and of different groups of workers, often diverge. The right of a child to inherit the job of a retiring worker is widely accepted throughout China.[10] At Anshan Iron and Steel Corporation, for example, 17,000 children replaced retiring parents during 1980–83. Managers often complain that workers with several children may ask the enterprise to employ the child with the worst employment prospects. Moreover, because some children have needed jobs before their parents reached retirement age, some workers have retired early, thus depriving enterprises of skilled, productive workers in return for the services of untrained workers with poor employment prospects elsewhere. The authorities have now cracked down on premature retirement.

Rules on hiring children to fill quota allocations vary by industry, location, and year. Many extractive industries (timber, coal, and petroleum) have considerable latitude in hiring children. Direct hiring of children (other than to replace retiring workers) is a subject of constant bargaining in other industries. Most enterprise managers wish to hire children of workers, but they want to have some control over which children they hire. The managers usually achieve this control by subjecting all job applicants to standard tests but giving preference to children of workers. In the sample enterprises the proportion of children of workers employed directly as state employees ranged from 5 percent to nearly 40 percent of regular state employment.

Although the direct hiring of dependents and their replacement of retiring workers do not affect the total number of quota workers, many enterprises have been able to get around labor quotas by setting up collectives to employ dependents of workers (table 4-1). The ability to do this depends on local policy. Collectives are particularly numerous in the northeast but rare

Table 4-1. *Employment in Dependents' Collectives Set Up by the Parent Enterprise, 1982*

Enterprise	*Total state employees in parent enterprise*	*Employment in collective enterprises set up by the parent enterprise*
Anshan	194,638	160,549
Baoji	1,984	81
Chengdu	4,744	1,380
Chongqing	4,287	n.a.
Jiangmen	638	0
Jinling	23,716	n.a.
Mindong	3,335	303[a]
Nanning	3,159	n.a.
North China Petroleum	79,053	6,614[b]
Northwest Cotton	6,452	n.a.
No. 2 Auto	53,062	7,621[c]
Qingdao	1,561	95
Qinghe	3,322	n.a.
Qingyuan	6,218	n.a.
Sanchazi	10,029	8,754
Shanghai Cotton	9,805	n.a.[d]
Shanghai Oil Pump	437	n.a.
Shenyang	6,770	5,777
Tianjin	12,612	125
Xiangxiang	2,320	232

n.a. = not available.

a. The number reported for 1984 was 1,746.

b. This is the figure for 1984.

c. The number reported for 1984 was 9,000.

d. The enterprise set up three collectives for dependents and had a one-time recruitment of a small number of workers in 1980–81.

in Shanghai, for example. Anshan has made the most remarkable use of collectives. In September 1984, Anshan had about 220,000 state employees in its mining and steel operations and more than 160,000 employees in collectives set up to employ dependents of workers. (Employment in Anshan's collectives alone is greater than the modern sector manufacturing employment of Kenya, a country of about 20 million people.) Anshan has 177 such collective enterprises, most of which have been established since 1979. They engage in more than twenty industries, including steel (ten small rolling mills), bricks (eight plants), cement (six plants), chemicals (five plants), construction, farming, soft drinks, clothing, catering, and commerce.

Dependents' collectives have costs and benefits for the parent enterprise. Theoretically, collectives are self-supporting and independent, but in practice the parent enterprise often provides land, buildings, supplies, administrative support, an investment subsidy, or a captive market for collective output. Anshan used 4 percent of its self-marketed output to obtain material supplies for its collectives in 1983 and also supplied them with scrap steel, slag, and other waste materials (for other examples, see chapter 8 in this volume). On the other hand, enterprises can use collectives to manipulate supply allocations, multiple prices, or tax differences to advantage. Enterprises can also use the somewhat laxer control by higher authorities over collectives to increase bonuses. And they can use collective workers to expand their labor force. Anshan uses 8,000 collective workers in its main plants, many in key positions. Qingdao and Shenyang have relied proportionally even more on collective workers in their main workshops (see Chen and others 1984; Byrd 1985). This practice is now discouraged by the central government.

A final way for enterprises to get around restrictive labor quotas is through mergers and associations. No. 2 Automobile Plant set up the Dongfeng (East Wind) Automobile Corporation to produce vehicles in its own and associated factories. Most of the Dongfeng-brand special vehicles (such as buses and fire engines) of the No. 2 Automobile Plant are produced in associated factories because assembly of these special vehicles is very labor-intensive. Usually, however, getting access to labor is (at best) a secondary objective of mergers (see the section on mergers later in this chapter).

As noted previously, reducing excess labor is much more difficult than expanding beyond quota allocations. Chongqing ran into severe difficulties when the clock market collapsed shortly after it had made a commitment to employ workers from a merged collective. Although Chongqing was able to renegotiate the future growth of employment to some extent, it was left with large numbers of redundant workers. Some were put on study leave, which meant that no bonus had to be paid, and some were forced to become commissioned door-to-door salesmen. But it was not possible to dismiss any workers (Byrd and Tidrick 1984, pp. 51–52).

Dismissing temporary workers is, in principle, easier, but only a few factories have many temporary or short-term contract workers. Even those that do may face obstacles in dismissing them. Shenyang Smelting is reluctant to dismiss its temporaries even though it has surplus labor, because temporaries fill some of the key positions. The Shanghai No. 17 Cotton Mill has the added constraint that it cannot simply lay off good temporaries during a lull in demand, because they would easily find jobs elsewhere in Shanghai. Locally controlled factories such as Jiangmen Foodstuff are among the few with any significant degree of downward flexibility. The new contract labor system has the potential for increasing flexibility, but it remains to be seen how it will evolve.

Labor Incentives

The wage and bonus system is just as rigid as the labor allocation system in theory and nearly as rigid in practice. Wage scales are centrally prescribed, and enterprises have almost no authority over the number of workers to be paid a given scale or even over promotion of workers. Promotions and wage increases were common through 1957, but wages have since been frozen for long periods, and promotion of individual workers for any reason other than length of service has been rare. Wage increases in recent years have mostly moved all workers up a grade in the eight-grade scale. The structure of wages is fairly egalitarian, and worker attitudes generally stress egalitarianism.

In recent years bonuses and piece rates have been reintroduced. In theory the average bonus for a factory has been limited to about three months of basic wages, with no restrictions on individual variations. In practice, the reverse has occurred. Many enterprises have exceeded the average bonus limit, although individual variations in bonuses have been relatively small. (See table 2-7 for the average bonuses paid in the twenty sample enterprises.) These figures include bonuses for special awards, usually exempt from the ceiling. Still, it is clear from interviews that many enterprises, especially those controlled by lower levels of government, have exceeded the ceiling on regular bonuses.

The link between bonus payments and plan performance is also weak and subject to negotiation (see chapter 8 in this volume). A new bonus tax scheme introduced in 1984 has met with widespread evasion. Managers have the formal authority under the scheme to base individual bonuses on performance, but they rarely use it because of the strong egalitarian ethos. Most workers in a group fall into a narrow band of variation. About the only way a worker can lose, or face a big reduction of, his bonus is through absenteeism (including sick leave), so bonuses have effectively become a general wage supplement. Managerial bonuses are seldom much above the enterprise average and are often below it. Such rare exceptions as the Nanning Textile Mill enjoy large, special managerial bonuses set by the city; managers would not dare award themselves such bonuses.

One curious development associated with increased use of bonuses is that workers expect to be paid extra for ordinary tasks which would be part of the normal job in most countries. Equally curious is that managers seem to accept this expectation. The Shanghai No. 17 Cotton Mill complains that it lacks the authority to raise bonuses to provide an incentive to save materials. "Cement bags require a Y0.32 deposit, with Y.02 being returned when the bags are returned. The workers think this is too little and rip the bags up. If this incentive can be raised to Y0.05, each bag would cost Y0.03 more, but Y0.27 can be recovered." Although enterprises can use bonuses to "raise the enthusiasm" of workers in such cases, it does not augur well for future productivity growth if they have to use them that way.

Egalitarian pressures have also limited the use of piece rates and other payment-by-results schemes. The typical piece-rate system permits average payment of 130 percent of the basic wage (not much above the bonus limit), with individual payment based on individual output. Often the piece-rate share of the wage is restricted to output above the quota. In many enterprises, workers have successfully resisted such schemes, because they lead to harder work, increased individual competition, and little more pay on the average. Managers have also abandoned some piece-rate schemes (at Chongqing, for example) because even though the line or section using piece rates had higher output per worker, the increase had little effect on overall enterprise productivity, owing to bottlenecks in other sections not using piece rates. Some of the sample enterprises, especially textile mills, have successfully introduced piece-rate systems, but the schemes still appear to be far less common than in other countries, including other socialist countries.

Other wage reforms have had mixed results. In one common floating-wage scheme, the enterprise withholds 20 to 30 percent of the basic wages and puts the money into the bonus pool. This type of system generally meets the same resistance as piece rates and regular bonus schemes. It is not clear that it has had a strong incentive effect. But the incentive systems that increase the resources available for wage and bonus payments, even if distributed in an egalitarian fashion, seem to stimulate additional effort by workers. At Chongqing, Nanning, and Jiangmen, links between performance (profits or plan targets) and worker promotion have worked as strong incentives.[11]

Effects of Labor Allocation and Incentives

China's unusual system of labor allocation and incentives has some obvious shortcomings. The social security and welfare functions of enterprises result in extreme immobility of labor. This immobility is generally bad for economic growth and for individual worker welfare. Workers would be inherently better off, and better motivated, if they had more say over their first job assignment and more options to move. The economy would also benefit. China's stagnant total factor productivity is partly related to slow diffusion of best-practice techniques (Tidrick 1986), and labor mobility (especially of skilled workers and technicians) is an important source of technological diffusion in most countries.

Enterprises have little control over hiring, firing, or paying workers. Greater flexibility in shedding surplus workers would be especially beneficial, since the inability to dismiss surplus labor may increase the risk aversion of enterprise managers. Because it is easier to expand than to contract the labor force, enterprises may refrain from undertaking risky ventures that would leave them with the permanent liability of a larger labor force in case of failure. Another serious problem is the inability to discipline unproductive workers through dismissal. This inability means that incentives for productivity increases are lopsided—all carrot and no stick. More generally, enterprises must face some threat of closure or reorganization if they are inefficient. This threat would provide a continuing stimulus for innovation and cost reduction. It would also ensure that inefficient enterprises do not occupy scarce land, capital, workers, and markets, which more efficient enterprises could use better. Closing such enterprises would promote the growth of more efficient enterprises, which would create new jobs for displaced workers (World Bank 1985, chap. 7). But as long as workers are tied to one enterprise, none of these beneficial changes can occur. To increase labor mobility and enterprise flexibility, responsibility for worker welfare (including support of redundant workers) needs to shift from enterprises to the government.

Giving enterprises greater autonomy over hiring and wage decisions is more of a problem because of the way these decisions interact with the enterprise objective function. Rules for hiring the children of workers, or setting up collectives for dependents, have a big effect on enterprise behavior. The combination of egalitarianism, strength of the family motive, and a weak constraint on bonus ceilings would almost certainly lead to sharp increases in wage and bonus payments if enterprises were unrestricted. On the other hand, evidence from the sample of enterprises suggests that an increase in worker benefits, even if distributed in an egalitarian way, might well raise the productivity of labor.

Should wage and bonus payments be linked to productivity increases? The dilemma is that wages have three functions: allocation, distribution, and incentives. Wages affect the allocation of resources and, in particular, the substitution between capital and labor. Higher wages give an incentive to substitute scarce capital for relatively abundant labor, thus aggravating China's employment problem. Wages also affect the distribution of income: urban workers have higher incomes than most peasants and rural workers already; further wage increases would widen the urban-rural gap. But increased wages and bonuses can be linked to performance so that they have an incentive effect. They can thus pay for themselves in increased output per worker.

The three functions of wages—allocation, distribution, and incentives—are often incompatible. Linking wages to productivity may raise output per worker, but it will worsen the distribution of income and may set a wage standard that encourages substitution of capital for labor. Linking wages and bonuses to enterprise productivity or profitability has several potential dangers in China's half-reformed system. Workers may be rewarded for increased profits from price or other extraneous factors; enterprises may be given an incentive to reduce employment through mechanization; and enterprises may be able to bargain for higher benefits unmatched by productivity increases. In China today, greater enterprise control over wage and bonus payments would probably lead to higher wages, lower employment, and a worse income distribution—and to uncertain increases in labor productivity and to dubious benefits for total factor productivity and the economy.

Land

Land is much more restricted as a productive factor in industry than in agriculture. Nevertheless, insufficient space for facilities and storage can severely constrain production, expansion, and efficiency. The allocation and use of land are also tied to location, which can affect transport costs and marketing. For Chinese industrial enterprises, land is often a crucial determinant of production and a key constraint on their development potential. The rigid Chinese system of land allocation aggravates the shortage of land.

The System for Allocating Urban Industrial Land

There is no open market for urban land in China: its allocation for industrial use is handled primarily by administrative mechanisms, particularly in the case of new plant construction. But municipal authorities must also at least nominally approve transfers of land between enterprises. Administrative delays and difficulties discourage many enterprises from even trying to get more land through regular channels. The Northwest No. 1 Cotton Mill reported that it takes one to two years of negotiations to get land to build new facilities.

In this framework of administrative allocation, implicit property rights for urban land held by enterprises and institutions appear to be well established. These rights are probably based more on "customary practices" that have developed over the past several decades than on explicit legislation. Land cannot be freely alienated, yet state-owned institutions and rural collectives pay no rent for the land they occupy. Moreover, it is extremely difficult to take occupied land away from the holder without the latter's agreement, which usually requires satisfactory compensation. This makes the administrative transfer mechanism a weak and expensive instrument.

Monetary compensation is in principle related to the income-producing potential of the land. Compensation also takes the form of providing employment for some or all of the people "displaced" by the land transaction (often with jobs in the unit acquiring the land). Similarly, those who lose their dwellings as a result of land acquisition or transfer should get new housing. But in practice the amount of employment or housing provided is often subject to intense bargaining and negotiations, and it may bear little relationship to displacement in the unit giving up the land. Land for industrial use thus carries a "price" of sorts, and that price can affect demand and perhaps even supply.

Recent economic reforms have not greatly changed the basic system of urban land allocation. But the price of land (the costs to enterprises of acquiring more land for their own use) appears to have risen sharply. Moreover, the risk entailed by making commitments to hire large numbers of additional workers—a usual part of a land deal—is now very evident, particularly in industries that face excess supply and need to hire large numbers of workers' children anyway. For example, the Chongqing Clock and Watch Company acquired a large plot of land from a suburban commune to provide a new site for its watch factory and ease congestion at the original site. But it had to commit itself to hiring large numbers of unskilled commune members as temporary workers in perpetuity. Shortly afterward the clock market collapsed, leaving Chongqing with a heavy, almost unmanageable burden and financial drain. Under these circumstances, enterprises may well be increasingly deterred from obtaining land, even when it is available.

Several features of China's economic system tend to worsen the shortage of land and contribute to the inefficiency of land use. The concentration of industry (particularly heavy industry) in large cities crowds industrial enterprises on restricted sites and generates excessive pollution (Henderson 1986, pp. 32–39). The reluctance to close inefficient enterprises squeezes the more successful enterprises, which could otherwise expand onto the land vacated. The responsibility of enterprises to provide housing for workers and their families (more often than not on the factory site) further tightens land constraints and possibly obstructs relocation. The tendency of enterprises to hoard inputs in short supply puts another strain on their land (because of the storage space required). And the lack of coherent urban zoning permits many inefficient practices to develop unchecked.

Examples of Space Constraints and Location Problems

One type of land constraint is inadequate space, which interferes with production, prevents expansion, or both. This constraint is felt very unevenly across the enterprises in our sample. Some firms have a surfeit of available space because of generous initial endowments or large later additions. Others, particularly those located in the central areas of cities, are severely constrained by the shortage of land. In a few cases, like Shenyang Smelting, land may even be a binding constraint on production in the short run. The Qinghe Woolen Textile Mill had such a crowded site that it was not interested in a major 4,800 spindle expansion project, which eventually was forced on the enterprise by the Ministry of Textile Industry. The Shanghai Oil Pump Factory feels such a severe space constraint that it proudly reports its profits per square meter of floorspace. At the Anshan Iron and Steel

Corporation, which was forced to modernize facilities while maintaining production, space is so restricted that large-scale construction equipment cannot be used; earthwork chronically runs into a dense network of underground pipes; and any expansion of a workshop requires moving neighboring facilities elsewhere (moving costs typically account for about half of total project investment costs).

Problems with poor location are just as ubiquitous as space constraints. Shenyang Smelting, engaged in highly energy-intensive refining of nonferrous metals, is located in one of the most energy-deficient parts of China. The No. 2 Automobile Plant has workshops scattered in mountainous terrain, it suffers from floods, and it has access to only one, very crowded single-track railway line; as a result, it incurs high transport costs both within the plant and in transactions with other enterprises. The Mindong Electrical Machinery Plant was originally located in Fu'an, a remote part of Fujian Province that had poor transportation and communication facilities; it faced great difficulties in marketing and particularly in export dealings. Some location problems (those of No. 2 Auto, for example) are due to faulty original siting decisions; in other cases (like that of Shenyang) the original site may have been appropriate at the time the factory was set up, and problems have arisen because of a failure to relocate when changing circumstances warranted doing so.

Overall, a fragmented, almost patchwork pattern of micro imbalances and specific arrangements has emerged. For example, in the case of the Chengdu Locomotive and Rolling Stock Factory, some land within the factory site is owned by peasants, and high costs (in terms of money and employment provision) have deterred the plant from taking it over even though it is needed. The Qingdao Forging Machinery Plant, on the other hand, has a spacious site and could expand onto neighboring agricultural land if necessary. Shenyang Smelting is hemmed in by other factories on all sides; has insufficient space to store incoming raw materials; and cannot find room for additional workers' apartments on its own land. The evident unevenness in factor endowments is not surprising given the arbitrariness of initial land allocations when enterprises were set up, the lack of an open market in urban land, and the weakness and high cost of administrative reallocation mechanisms.

Means of Obtaining Land

Enterprises have found ways to ease or get around land constraints. One of the most obvious is to pad the original request for land when a factory is first set up. This is easiest to do in the process of urbanization, when large amounts of land are shifted from agricultural to urban industrial use and particular factories usually are not individually responsible for compensation.

Many heavy industrial enterprises set up in the 1950s and 1960s appear to have been able to get comfortable endowments of land in this way, but the situation may be tougher for newly established enterprises today. Once gained in this way, surplus land is simply hoarded against future need.

A second way is direct land acquisition through administrative processes. This method has become increasingly difficult, and only very rarely does it result in an appropriate site. Much depends on the land situation in the immediate vicinity of the existing site. The Nanning Textile Mill was, with some delay, able to obtain land for a new workshop from an adjoining nonferrous metal smelter, but most factories do not have this option.

A third way is to move part of the production process out of the original site by means of subcontracting, often with smaller, rural factories that have considerable space (and labor) available. The feasibility of subcontracting depends greatly on the technical character of production. For example, it usually is not possible in continuous-process industries (petrochemicals), but it is often suitable in the textile industry. One problem with subcontracting is that supply relationships may be unreliable if subcontractors are at arm's length.

A fourth way of increasing the land endowment—apparently the most common—is to merge or enter into joint ventures with other enterprises; the frequent use of this method may be because landholders insist on a merger as a "reward" for providing land. The method can be expensive, however, and it generally does not result in the best possible distribution of land, since the willingness of landholders to engage in joint ventures depends on many factors. (See the later section "Mergers, Joint Ventures, and Associations.")

Wholesale relocation appears to be rare, being done only by enterprises in extreme distress or by those with very aggressive management. Mindong's move from Fu'an to Fuzhou is an example, but the limits of this approach are apparent in the need for Mindong to maintain production and employment at Fu'an. Because of China's highly restrictive urban registration system, Mindong's original workers could neither move with the enterprise, even though they had urban household status in Fu'an County, nor be laid off. Even the leading cadres of the enterprise faced great difficulties in having their residency changed and bringing their families to Fuzhou.

Implications

The most obvious effect of the allocation system for urban land is to make factor endowments rigid and extremely uneven across enterprises, with no built-in mechanism for transfers that would improve the distribution of land. As a result, profit-oriented enterprises have strong incentives to circumvent land constraints, increasingly through mergers and joint ventures. The system for land allocation may thus be stimulating mergers and joint ventures, particularly between urban and rural enterprises. These arrangements, however, are likely to be more rigid and costly than straightforward market transactions.

Another obvious result of the land allocation system is the widespread hoarding and waste of land. State enterprises pay no rent or other charges for the land they use (except for an urban property tax), so they have little incentive to give up surplus land, except when offered deals that benefit them exorbitantly. Paradoxically, given the lack of an open market in urban land, the effective price of land appears to be difficult to control, and the cost of land acquisition may have become so high as to dampen demand.

A combination of microlevel administrative controls and lack of overall regulation and guidance thus characterizes China's urban land allocation system. Authority over land allocation is highly fragmented, yet no free market in urban land has been allowed to emerge. Because of the obvious externalities involved, industrial market economies almost universally develop some kind of land-use plan (at least at the local level) and enforce it through zoning regulations. Combined with well-functioning land markets, this government intervention seems to generate reasonably efficient patterns of land use.

China could move toward a more efficient pattern of land use by reducing local government administrative controls over land transactions and instituting a land-use charge. That change would make the financial cost of holding land reflect its opportunity cost and encourage enterprises with surplus land to get rid of it. Such a charge would have to be differentiated according to the economic value of the land concerned and supported by coherent land-use plans and zoning policies.

Investment

The allocation of investment resources across projects, enterprises, industries, and regions is a crucial determinant of efficiency, growth, and long-term economic development. One of the main causes of inefficiency in China has been misallocation and waste of the massive investment resources mobilized through the fiscal system. Since the late 1970s, China's system for industrial investment has changed greatly, particularly in investment financing. Yet the underlying control mechanisms and formal procedures persist.

Investment Control Mechanisms

Enterprise investment decisionmaking in Chinese state-owned industry is subject to a seemingly formidable array of administrative controls, most of them enforced through the project approval process, which is long and cumbersome and involves numerous government organizations. Several overlapping controls augment the established project approval procedures. These controls include annual fixed investment plans and ceilings, multiyear investment plans, fund allocation processes, and even administrative controls over the allocation of investment goods. As a result, investment decisionmaking is both bureaucratic and politicized, and there is much red tape to limit enterprise autonomy. The enterprises in the sample cite long delays in approval, funding, and implementation of investment projects as serious problems.

But Chinese administrative control mechanisms are often much weaker than they appear to be on the surface. They are fragmented both territorially and between different government agencies. There is considerable compartmentalization of decisionmaking and funding, which weakens the ability of central planning authorities to exert tight control. And if enterprises are "allied with" their immediate supervisory agency on many issues, they may have more de facto independence in investment decisionmaking. Investment ceilings are a crude and unwieldy tool; they appear virtually never to be passed down all the way to the enterprise level, so their impact in any case can be felt only through the project approval and implementation process. Ceilings on investments have high costs because they are enforced by means of across-the-board cutbacks, the suspension and delay of ongoing projects, and the holding up of even urgently needed new projects. With the fragmentation of controls and expansion of the role of the market in China's material supply system, the planned allocation of investment goods is not an effective vehicle to achieve control over investment: there are simply too many sources of investment goods outside the material allocation plan, including goods in short supply, like cement and steel, as well as those in excess supply, like many types of ordinary machinery (see chapter 10 in this volume). Multiyear investment planning may not be an effective deterrent to enterprise autonomy, either. The project approval process undoubtedly can constrain enterprise investment decisionmaking and delay or interfere with project implementation. But it, too, is weakened by fragmented and multilevel control and is probably far less effective in controlling enterprise investment projects than in controlling large new capital construction projects.

This leaves only the funding process as a potentially strong form of external administrative control. But even here control over the use of funds in the hands of firms appears to be rather weak. Indeed, such control prevented no enterprise in the sample from carrying out a small or medium-size investment project that it could fund entirely from its own resources.[12] Some enterprises have spent considerably less of their retained profits on productive investment than the guidelines stipulated—and correspondingly more on workers' welfare benefits and facilities. They have also used major repair funds and trade credit to finance fixed investment. The Tianjin Color Textile Corporation has even used bank loans and technical transformation funds to finance the construction and repair of workers' housing.

Nevertheless, many enterprises (like Shenyang Smelting) cite as the binding constraint on their investment activities the availability of funds, not the supply of construction materials or even the approval of investment projects. A number of Shenyang's approved and urgently needed investment projects were delayed or could not be implemented owing to the failure of banks or government agencies to provide funding as promised. A good example is a project for using slag from the lead smelter, a key technical improvement project that the State Economic Commission approved in November 1982. The approved cost estimate was Y11.5 million, of which Y3 million was to be financed by state grants and the rest by bank loans. But due to a policy change that allowed Shenyang Municipality to retain for its own use depreciation funds previously remitted to the central government, the state grant (to come from these remitted depreciation funds) disappeared. Under these circumstances the bank was understandably reluctant to provide any loan funds, and in the end grudgingly granted in the autumn of 1983 a loan of only Y1.3 million. In late 1984 national authorities finally agreed to provide Shenyang Smelting with a grant of Y2 million and a bank loan of Y3 million for the project in 1985, but this total amount is still far from sufficient to pay for the entire project, and there have been cost overruns and price increases in the interim.

As the example of Shenyang suggests, many delays and problems stem from conflicts over funding rather than bureaucratic procedures. Xiangxiang Cement Plant has run into its share of such difficulties. In one major project, railway authorities refused to expand facilities to handle the increased transport of cement out of the plant; as a result, the enterprise eventually had to increase the project investment cost by Y2.9 million to pay for the additional tracks needed. A different expansion project required additional electric power, but the electricity bureau claimed it had no funds and forced the enterprise to invest Y2.3 million in power facilities. Still another project (with an estimated total investment cost of over Y50 million) was approved by the State Planning Commission at the end of 1982. Hunan Province, however, which originally was supposed to cover one-third of the project cost, refused to do so, and as of the middle of 1984 this issue had still completely stalled the project.

Higher authorities can exert some control by affecting the availability of funds to enterprises. To do so, they have a number of instruments at their command: credit controls and allocation of credit for specific investment projects; provisions of profit-retention schemes; depreciation rates; regulations governing the uses of retained profits; various types of levies on enterprise funds, including remittance of a portion of depreciation funds (a long-standing practice), the levy on enterprise profits and other extrabudgetary funds to finance key energy and transport projects (started in 1983), and mandatory purchases of government bonds (started in 1981); taxing of enterprise self-financed investment projects (a 10 percent construction tax applicable to certain types of self-financed projects starting in 1983); predeposit requirements for enterprises wishing to undertake substantial self-financed investment projects; and direct controls over the use of funds, such as freezing or even confiscating enterprise bank deposits.

The authorities can implement some of these financial controls—credit controls, levies on enterprise retained funds, and mandatory purchases of government bonds—fairly easily through the banking system. Others, like freezing bank deposits, may be effective in the short run but cannot be maintained for any length of time without causing great disruption.[13] Still others, like guidelines on the uses of retained profits, appear to be somewhat ineffective, as has already been noted. Moreover, some controls that in theory should be effective—like provisions for profit retention and depreciation—are not used to limit enterprise investment activities.

Enterprise profitability should be very important in investment decisionmaking, since more profits probably mean more internal resources for investment, and since high profitability almost certainly makes it easier for an enterprise to obtain bank loans and government grants for investment projects.[14] Data from the sample show that during 1980–82, enterprise profitability had a weak influence on enterprise investment activity but a much stronger effect on the investment financed by bank loans. For an enterprise with average profitability, a 1 percent increase in profits was associated with about a 0.5 percent increase in investment. Moreover, it appears that the relationship between investment and profitability dates only from the late 1970s. Thus, one hypothesis is that the economic reforms have made enterprise profitability a much more important determinant of investment decisions than before, which, if true, would magnify the adverse impact of China's distorted price structure.

In addition to influencing investment decisions, profitability may also affect the degree of enterprise autonomy in investment decisionmaking, with highly profitable enterprises given a freer hand. Enterprise autonomy in investment decisionmaking may also be closely linked to the priority that planning authorities accord to the firm's industry. If planners respond to profitability, the influence of the firm may be reinforced. Enterprises in high-priority industries may in any case have great freedom in deciding which projects to undertake and how much to invest. Chongqing, during its expansion phase (1980–81), appears to have been almost entirely unfettered in its investment plans and activities (Byrd and Tidrick 1984, pp. 38–41). Priorities can change, however, and can even be affected by market conditions. The manager of Tianjin noted that "the endorsement of capital construction projects was fairly easy to get previously, when there was a rush to develop light and textile industrial enterprises, but not now."

The relationship with supervisory authorities and the extent to which an enterprise benefits from preferential treatment also influence enterprise autonomy in investment decisionmaking. In this context, model or advanced enterprises may well have greater access to funds and more autonomy in investment decisionmaking than other enterprises. Patronage is also important: when an enterprise has only one supervisory agency and the relationship between the two is good, the enterprise may be relatively free to engage in smaller investment projects, and the supervisory bureau may invariably support enterprise proposals for larger projects. Enterprises under multiple leadership, such as Shenyang Smelting, may be much more restricted.

Changes in Investment Financing Sources

The sources of finance for fixed investment in China have changed greatly since 1978. The share of the government budget in financing fixed investment in the state sector declined from a peak of 66 percent in 1978 to 31 percent in 1982, before rebounding slightly in 1983–84. Investment financed by enterprises, supervisory agencies, and local governments (outside the budget) rose from 32 percent in 1978 to 45 percent in 1982. These investment funds consist primarily of depreciation funds and profits (some retained by enterprises, some controlled by supervisory authorities). Investment financed by domestic bank loans and by foreign loans or direct foreign investment, negligible before 1978, accounted for close to a quarter of the total in 1982. Changes in the financing of investment in state industry are probably even greater than the aggregate changes.

The experience of the twenty enterprises in the sample is not as clear-cut as the overall trend. The sources of fixed investment financing are compared in table 4-2 for each enterprise before the reforms (1975–77) and in a period of fairly widespread reform (1980–82). There are great differences across industries and subsectors and even between enterprises in the same industry. For example, among the four textile producers for which data from both periods are available, the share of bank loans went up in three of them but fell from about 20 percent to zero for the Northwest No. 1 Cotton Mill. In some cases trends in enterprise investment financing have been diametrically opposed to national trends. The share of government grants went up in six of the sixteen enterprises for which information is available, whereas that of bank loans stayed the same (at zero) or went down in six. In nearly half the firms, retained profits accounted for 10 percent or less of total fixed investment in 1980–82; only in four did it account for more than a quarter of total fixed investment. Only five enterprises conform closely to the national pattern by showing a significant decline in government grant financing and large rises in bank loans and self-financing.

This diversity is not surprising, particularly since changes in financing the expansion and modernization of enterprises may have differed somewhat from developments in financing of capital construction projects. Self-financing (from retained depreciation and major repair funds) was an important source of investment finance all along. Bank loans and retained profits were negligible for nearly all enterprises in 1975–77; reforms allowed many enterprises to rely more on these sources in the 1980s. But the reliance on bank loans appears to have been sector specific: six of the seven enterprises with a share of bank loans above 20 percent in 1980–82 were in consumer goods.

Reforms have had a contradictory influence on the shares of internal and external financing in total investment. Reductions in government grants, use of profit retention to finance investment, and higher depreciation rates and retention rates from depreciation funds have tended to increase the share of internal financing, while greater reliance on bank loans has tended to decrease it. Between 1975 and 1977 and between 1980 and 1982, the share of internal financing went up in about half the enterprises for which data are available, down in the other half. Overall, the average share rose from 62 percent to 67 percent. More than two-thirds of the enterprises in the sample relied on internal sources to finance at least half their fixed investment in 1980–82. The fluctuations for individual enterprises have been violent, however.

Thus despite national trends, changes in investment financing have been idiosyncratic and largely enterprise specific. Few consistent patterns are observable, so a relatively clear picture at the macrolevel becomes much more muddled and diversified at the microlevel. In investment finance as in other spheres of activity, it appears that the system operates very much on an ad hoc and case-by-case basis.

In addition to greater reliance on bank loans and retained profits, some innovative and more or less new means of financing investment have emerged in Chinese industry. Among the more important ones are trade credit to finance investment and support partner enterprises (which undoubtedly has antecedents in the prereform period); equity joint ventures between Chinese firms; issuance of stocks to individuals, who are often employees of the concern involved; leasing; and various forms of compensation trade. (See the section "Mergers, Joint Ventures, and Associations" later in this chapter.)

These "new" methods of investment financing are still very much at the fringe of China's industrial investment system. They appear to be arranged largely on an ad hoc, enterprise-specific basis. Moreover, they are often

Table 4-2. *Source of Financing Enterprise Fixed Investment, 1975–77 and 1980–82*

Enterprise	Percentage share, 1975–77					Percentage share, 1980–82				
	Government grants	Bank loans	Retained profits	Depreciation and major repair funds	Other	Government grants	Bank loans	Retained profits	Depreciation and major repair funds	Other
Anshan	55.3	0	0	44.7	0	25.1	10.8	15.8	44.7	3.6[a]
Baoji	0	0	0	100.0	0	1.7	0	1.6	96.7	0
Chengdu	31.1	0	0	68.9	0	40.3	0	12.3[b]	47.4	0
Chongqing	100.0	0	0	0	0	16.2	37.4	26.8	15.8	3.8[c]
Jiangmen[d]	38.5	0	0	61.5	0	1.2	10.9	44.9	43.0	0
Jinling[e]	—	—	—	—	—	17.5	30.5	26.1	25.9	0
Mindong	n.a.	n.a.	n.a.	n.a.	n.a.	n.a.	n.a.	n.a.	n.a.	n.a.
Nanning	0	0	0	100.0	0	2.5	64.6	18.9	14.0	0
North China Petroleum[f]	69.3	0	0	30.7	0	45.8	0.9	0	53.3	0
Northwest Cotton	35.6	19.3	0	43.0	2.1[g]	1.0	0	38.7	60.2	0
No. 2 Auto[h]	100.0	0	0	0	0	4.8	2.4	18.9	43.7	30.2[i]
Qingdao	16.3	2.4	0	35.3	46.0[j]	12.3	0	4.2	56.9	26.6[j]
Qinghe	10.1	0	0	86.7	3.2[k]	12.5	70.4	10.0	7.1	0
Qingyuan	66.0	1.7	0	24.6	7.7[l]	1.6	48.9	12.6	25.7	11.2[l]
Sanchazi	4.6	0	0	95.4	0	20.4	0	2.3	77.3	0
Shanghai Cotton[d]	2.8	7.0	0	35.0	55.2[m]	1.7	21.8	0	38.4	38.1[m]
Shanghai Oil Pump	29.9	0	0	70.1	0	39.6	0	6.2	54.2	0
Shenyang	15.6	0	0	77.8	6.6[n]	6.3	2.1	11.1	60.0	20.5[n]
Tianjin[o]	—	—	—	—	—	5.0	56.7	8.7	19.5	10.1[p]
Xiangxiang	n.a.	n.a.	0	n.a.	n.a.	82.7	0	5.2	11.9	0.2

n.a. = not available.

Note: Dashes indicate that data are not applicable.

a. Loans from the Ministry of Metallurgy and State Economic Commission and funds for pollution control and waste treatment.

b. Based on the figure for retained projects put into the enterprise's production development fund.

c. A loan from the local government, part of which was later changed into a grant.

d. Very rough estimates.

e. 1981–82 only (enterprise was formed in 1981).

f. The earlier period is 1976–78 rather than 1975–77. The "government grants" category includes several types of investment funds allocated by the Ministry of the Petroleum Industry.

g. Money drawn from the enterprise's welfare fund.

h. The enterprise was still under construction in 1975–77.

i. This was apparently part of some kind of special deal with the central government, under which part of the profits the enterprise otherwise would have remitted to the government could be used for investment on a repayable basis.

j. Profits from custom-design projects based on orders from other factories.

k. Other enterprise funds plus residual.

l. Includes loans from the local government and other government agencies and a compensation trade deal between the provincial building materials bureau and the county cement plant.

m. Profits from processing work done for other factories and technology transfers as well as loans from the Shanghai government.

n. Includes profits from production of sulphuric and earmarked for investment in pollution control projects and pollution fees returned to the enterprise for the same purpose.

o. The Tianjin Color Textiles Corporation was established in its present form only in 1978. The 1980–82 figures are very rough estimates based on fragmentary data.

p. Loans from the local government.

stimulated more by shortcomings or gaps in the administrative system than by economic considerations. Compensation trade is sometimes little more than a surreptitious means of raising effective prices for goods that are subject to administrative price controls. Similarly, administrative restrictions on the direct acquisition of factor inputs often appear to be the main motive for mergers and joint ventures. The Shanghai No. 17 Cotton Mill turned to leasing to stretch out the effective maturity of its borrowing (the maximum term for most bank loans is five years).

Investment Incentives

Given that they appear to have some autonomy in investment decisionmaking, how do enterprises decide how much to invest in various projects? And how do they decide to finance their investments? The first question concerns the extent to which market-oriented reforms and the emergence of buyers' markets for some commodities have modified or weakened the chronic "investment hunger" of investment decisionmakers. The second question concerns the choice of financing sources, particularly the choice between self-financing and bank loans for investment projects.

Investment demand. According to the experience of the enterprises in the sample, investment hunger is alive and prospering despite the recent reforms. Indeed, its influence may have increased with the emergence of new financing sources subject to weaker administrative controls. Enterprises are still willing to invest all the funds available to them, regardless of the market conditions they face. And if they fear that the administrative hierarchy will impose controls to prevent overinvestment in their industry, they may even preemptively build up capacity to give them more leverage in later bargaining with authorities. Further stimulating the hunger for investment is the practice of including housing and other facilities in the investment cost and financing plan of projects, which makes such projects an easy means of justifying and financing workers' housing construction.[15]

Some caveats to this general observation are in order, however. Many enterprises prefer to spend their retained profits on collective welfare and workers' bonuses rather than on investment, and they do so to the extent that they can get away with it. This means that the drive to expand production is mitigated by the desire to increase workers' incomes and benefits in the short run. For enterprises facing a buyers' market, investment demand may not be greatly reduced. But the emphasis shifts away from expansion of output toward projects that enhance competitiveness without necessarily generating increased output (like increasing varieties or improving quality or styling).

Perhaps most important, the cost of investment funds is still very low in China. That makes it difficult to distinguish between true investment hunger (which disregards the cost of funds) and rational behavior of enterprises (which should demand investment funds if the cost is low). In some cases, higher borrowing costs have greatly dampened the investment demand of Chinese enterprises. For instance, when bank loans have to be repaid from after-tax profits rather than from before-tax profits, the effective cost of capital is raised sharply, and enterprises facing this situation will often refuse to borrow. Market conditions also affect the willingness of enterprises to borrow at high interest rates. It is doubtful that Chongqing would borrow at 13.5 percent a year today, though it did so quite willingly in 1980 when the market was not a constraint and the company had ambitious long-term growth plans.

Choice of sources of investment finance. Choosing a source of investment is obviously influenced by the relative costs of funds from different sources. But the opportunity to use funds for other purposes is also very important. For instance, retained depreciation and major repair funds for the most part cannot be used to finance workers' bonuses or collective welfare facilities, so enterprises are quite willing to use them for productive investment. But control over the uses of retained profits is relatively weak, so enterprises often try to divert some retained profits from production development to workers' bonuses or welfare expenditures. Another important consideration is the ease and speed with which funds can be obtained. Both bank loans and government grants require a great deal of red tape and frequently delay the implementation of a project. The use of retained profits and depreciation funds is generally easier, as is the reliance on unconventional sources of finance.

Some features of the Chinese accounting system—particularly those for loan repayments, depreciation funds, and (where applicable) fixed-asset charges—very much affect the cost of funds from different sources. Bank loans that finance fixed investment are generally repayable from the before-tax profits of the new project, which means that the government rather than the enterprise, in effect, makes a considerable portion of principal repayments (half of them if the profit tax rate is 50 percent). If these profits are insufficient, the enterprise can repay loans from depreciation funds from the fixed assets of the project, from charges on these assets (if any), and in some cases from indirect taxes on the output of the project. Since the maturity of fixed investment loans is only about three years on average, even very profitable projects generally cannot service loan obligations from newly generated profits alone. So they must draw on depreciation funds (part of which would otherwise be turned over to the government) and taxes (all of which would otherwise be turned over to the government).

The requirement that enterprises turn over a portion of depreciation funds generated by all their assets to government authorities—regardless of whether government grants, bank loans, or the enterprises' own funds created the assets—is another peculiarity of enterprise finance in China. This practice decreases the attractiveness of both of the latter two sources of investment finance, as do fixed-asset taxes for those enterprises required to pay them.

The overall net effect of these accounting and taxation provisions depends on the enterprise's profit-retention system. In general, the provisions reduce the net cash flow from self-financed investment and raise the net cash flow from investment financed by bank loans.[16] This situation naturally makes bank loans more desirable than self-financing for enterprises, particularly since enterprises have attractive alternative uses for retained profits (like collective welfare and workers' bonuses). But projects are generally not eligible for bank loans unless they increase net profits, something easiest to achieve through increased production. Thus, enterprises may be encouraged to expand rather than to replace facilities, even when expansion is not the best alternative. Low indirect tax rates are another deterrent to borrowing, particularly in producer-goods industries.

In practice, it is very difficult to separate the incremental profits of a new project from those that would have been earned by the enterprise without the project, so loan repayment procedures that look neat on paper break down in practice. An enterprise's annual loan repayments may well be determined more by negotiations with banks and financial authorities than by the terms of the loan contract. In particular, local governments sometimes request that loan repayments be delayed to avoid an adverse impact on their revenue. This phenomenon of delayed, uncertain, and annually negotiated loan repayments appears to be fairly widespread. It was common practice in Nanning Municipality. In Qingyuan County, only 30 percent of fixed-investment loans due to the local branch of the People's Bank of China were repaid in 1983, and the figure was to drop below 20 percent in 1984.

Raising the cost of investment funds. There have been attempts in recent years to raise the cost of capital to Chinese industrial enterprises, but they have not been very successful. Interest rates on bank loans have been raised considerably, but because of the short maturity of most loans, the higher rates have had only a small effect. Moreover, the Bank of China's interest rates on loans to finance imported equipment have fallen in line with the decline in world market rates. The campaign to have bank loans replace government grants for capital construction projects undoubtedly has raised the cost of capital (considering that these funds previously were grants). But interest rates remain lower than those for ordinary bank loans for smaller fixed-investment projects, and repayment from before-tax profits remains the norm.

The fixed-asset fee was another major attempt to raise the cost of capital to enterprises. Even if low, its potential impact is much greater because it affects all fixed assets rather than just newly acquired ones. But it appears to have been precisely this impact on enterprise finances—and the wide differences in enterprise profitability due to distortions in the structure of relative prices in China—that caused the fixed-asset fee to be left out of the new profit tax system instituted in 1983–84. Thus, many firms that once paid the fee no longer do so.[17]

Another example of backsliding on the cost of capital is a subsidy introduced in 1984 for loan repayments at Nanning and other enterprises. Enterprises and their workers had complained that using all the incremental profits from an investment project to repay bank loans meant that no additional retained profits would be available for workers' bonuses or collective welfare. If a project involved expansion and generated more employment in the enterprise, this practice would reduce the average level of bonuses and welfare per worker: either new workers would get none of these benefits, or the benefits of existing workers would have to decline. The solution was to let enterprises retain additional profits based on the amount of loan repayments made from profits in a given year (Ministry of Finance 1984, p. 802). In Guangxi Autonomous Region, enterprises were to be allowed to draw 40 percent of their base profit-retention rate times the value of their loan repayments made using profits (presumably on the basis of guidelines that enterprises should spend no more than 40 percent of their retained profits on bonuses and workers' welfare combined). In Nanning Municipality this was increased to 50 percent, because the share of collective welfare and bonus payments in the retained profits of municipal enterprises was typically higher. This added benefit to enterprises comes on top of the lucrative method of allowing loans to be repaid from before-tax profits.

These examples show some of the difficulties China faces in raising the cost of capital to enterprises: murky accounting practices, loan repayment procedures, and negotiated arrangements for the distribution of profits. In addition, enterprises strongly oppose measures to increase the cost of capital, particularly when such increases would affect workers' benefits. And their supervisory agencies are likely to support them.

Implications of China's Industrial Investment System

Still embryonic, capital markets in Chinese industry lag far behind goods markets. Compartmentalization and impediments to horizontal flows of funds remain a serious bottleneck. The banking system, still heavily influenced by administrative controls, is not yet functioning as a true financial intermediary. Enterprises are restricted by the types of financial assets they can hold and by their ability to diversify into new product lines. Of course, without price reform and without measures to make the cost of capital to enterprises reflect its opportunity cost to the economy, free capital flows to the highest financial returns could result in inappropriate investments and waste. This problem has already become serious as enterprises, banks, local governments, and other administrative entities making investment decisions become more and more responsive to profitability. Nevertheless, with reform, the need for and benefits of allowing more flexible flows of investment funds will become greater.

With fragmentation of investment flows and the near absence of a capital market, financial resources will continue to be a prime constraint on investment activity. Funding constraints will often lead to suboptimal project scale, a problem less evident in modernization than in new construction. In modernization, the best solution is often large-scale expansion of one plant rather than simultaneous expansion by several producers, but funding constraints encourage the latter.

Another problem is that endowments of physical capital are likely to vary greatly across enterprises in relation to needs, and there are only limited and crude mechanisms for ameliorating such imbalances. The situation is much the same as that for land and to a lesser extent for labor. Such imbalances naturally breed waste and divert capital to uses having a lower priority. They also force enterprises to engage in various machinations to get around capital constraints.

Other features of the investment system have more positive implications. Raising the cost of funds substantially reduces enterprise investment demand, which means that price changes can curb investment hunger in China. Similarly, a strong buyers' market can deter enterprises from continuing to invest in expansion and shift their orientation toward investments that increase competitiveness and improve consumer benefits. And some new, innovative forms of investment financing have great potential if future reforms proceed as planned.

Mergers, Joint Ventures, and Associations

Interenterprise relations in China go beyond the merely commercial. They include simple subcontracting, processing raw materials on behalf of another enterprise, compensation trade, joint ventures involving profit sharing, and even mergers in which one factory completely absorbs another. More than half the twenty enterprises in the sample have had close interenterprise relations of various kinds.[18] Distinct but often related is the widespread emergence of industrial corporations. In some cases the enterprises that become part of these corporations form them voluntarily. But more often, the corporations are attempts at industrial reorganization imposed from the top down.

A Diversity of Forms and Arrangements

The Nanning Textile Mill started engaging in processing relationships with five smaller enterprises in 1983–84.[19] In some cases the outward form of the relationship is purely commercial, and in others a processing fee is paid for work done. The associated enterprises remain financially and operationally independent. Nanning, however, provides circulating capital in a disguised manner by settling accounts only when the finished products are returned. Moreover, Nanning sometimes pays a higher price than the going market rate and often provides free technical expertise and manpower. These kinds of arrangements were fairly common in Chinese industry even before the late 1970s, and in many cases they formed the foundation for mergers and joint ventures.

Compensation trade is a more recent development. It generally involves only an arm's-length financial relationship and is a means of obtaining supplies outside the plan for the medium or long term. For example, Shenyang Smelting provided a fifteen-year interest-free loan of Y1.7 million to a small cement plant, along with an old zinc-making rotary kiln that it had converted to a cement kiln. In return, the small plant guaranteed the smelter 10,000 tons of cement a year for fifteen years. In some other cases, compensation trade has verged on extortion by producers of underpriced raw materials in short supply; alternatively, such deals could be viewed as raising the effective price of low-priced materials subject to price controls.[20]

Joint ventures involve equity investment by partners and shared profits in accord with investment shares. These appear not to have been allowed before the recent reform period but are now fairly widespread. In some cases the partners set up a new enterprise with contributions (often partly in kind). More commonly, the smaller partner "becomes" a joint venture, with its original facilities and resources considered as its contribution. Joint ventures vary greatly in the control the dominant partner exercises, and the distinction between tightly supervised joint ventures and outright merger or acquisition is fuzzy.

One joint venture in the sample is interesting because it involves the issuance of stock to individuals. In 1980 the Shanghai No. 17 Cotton Mill entered joint ventures with two suburban communes to set up collectively owned textile mills, and it issued stock to its employees to cover part of the financing needs. Shanghai Cotton permitted each of its employees to purchase up to five nontransferable, nonredeemable shares for Y50 a share, with an annual dividend of 12 percent. About 8,000 shares worth Y400,000 were sold to 3,000 employees (roughly a third of the labor force). But a dispute over how the joint venture should repay its bank loan resulted in the dissolution of the stock scheme and the new enterprises after two years. Originally, the venture was to repay both principal and interest for the bank loan from before-tax profits, the normal practice for state-owned enterprises. But the bank later applied the rule for collective enterprises—loan repayment from after-tax profits. This switch made the repayment burden so heavy that the joint ventures liquidated their assets to repay the bank and the stockholders. No stockholders lost money, however, since they received dividends for two years and then were repaid principal on liquidation.

Mergers and acquisitions of one enterprise by another are often a further step to increase control and supervision over loosely associated enterprises. Chongqing was an amalgamation of seven factories when it started in 1980. In addition there were sixteen joint ventures and two firms with which Chongqing had only a processing relationship. In 1983 the eight "associated enterprises" in Chongqing Municipality were put directly under Chongqing, and the ties with their former supervisory agencies were severed.[21] When the Mindong Electrical Machinery Corporation was established in 1981, it instituted rather tight control over all subordinate factories, including joint ventures with the former Mindong Electrical Machinery Plant.

Industrial corporations are in some cases a logical culmination of the integration of smaller "branch" enterprises under a dominant central concern. Both Chongqing and Mindong took on the corporate form in this manner. But there are several other types of corporation.[22] One such type is a loose amalgam of large, powerful enterprises under a relatively weak administrative apparatus, with powerful centrifugal forces at work (Jinling Petrochemical General Corporation). A second is a strong administrative corporation of long standing, which can control production and supply rather tightly (Shanghai No. 17 Cotton Mill and the Shanghai High-Pressure Oil Pump Factory under their respective corporations). A third type is a national umbrella corporation, set up in industries for which greater centralization was deemed desirable (the nonferrous metals and petrochemical industries, for example). In addition, some corporations are loose associations of enterprises in the same line of business or with close production-supply relations. Such enterprises are often widely scattered, and they form the associations more or less voluntarily. An example is the Dongfeng Automobile Corporation, set up under the aegis of the No. 2 Automobile Plant in 1981. Dongfeng now has 103 associated factories in different parts of China, the bulk of which have only a production contracting or processing relationship with No. 2 Auto.

The Mindong Electrical Machinery Corporation provides a striking illustration of the uses to which mergers, corporations, and joint ventures can be put. Formed on a shoestring in 1958, Mindong merged with a defunct tea-service factory in 1964 to acquire needed land and warehouses. After a period of stagnation during the Cultural Revolution and its aftermath, Mindong acquired two failing local machinery plants in late 1979, and its gross output value nearly doubled in 1980. The grand design of its later mergers and joint ventures was to move the heart of the enterprise from the remote and mountainous Fu'an to Fuzhou, the capital of Fujian Province, which has excellent transport and close connections with the outside world. At the end of 1981, Mindong merged with two Fuzhou machinery enterprises that could not make ends meet, and it changed from an enterprise to an industrial corporation. Since then, Mindong has aggressively used mergers, joint ventures, and the corporate form to expand, relocate, and enter new lines of activity. One of its factories, formerly a shipyard, now dismantles old ships to recover scrap steel and other materials. Mindong also hopes to develop a furniture factory that uses recovered materials. And it eventually plans to build steel-making and steel-rolling facilities to process the scrap steel it recovers—facilities whose power plant will use ship generators and will be fueled by waste oil from the ships being dismantled.

Motives

The motives for mergers, joint ventures, and other associations are as varied as the arrangements. Perhaps the most powerful one is to overcome severe space constraints on an enterprise's existing site. Chongqing made a very costly arrangement with a suburban commune to get a new site for its clock factory. The Qinghe Woolen Textile Mill tried unsuccessfully to form a joint venture with local rural production brigades to use their land for weaving facilities. More generally, enterprises often form joint ventures and associations to augment their factor endowment, whether it be land, labor, or, less commonly, financial capital. A good example is the Shanghai Oil Pump Factory, which has seven associated operating sites in the suburbs. It hopes to transform three of these enterprises into branch plants, presumably more tightly controlled.

Another powerful motive is to gain access to needed supplies. This motive spawns two types of arrangements: compensation trade and other arm's-length deals, and mergers and joint ventures to increase backward integration (see chapter 8, this volume). The first type may be more suitable as a means of obtaining energy or raw materials, which are often under the jurisdiction of a different ministry. The second type appears to be the preferred method of backward integration into the production of parts and components. At the earlier stages the enterprise generally sets up new production facilities. Later it enters joint ventures with existing producers and perhaps eventually merges with the partners.

A third motive of enterprises is to improve market position. Joint ventures and associations with shops or other commercial entities invariably have the goal of penetrating new markets or maintaining a strong position in local markets. Chongqing's joint ventures with watch factories in Yunnan and Guizhou provinces helped it to maintain a dominant position in those markets.[23] Similarly, the No. 2 Automobile Plant's leadership of the Dongfeng Automobile Corporation had as one of its goals the opening of previously protected local markets. Mindong, too, wanted to improve its competitive position by changing location.

Why would small enterprises or collectives get involved in close relationships with larger enterprises? One reason is to allow a failing concern to stay in business. Another is to provide employment for surplus members of the organization. And a third is to obtain a financial windfall in return for making some scarce resource available to the partner (which cannot be sold directly for what the market will bear). Even if a smaller enterprise does not get extraordinary financial benefits from becoming involved with or absorbed by another firm, it often gains employment for its members in the larger enterprise or in the venture established.

Immediate financial benefit is rarely a primary motive for the larger partner. Indeed, some of the enterprises in the sample have lost money from joint ventures and associations. No. 2 Auto delivers engines and chassis for vehicles to associated enterprises, earning only negligible profits, compared with a profit of about Y5,000 per assembled truck it makes itself.[24] Chongqing had to support partners financially in various ways, as did Mindong. In these cases, it could be argued that the activities were intended to maximize market share and perhaps profits over the very long run. But short-term financial returns clearly were not a dominant consideration.

Similarly, increased benefits for workers usually are not a major consideration for the merger partner in joint ventures or mergers. Workers' housing in some of Chongqing's collectively run associated enterprises is considerably better than in the core factories. It is doubtful that Mindong's move from Fu'an to Fuzhou was in the best long-term interest of the original workers. On the other hand, workers at the Shanghai No. 17 Cotton Mill at least temporarily were permitted to earn a much higher return on their savings through the joint ventures involving stock issuance discussed earlier. Mergers with enterprises previously set up to employ children and dependents of workers also fit well with the worker-family motive.

Finally, some associations have involved forward integration or simply an evening of imbalances in capacity at different stages of production. The small steel-rolling mills of Anshan and the sales outlets of such market-oriented enterprises as Chongqing and Mindong are examples of forward integration. Nanning is a good example of evening capacity imbalances. There is an obvious trade-off between the flexibility that enterprises retain in purely commercial or processing arrangements and the control they generally maximize in mergers or tightly supervised joint ventures.

Achievements and Problems

The mergers, joint ventures, and associations of the enterprises in the sample are too young to allow conclusive evaluation. It is, however, fairly easy to assess many of them as socially beneficial, at least in the short run. A good example is Nanning's associations: no long-term commitments were entered into, and in the short run the arrangement is profitable for all concerned. In contrast, Chongqing undoubtedly lost in the deal with the suburban commune to acquire a new site for the clock factory (in return for which it had to take on a large number of commune members as temporary workers "in perpetuity"). The commune gained, but the arrangement probably was socially harmful since a large plot of land with a high opportunity cost was lost for other uses. More generally, given the lack of well-functioning factor markets, it sometimes is difficult to ascertain whether a joint venture or association is economically beneficial from a national perspective. Many mergers, joint ventures, and associations would be inferior to solutions that rely on the market mechanism, since the former usually are less flexible and require added real resources.

It is also instructive to look at instances where a merger or joint venture failed or was not able to get off the ground. As part of a 4,800 spindle expansion project, the Qinghe Woolen Textile Mill wanted to enter into a joint venture with some rural production brigades to establish facilities for weaving with 100 looms. Qinghe hoped thereby to reduce the amount of civil construction required on its already crowded site, easing space constraints and perhaps gaining other benefits. In the end the parties never struck a deal because of their inability to agree on profit-sharing arrangements and Qinghe's fears about the lack of technical skills of workers from the rural collectives. In this case at least, the obstacles were not external or administrative: government authorities were neutral throughout.

The failure of the joint ventures between the Shanghai No. 17 Cotton Mill and suburban communes, on the other hand, is traceable directly to conflicts with local authorities over loan repayment. These conflicts may have been a guise for ideological concerns about the issuance of stock to Shanghai Cotton's employees. Local governments in charge of smaller enterprises have sometimes resisted joint ventures that might encroach on their authority or threaten the protected markets of other local enterprises. Fuzhou municipal authorities opposed the expansion of Mindong into the Fuzhou area, fearing that it would threaten inefficient small local producers of electrical machinery.

All in all, the various interenterprise relationships provide some needed flexibility to the system of factor allocation in China. They often help enterprises get around perceived or actual constraints on expansion. The social benefits can be large, particularly when the enterprise for which the constraints are eased is efficient and well managed. But administrative obstacles sometimes hinder or even prevent the consummation of arrangements. Moreover, government authorities may try to promote extraneous goals like creating employment or propping up troubled enterprises. In any case, most of these arrangements are the result of distortions in the system of factor allocation and might not be necessary if markets were to play a greater role. This is not to say, however, that various kinds of interenterprise arrangements would not occur in a well-functioning market system with a minimum of administrative intervention (Williamson 1975).

Conclusions

One notable feature of factor allocation in China is the considerable autonomy of enterprises, despite nominally rigid controls over land, labor, and capital. This autonomy is partly the result of the fragmentation of administrative authority. It is also due to recent reforms that have granted greater decisionmaking powers to enterprises and further decentralized or fragmented administrative controls (most notably in financing investment and supplying capital goods). Enterprises in the sample have found ways to evade administrative restrictions and to obtain control over additional factor inputs wanted for expansion or for other reasons. In these efforts, they have been more successful with labor and investment funds than with land. Rigidity is greater in selling land, scrapping or selling obsolete or worn-out equipment, and especially laying off excess labor: that is, in getting rid of unneeded factor inputs.

Another remarkable feature of China's economy is the substantial territorial decentralization of administrative authority over factor allocation. Landholders, particularly when they are such social institutions as rural communes, appear to exercise considerable administrative powers. In any case, most decisions about land allocation are probably approved by a level of government no higher than the municipality. Labor allocation is similarly under local control.

Given the extent of enterprise autonomy, enterprise objectives influence the pattern of factor allocation and use, especially in determining the increments to existing factor endowments. Enterprises want land not only for production but also for housing and other facilities for their employees. They make capital investments to earn profits, increase capacity (as part of the expansion drive), make working conditions easier, and sometimes provide jobs for their workers' children. External constraints and incentives affect these objectives, as do the goals of the enterprise's workers and managers. This interaction is most evident for labor, where a rigid system of quota allocation and strong concern for worker and community employment generate incentives and behavior that sometimes are paradoxical. The family-oriented firm will expand its labor force as long as many of the new workers hired are children of existing workers. Enterprises often use mergers and joint ventures to create employment for the partner that contributes land or market access. And the close, usually life-long attachment of workers to their enterprises does not, under present circumstances in China, lead to greater effort and productivity.

Common to land, labor, and capital is the interesting combination of a weak, often nonexistent market mechanism for factor allocation and a fragmented, often ineffective set of administrative control mechanisms. Enterprises find it impossible to go out and buy or sell land directly. But government authorities cannot reallocate land to enterprises and institutions without expensive, often prohibitive compensation. There is no labor market, but this does not mean that workers or professional staff can easily be moved from one enterprise or town to another by administrative fiat. Capital markets are embryonic, yet administrative control over enterprise investment is haphazard and fragmented. Even when enforced, the controls are ponderous and unwieldy.

Overall, China's system of factor allocation still suffers from inflexibility and severe imbalances, which lead to costly inefficiency. The deficiencies are only partly the result of rigid administrative controls. They are also the result of enterprise objectives and the lack of factor markets and of pressure or incentives for enterprises to relinquish excess factor inputs they do not need. Chronic shortages obviously play an important role by inducing enterprises to hoard even unneeded factors against future requirements.

All these elements suggest that reforms in the system of factor allocation have not yet progressed far enough to improve efficiency and increase flexibility. Relaxed administrative controls and expanded market mechanisms are obviously needed to achieve greater flexibility. And to improve efficiency, the prices that enterprises pay for factor inputs must reflect true economic costs more fully. But reforms of labor and wages must proceed carefully, given the complex interaction of enterprise objectives, incentives, and constraints in this area, and considerable administrative control may still be needed in the near future.

Notes

1. Four-year fixed-term managerial appointments were introduced in 1984. Some critics feel this change has made managers overly concerned with short-term profits and bonuses.

2. An enterprise maximizing net product per worker will be more restrictive with respect to employment because it will want to employ an extra worker only if his marginal product is greater than the firm's average product, whereas a profit-maximizing firm will want to employ an additional worker as long as his marginal product is greater than his wage. Since the wage is normally less than the average product (wage plus profit), the labor-managed firm will employ fewer workers in equilibrium than the profit-maximizing firms. Ward 1967 introduced the theory of labor-managed enterprise behavior. See also Meade 1972 and Bergson 1982.

3. Chongqing Clock and Watch Company wanted to maximize total net product because it would also provide greater housing benefits and floating wage increases. The assumption that net product is the maximand is a simplification. Workers may attach different weights to wage and profit components, depending on tax rates and other regulations. See Byrd and Tidrick 1984, pp. 30–33.

4. Hicks 1935 noted that a "quiet life" is the ultimate benefit of monopoly in a capitalist economy.

5. The Daqing Oilfield developed into a widely emulated national model during the prereform period. In the late 1970s there was a major campaign for industry to learn from Daqing, and enterprises strove for recognition as "Daqing-style enterprises" or "advanced enterprises in emulating Daqing."

6. The coefficient of variation (standard deviation divided by mean) for the ratio of profits to total fixed assets in our sample in 1980–82 was 0.77; for retained profits over fixed assets it was 0.69, only a slight drop. One possible explanation would be that retention rates are set to provide a certain level of bonus per worker, but this cannot be confirmed from our sample. The coefficient of variation of retained profit per worker during 1980–82 was 0.50, still relatively high. It is interesting to note that in Hungary, however, the coefficient of variation for both preredistribution and postredistribution profitability was far higher than in our sample (chapter 13, this volume).

7. The management of No. 2 Auto has been careful to expand bonuses gradually each year rather than to pay high bonuses in a single year, which might not be sustained and which could create discontent among workers.

8. For the effect of different tax systems on incentives under different objective functions, see Byrd and Tidrick 1984, p. 33.

9. North China Petroleum was also not allowed to hire the children of workers who still had rural registration, and Nanning Textile Mill faced similar restrictions. This anomaly arises because of Chinese policy on urban-rural migration. Enterprises are sometimes allowed to hire workers with rural registration as a special exception, but these workers retain their rural registration and are ineligible for an urban grain ration. Their children are therefore ineligible for urban employment unless another special exception is made.

10. Children of course do not step right into their parent's job, but they are entitled to be assigned to some permanent job in the enterprise.

11. For details on Nanning, see chapter 8 in this volume, and on Chongqing, see Byrd and Tidrick 1984, p. 29.

12. Projects larger than a certain size must be approved by planning authorities regardless of their source of funds, and approval procedures for the self-financed investment projects of enterprises appear to have been tightened in the past two to three years. Nevertheless, at least among the enterprises in the sample, self-financed projects seem never to have been turned down. Of course, most enterprise investment projects rely on some external financing, which opens the possibility for effective external controls.

13. Some enterprises had their bank deposits frozen as part of a general macroeconomic stabilization program in early 1981. But this had only a small and short-lived impact on the enterprises in the sample, except that it caused some customers to cancel orders.

14. Even if a large share of profits is siphoned away by indirect taxes, these same profits can often be used for loan repayment, thus making an enterprise a better credit risk.

15. This link between capital construction investment projects and workers' housing and other facilities apparently started only during the recent reform period. The authorities instituted it "to avoid new debts on housing to the workers."

16. Byrd and Tidrick 1984, pp. 34–38, provide a more detailed discussion of this subject, particularly the effect of loan repayment provisions on incentives. Though this analysis is based on the Chongqing Clock and Watch Company, it appears to be

applicable except in the few cases where banks or local authorities force enterprises to repay loans from after-tax profits.

17. Some enterprises in the sample that are subject to separate multiyear financial incentive schemes (like Chongqing and Jiangmen) must still pay this charge. Other enterprises (like North China Petroleum) have instituted an "internal fixed-asset fee" to encourage subunits to economize on their use of fixed capital.

18. Another common relationship, already discussed, is that between state-owned industrial enterprises and the subordinate factories (nominally collectively owned) they set up to employ workers' children.

19. One of the relationships involved degumming ramie, which Nanning provided along with equipment and technical expertise. Another involved spinning blended cotton-linen yarn, with Nanning providing ramie. The other three involved various kinds of weaving, using yarn that Nanning provided.

20. In processing deals and compensation trade, it is common for financing to be arranged through trade credit, usually covered by short-term bank loans and listed as "receivables" in enterprises' circulating capital accounts. See chapter 8 in this volume for some other examples of compensation trade from our sample.

21. This was part of a reform of industrial administration in Chongqing, a reform that abolished the supervisory authority of district governments over their enterprises. See Byrd and Tidrick 1984, p. 18.

22. Industrial corporations are discussed in more detail in chapter 11 in this volume.

23. By establishing a close relationship with provincial watch producers, Chongqing gained a market for its components and for the types of watches it could produce but the joint venture partners could not. See Byrd and Tidrick 1984, p. 20.

24. Engines are the binding constraint on No. 2 Auto's vehicle production, so it really was sacrificing profits. In 1983 the plant delivered about 3,000 complete engines and chassis to associated factories, above and beyond its mandatory plans, forgoing profits of about Y15 million.

References

Bergson, Abram. 1982. "Entrepreneurship under Labor Participation: The Yugoslav Case." In Joshua Ronen, ed., *Entrepreneurship*. Lexington, Mass.: D.C. Heath.

Byrd, William. 1985. *The Shenyang Smelter: A Case Study of Problems and Reforms in China's Nonferrous Metals Industry*. World Bank Staff Working Paper 766. Washington, D.C.

Byrd, William, and Gene Tidrick. 1984. "Adjustment and Reform in the Chongqing Clock and Watch Company." In *Recent Chinese Economic Reforms: Studies of Two Industrial Enterprises*. World Bank Staff Working Paper 652. Washington, D.C.

Chen Jiyuan, Xu Lu, Tang Zongkun, and Chen Lantong. 1984. "Management and Reform in the Qingdao Forging Machinery Plant." In *Recent Chinese Economic Reforms: Studies of Two Industrial Enterprises*. World Bank Staff Working Paper 652. Washington, D.C.

Denison, Edward. 1967. *Why Growth Rates Differ*. Washington, D.C.: Brookings Institution.

Granick, David. 1975. *Enterprise Guidance in Eastern Europe.* Princeton, N.J.: Princeton University Press.

Henderson, Vernon. 1986. *International Experience in Urbanization and Its Relevance for China.* World Bank Staff Working Paper 758. Washington, D.C.

Hicks, J. R. 1935–36. "Annual Survey of Economic Theory: The Theory of Monopoly." *Econometrica* 3/4 (January):1–20.

Kornai, Janos. 1979. "Resource-Constrained versus Demand-Constrained Systems." *Econometrica* 47, no. 4:801–19.

———. 1980. *Economics of Shortage.* 2 vols. Amsterdam: North-Holland.

McKinnon, Ronald I. 1973. *Money and Capital in Economic Development.* Washington, D.C.: Brookings Institution.

Meade, J. E. 1972. "The Theory of Labour-Managed Firms and of Profit Sharing." *Economic Journal* 82 (March Supplement):402–28.

Ministry of Finance. 1984. "Guoying Qiye Dierbu Ligaishui Shixing Banfa" (The trial method of the second stage of substituting taxes for state enterprise profit remittances). *Zhonghua Renmin Gongheguo Guowuyuan Gongbao* (Bulletin of the State Council of the People's Republic of China) 23 (October 10):798–803.

Tidrick, Gene. 1986. *Productivity Growth and Technological Change in Chinese Industry.* World Bank Staff Working Paper 761. Washington, D.C.

Ward, Benjamin N. 1967. *The Socialist Economy: A Study of Organizational Alternatives.* New York: Random House.

Wells, Louis T. 1975. "Economic Man and Engineering Man: Choice of Technology in a Low-Wage Country." In C. Peter Timmer and others, *The Choice of Technology in Developing Countries.* Studies in International Affairs 32. Cambridge, Mass.: Harvard University, Center for International Affairs.

Williamson, Oliver E. 1975. *Markets and Hierarchies: Analysis and Antitrust Implications.* London: Free Press.

World Bank. 1985. *China: Long-Term Issues and Options.* Baltimore, Md.: Johns Hopkins University Press.

5

The Industrial Environment in China and the CMEA *Countries*

David Granick

THE ENVIRONMENT FOR STATE-OWNED industrial enterprises in China differs in important ways from that in the European countries of the Council for Mutual Economic Assistance (CMEA).[1] First, in China, much more trade in producer goods takes place in markets equilibrated by marginal prices. The CMEA countries, by contrast, use a system of rationing for the physical allocation of producer goods to enterprises. Second, the opposite is true for the allocation of labor: labor markets are weak in China, but they are genuine in, say, the U.S.S.R. Third, Chinese enterprises attribute much less significance to plans for regulating their current operation than do the CMEA countries (except Hungary). Fourth, regional authorities in China exercise much more power than do their counterparts in the U.S.S.R.—in social spending, in raising funds, and in supervising production. This chapter spells out the details of these differences and comments on the relevance of the last difference to marketization.

Distribution Mechanisms for Producer Goods

The student familiar with the U.S.S.R. and other European CMEA countries (with the possible exception of Hungary) is struck by how much trade between industrial enterprises in China is in markets equilibrated through price. For such trade, disequilibrated sellers' markets seem to be exceptional rather than the rule. Market balance is obtained by the use of a multiprice system, one rarely employed in CMEA countries for purchases by industrial enterprises.

Distribution in the European CMEA Countries

The distribution system for most producer goods in European CMEA countries other than Hungary rests on a rationing system of physical allocation to the enterprise. Goods are obtainable only with an allocation order accompanied by the payment of money.[2] A single-price system applies. Because it would be pointless to have an allocation system if markets cleared at existing monetary prices, we find what might be expected: unsatisfied demand for producer goods when demand is expressed solely in monetary terms. But such demand is not "effective demand" if unaccompanied by allocations. Thus, excess demand in the monetary sense does not, in itself, lead to sellers' markets.

Sellers' markets exist for two reasons. First, allocations frequently seem to be given in larger volumes than the available supply of the items—a failure of "balancing." Second, and more important, allocations are of necessity highly aggregative.[3] Within a given aggregate that enters both the production plan of producers and the allocations to users, producers naturally prefer the product mix most advantageous for meeting their various success indicators (which are plans). Although producers, of course, give some attention to the product-mix needs of users, their own plans are sufficiently taut, and enterprise incentives for fulfillment and overfulfillment are sufficiently great, that user needs are given a distant second priority.[4] Users must take whatever mix the producer chooses within an allocated aggregate, since additional allocations will always be granted to some other user if such allocations are required to absorb unsold goods.

During the Stalin period, a large group of users could be protected at least against the failure to receive their total allotment within each aggregate. This was due to the heavy reliance on the "priority" principle in the execution of plans. Priority users received their full allotments or more; shortfalls were concentrated on nonpriority users. In this fashion, heavy industry and most of the engineering industry—which Soviet planners viewed as the core of the rapid industrialization program—were virtually guaranteed the critical material inputs.

Since the mid-1950s, however, the concept of a priority sector in the U.S.S.R. has been so expanded (to agriculture and to many consumer goods) that it has lost almost all meaning. The incentives of producer enterprises have also become more tightly linked to preselected quantitative success indicators. Thus, it appears that the existence of sellers' markets for producer goods now applies much more broadly (if less sharply) throughout almost all the economy. (Military production presumably is still protected, but we know too little about such production to be sure.)

Distribution in China

Enterprise interviews in China indicate the existence of a system of distribution radically different from that in European CMEA countries throughout the reform period from 1979 on and suggest that this system also held—although to a lesser degree—prior to the reforms. The critical distinctive elements in China are discussed below.

Allocation priorities. The allocations of inputs to an enterprise are usually intended to supply only part of its needs. This is true not only when the economy is overheating but even when cutbacks of investment reduce the short-term need for materials relative to supply. In mid-1982, apparently a period of relative ease in supply conditions, a representative of the planning bureau of Shanghai stated that normally only 70 percent to 80 percent of that city's consumption of goods allocated by national ministries and by higher national bodies is covered through any type of allocation. Judging by the interviews in our sample enterprises, such relatively low coverage is typical of Chinese industry in general.

Enterprises that produce products allocated by central state organs above the level of individual central ministries, and that are directly supervised by central bodies rather than solely by provincial or lower regional authorities, seem to be in a privileged position with regard to receipt of the small number of critical items that are allocated at this central level.[5] They seem much more likely than other enterprises to receive the full amount of such items required to produce their planned output. (But they do not seem to be favored to receive materials needed to produce above-plan output or to produce the portion of their planned output that is not centrally allocated. Moreover, in a sample of four enterprises, there seemed to be at least one exception to the situation of privilege.)

Such centrally supervised enterprises do no better than others, however, and may indeed do worse, in receiving their requirements of goods allocated at the provincial and municipal level: one sample enterprise that recently shifted from local to central control reported a reduction in the proportion of its needs covered by local allocations. "Priority," as indicated by the level to which the enterprise is subordinated, seems a poor guide to the coverage of needs by allocations handled locally.

Materials problems. Enterprise complaints about the insufficiency of desired material inputs are minor by Soviet standards. The main Chinese complaint concerns electricity. The shortage of electricity is pervasive, leading to the closing of plants and the rescheduling of operations. Aside from this shortage, one enterprise's complaint is indicative. It could not purchase copper scrap—not because there was not enough scrap, but because it could not afford to compete for scrap in a market where prices were virtually free. It was for this reason that the enterprise did not even attempt to procure more than a nominal amount of the scrap.

As one would expect, enterprises encountered much more difficulty in obtaining a desired product mix and products of their precise specification than in meeting demand for broader aggregates of supplies. But even at this level, my impression is that the Chinese enterprise's problems are mild compared with those of its Soviet counterpart. This remark must be treated cautiously, however. An enterprise accustomed to obtaining a product mix that only roughly approaches the specifications desired may register no complaints when reality accords with its expectations.[6] I recall interviews in 1960 with American managers of engineering plants in Great Britain who complained bitterly as to the total lack of local suppliers who could and would meet desired specifications. Yet no one would claim that the British situation in that regard in 1960 was objectively worse than the one in China today.

Pricing policies. Prices paid by the same enterprise—particularly calculated with cost, insurance, and freight (CIF) but also freight on board (FOB)—vary considerably within the same period. The variance depends partly upon the administrative status of the supplying enterprise. "Small cooperatives" are least constrained in their pricing policy, whereas among the state-owned enterprises there is a gradation of prices that corresponds to the level of government to which an enterprise is responsible. In addition, however, an enterprise has frequently been permitted to charge a higher price for the portion of its output that is above plan than for that part produced to meet planned output targets. By mid-1984 state-owned industrial enterprises in general were allowed to raise their prices up to 20 percent for their above-plan production (Provisional Regulations of the State Council, May 11, 1984).

What does this variation in price amount to overall? The best single figure comes from a huge enterprise producing centrally allocated items. The above-plan output of its major product can be calculated to use materials that are bought CIF at prices that average 25 percent higher than those paid for goods used in the production of that part of the enterprise's output that is planned and allocated. Since at least the major single item among these supplementary materials is bought at the standard price because of barter arrangements entered into by the enterprise, the average price increase for the supplementary materials that are truly purchased is clearly much more than 25 percent.

This variation in prices for an identical product seems to permit market clearing, with money rather than allocations constituting both the medium of exchange and the unit for measuring "effective demand." With rare exceptions, the receipt of a larger allocation of a given input has financial importance for the receiving enterprise—but no effect on its output except through considerations of cost.

Compensatory trade. At least since 1982, Chinese enterprises have been able to engage in "compensatory trade." One of our sample enterprises, centrally directed and producing centrally allocated products, made a purely monetary investment (a fifteen-year interest-free loan) in another enterprise. In return, it would get assured delivery at a low price of a specified annual volume of a locally distributed product produced by the other enterprise. This "trade" is a form, extended over time, of paying a higher price for nonallocated supplies. It entails, however, a special political risk. The supplying enterprise may be taken over by a higher level of government, and its planned production then may be subject to the allocation procedures normal for the product.

Barter. Chinese enterprises also engage in "exchange," or barter. What substantively differentiates such barter from that in the U.S.S.R. is that almost all of it consists of exchanges of final products of two enterprises. In contrast, Soviet barter consists primarily of exchanges of allocated inputs between two enterprises. Soviet enterprises are not allowed to self-market even their above-plan output, which is allocated to users in the same fashion as is their planned output (Manevich 1973, p. 32). Exchanges of final products among these enterprises thus is possible only by not declaring the production of these items to higher authorities. The relative tautness of production plans sharply limits the scope for such action, however.

The use of markets. The foregoing observations about the Chinese system of distribution of producer goods support the view frequently asserted in China that the plan directive should be the main instrument, and the market an assisting factor, in determining production and materials distribution. The official allocation is related—even though rather stochastically between enterprises—to planned production; the prime significance of such allocation is that supplies are purchased at a relatively low price. But additional supplies are also available to the enterprise at higher prices. Most purchases and sales of at least those state enterprises under the administration of an organ of the municipality, the province, or the central government will be at the official price and determined by plan. In this sense, the plan directive exerts the dominant influence. But the clearing of producer-goods markets through prices alone gives the market a role that it does not have in the U.S.S.R. or in any of the other European CMEA countries where plan directives reach the enterprise level.[7]

In fact, one could make a good case that the market plays a stronger role in this regard in China than it does even in Hungary. Hungarian economists seem agreed that, despite the absence of allocations, their economy even today is characterized by interenterprise sellers' markets that remain uncleared. (See, for example, Kornai 1983, pp. 244–45, and Bauer 1983, p. 307.) Thus, distribution is to a considerable degree determined by factors other than the willingness and ability of an enterprise to outbid others for the goods. In this sense, Chinese market influences may be stronger than Hungarian on the margin—that is, for the last units of a material used by an enterprise.

Chinese markets are, of course, very imperfect. There are strong aspects of regional monopolies, and regional protectionism is a major force segmenting the national market. Competition is often treated as cutthroat and as leading to "untidy" markets that should be regulated. Central efforts to expand competition have only begun to become effective.[8] But none of these facts limits the impact of markets on the economy. Instead, they reflect the limits to competition in these markets.

Furthermore, the system of multiple prices—different from the CMEA system and from that found in capitalist countries—has multiple disadvantages. Different state enterprises in the same industry, even those subordinate to the same administrative body, receive allocations of given materials (and thus the right to purchase them at low prices) that cover very different proportions of their requirements for producing their planned output. These anomalies may reflect historical accident, such as the earlier supervision of an enterprise by a different administrative body. Or they may reflect differences in the rate of growth of planned output, with rapid growers "penalized" by being assigned a lower ratio. Furthermore, costs reflect the enterprise's production plan. Other things being equal, the higher the production plan relative to actual output, the lower the per-unit variable costs. Relative profits of two enterprises also reflect the level of each enterprise's production plan in another fashion. Other things being equal, the higher the production plan relative to actual output, the lower the per-unit sales receipts. There is no reason to expect that these two effects of a comparatively high production plan will cancel out. It is for good reason then that the Central Committee of the Chinese Communist party, in its October 20, 1984, statement, asserted that "reform of the price system is the key to reform of the entire economic structure."

How do these conditions compare with those before the reform? In only two of the sample enterprises was there discussion in the interviews as to continuity with the prereform period. In one, a specific comparison was made between the enterprise's experience during 1976–78 and 1979–82. This comparison was carried through systematically for each of the major materials purchased. Product by product, allocations in the two periods covered much the same proportion of total materials purchased. Price differences existed for products purchased under allocations and those bought on the open market during 1976–78: the products included lumber, coke, coal, and paint. The proportion of nonallocated supplies obtained through barter was much the same in both periods. During 1976–78, half this barter was conducted through exchange by the enterprise of its final product. This comparison, far more detailed than that presented by the second enterprise, suggests that multiprice market equilibria existed before 1979 as well as after. In this respect, the reform movement would seem irrelevant.

In the second enterprise, in contrast, the 1979–84 years were treated as similar to the 1958–63 period but as radically different from 1964–78, when, it was claimed, absolutely everything was obtained through allocation and was purchased at a single price.

Both of these answers suggest that the use of markets and of multiple prices for producer goods to equilibrate supply with effective demand as expressed in money is no innovation of the current Chinese government. The importance of markets and of market clearing for the treatment of producer goods seems to go back a long time in the history of the People's Republic. On the other hand, I have gained the impression from the tone of the interviews in the enterprises taken as a whole, although I have no data to back it up, that the period since 1978 has seen a significant expansion in the market-clearing practices described above.

Factor Markets for Labor in the State Industrial Sector

We have seen that producer-goods markets seem fairly well equilibrated and that the market mechanism is the device used for determining the distribution of these items in China. Casual observation of retail establishments in a few cities suggests that the same is also much more true for consumer industrial goods in urban areas than is the case in the U.S.S.R. or in most of the European CMEA countries. (This observation is supported by data from the only two enterprises in our sample that entirely or primarily produce consumer goods. But this evidence is very weak, because their subsectors are minor in importance and might well be unusual within the total sector of industrial consumer goods.) Thus, the market mechanism plays a very different allocative role in product markets in general in China from the one it does in the U.S.S.R. or in any of the other European CMEA countries with the possible exception of Hungary.

The exact opposite, however, pertains to the factor markets for labor in the state industrial sector. Within the European CMEA countries, and in the U.S.S.R. specifically, these factor markets are genuinely self-clearing. Relative earnings for different types of labor are determined primarily by forces of supply and demand rather than by central edict.[9] In China, in contrast, market factors play only a very small—although growing—role. The distinction between the U.S.S.R. and China regarding the role of market forces in the allocation of products versus labor could not be greater.

The Soviet Labor Market

Four main points should be made about labor markets in the U.S.S.R. First, the Soviet labor market is a genuine market. For the entire state sector in 1980, 68 percent of all hiring was done directly by enterprises or other organizations (at the factory gate in industry). Another 10 percent was done through municipal labor exchanges that acted as simple intermediaries between the job seeker and would-be employer, both of which had the right to refuse the suggested labor contract without giving any explanation. Of the remaining 22 percent of hirings, 14 percent involved the placement (normally for about three years) of recent graduates of full-time professional educational institutions, including universities (Kotliar 1984, pp. 53 and 56). The major exception to a voluntary market relationship in labor employment is the sending of state employees to work in agriculture for roughly one month a year. In 1982 some 11 million urban state employees (about 15 percent of all urban state employees) were sent for such obligatory work. The quantity of this exception has grown rapidly and continuously during the 1950s and 1970s. Nevertheless, the phenomenon can still be regarded as minor.

Second, the Soviet labor market is very active. Until the end of the 1970s Soviet state employees could quit a job on two weeks' notice; today the required notice is two months. In 1978 in the Russian Republic, 16 percent of all industrial manual workers quit their jobs during the year.[10] This figure is close to that from American data for all full-time employees in manufacturing. Although no reliable figure exists as to total separations for any reason of manual workers in industry, labor economists in the U.S.S.R. commonly accept the estimate of 30 percent a year.

Third, separations on the Soviet labor market occur overwhelmingly as a result of employee rather than employer decisions. Dismissals of state employees for disciplinary reasons (for example, for absenteeism or drunkenness on the job) appear to total 1 percent to 2 percent per year. Dismissals for incompetence, or obligatory permanent transfers to other work within the same plant, are virtually nonexistent (aside from managers and professionals) after a probationary period that for the vast bulk of employees is limited to between one week and one month. Redundancy dismissals and obligatory transfers for redundancy reasons to other work within the same plant, judging from a major Soviet study covering 1976–80, seem to be less than 1 percent per year (Fil'ev 1983, p. 59). It seems safe to conclude that the total of all dismissals, plus obligatory job transfers within an enterprise, constitute something less than 2 to 2.5 percent annually of the Soviet industrial labor force.

Fourth, demand by employers on the Soviet labor market in the state sector is such that workers and employees can count on finding a new job very quickly in the same locality if they quit their job and that new entrants in the labor market similarly have no difficulty in finding work in the state sector. Much of Soviet urban housing is owned by individual enterprises; however, just as seems to be the case in China, workers who leave their original enterprise will not in practice be dispossessed from their current housing. Still, there is no guarantee that available jobs will be at the skill level of the particular workers or employees applying. It is striking that in Soviet industry as a whole in 1975, a third of the employees holding diplomas of secondary specialized education (usually requiring two years of study after completion of normal secondary education) were working as manual workers.[11]

Faced with the labor market described above, Soviet industrial enterprises are forced to compete with one another for their labor supply. Such competition takes various forms. One is labor relations: the provision of good training on the job, of safety, and of efforts to design the work environment so that it is pleasanter and the jobs more interesting. The second is fringe benefits: housing, canteen meals, enterprise-operated retail stores, and the like. The third, discussed below, is monetary earnings. These are paid primarily from the wage fund but also from a special incentives fund created from a specified portion of retained profits. For manual workers in industry, some 67 percent to 81 percent of all earnings above base wages are paid from the wage fund, and almost all of the residual is paid out of retained profits.[12]

The individual Soviet enterprise, like the Chinese, receives a planned wage fund for a given year. The actual wage fund made available in the Soviet case, unlike the Chinese, will be greater or less than planned according to whether the actual output produced during the year is greater or less than the planned volume. But the difference between the actual and planned Soviet wage fund is normally quite small.

From the wage fund, the Soviet enterprise must first meet its obligation to pay personnel their basic wages plus any overtime—all of which is calculated from centrally determined wage rates calibrated according to the industry and skill level. To this obligation is added a set of other centrally determined supplements reflecting the conditions of work faced by the individual worker, supplements for various regions, and so on. The remainder of the enterprise wage fund is available for the payment of incentives—payments to piece workers for producing more than a standard output, and various bonuses that go almost entirely to manual workers.

The wage fund available per worker and employee increases fairly regularly by several percentage points per year to cover inflation and to provide improvements in real earnings. But the wage rates and rate supplements typically remain constant for about fifteen years (except for the minimum wage rate, which has changed more frequently), at which point they are increased considerably. The reconciliation between a wage fund per capita that is increased each year and wage rates that move upward only at very infrequent intervals is achieved by variation in the incentive portion of the wage fund. For manual workers in Soviet industry as a whole, this part of the wage fund fell from an estimated 35 percent to 16 percent between 1957 and 1961, an interval during which wage rates were increased. By 1972, shortly before the next wage-rate increase, the incentive portion had again risen to 32 percent (McAuley 1979, pp. 247–49).

When one also takes account of incentive payments made to manual workers in industry out of retained profits, we can calculate that some 20 percent to 42 percent of total earnings of manual workers in all Soviet industry consists of incentive payments. We can see, as well, that this percentage varies cyclically in relation to the timing of wage-rate increases. Almost as large a percentage of the earnings of white-collar employees, professionals, and managers also comes from such payments, although for them such supplementary earnings are paid virtually entirely out of retained profits. Total incentive payments constitute a large "pot" that the enterprise management and trade union can distribute as they see fit.

How is this pot of incentives used? Partly, of course, it is used simply to increase general monetary earnings annually in the face of wage rates that are stable over long periods. This usage introduces no differences between relative wage rates and relative earnings. A second use is the one for which incentives are officially established: to reward individuals and small groups of individuals. Viewed on the scale of a ministry as a whole, this usage should also have no significant effect on the relative earnings of different trades or skill groups. A third usage, however, does have a major effect. It is the use of this pot by the enterprise to compete with other firms for workers who are in relatively short supply either within the particular enterprise or overall in industry. Commenting on the observed deviations between relative earnings and relative wage rates within the same enterprise, a Soviet author writes, "any other relationship in the enterprise would lead to many categories of personnel simply disappearing from the enterprise; production would stop" (Shkurko 1983, p. 75). Many Soviet specialists in wage administration are said to believe that future changes in wage rates should follow, rather than attempt to direct, the skill variations in earnings. Indeed, in 1982 centrally determined changes in relative wage rates within underground coal mining tended to follow the observed earnings differentials between skill categories (Kheifets 1982, pp. 37–38).

It is true that the distribution of the incentive portion of the wage fund is formally restricted to individuals who have "earned" the bonuses/piece rates according to centrally specified criteria. But it is doubtful that such restrictions have ever been operational. Since the mid-1970s, their application even as a matter of form has been increasingly relaxed. In 1982 a Soviet writer could declare that savings out of an enterprise's wage fund simply do not occur. When the management sees that it may have such savings in a given trimester, it takes all measures needed to avoid them, "all the more since such liquidation of savings is not difficult" (Zaitsev 1982, p. 120).

Indeed, incentive payments are so sharply differentiated among people of different trades and skills that, in an investigation conducted in the early 1980s in the largest Soviet civilian engineering ministry, virtually no correlation could be found between skill grade and earnings within any of the four trades of manual workers studied. Within a given skill grade, the differences in earnings between trades are striking (although there should be none on average according to the formal system of wage rates and supplements). Furthermore, these differences are not systematically related to the possibilities for skill improvement within the trade and thus to investment by workers in improving their own human capital (Shkurko 1983, p. 76). Because the investigation covered all workers in these four mass trades in this major national industry, it is difficult to believe that purely random events explain the above result. It would seem reasonable for us to follow the Soviet author who presented these data and to attribute the result to market forces of supply and demand within the labor market.

Workers and employees of given trades and skill levels that are in short supply in the particular enterprise receive disproportionately high shares of the incentives pot. The higher shares reduce their quit rate from what it would otherwise be and encourage workers with the same trades and skills in other enterprises to leave their existing enterprise and to join the one attempting to attract them. Workers receiving disproportionately low shares of the incentives pot are, in effect, being encouraged to quit and take jobs elsewhere, since their numbers are comparatively high in this enterprise. In addition, this use of the incentives pot encourages workers and employees in all enterprises to learn new trades that are generally in short supply in the locality and to change over to working in these trades.

Thus, within any given Soviet enterprise, relative earnings are determined primarily by market forces rather than by central authorities. True, the relative earnings of groups such as textile loom operators and underground coal miners are set essentially by central authorities. The reason is that workers in these trades are completely segregated into different industries and enterprises, and the total wage fund of each enterprise is decided by the center rather than by market relations. But most industrial workers are employed in trades that are found in a wide variety of subbranches; for them, it would appear that central authorities have no more influence over relative pretax earnings than such authorities have in capitalist countries. Indeed, the main influencing mechanism is the same in both types of societies: legislation of a minimum wage rate. Within the state sector of the U.S.S.R., the ability of central authorities to determine the distribution of income coming from wages and salaries seems to be quite limited.[13]

The Chinese Labor Market

The distinction between Chinese and Soviet labor conditions originates in the radical differences between the two countries in the number of urban citizens with both the capability and the desire to work in the state sector, in relation to the feasibility of the state's providing such work given the capital resources of each country. In commenting on the Chinese scene we must start from the position that, even if Chinese state enterprises were to hire freely at the gate according to their needs and available wage funds, one could not expect a quit rate that would be within an order of magnitude of the Soviet. So long as social considerations in China keep the dismissal rate exceedingly low by international standards (this is a phenomenon found in all European CMEA countries and in Yugoslavia), an active labor market in the state sector will not be possible.

A basic conclusion from this assumption is that it would not be possible for the wage funds of Chinese state industrial enterprises to be used as they are in Soviet industry. That is, they could not be spent so as to permit changes in relative earnings of different types of labor in the enterprise that reflect changes in the relative supply or demand for these kinds of labor. This use would be conceivable for very specialized managerial and professional employees but not for any large part of the labor force. Thus, relative earnings within the state industrial sector could not reflect the play of market forces, even if Chinese authorities wanted them to do so.

One might argue that the quit rate in a variety of trades within many large capitalist enterprises in developed countries is also very low and that relative earnings are determined by some form of job evaluation. But such job evaluation is always linked to market relations, and these enterprises are always careful to keep in close touch with the relative wages paid in competing enterprises. The market place thus serves here as the foundation for job evaluation in a way that would scarcely be possible in Chinese industry.[14]

Discussions of personnel matters in Chinese enterprises are filled with complaints as to the difficulty of rewarding people according to their worth. Although suggestions for improvement are usually couched in terms that imply that such a system of reward would reduce income egalitarianism within a given enterprise, this implication is in fact unwarranted. Differences in earnings among the bottom 90 percent to 95 percent of earners in a Chinese enterprise must be as great as they are within a typical American firm. The issue is not the range of difference. Rather it is the basis for placing an individual at one point or another within the range. In the Chinese enterprise, ever-increasingly from the mid-1950s to 1979, the criterion was neither that of the labor market nor that of job evaluation nor even that of personal favoritism. Instead, placement was primarily on the basis of seniority in the firm, and only seniority accumulated prior to the mid-1950s had weight.

As a generalization, one can say that normal upward reclassification of manual workers (other than apprentices) and white-collar employees ceased in China in the mid-1950s and did not begin again until 1979.[15] Although, of course, many people progressed in skill and managerial authority, for a quarter of a century such movements could rarely be recognized by upward movement on the pay scale. Piece-rate payment and bonuses were also as a rule nonexistent until 1978. Although there may have been some "subsidies" given for managerial positions, they cannot have amounted to much.[16] Only in 1979, and again in 1983, could higher percentages of employees be promoted.[17]

The Deng regime thus inherited a most unfavorable situation in state industry: substantial inequality of incomes distributed in a way that bore little correlation to responsibility, skill, or effort. Incomes in state industry had to be restrained because of their inflationary impact. But employee earnings across the board increased substantially to keep up with inflation and to follow the increases in real incomes in the agricultural and cooperative sectors. Thus, most of the bonus payments (substantial since 1979) and much of the added earnings from promotions amounted to across-the-board increases.

Thus, it is not unexpected (and, to explain it, no appeal need be made to egalitarian Chinese traditions) that progress has been slow over the bare five years of reform in moving toward a differentiation of earnings within the state enterprise according to skill, position, and effort. Indeed, without pressure from the labor market for such differentiation, the progress in many of the sample enterprises is surprising. True, much of it has been accomplished by various subterfuges of enterprise management rather than through promotions or through bonus differentiation. Nevertheless, by 1984 at least two of the sample enterprises had schemes in force according to which top managers could receive open bonuses of a substantial amount. In one of these enterprises, the bonus offer for one year amounted to 150 percent of the sum of base salary plus past normal bonus.

Certainly much more can, and presumably will, be done in the direction of such differentiation. Without any labor market, however, we may be skeptical of the ability of any enterprise to draw up patterns of income differentiation that will win wide acceptance among its labor force in the long run. Job evaluation, in its very nature, seems to me to be too arbitrary a technique—because of the problem of determining the weighting of the different factors used in the evaluation process—to bear the weight that would have to be placed upon it.

What, then, of the creation of a labor market in Chinese state enterprises? The set of obstacles to moving from one urban area to another, let alone from a rural to an urban area, seems to have remained constant throughout the reform period. All workers and white-collar employees, including top managers, who were transferred inside the same sample enterprise from one town to a city in the same province had to leave their families behind. Urban workers who had married rural residents could not, in effect, bring their spouses to the urban area; or, rather, the latter could be registered as urbanites and receive urban rations only after many years of living in the cities without a ration card.

Interviewees in two of the sample enterprises discussed voluntary transfers of people with higher education between organizations. One enterprise was a net loser, and the interviewee here complained of constraints imposed by higher authorities that prevented the enterprise from being competitive. The second, a producer of a very banal product, had made itself so attractive to possible transferees that a full 4 percent of its personnel were university graduates.[18] Interviewees in other enterprises discussed the issue of ordinary workers' quitting and indicated that no obstacles would be put in their way. However, aside from arranged transfers between state enterprises within the same city (mostly to bring a newly married worker's job closer to his or her new housing), the issue of such resignations appears to be theoretical because of the difficulty of finding another state-employee job, something less likely to apply to industrial personnel with higher education.

Regular state employees are almost immune from dismissal. Nevertheless, two of the enterprises in the sample had procedures that mimicked dismissal. One consumer-durables enterprise, when its production had to be cut because of lack of demand, compelled some of its manual workers to peddle the product to local residents. If the workers' sales were insufficient, their monthly earnings were reduced sharply below the base pay for their grade. The second enterprise had just reduced the earnings of a few workers to 60 percent of the base pay for their grades. It has also been stated that national policy since 1982 permits dismissals for excessive absenteeism.

All these practices seem to be new developments, indicating small changes of traditional policy. But dismissals (in what was presumably, but not certainly, then a state enterprise) occurred as far back as 1964 in a predecessor organization of one of the enterprises in the sample. The occasional dismissals in the 1980s may have had counterparts in earlier decades, and they may represent no real change within Chinese state industry.

More significant as a movement toward a labor market than what has been discussed above is what has been reported to be a new national policy, one that is certainly being implemented in a number of the sample enterprises. This is the policy of engaging most additional workers through limited-term but multiyear contracts rather than as permanent workers. The clear purpose is to make it possible for the enterprise to dismiss workers for individual fault, as well as to cut back staff in reaction to changes in conditions in the enterprise's markets. It is much too early, however, to tell whether the new system will in fact reduce the inflexibility inherent in permanent employment.[19]

The problem facing Chinese industry is that, given the limitations in employment opportunities within state industry and the superiority of such jobs to those in urban collectively owned enterprises, the only way to create an active labor market is by permitting dismissals on an extended scale.

Soviet industry, in contrast, enjoys an active labor market along with a dismissal policy that has been almost as rigid as the Chinese practice currently appears to be. The difference between the two countries is in the proportion of the labor force that quits annually, and it seems unlikely that this difference will change drastically over the medium run.

Plans for Regulating Current Operations

A third major difference that seems to exist between state-owned enterprises in China and those in the CMEA countries is the significance of plans for regulating the current operations of enterprises. (Investment plans are not discussed in this chapter.) Among the European nations in the CMEA, Hungary is a case apart since no plans are given to the enterprises. The other countries, although differing considerably among themselves,[20] appear to give much more operational significance to the plan as a means of directing enterprises' activities to particular goals than is the case for the Chinese enterprises in our sample.

Soviet enterprises receive annual production plans, along with physical allocations of material inputs and wage funds linked to these plans, that are intended narrowly to circumscribe the domain of choice left to enterprise management. Labor productivity and profit plans further circumscribe this domain. It is true that the various plans that an enterprise receives are frequently inconsistent, even though they are all issued by the same superior organization. But that organization is administratively responsible for all of the enterprise's activities, for the appointment and dismissal of its director, and for the settlement of differences as to the entitlement of the enterprise to various types of financial award related to plan fulfillment. Thus, at a minimum, there is an organizational unity that does not exist for most of the Chinese enterprises in the sample.

Four questions may be usefully posed as to the operational significance of annual plans: (1) To what degree is plan fulfillment important to the enterprise? (2) To what degree are the plans in fact determined by the enterprise whose activities are being planned, with approval from the "planning" body required only as a matter of form? (3) To what degree does actual performance of the enterprise match its plan? (4) To what degree is the plan adjusted during the course of the year, with the adjustments reflecting performance during the part of the year prior to revision?

Soviet Enterprise Plans

For Soviet enterprises, the fulfillment of plans is very important, because the incentives fund and, to a lesser degree, the wage fund depend heavily on plan fulfillment.[21] The answer to the second question is equally clear: the superior organization plays a decisive, not formalistic, role in setting the enterprise plan.

The third question, as to the matching of performance and plan, is more difficult to answer. Annual data for all industrial enterprises in either the Russian Republic or the entire U.S.S.R. show the following percentages of enterprises that failed to meet their plans as these existed at the end of the year: sales, 6 to 7 percent (1976–77); labor productivity, 16 percent (1976); profits, 18 to 22 percent (1966–70 average and 1975–76); costs, 21 percent (1961–65 average). (See, respectively, Kosygin 1976, p. 9; Triain 1978, p. 97; Dadashev 1979, p. 45; and Duginov 1979, p. 97.) Aside from sales, these figures are substantial. Although we do not have data on the proportion of enterprises overfulfilling their plans by different amounts, it would appear that an overfulfillment by more than 5 percent—and certainly by more than 10 percent—would be highly exceptional. In Romania and in the German Democratic Republic, plan underfulfillment by industrial enterprises appears to be much rarer than in the U.S.S.R., and the proportion of enterprises achieving substantial overfulfillment seems no larger (Granick 1976, chaps. 4 and 6).

The fourth question, as to the degree of plan adjustment, is still more difficult to treat. During 1976 "plans" (which plan is not specified) of one-fourth of all Soviet industrial enterprises and associations were reduced, half of them during the last month of the year (Brezhnev 1979, p. 454). Annual data for 1977–79 covering the U.S.S.R. as a whole show that the number of enterprises failing to fulfill their plan for the first eleven months of the year was 221 percent to 236 percent of the number that did not fulfill their annual plan. The Soviet author who presented these figures explains the discrepancy primarily by changes in the annual plan made during December.[22] Furthermore, sample data suggest that plan changes downward for some enterprises are, at the industry level, compensated by plan changes upward for others (Shaikin 1974, pp. 98–109).

The above figures suggest that revisions are on a scale that makes the fulfillment of the final plan a meaningless indicator of success. Presumably, revision primarily reflects performance during the part of the year prior to revision, which is indeed the conclusion of Shaikin (1974, pp. 98–109), the only economist to investigate the matter with sample studies. But there are three arguments against this conclusion of meaninglessness.

The first counterargument is that it is unclear where the 1976 data came from; Shaikin—although writing three years earlier—said that ministries keep no figures on the degree of plan fulfillment according to the original plan (1974, pp. 98–109). The second is that the 1976 data may mean that one-fourth of all enterprises had one or more of their many plan indicators reduced during the year. If this is the meaning, the relevant proportion for any single indicator could well be under 10 percent. The third and most

Table 5-1. *Fulfillment for the Year as a Proportion of the Final Annual Plan*
(percentage of observations)

Measure of plan and performance	*Number of annual observations*[a]	*Percentage of plan fulfillment*[b] <98	98–100	100–110	110–120	120–130	>130	Total
Profit								
Reform years[c]	54	4	4	22	17	13	41	101
Earlier years	34	18	0	21	38	6	18	101
Output[d]								
Reform years[c]	72	0	6	44	31	8	11	100
Earlier years	75	12	3	56	21	4	4	100

a. During the pre-reform years there are three cases in which profits were made when losses were planned, or vice versa. These observations were excluded from the table.

b. A percentage of plan fulfillment that is exactly on the borderline between two categories is placed in the higher one.

c. 1979 and later.

d. For output, 23 observations (in 11 years of enterprise records) during the reform years, and 31 observations (in 17 years of enterprise records) during the earlier period, were for physical output of major products. The remainder of the output observations were for total output measured in constant prices. The physical output observations all fell into the 100 percent to 120 percent range of plan fulfillment; thus their inclusion biases the table's results for the fulfillment of the output plan away from the extremes, if one believes that the proper measure should be the number of enterprise years for which data are available.

important argument is embodied in two questions. Why, if plan fulfillment is so meaningless, do Soviet authorities persist in attaching bonuses for all white-collar personnel primarily to these success indicators? And why do Soviet managers and economists endlessly bemoan the perverse incentive effects of plan indicators that are poorly constructed? A sufficient degree of revision linked to past results would eliminate all effects, whether perverse or not.

Chinese Enterprise Plans

According to data from the sample enterprises, there is no reason to believe that the answers to questions on the authority for initiating the plan and the degree of its revision—the second and fourth questions posed above—differ much between Soviet and Chinese state industrial enterprises. Discussion is thus limited to the importance and level of achievement of the plan—the first and third questions.

With regard to the question on the degree of plan fulfillment, table 5-1 shows data for the sample, and table 5-2 reduces the data to enterprise years. The tables show two things of interest. The first relates to the number of cases in which enterprises failed to fulfill their plans: this number is reasonably

Table 5-2. *Output Data Reduced to Enterprise Years*
(percentage of observations)

Measure of output	*Number of observations*	*Percentage of plan fulfillment*[a]					
		<98	*98–100*	*100–120*	*120–130*	*>130*	*Total*
Reform years[b]	60	0	7	70	10	13	100
Earlier years	61	15	3	72	5	5	100

a. A percentage of plan fulfillment that is exactly on the borderline between two categories is placed in the higher one.
b. 1979 and later.

substantial (18 percent of the cases) through 1978, but only 7 to 8 percent (depending on the measure used) during the reform years. In this respect, the Chinese sample seems to depart from the Soviet standard of comparison only from 1979 onward. Far more striking is the proportion of cases in which enterprises grossly overfulfilled their plans (by 20 percent or more). This proportion was 10 to 24 percent in the earlier period and 19 to 54 percent thereafter. The Chinese sample here departs greatly in both periods from the Soviet standard, but it does so far more sharply during the reform years.

The high degree of overfulfillment suggests that Chinese enterprises are not seriously influenced in their behavior by fear of the "ratchet effect" of plan increases in the coming year as a result of performance increases in the current year. This lack of influence is all the more striking because, whereas failure to meet plans has in itself some negative effect on the ability of enterprises to pay bonuses, there is no reward with regard to the degree of plan overfulfillment for any indicator except profit.[23] One would suspect that the ratchet principle has so little effect on enterprise behavior in China, in comparison with the strong effect it is widely believed to exercise in the U.S.S.R., because Chinese enterprises are normally confident that they will in the future be able to reach any likely plan target. This confidence stems from the considerable slack apparently built into the plan in most years. Furthermore, in comparison with Soviet enterprises, the Chinese enterprises seem to have more of a basis for confidence that, if they are threatened with plan underfulfillment and are unable to persuade higher authorities to reduce their plans, the authorities will take informal action to eliminate the legislated effects of failure. In this last respect, Chinese enterprises seem to be rather similar to Romanian enterprises of about 1970.

A much more important conclusion from the tables is that a high proportion of state enterprises must have found that plans did not work either as binding constraints on their behavior or as motivating parameters, particularly since 1979. Their problem was not one of meeting the plan; that was relatively assured. Neither was there any advantage to exceeding the plan (except that of profits) by 20 percent as opposed to 1 percent. It is in this sense that plans may be considered irrelevant to many Chinese enterprises.

A striking illustration of this irrelevance is the treatment of the output plan of one of the sample enterprises. In the early part of a recent year, the enterprise was aiming to produce only 60 percent of its annual plan for one major family of products but 133 percent for a second and much larger family. Both the plan given to the enterprise by its superior body and the enterprise's own objectives were founded on forecasts of market demand. Even though allocations of materials were based on the plan and despite the fact that material requirements differed considerably between these two product families, the enterprise felt no compunction about such projected deviations from the plan. Furthermore, and perhaps most striking, representatives of the superior body seemed to feel that the enterprise's behavior was reasonable provided that the enterprise's prediction of market demand turned out to be correct.

Of course, irrelevancy in the sense indicated above does not indicate that the plans have no effect. Allocations of materials are related to output production plans. At a minimum this holds down unit production costs for the planned volumes. On the other hand, above-plan production—when market conditions permit—generally can be sold at higher prices than planned production. The relative weight of these factors in particular instances may have a major effect on the volume and even on the sign of retained profits obtained by an enterprise from marginal output as its total production moves above plan.

In contrast to the effects on obtainability and especially on prices of materials, there is no indication from the interviews in the sample enterprises that labor force allotments are closely linked to the size of production plans. In this latter respect, Chinese enterprises are in a radically different position from that of their Soviet counterparts.

The relationship between planned output expansion and net labor recruitment is lacking in China because recruitment of state employees is conducted overwhelmingly from youths who are new or recent entrants into the labor market. The expectation appears to be that their first few years on the job (and especially their first year, which is the one for which the enterprise receives a production plan) will be spent primarily in an apprenticeship or other training role, and that their contribution to the expansion of production will be minor.

Recruitment quotas for enterprises seem to rest on two distinct bases. The first is a combination of national, provincial, and municipal policies as to the appropriate creation of new jobs in the urban state sector during the current year. Such policies reflect the consideration of employment creation and counterconsiderations of inflation restraint and labor-productivity improvement. They also reflect strategy for the appropriate mix of state-employed and collectively employed urban workers and the mix of urban and rural industrial expansion. The second basis is the expectation of growth in the enterprise's production over many years—enough so that this year's recruits can become effective. Neither basis is closely linked to the enterprise's planned output expansion, which is limited to a one-year period.

State-owned industrial enterprises also recruit labor for collectively owned subsidiary enterprises. Governmental bodies control such recruitment much less than they do the recruitment of lifetime state employees. The extent of this collective recruitment seems to be heavily influenced by the financial position of the enterprise, since most of the work of recruited employees is in auxiliary operations (factory canteens, for example) rather than in production. Because some recruits are believed capable of making an immediate contribution to production, it will also reflect the expected short-term expansion in output and thus, perhaps, of labor needs. But even this last component of recruitment, which today still appears to be minor, is not a reflection of enterprise plans as such.

An aspect of the lack of expectation by Chinese supervisory authorities of a close relationship between an enterprise's output and its labor force is the treatment of the wage fund. As in the Soviet enterprise, the wage fund is a monetary quota given to each enterprise by the agency to which it is subordinate. This fund is used as a limitation on cash that can be paid out by the bank to the enterprise to cover basic earnings. In the U.S.S.R., however, the planned figure for the year reflects the planned output and planned labor productivity. The actual sum made available depends upon actual output relative to planned output. The Soviet enterprise can recruit and make incentive payments to its manual workers within the constraint of its wage fund.

In contrast, the Chinese enterprise's wage fund reflects its actual number of state employees and their skill grades approved for the year. As actual output moves above or below planned output, the Chinese enterprise's wage fund is unaffected (or almost so).

This national difference between the effect of the output plan on the planned size of the labor force and of the wage fund may be a reflection of two factors at work. One is the lower probability in China than in the U.S.S.R. that enterprise activity will be close to plan. But the second factor is by itself a condition sufficient to explain the observed difference. It consists of several intertwined facts: the amount of Chinese labor recruitment is heavily influenced by decisions about job creation made to alleviate what would otherwise be local unemployment; labor mobility is low because of the shortage of jobs; and recruitment is heavily concentrated on juveniles expected to make little contribution to production in their first year. In sharp contrast, Soviet enterprise labor recruitment is essentially uninfluenced by considerations of job creation, and most hiring is of people who are already in the labor force, have skills, and come from other enterprises that they have voluntarily quit. Thus most new recruits to an individual Soviet enterprise's labor force are able and expected to make immediate production contributions.

It is noteworthy that none of the sample Chinese enterprises received formal multiyear output plans, although some did receive multiyear financial plans in the form of a statement of the amount of tax or profits they must provide each year to higher authorities. In contrast, efforts have been made since 1970 (although with limited success) to give all Soviet industrial enterprises output plans covering a five-year period, with the plan broken down into annual divisions. This Soviet attempt explicitly reflects concern with what is viewed as the holding back of above-plan output by enterprises in the current year because of their managements' expectations about the effect that such expanded output would have on the enterprise plan for the coming period.

The absence of such efforts at multiyear planning for Chinese enterprises may reflect nothing more than the primitive state of planning in China versus the U.S.S.R., or the greater Chinese realism about what planners in any country may be expected to accomplish. But it may well also reflect that Chinese enterprises do not fear the ratchet effect in plan making and, thus, do not restrain themselves from massive overfulfillment. Why? Because plans are neither binding constraints nor binding incentive parameters for most Chinese industrial enterprises, whereas they are for Soviet enterprises. This hypothesis is consistent with the fact that in the case both of profit payments to higher authorities and of tax levies, efforts have been made in China (often unsuccessfully, as in the U.S.S.R.) to have decisions made for multiyear periods. Such financial decisions seem to be of real importance to Chinese enterprises, and thus there could be enterprise reactions to an expected ratchet effect in this area if decisions are taken annually by supervisory bodies.

The Role of Regional Authorities

The economic role of provincial and subordinate regional authorities appears to differ significantly between the U.S.S.R. and post-1978 China. Regional authorities in China exercise much more authority over the amount of their social expenditures, and they have to raise a larger share of the funds to finance them. Furthermore, regional authorities in China supervise a much higher proportion of industrial enterprises and of industrial production. The need for these regional authorities to find their own financing affects the incentive system they use to direct Chinese industrial enterprises.

Centralization in the U.S.S.R.

The state budget in the U.S.S.R. apparently is much more unified than that in China. Soviet republics and lower regional bodies do have certain funds allocated to them (the most important are the profits of enterprises under the control of these authorities), the volume of which depends upon the sectoral composition and quality of management of their industry. But the U.S.S.R. essentially appears to have centralized the decision as to the sum of social expenditures in each region. When greater funds are raised from enterprise profits, they are presumably heavily counterbalanced by decreases in the resources directed from the national budget. Generally they are not accompanied by increased social expenditures (see Davies 1958, pp. 297–98 and 302–4; see also Gallik and others 1968, p. 55, and Garvey 1977, pp. 85–86). This financial centralization is not surprising, given that allocation of materials and capital goods is carried out primarily on the national level. It would be of only limited value to individual Soviet regions to have increased monetary income if it were unaccompanied by allocations.

It is true that enterprises under regional rather than under national subordination produce a large part of gross industrial production in the U.S.S.R.: 46 percent in 1981 (TsSU SSSR 1982, p. 151). But the situation in the coal industry seems to typify the limited significance of such regional administration. There exists both a national coal ministry and a special republic-level ministry in the Ukrainian Republic. The Ukrainian ministry seems, however, to have no more authority than does the industrial association for the Kuzbass region, which is directly under the national ministry rather than under the jurisdiction of its own republic. For example, the Ukrainian ministry has the right to set additional tasks for output and profits for units under its administration—but they can add up to no more than 1 percent of the plan that the national ministry approved for the Ukrainian ministry. It would appear that only for financing construction is the Ukraine in a different position. Financing is done from the budget of the Ukrainian Republic, and thus there is need for coordination between the national coal ministry and the Council of Ministers of the Ukraine in presenting development plans for the Ukrainian coal industry. But even these proposals go for decision to the national-level State Planning Commission of the U.S.S.R. (Tsimerman 1984, pp. 5–6, 36, 53–54, 61–62, 146–47).

Localism in China

Unlike the situation in the U.S.S.R., both the social expenditures and investments of Chinese provinces and municipalities depend considerably on sales tax and profit revenues received from industrial enterprises under local subordination.[24] Furthermore, as already seen, national allocation of materials and capital goods constrains what the regional authorities can do with their revenues less in China than in the U.S.S.R. Thus, Chinese provinces and municipalities have both more incentive and more opportunity than their Soviet counterparts to administer the enterprises under their control in the interest of increasing local budgetary revenue and the number of local jobs in state industry.

The current result of such localism may well be to reinforce the role of the market in regulating Chinese industry. (Although localism must have been at least as important during the previous two decades, it then presumably took other forms.) Chinese provinces and municipalities do take actions that tend to hold down the profits of the enterprises they regulate: for example, by attempting to insist that supply come from local sources to generate more local employment and increase the profits (or reduce the losses) of other enterprises under the same regional authority. And Chinese managers are concerned with the purely physical production of items that they themselves are then allowed to allocate within their own area. But on the whole, their interest appears to be primarily financial and is on an enterprise-by-enterprise basis. The greatest concern of supervising regional authorities seems to be the profit earned by the enterprise rather than the provision of physical output or output mix in accord with plans. Regional authorities seem normally to accept departures from production plans if such departures can increase the enterprise's profits.

Two phenomena may constitute reactions by the national authorities to this practice. The first is a system in which different authorities give output plans that cover the same period to a single enterprise, a system that applies among others to some enterprises that produce centrally allocated goods. They may receive from the center an annual output plan that requires only part of the enterprise's capacity, and for which the center itself provides most or all of the centrally allocated materials and fuel that are required. The enterprise must sell output planned in this fashion in accord with the center's allocation system. Production above this amount is also planned—but by the regional authority to which the enterprise is subordinate. The center takes no responsibility for the centrally allocated materials and fuel needed for such auxiliary output.

The second phenomenon (more likely to be an artifact of the sample) is a move during the 1980s to transfer enterprises from dual control by both the center and the regional authorities to control solely by the center. Of seven sample enterprises in which the center currently does at least some direct planning and administration, three are under mixed control of the center and province. One was under sole central control before 1979 and continued to be so. But three of the seven had been transferred during the first half of the 1980s from mixed control to sole control by the center. In no sample cases was the change in the other direction.

Here we may well be observing efforts by the central authorities to protect more of the economy from domination by market incentives during a period when the price system is believed to be so ridden with anomalies that it cannot play a proper allocative role.

Performance and Incentives

In the U.S.S.R., the top management of enterprises has had little choice but to direct efforts of their work force primarily to performing well in accord with whatever plan-fulfillment criteria are set for them. The management's income is volatile and highly dependent on bonuses rewarded for such performance, as is the income of the entire labor force. Given an active labor market, an enterprise that performs badly will soon find its better manual workers and white-collar employees resigning.

The results of such direction of effort and resources have been twofold. Management and workers have been stimulated to harder work by the carrot and stick of fluctuating earnings. But neither group is strongly motivated to achieve production that is important to the economy but that is poorly reflected in the plans that determine wage funds and retained profits. This second consideration is one with which Soviet administrators have been unsuccessfully wrestling with for at least as long as the lifetime of the People's Republic of China.

In China, before the recent reform years, the performance of the enterprise affected the income of neither top managers nor the labor force. Although this lack of influence on income killed motivation (something much bemoaned in the sample enterprises), it also meant that the enterprises were less likely than were Soviet enterprises to channel their production effort in directions clearly harmful to the regional and national economy.

It seems likely, although this historical perspective does not show up in the interviews in the sample enterprises, that the beginning of the destruction of the "iron pot" for Chinese state industry as a whole is making Chinese management decisions more responsive to the success criteria set for state enterprises. Chinese managers are not forced to such responsiveness by the requirements of an active labor market; rather, the demands of their workers and employees for higher incomes place pressure upon them that is difficult to resist. Therefore the malfunctions of such success criteria—and increasingly in Chinese state industry this means the inappropriateness of relative prices rather than of plan indicators—may be expected to have ever more deleterious effects on the economy. Suppliers of allocated goods will probably go even further in determining their product mix according to the relative profitability of different items at state-determined base prices rather than according to the needs of the using enterprises. Such distortions, which for good reason are typical of Soviet industry, may for the identical reason become more widespread within the planned and allocated quotas used in Chinese state industry.

Data from sample enterprises are not conclusive in showing that worker income or even managerial income has been strongly dependent during the reform period on enterprise performance as measured along any dimension. Yet it seems reasonable to conclude from the interviews that the process is at least beginning. This development provides good opportunity for improvement in enterprise performance, although one that will probably continue to be restricted by the absence of a genuine labor market within the state sector of industry. This process underlines the appropriateness of the October 1984 assertion of the Central Committee of the Chinese Communist party that "reform of the price system is the key." Without such reform, increased incentive could backfire.

Notes

1. In this comparison of China and the European countries of the Council for Mutual Economic Assistance (CMEA), the U.S.S.R. is given the main attention. This is partly because the U.S.S.R. and China, as very large nations, face similar pressures to decentralize planning and the supervision of enterprise operations, as well as to formalize procedures, that are of a different magnitude from those felt by the smaller CMEA countries. Informal central direction of enterprises in Hungary, for example, has attained a dimension utterly impossible in either China or the U.S.S.R. A second reason for concentrating on the U.S.S.R. as a standard of comparison is that the economic system of Hungary, the other most interesting standard to use, differs too radically from that of China. The Hungarian system includes neither production plans for enterprises nor the allocation of materials.

Comparative data for the CMEA countries are from their national literature and from interviews conducted during 1970–71 in Hungary, Romania, and the German Democratic Republic (GDR) in enterprises and at higher administrative levels (for interviews, see Granick 1976).

2. It is true that in the German Democratic Republic in 1970, one garment enterprise was able to obtain 20 percent of its inputs of cloth outside the materials allocation system (Granick 1976, pp. 184–85). But it was probably a great exception, and such purchases would be much less likely after 1972.

3. Soviet annual production plans and allocations are in aggregates that number 16,000 or 67,000, depending on the period and source. (Berliner [1976, p. 64] gives the figure of 16,000 for 1968; Iun' [1983] suggests a figure climbing to 67,000.) The number of individual industrial items produced is said, depending on the source, to range from 12 million to 25 million (Subotskii 1981, p. 18, and Ukrainskii 1984, p. 39).

4. Both of these reasons, and the accompanying result, seem to apply much less to the German Democratic Republic than to the U.S.S.R. (see Granick 1976, chaps. 6 and 7).

5. In China, only a very small number of aggregates are centrally allocated: 24 in the early 1970s and some 200-odd in 1984. In contrast, some 2,000 aggregates have been balanced and aggregated in the U.S.S.R. at the comparable level of the Council of Ministers and the State Planning Commission. (Soviet data are for 1966, 1977, and the early 1980s as given in Berliner 1976, p. 64, Drotsenko and Soloveichik 1977, p. 39, and Iun' 1983, p. 26.)

6. Personnel in a plant in the center of China had no complaints about the materials received. Yet the manager charged with cost reduction estimated the enterprise's use of materials as 30 percent higher per unit of output than in counterpart enterprises in Shanghai, even though the rejection rate of subassemblies and final products was believed to be little higher. Presumably, the product-mix difference in the materials explains the variation between the plants' performances.

7. One may well ask how the argument offered here for equilibrium in producer-goods markets can be reconciled with William Byrd's discussion of buyers' and sellers' markets (chapter 10 in this volume). The answer would appear to be that Byrd's discussion—at least of sellers' markets—refers solely to that portion of the market composed of those quantities of a given product that are subject both to obligatory plan for producers of the product and to allocation for the users of the product. In contrast, the discussion in this chapter refers to marginal production in the market as a whole. When sellers' markets exist for planned output, prices for marginal output are higher than for planned output.

8. See the decision on reform of the economic structure, made by the Central Committee of the Chinese Communist party on October 20, 1984. In this statement, it was argued that competition among Chinese enterprises should go so far that only the best enterprises would survive.

9. Data supporting this statement are from Granick (forthcoming) and relate entirely to the U.S.S.R. during the last two decades. Because the reality of market determination of relative labor earnings is quite different from formal determination in countries other than Hungary, it is difficult to be certain as to the reality in the other CMEA nations without specific investigation of the situations in these lands. In particular, the relatively low rate of labor turnover in the GDR that is indicated by sample studies (see especially Belwe 1982), and the extent of the financial penalties for such turnover imposed in 1983 in Romania (see *Le Monde*, September 7, 1983, p. 6), suggest that the importance of the labor market may be less in these countries than in the U.S.S.R. See, however, Granick 1976, p. 187, and Adam 1982 for materials suggesting that the Soviet situation may be generalizable to other CMEA countries. The reader should be aware that various other scholars (for example, Kirsch 1972 and Janet Chapman in Kahan and Ruble 1979) have given much more weight than I do to the formal determination of wages in the U.S.S.R., and they thus present a different picture of market forces operating in that factor market.

10. Kartashova 1984, p. 84. These quit figures do not include departures for military service, full-time studies, or retirement.

11. Geliuta and Staroverov 1977, pp. 74–75. The authors base this percentage figure on materials of the Central Statistical Office of the U.S.S.R.

12. See Vasil'ev and Chistiakova 1972, p. 124, Artemov 1975, p. 40, and Nazarov 1975, pp. 271–72. The percentage from retained profits rises sharply in the period immediately after the setting of new wage rates for reasons explained below.

13. These last statements, as the reader will appreciate, treat the central authority's demand pattern for goods and services, as well as both aggregate investments and their distribution, as part of "other things being equal."

14. There is indeed a political effort in America to increase female wages sharply in relation to male wages by introducing a type of job evaluation that is completely

divorced from the marketplace. But to my knowledge, little so far has come of it in practice outside of employment by the various states.

15. One enterprise, however, reported that its manual workers received, as a matter of principle, regular increases in grade during 1958–62. In a few other years, the central government allowed a small percentage of the workers and employees in each enterprise to move up one grade.

16. Subsidies were given in a number of our sample enterprises in the 1980s. For only one, however, do we know of their existence in the earlier period (1962–64 for section chiefs).

17. In 1979, judging at least from one enterprise, promotions were substantial (40 percent of the labor force) but not universal. In 1983, on the other hand, promotions by one level seem to have been virtually universal—at least for employees with five years seniority, as seen in one sample enterprise. Thus, the 1983 "promotions" should better be viewed as constituting a national wage increase for all except those at the top grade. One sample enterprise also indicated substantial promotions (30 percent) in both 1981 and 1982.

18. This enterprise was described as the best performer in its industry in the country, and it received production targets from the center rather than from its province or municipality. Thus it was exceptional.

19. To see why it might have no effect, it is worth recounting an experience with what was described as a previous national policy. In 1982 it was determined that all collectively employed workers active in a state industrial enterprise should be isolated into one or more separate accounting units. The purpose was to ensure that their incomes would vary with the results of their unit. In one of the sample enterprises, however, in 1983 subsidies from the state enterprise were being provided to such newly formed collective units. The enterprise management intended that these subsidies should be paid in such a way that the earnings of the collectively employed workers would not be affected by the administrative change.

20. See Granick 1976 for an examination of such plans in the German Democratic Republic and in Romania in the early 1970s and for a comparison of them with enterprise plans in the U.S.S.R.

21. A study covering thirty-six enterprises of the electrical cable industry during 1971–75 was conducted by the Soviet Labor Research Institute. The seven most effective enterprises were distinguished from the seven least effective, and it was the second category that had a higher ratio of incentives fund to wage fund. The reason for this perverse result was that the more effective enterprises were given more difficult plans, which they fulfilled to a lesser degree (Markov 1980, p. 172). On the other hand, interview data for Romania suggested that plan fulfillment was unimportant for the industrial enterprise in the early 1970s, the degree of fulfillment being viewed primarily as a reflection of the ability of ministerial planners to make good predictions of performance (Granick 1976, chap. 4).

22. See Krylov 1980, p. 22. It is unclear whether these data refer only to industry or to a larger segment of the economy, and there is no indication which plans are involved.

23. In many profit-retention schemes, as well as in the current national tax scheme, the enterprise can retain a higher proportion of those profits that are above

plan (or above a proxy for the profit plan). In the U.S.S.R., the degree of plan overfulfillment very much affects profit retention and the creation of the incentives fund. The same is true in the German Democratic Republic, though not for some years before 1972 (Granick 1976, chap. 6 and p. 219). There have been mixed statements from two of the sample enterprises as to the theoretical effect upon bonuses of failing to meet plans. It seems unlikely, however, that the actual effect is great in Chinese enterprises.

24. The situation is heterogeneous, however. The municipality in which one sample enterprise is located relies on the province for budgetary allocations, thus operating under the Soviet-type system. It is possible that the same is also the case for the municipalities of some other sample enterprises.

References

Adam, Jan, ed. 1982. *Employment Policies in the Soviet Union and Eastern Europe.* London: Macmillan.

Artemov, Iu. 1975. *Voprosy Ekonomiki* 8.

Bauer, Tamas. 1983. *Journal of Comparative Economics* 7 (Sept.): 3.

Belwe, Katharina. 1982. *Die Fluktuation Werktätiger als Ausdruck sozialer Konflikte in der DDR.* Bonn: Gesamtdeutsches Institut Bundesanstalt fur gesamtdeutsche Aufgaben.

Berliner, Joseph S. 1976. *The Innovation Decision in Soviet Industry.* Cambridge, Mass.: MIT Press.

Brezhnev, L. I. 1979. *Ob osnovnykh voprosakh ekonomicheskoi politiki KPPS na sovremennom etape.* 2d ed. Vol. 2. Moscow: Politizdat.

Dadashev, A. 1979. *Voprosy Ekonomiki* 8.

Davies, R. W. 1958. *The Development of the Soviet Budgetary System.* Cambridge: Cambridge University Press.

Drotsenko, O. D., and D. I. Soloveichik. 1977. *Ekonomika i organizatsiia promyshlennogo proizvodstva* (hereafter cited as EKO) 2.

Duginov, A. 1979. *Planovoe Khoziaistvo,* 8.

Fil'ev, V. 1983. *Voprosy Ekonomiki* 2.

Gallik, David, C. Jesina, and S. Rapawy. 1968. *The Soviet Financial System: Structure, Operation and Statistics.* U.S. Bureau of the Census, Washington, D.C.: Government Printing Office.

Garvey, George. 1977. *Money, Financial Flows, and Credit in the Soviet Union.* Cambridge, Mass.: Ballinger.

Geliuta, A. M., and V. I. Staroverov. 1977. *Sotsial'nyi oblik rabochego-intelligenta.* Moscow: Mysl'.

Granick, David. 1976. *Enterprise Guidance in Eastern Europe.* Princeton, N.J.: Princeton University Press.

———. Forthcoming. *Job Rights in the Soviet Union: Their Consequences.* Cambridge: Cambridge University Press.

Iun', O. M. 1983. *EKO* 8.

Kahan, Arcaduis, and Blair A. Ruble. 1979. *Industrial Labor in the USSR*. New York: Pergamon Press.

Kartashova, L. 1984. *Planovoe Khoziaistvo* 9.

Kheifets, L. 1982. *Voprosy Ekonomiki* 6.

Kirsch, Leonard J. 1972. *Soviet Wages: Changes in Structure and Administration since 1956*. Cambridge, Mass.: MIT Press.

Kornai, Janos. 1983. *Journal of Comparative Economics* 7 (Sept.): 3.

Kosygin, A. N. 1976. *Current Digest of the Soviet Press*, April 7.

Kotliar, A. 1984. *Ekonomicheskie Nauki* 3.

Krylov, P. 1980. *Planovoe Khoziaistvo* 6.

McAuley, Alastair. 1979. *Economic Welfare in the Soviet Union*. Madison, Wis.: University of Wisconsin Press.

Manevich, E. 1973. *Voprosy Ekonomiki* 12.

Markov, V. I. 1980. *Oplata truda v sisteme upravleniia ekonomikoi razvitogo sotsializma*. Moscow: Ekonomika.

Nazarov, M. G. 1975. *Mnogofaktornyi analiz proizvoditel'nosti truda v tekstil'noi promyshlennosti*. Moscow: Legkaia industriia.

Shaikin, V. P. 1974. *Ekonomika i Matematicheskie Metody* 1.

Shkurko, S. 1983. *Planovoe Khoziaistvo* 6.

Subotskii, Iu. V. 1981. *EKO* 11.

Triain, A. 1978. *Planovoe Khoziaistvo* 3.

Tsimerman, Iu. S. 1984. *Deiatel'nost' khoziaistvennykh organov ugol'noi promyshlennosti*. Moscow: Nedra.

TsSU SSSR. 1982. *Narodnoe khoziaistvo SSSR 1922–1982*. Moscow: Finansy i statistika.

Ukrainskii, D. 1984. *Planovoe Khoziaistvo* 2.

Vasil'ev, E. K., and L. M. Chistiakova. 1972. *Effektivnost' oplaty upravlencheskogo truda v promyshlennosti*. Moscow: Ekonomika.

Zaitsev, A. P. 1982. *EKO* 9.

6

The Reform of China's Industrial System

Gao Shangquan

IMPLEMENTING A PLANNED ECONOMY in a socialist society based on public ownership of the means of production requires a corresponding planning system. The scope of the planning system is broad: it includes production, construction, circulation, distribution, and other areas. There is some truth to the saying that the planning system is the core of the economic system. Reform of the planning system thus influences the reform of the overall economic system.

Reform of the Planning System

During the first five-year plan, a centralized and unified planning system was formed, modeled basically after that of the U.S.S.R. This system has persisted more or less intact until the present. First, the state assigns mandatory plan targets for important economic activities and relies on administrative measures to ensure the implementation of plans. Second, administrative departments at all levels hold the power to make planning policies. Moreover, targets are assigned to departments and localities, and management is exercised at each level. Enterprises lack the necessary power to make planning policies. Third, planning gives priority to product targets. The fulfillment of quotas for goods has become the main standard for evaluating successful results of work in departments, regions, and enterprises.

Success has been tremendous in implementing the planned economic system; in amassing large quantities of financial, material, and human resources; and in carrying out large-scale socialist construction. In a short period of time China has established an independent and fairly comprehensive industrial system and a national economic system. The people's material and cultural lives have improved substantially, and the profound changes in

China over the past thirty-six years have already begun to reveal the superiority of the socialist system. Nevertheless, this superiority has not yet developed as it should. One reason that it has not is that a rigidity in the economic system does not meet the requirements of social productive forces.

The Need for Reform

The planning system has four main flaws. First, centralization is excessive, management is excessive, and the scope and proportion of command plans are too great. Enterprises need more autonomy. Second, commodity production, the law of value, and the role of the market are overlooked. We have emphasized "putting planning first, the law of value second," and we have separated the planned economy from the law of value and even set them in opposition to each other. This one-sided emphasis on command plans makes enterprises unwilling to take the initiative in learning about the market. Thus, because scarce products are not increased, supplies chronically fail to meet demand, and because surplus products are not decreased, production needs are seriously out of line. This situation leads to massive overstocking and waste. Third, economic leverage has not been fully applied. Since command plans rely excessively on management, the state is responsible for issuing enterprise production tasks, distributing products, allocating equipment, supplying materials, assigning personnel, collecting profits, and assuming losses. With enterprises lacking both vitality and incentive, it is difficult for economic levers to play a role. Fourth, a strict system of responsibility in planning has not been established. Input does not link up with output, and the phenomenon of eating out of "one big pot" is widespread, since capital funds are supplied free and goods are supplied at par. This situation has prompted people to scramble enthusiastically for investments, projects, and materials, giving rise to "investment starvation," long construction time for projects, and poor investment benefits. Production costs are high, expenditures are great, and profits are low. Furthermore, the commodity turnover cycle is slow and expenses are high.

Beginning in 1958 China's planning system went through several changes and reforms, but they were confined to enterprise status and affiliation. The reforms inappropriately advocated that quotas be raised at each level; there still was no comprehensively balanced, planned economic system. Thus enterprises lacked vitality, economic levers did not function, and the macroeconomy repeatedly became imbalanced.

Since the Third Plenary Session of the Eleventh Party Congress in December 1978, the rural and the urban economic systems have been reformed. The regulative role of the market is beginning to develop, and attention is being given to the application of economic levers. But the steps in the reform of the planning system are small, and the defects of the original system still have not been ironed out. Many problems still exist, and we are far from being able to meet demands for revitalizing the domestic economy and opening up to the outside world.

Basic Principles and Direction of the Reforms

The basic key points of the socialist planning system must be upheld. The "Decision of the Central Committee of the Communist Party of China on the Reform of the Economic Structure," approved by the Third Plenary Session of the Twelfth Party Congress in 1984, summed up the positive and negative experiences in China's socialist construction.[1] In particular, the resolution addressed reforms in the economic system in urban and rural areas over the previous few years. It provided an outline of the basic points of the planning system:

> First, generally speaking the planned economy that we have implemented is a planned commodity economy, not a market economy that is completely regulated by the market. Second, in production and exchange, which are totally regulated by the market, the major labor tasks involve certain agricultural products, articles of daily use, and service and repair industries. These all play a supplementary yet essential role in the national economy. Third, implementing a planned economy is not equivalent to giving priority to mandatory plans. Mandatory plans and guidance plans are both essential to a planned economy. Fourth, guidance plans are primarily to be used as economic levers while command plans are compulsory, but they must also follow the law of value.

When we are carrying out reforms in the planning system, it is necessary to support these basic points, because they clearly demonstrate the direction of progress in the reform of the planning system.

The socialist planning system must consciously rely on and apply the law of value. The resolution of the Central Committee of the Chinese Communist party presents two significant breakthroughs in the reform of the planning system. First, it challenges the idea that a planned economy conflicts with the commodity economy. Second, it changes the idea that the implementation of a planned economy conflicts with the application of the law of value. The basic significance of these two major breakthroughs is that, in integrating theory and practice, it solves the problem of how to establish a socialist economic system that is Chinese and full of energy and vitality. At the same time, it indicates a clear and specific course for the reform of the planning system.

In the past there existed the incorrect view that if we implement a planned economy, we cannot have a commodity economy or apply the law of value.

Now it is recognized that a commodity economy is an unavoidable phase in the development of a socialist economy; it is a necessary condition for achieving the four modernizations. Only by fully developing a commodity economy is it possible truly to invigorate the economy, spur an increase in productivity in all enterprises, make management more flexible, and be sensitive to the complex and varied needs of society. These aims cannot be achieved by relying purely on administrative measures and mandatory plans. To understand a socialist planned economy clearly, it is necessary to apply consciously the law of value and to establish a commodity economy based on the system of public ownership.

A socialist planning system should be unified and flexible. China is a vast country, the population is large, communication is difficult, information is not up-to-date, economic and cultural development is uneven, and the commodity economy is not well developed. Given these conditions, it is necessary for our planning system to be both unified and flexible. On the one hand, since the national economy concerns itself with the whole, no department, region, or enterprise can do things its own way and concern itself only with the needs and interests of one part while obstructing the interests of the whole. On the other hand, it is also necessary to develop fully the initiative and creativity of each department, region, and enterprise. In particular, enterprises must not be excessively controlled; it is essential to give them ample flexibility. Along with the development of scientific technology and the economy, and the steady improvement in the people's standard of living, the needs of society have become increasingly complex, varied, and diversified.

Many situations arise from changes in the national economy that are difficult to predict. For example, pharmaceutical plants in some areas have for many years produced drugs for treating gastric disorders according to assigned plans. Suddenly, in the last two or three years, there has been a vast amount of overstocking. After investigation, it was discovered that for many years local residents ate sweet potatoes, which caused gastric disorders. But in the past few years, in keeping with rural reforms, wheat has become abundant. The dietary habits of residents have therefore changed, and gastric disorders have afflicted fewer people.

A planning system must thus have flexibility. It is pointless to include all socioeconomic activities in plans while overlooking the importance of economic forces and market regulation. Generally speaking, our economic plans should be broad in outline and flexible in detail. Once a comprehensive balance in planning is achieved and economic levers are in place—with the important aspects under control and the minor aspects being relaxed and freed—the national economy may then generally develop in a proportionate, harmonious manner.

The Key Steps in the Reform

Reduce the scope of mandatory plans and further transfer the jurisdiction of planning management to a lower level. Although we must implement mandatory planning for the major economic activities, we must implement guidance plans or market regulation, according to the differing circumstances, for other economic activities and for large numbers of products. An increase in enterprise vitality is the central link in the reform of the economic system, and it must also be included in the reform of the planning system. To improve enterprise vitality, particularly the vitality of large and medium-size enterprises owned by all the people, the jurisdiction of planning management must be transferred to lower levels, level by level. The Chinese government has already determined the first steps in the reform of the planning system: fully implement guidance plans in agricultural production; reduce the number of products in industrial production under mandatory plans from 123 to about 60 products; reduce materials uniformly allocated by the state from 256 to 65; greatly reduce the mandatory plan targets in commerce and foreign trade; relax the control of self-funded investments in fixed-asset investments; and transfer to lower levels the authority to examine and approve capital construction and technological transformation projects.

Reform the planning management system of the macroeconomy. The Central Committee must determine such macroeconomic issues as the rate of economic development, the rate of industrial and agricultural accumulation and expenditure, the issuance of currency, the scale and direction of fixed-asset investments, the development of major economic and technical policies, foreign economic relations, and the improvement of the people's standard of living. To consolidate the comprehensive balance of the national economy, we must change our focus from achieving a balance of commodity targets to achieving a balance of value targets and expand our focus from achieving a balance in planning, in budgeting, and in enterprises. We must emphasize the balance of total supply and demand in society. China is now replacing the old economic system with the new. The drawbacks of the old system have not yet been systematically established. Under such circumstances demand-induced inflation and macroeconomic imbalances may easily occur. Experience shows that the more we revive the economy, the more we must strengthen macroeconomic management so that invigoration does not lead to disruption, and management does not lead to suffocation.

Comprehensively apply economic regulative measures. Guidance plans primarily rely on the application of economic levers. Those who determine plan targets must study and suggest economic regulative measures for fulfilling them. We must consolidate the comprehensive study and application of economic levers on price, taxation, credit, wages, and the exchange rate and consider them significant and integral parts of planning. We have just adopted administrative, legal, economic, and other readjustment measures—especially economic regulative measures—to strengthen credit management, control the issuance of currency, improve control of the consumption reserve fund, avoid uncontrollable increases of such funds, improve management of capital construction, and control the scope of investment in fixed assets. To revive the economy and ensure the orderly and harmonious development of economic activities, we must improve economic legislation, supervision, and judicial work. It is essential to formulate various economic laws and management regulations; to improve auditing, taxation, industrial and commercial management, banking, and other departments at all levels; and to develop fully their role in economic supervision.

Annual and Long-Range Plans. Annual plans, based on the requirements of the five-year plan, should be primarily determined by economic contracts between enterprises. This mode of operation would enable planning departments to break away from the details of daily routine. We should link current work with the implementation of long-range social and economic development plans. And we must stress the prompt collection, collation, and dissemination of all kinds of economic information. We must also improve economic forecasting in order to increase the scientific nature of planning.

Reform of the Pricing System

The reform of the pricing system is the key to the success or failure of the reform of the economic system. There exists a fairly jumbled situation in the pricing system in China because we formerly neglected the role of the law of value. The prices of many commodities fail to reflect value and the relationship between supply and demand. Since the Third Plenary Session of the Eleventh Party Congress in 1978, we have implemented the following readjustments and initial reforms of commodity prices:

- We have substantially increased the purchasing price of primary agricultural products.

- We have properly increased the retail prices of meat, poultry, eggs, aquatic products, and eight kinds of primary nonstaple foods. At the same time, we have given subsidies to workers.

- We have increased the price of coal, pig iron, and other products while decreasing the prices of some electrical appliances.

- We have increased the prices of tobacco, alcohol, and leather goods while decreasing the prices of televisions, wristwatches, and so on.

- We have decreased the prices of synthetic textiles and raised, as appropriate, the prices of cotton textiles.

- We have adjusted costs for some rail and water transport.

- We have begun to reform the pricing system—that is, to change former unitary planned prices to state unified fixed prices, floating prices, negotiated purchasing and selling prices, market trading prices, and various other forms.

The price readjustments and initial reforms play a big role in promoting readjustment of the industrial and agricultural productive structure, in revising production and circulation, and in spurring the development of the national economy. Nevertheless, we must acknowledge that these readjustments and reforms are still in the early stages. We have not yet systematically reformed the pricing system; consequently, it is still seriously irrational.

First, the comparative prices of different commodities are irrational. In particular, the prices of certain mineral products and raw materials are low, which deters the development of basic industries, the promotion of technological advancement in processing industries, and the improvement of economic results. The low prices have also retarded the rationalization of investment, product, and consumption structures and have affected the healthy, coordinated development of the national economy.

Second, price differences between similar commodities of different quality are not spread out. As a result, we do not have higher prices for better quality goods and lower prices for lower-grade goods. This lack of differentiation seriously hinders technological advancement and the development of new products.

Third, the buying and selling prices for primary agricultural by-products are topsy-turvy, for the selling prices are lower than state procurement prices. The more agriculture flourishes, the more the commercial departments purchase, the greater the losses incurred, and the heavier the financial burden of the state. Financial subsidies now constitute nearly 30 percent of state financial revenue. The topsy-turvy state of the purchasing and selling prices of primary agricultural products and sideline products is detrimental to the rational adjustment of the agricultural production structure and to the turnover of commodities.

Fourth, the prices charged by "tertiary industries" are low. The food enterprises lack vitality, development is slow, and some businesses are withering and drying up. If price readjustment is not carried out, they may not survive.

These four conditions clearly demonstrate that an irrational price system hurts the smooth development of the national economy, the improvement of economic results, the revival of the domestic economy, and the further opening to the outside world.

Price is the most effective means of regulation. To apply the law of value, we must make good use of this regulatory mechanism. Our main objective is to increase enterprise vitality. To use pricing to match enterprise production to the needs of society, so that prices regulate enterprise operations, it is necessary for enterprises to be able to compete under largely similar conditions. If the pricing system is not reformed, it will be difficult to implement other reforms, including the reduction of command plans, the expansion of guiding plans, and the reform of the wage system. Consequently, reform of the pricing system is the key to the success or failure of reforming the whole economic system.

Characteristics of Implementing Price Reform

First, the reform of the pricing system began with agriculture and agricultural products. The system of compulsory procurement and distribution of agricultural products that China had implemented for thirty years has basically been eliminated. We have applied the law of value, expanded the scope of market regulation, and are gradually relaxing prices. Keeping the peasants well informed and guiding them in carrying out production according to market demands is beneficial to the readjustment of the structure of agriculture and to promoting the harmonious development of agriculture. In terms of the actual circumstances in China, it is correct that the reform of the pricing system should proceed from agriculture and agricultural products. Agriculture is the basis of China's national economy, and agricultural and related products are the most important necessities in the people's daily lives. Sound pricing of agricultural by-products encourages peasant initiative and the harmonious development of agricultural production and creates very beneficial conditions for price reforms of capital goods in urban areas.

The reform of China's economic system began in rural areas, where the responsibility system was promoted to solve the problem of eating from "one big pot." The system was then introduced in urban areas. In 1979 the index of procurement prices for agricultural and sideline products increased 20 percent. In 1980 it increased 7 percent more. As a result of increased production and higher prices, the income of peasants from sales of agricultural products reached Y26 billion. In 1985 we must readjust purchasing and selling prices for rural foodstuffs and purchasing prices of cotton. We must also implement contract quota purchasing, gradually readjust prices of other agricultural products, and implement market regulation.

Second, we have implemented a dual-price system for the means of production that eventually must approach market price. In the last few years we have had a dual-price system for coal—that is, we retained some planned prices and implemented an increased price for production that exceeds plans. In the future it will be necessary to decrease gradually the role of state-set prices, to increase gradually the emphasis on market regulation, and to increase planned prices bit by bit. Because we have a two-tiered price system, the effects of gradually increasing prices are small, the social reverberations minor. The Chinese people are familiar with the dual-price system and are receptive to it. Of course, such a system may also give rise to fraudulent buying and selling and other speculative activities. We are now adopting effective measures that will halt speculation and profiteering and check new unhealthy trends.

Third, the state participates in market regulation, and its supervision of commodity prices must be enhanced. The relaxation of prices does not mean that the state will have nothing more to do with prices. The state still purchases large amounts of grain, cotton, and other staple products at preferential prices. Between 150 billion and 160 billion jin of grain (1 jin = 0.5 kilogram) are purchased at an "inverted 3:7" proportional price schedule (30 percent based on former state-controlled procurement price; 70 percent on former above-contract sales price). Market prices, which fluctuate freely, are in effect for surplus amounts. If market prices fall below the procurement price, the state adopts protective prices—that is, purchases are based on the controlled procurement price so as to protect peasant interests. With state participation in market regulation, materials are bought and sold in large quantities, commodity prices are kept down, and wild fluctuations due to blind market forces are avoided. To ensure supplies in urban areas, state participation in the market regulation of certain commodities through subsidies will prevent infringement of consumer interests. To maintain basic stability of market commodity prices, it is necessary to improve commodity price inspection, to establish a mass consumer supervision system, and to strengthen commodity price supervision by auditing, financial, banking, and industrial and commercial management departments.

Guidelines and Principles for Price Reform

After much serious comparison and calculation, a decision was made to adopt the guideline of "combining relaxation and readjustment of prices and advancing by small steps" in the reform of the pricing system. The relaxation of prices refers to relaxing gradually the prices of certain commodities, allowing market regulation, and having negotiated buying and selling. The readjustment of prices refers to implementing gradually state unified price readjustments for commodities closely linked to the national economy and the people's livelihood, so that they become more rational. It is not advisable for the steps in price reform to be unduly large. We must take one step and look around before taking another. We must think as we go, and we must feel our way rock by rock as we cross the river. Why is it necessary to take small steps in price reform? The pace is determined by the state's financial capacity, by the ability of enterprises to assimilate reforms, and by the receptivity of the people. Given these determinants, we must understand three principles in the reform of the pricing system.

First, when structural readjustment is implemented, commodity prices fluctuate. This does not mean that everything will increase in price but that whatever should decrease in price will decrease and whatever should increase will increase. As a result, the prices of all sorts of products will become more rational, and more rational prices will play a role in encouraging production, reviving circulation, and guiding consumption. Still, the extent of price increases should not be so great as to lead to overall price increases. To this end, it is necessary to gauge what is possible and to act accordingly and with caution.

Second, when raising the prices of some mineral products and raw materials, processing industries must strive to decrease consumption so that they can absorb the increased production costs that result from price increases. Reduced taxes could solve part of the problem. The containment of increased production costs within industries will make increases in the market price of industrial consumer products unnecessary. At the same time, the enterprise's ability to absorb increased costs must be taken into consideration.

Third, during price readjustment, measures need to be adopted to ensure that the real income of vast numbers of urban residents does not drop because of the readjustment. To offset the increases in prices, the state must provide certain subsidies to the people, but not everything can be subsidized. This point touches upon the matter of the vital interests of the masses. It is necessary to consider the receptivity of the masses and to control the increases in commodity price.

Based on these guidelines and principles, the primary terms of the 1985 price reform are:

- To readjust rationally the purchasing and selling price of grain and the purchasing price of cotton in rural areas while implementing contract purchasing, to relax gradually the prices of other agricultural products, and to allow market regulation so as to motivate the development of the rural commodity economy and the readjustment of the agricultural production structure.

- To increase properly the cost of short-distance rail tariffs so as to promote the readjustment of the transportation structure, and to develop fully the role of highways and water transport.

- To spread out, as appropriate, quality price differences and regional price differences, to reduce or eliminate second-rate but expensive products that do not meet market demand, and to promote the rapid increase of top-quality, name-brand products.

- To retain the prices of raw materials, fuels, and other primary production materials distributed according to plan, to allow market regulation for materials independently marketed by enterprises as stipulated, and to promote the entrance of the means of production in the market.

Careful study of this plan shows that the risks in implementing it are minor. The plan is constructive, reliable, and beneficial to the establishment of a rational pricing system under the premise of preserving overall economic stability.

Under socialist conditions, it is necessary to uphold the policy of basically stable commodity prices and to avoid large-scale price fluctuations. Nevertheless, stable commodity prices do not mean frozen prices. We must readjust prices in a planned, controlled, and rational manner, according to the law of value and changes in supply and demand. We must also invigorate prices and, at the same time, successfully manage the relationships between stability and readjustment and between price changes and increases in the people's income. Such reforms will benefit the development of the economy and improve people's livelihood.

In sum, rational planning and pricing systems are needed to ensure that the national economy will be invigorated but not turned topsy-turvy. Reforms of the planning and pricing systems are thus the keys to the success or failure of the reform of the overall economic system. Reform of the planning and pricing systems is a very complex, systemic project that involves every aspect of the national economy and is closely linked to hundreds of millions of people. Thus, it is essential to be resolute in the objectives and direction of reform and to be cautious in the methods of reform. The Chinese people have complete confidence. We will strive for victories in reform.

Note

1. Published in English in *China Daily*, October 23, 1984.

PART TWO

Planning, Supply, and Marketing

An analysis of planning, supply, and marketing is critical to understanding the Chinese industrial system. It is these closely linked areas in which the greatest changes have occurred and in which China differs most from other socialist countries. The four chapters in this part take different analytical approaches and cover different aspects of the planning-supply-marketing nexus. Chapter 7 is mainly theoretical and prescriptive; the other three chapters are mainly empirical. Chapters 8 and 10 are complementary, with one analyzing planning and supply, the other marketing. Chapter 9 covers supply and marketing and thus partly overlaps with both chapters 8 and 10, but the coverage of issues differs somewhat. Moreover, chapter 9 provides more institutional detail, whereas chapters 8 and 10 are more schematic in their analysis.

Chen Jiyuan's largely theoretical discourse on the proper role of planning in a socialist system draws on the survey of sample enterprises. Chen argues that a socialist economy is a commodity economy in which exchange should be carried out in accord with the law of value. With this argument as his premise, he then considers two fundamental relationships: that of the state-owned enterprise and the state and that of planning and markets. He accepts as legitimate the view that government and enterprise are inseparable in socialist state-owned enterprises. But this does not imply that the two are inseparable in organizational form. Enterprises should not be minisocieties, and the state need not be directly involved in production decisions to perform its leadership role. Nor do state-owned enterprises need to be state operated. Turning to the second fundamental relationship—that between planning and markets—Chen argues that it is too frequently seen as contradictory. He feels that methods of economic management are neutral and that it is wrong to identify planning with socialism and markets with capitalism. As experience in the sample of twenty enterprises has shown, failure to use the market mechanism creates problems of inadequate information, motivation, and pressure for enterprises to improve performance. Every part of a socialist economy should be subject to both plan and market regulation, with plan regulation usually being carried out through the market mechanism.

Chen concludes that mandatory planning should play a smaller role in the future. Mandatory plans have not worked well in most of the sample enterprises because plans were unrealistic, often revised, and therefore essentially meaningless. China's huge population and territory mean that interests are too divergent and information requirements too great for universal mandatory planning—even if computers and better planning methods are used. What is required is a separation of ownership and operating authority and a greater use of nonbinding guidance plans. Mandatory plans will still be necessary in two cases: for products of mainstay enterprises that are in the national plan and affect the people's livelihood and for products whose demand exceeds supply. Even in these cases, however, guidance plans may work better if the state cannot accurately forecast demand. Over time, the scope of mandatory planning should shrink because shortages of many goods will be eliminated through increased production. But since some products will always be in short supply, mandatory planning can never be eliminated.

Some other conclusions emerge from Chen's analysis. Because enterprises have too many mothers-in-law (supervising authorities), their plan targets often conflict, and their supply, labor, and marketing plans often are uncoordinated. These problems can best be solved by reducing the detail of plans rather than by instituting administrative reforms. Similarly, the problems of raising plan targets of good performers (called the "ratchet effect" in the West and "whipping the fast ox" in China) can best be corrected by changing the method of planning assessment. Enterprises should be allowed to market their own products and purchase inputs freely.

In chapter 8 Gene Tidrick analyzes planning and supply in the twenty sample enterprises. Although China's system is a recognizable variant of the Soviet model, Tidrick shows that central planning is far narrower in China. The central authorities allocate only a few broad categories of products. Moreover, even such key materials as steel and coal have long been partly controlled by local rather than central authorities, giving rise to separate planning and allocation subsystems at the provincial and local levels. These subsystems have traditionally striven for autarky, and, therefore, China has regionalism (local protectionism) as well as the departmentalism (ministerial self-sufficiency) commonly associated with Soviet-type economies. Recent reforms have substantially modified this cellular planning and allocation system by increasing the share of production allocated outside the plan through market or quasi-market mechanisms. Each of the three main allocation channels—central plan, local plan, and market—often has a different price for the same product.

Plan targets handed down to the enterprise are neither taut nor firm. Although bonus payments are nominally linked to plan fulfillment, no enterprise in the sample lost its bonus for failing to meet its targets. Tidrick argues that, because bargaining is so pervasive and incentives are so manipulable, bonus and social welfare payments largely determine plan targets and profit-retention rates rather than the reverse. He concludes that the solution is not to tighten plans or to link incentives more closely to plan fulfillment. Such actions would only compound the conflicts and distortions of the existing planning system. But made-to-measure incentives are also pernicious because they encourage rent-seeking behavior (efforts to obtain income through regulations which confer privilege, rather than through productive activity) and erode financial discipline. The solution is to reform prices so that stable and universal incentives can be established for enterprises.

One of the most striking features of the Chinese system is that both allocated supplies and allocated output may be less than the production target. Tidrick reviews the relationship of allocation to plan targets (both guidance and mandatory plan targets) and shows how, despite deliberate underallocations of inputs, enterprises manage to obtain supplies through numerous mechanisms. In general, supplies constrained neither total output nor the product mix of sample enterprises. Tidrick argues that, because of the existence of multiple sources of supply, the formal system of planning and allocating supplies mainly affects the distribution of profits rather than the allocation of resources. At the margin, resources in Chinese industry are increasingly allocated through the market. Resource allocation is often inefficient, however, because markets are fragmented. And the multiple pricing system leads to predictable abuses, such as long cross-hauls and high-cost production by small-scale enterprises under local control.

In chapter 9 Tang Zongkun uses data and cases from the sample to analyze the supply and marketing system for state industrial enterprises. Tang outlines the main features of the material supply system, which allocates producer goods, and the commercial system, which markets manufactured consumer goods. The traditional allocation system is characterized by fragmented administrative responsibility, strictly vertical flows of both goods and information, and passive prices.

Tang argues that there are many contradictions between the traditional administrative system of product allocation and the development of a socialized economy. He attributes underallocations of supplies to systemic shortcomings rather than to poor planning. Because enterprises bear no risk, they always wish to overstock inventories. Overstocking inevitably leads to excess demand and underallocation. Administrative allocation also fails to provide enterprises with inputs of the required specification because administrators necessarily deal in broad aggregates. Although supply conferences help solve the problem of disaggregation, they are cumbersome and can be held only twice yearly. Supply allocation is thus difficult to synchronize with production planning, and neither allocation nor production planning can respond to changing economic conditions.

Tang also identifies numerous other problems that result from these systemic defects. Deliveries fail to meet contract specifications in either quantity or quality. Transport constraints compound supply shortages. Excess inventories of some goods coexist with shortages of others. Moreover, fragmented responsibility for allocation generates many irrational production and allocation decisions. Tang notes that China suffers from both regional protectionism and ministerial protectionism because of administrative fragmentation.

Because of these deficiencies of administrative allocation, enterprises have always tried to use barter or parallel markets to circumvent the system. Since 1979 the authorities have sanctioned many previously illegal parallel market activities, and the scope of such activities has expanded. Tang analyzes the main mechanisms for obtaining supplies outside the quota allocation system: barter, processing agreements, imports using retained foreign exchange, direct purchase from local enterprises and supply bureaus, and direct investment in mines or factories producing scarce inputs.

Reforms giving enterprises greater autonomy in obtaining supplies have been matched by reforms giving them greater authority to self-market their output. Tang describes and analyzes the principal changes in marketing. He argues that the reforms have had a beneficial but modest effect. For the most part, they are simply refinements of the existing system. The right to self-market is unstable, fluctuating with the overall market balance: when supplies become tight, the right to self-market is curtailed.

Tang concludes that the goal of reform should be to shift completely to a planned commodity economy. Enterprises should make all production, supply, and marketing decisions, and prices should be allowed to fluctuate according to market conditions. The transition should be gradual, however, using such interim mechanisms as government priority purchase orders and step-by-step relaxation of price controls and allocation quotas.

In chapter 10 William Byrd analyzes the effects of the many recent changes in industrial marketing. Since 1978 there has been a big increase in the role of the market mechanism, including self-marketing by enterprises. Equally important has been the emergence (and in some cases the subsequent disappearance) of buyers' markets for many commodities. Byrd discusses why buyers' markets emerged, the relationship between their emergence and the reforms increasing the role of the market mechanism, and the sustainability and economic impact of both marketing reforms and buyers' markets.

Byrd finds that buyers' markets have been more beneficial for customers and the economy than sellers' markets. The sample enterprises facing sellers' markets typically tried to expand output or focused on technical improvement in products or processes with little regard for cost or customer preferences. The typical response to a buyers' market, after an initial period of adjustment, has been a concerted effort to respond to customer needs—by improving quality, introducing new products, reducing prices, or selling a better product for the same price. Neither market has yet led to much cost reduction because enterprises can usually bargain for tax relief. But in most respects buyers' markets have oriented enterprises toward intensive growth, a major objective of the original adjustment and reform program. Byrd also analyzes how technology, self-marketing, product characteristics, financial considerations, and input market conditions affect enterprise response. He concludes that none of these factors is as important as the basic dichotomy between a buyers' market and a sellers' market in explaining enterprise behavior, though they may reinforce or inhibit the effect of market conditions.

The way the government responds to changing market conditions greatly affects enterprise behavior and economic performance. Byrd concludes that in a sellers' market the government typically restricts self-marketing and rations output. In a buyers' market the government usually abdicates responsibility for marketing, thus placing the full burden of adjusting to falling demand onto enterprises. When a buyers' market emerges, local governments often try to protect their enterprises from increased competition. Regional protectionism, in turn, has often encouraged enterprises to undertake joint ventures across regional boundaries to penetrate protected regional markets. Byrd concludes that buyers' markets have been more sustainable for consumer goods than for investment or intermediate goods, which are threatened by a resurgence in investment demand. To help promote buyers' markets, the government could subject enterprises to greater financial discipline, eliminate regional protectionism, and permit greater price flexibility.

7

The Planning System

Chen Jiyuan

PLANNING IS AT THE CORE of the socialist system of economic management, controlling and influencing other aspects of that system. In the scope of its control, the planning system has two parts: a macroplanning system and a microplanning system. The macroplanning system is within the sphere of society and includes state plans, sectoral plans, and regional plans. The microplanning system is primarily associated with a basic economic unit—that is, with an enterprise's production, supply, and marketing, and with its human, financial, and material resources. To analyze the entire microplanning system, we must examine the planning inside the enterprise, planning between enterprises, and planning between the enterprise and the state.

The relationship between the enterprise and the state is a key factor in determining the planning system for state-operated industrial enterprises. Moreover, it directly affects planning relationships within and between enterprises. This chapter will focus, therefore, on the planning relationship between the enterprise and the state, dealing with relationships within and between enterprises only to the extent necessary. The chapter will also integrate practice and theory. "Practice" here refers to the planning system for state industrial enterprises in China. The data from our survey of twenty state-operated industrial enterprises will serve as the main background material. But there will also be a comparison of China's system with those of other state-operated industrial enterprises. Applying this comparative method to the study of planning systems in state industrial enterprises will help in sifting and winnowing information, in clarifying the problems, and in discovering laws.

In Chinese economic circles, profound changes are occurring in the theoretical view of planning systems. The reform of China's economic system continues to break through some long-held concepts. As we accumulate experience in economic reform, new economic theories begin to take shape and become more important guides to implementing reforms. Therefore, criticisms will here be leveled at some traditional views, once considered unalterable principles. And some new economic theories will be expounded.

The Status of State Industrial Enterprises

In a socialist economy the state is the owner of a state industrial enterprise. This inference is both fundamental and general. Because the state is the owner of the state industrial enterprise, there are two contradictory sets of theory and reality—and two questions that need to be studied. The first question is whether a socialist state-operated industrial enterprise is a commodity producer; the second is whether the political structure can be separated from the enterprise organization.

On the first question, many socialist countries and many economists in China have long refused to acknowledge that a socialist economy is a commodity economy. In particular they refuse to acknowledge in a socialist economy under the system of ownership by the whole people that there is any relationship between commodities and currency. The logical inference must then be that a state-operated industrial enterprise is not a commodity producer. This basic inference regarding the status of the enterprise has given rise to a series of chain reactions. The enterprise takes all its orders from the planned assignments sent down by the state in determining what products and how many products it is to produce. The funds necessary for the enterprise's economic operation are entirely allocated by the state, and all the enterprise's income is turned over to the state. All products produced by the enterprise are subject to monopoly purchasing and marketing by the state. The enterprise's equipment and raw materials needed for production are also all provided by the state. This was the basic situation in the twenty state industrial enterprises we surveyed, whether in a key large enterprise producing the means of production (like the Anshan Iron and Steel Corporation) or in a small enterprise producing the means of consumption (like the Jiangmen Nanfang Foodstuff Factory). Therefore, under the original planning system and the inference that an enterprise is not a commodity producer, state industrial enterprises became an appendage of the state's administrative structure, without their own independent movement of funds and with the state taking full responsibility for profit and loss. These enterprises soon lost their initiative and enthusiasm.

After many years of traveling this winding road, we have learned that a socialist economy is a planned commodity economy based on a socialist system of public ownership of the means of production. The enterprises are the basic economic organizations, the cells that make up the national economy. Although the owner of industrial enterprises is the state, and the basic interests between the state and the enterprise and between one enterprise and another are identical, each individual enterprise has its own, relatively independent material interests. The supposition that the basic interests between state and enterprise and between one enterprise and another are identical determines that exchange at equal value is still to be carried out within an economy under the system of ownership by the whole people. Not only does there persist a commodity exchange relationship between the system of ownership by the whole people and the system of collective ownership, there also persists a commodity-currency relationship in the system of ownership by the whole people. Therefore, the state-operated industrial enterprise is a producer of material products and of commodities, and it must carry out its productive and economic activities according to the laws of movement in a commodity economy.

Naturally, the state-operated industrial enterprise has its own characteristics as a commodity producer. Commodity producers based on private ownership of the means of production are entirely independent and enjoy complete freedom. State industrial enterprises have only relative independence as commodity producers—independence that falls under centralized control. The enterprise's interests are to be respected and protected but not placed above those of society or of the state. The enterprise must see to its own interests while furthering those of the society and the state. This is of paramount importance in determining and coordinating the enterprise's responsibilities, authority, and interests—and in handling the relationship between state and enterprise.

On the second question—that of the mutual relationship between the state's administrative organs and the enterprise organization—the view has been that government and socialist state-operated industrial enterprises are inseparable. The reason is that a socialist state is not only an organization of political power but also an owner of the means of production representing all the people. Even though the state's management of a state enterprise may be administrative in form, it does not go beyond the economic relationships to impose a sort of administrative meddling. Instead, it is an internal requirement and manifestation of economic relationships in a socialist system of ownership by the whole people. Such relationships will always be present between the state and the various state enterprises. It would be impossible to sever all ties between the state and the state enterprises. Thus, in this sense, government and enterprise are inseparable.

What should be said about the foregoing viewpoint? With the state as the owner of state-operated enterprises, its relationship with the enterprises cannot and should not be severed. Indeed, the state must manage state enterprises to influence, determine, and control the enterprises' behavior and to realize better the state's interests. But state ownership of the enterprise does not imply that government and enterprise must be inseparable, with the government representing the enterprise. This perceived inseparability of government and enterprise, in which the enterprise becomes an appendage of the state's political organization, is one source of the many faults in the management system for state industrial enterprises in China and in many other socialist countries.

First, this inseparability of government and enterprise has severed internal relationships in the socialist commodity economy. The political organization has forced the enterprise's economic activities to adapt to artificially imposed administrative restrictions. This situation can only greatly hinder the enterprise's normal production operations and activities. Second, the inseparability means that the enterprises have lost their independent economic interests, so that the quality of the enterprise's production operations has nothing to do with its material interests. This loss of independent economic interests can only seriously weaken or even destroy the enterprise's economic impetus to improve its production operations. Third, the inseparability means that certain undertakings which should be carried out by the political organs are turned over to the enterprises, so that the enterprises become little societies. All the enterprises we surveyed provide commercial services, educational and health facilities, and various types of welfare. Some go so far as to operate public security bureaus, public prosecutor's offices and courts, and related services. These societal tasks can only dilute the enterprise's vitality, affecting its leadership and its production operations, and greatly lowering its economic returns.

Among socialist state-operated industrial enterprises, this inseparability of government and enterprise need no longer persist as an organizational form. It is only the product of certain historical conditions under socialism. It lacks universal applicability in the handling of relationships between the state and enterprises. And it is not an internal requirement and manifestation of the economic relationships in a system of ownership by the whole people.

Combining political structures and economic organizations, so that the political structures directly control economic organizations, is not the only way a socialist state can perform its economic functions. Nor is it the optimum one. A socialist state has economic and political functions, and the state owns the state-operated industrial enterprises. But these two facts cannot justify combining political structures and economic organizations into one.

There are two primary aspects to the economic functions of a socialist state: one is leading the transformation of all socioeconomic relationships; the other is organizing a leadership system and large-scale economic construction. Correct performance of the state's economic functions matters much in the smooth, healthy development of a socialist economy.

A socialist state's most elemental goal of economic management is to develop its productive forces. This means mobilizing laborers, taking full advantage of enterprise vigor, achieving a macroeconomic balance, and ensuring the planned, proportional development of the national economy. China's practical experience and that of other countries have shown that the inseparability of government and enterprise is of no assistance in achieving this goal. On the contrary, it may suppress the enthusiasm of the labor force, strip the enterprise of its vigor, and hinder development of the socialist economy.

Separating government and enterprise does not strip the state of its economic functions. It enables the state to perform its economic functions more effectively. After the separation of government and enterprise, the state is able to extricate itself from the morass of matters it handles poorly. Instead, the state should set a strategy for economic development and draft scientifically based national economic plans; determine the relevant economic policies; adjust and coordinate relationships of economic interest; include market mechanisms in planning mechanisms and use such economic levers as prices, taxation, profit margins, and exchange rates to adjust national economic development; draft complementary economic legislation to ensure the availability of statistics for the proper supervision and examination of the national economy; and provide economic news and technical consulting and other services to promote improved economic returns. This approach takes full advantage of the enthusiasm, initiative, and creativity of individual laborers and makes it possible to achieve a comprehensive macroeconomic balance on a vital, vigorous microeconomic basis.

In summary, these two points—that state industrial enterprises are relatively independent commodity producers and that political structures can and must be separated from economic organizations—are scientific determinations of the nature and status of socialist state-operated industrial enterprises. Only by clearly understanding these two points and by studying the reform of planning in state industrial enterprises can we start at the correct point.

Planning and Markets

Under China's previous economic system, the state-operated industrial enterprise was completely cut off from markets. The kind and amount of the many products the enterprise produced had nothing to do with market demand. Production was determined entirely by orders from the responsible higher authorities. After the products were produced, they were not sold by the enterprise in the marketplace but were subject to the state purchasing monopoly, with the state engaging in centralized marketing. The raw and processed materials and the technical equipment required by the enterprise to carry out production were also supplied centrally by the state. That is, no direct market relationship existed—nor was any allowed to exist—between the enterprise and the consumers, especially individual consumers. At the same time, no market relationship existed between the enterprise and other producers. There was a horizontal, mutual product-supply relationship among enterprises, and contracts had to be signed stipulating the varieties, quantities, and delivery times for the products to be supplied. But everything was determined by state plans. This state of affairs is fundamentally different from a free buy-sell relationship in the marketplace.

With enterprises dissociated from the market, acting according to the directives of the state plans, three problems were unavoidable. The first was information. For the information the enterprise needed for production, it relied solely on the relevant state organs. There was no way of ensuring the comprehensiveness, truthfulness, and timeliness of the information. The second problem was motivation. The production assignments sent down to the enterprise by the state relied on the conscientiousness of the enterprise's leaders and staff and workers. There was no impetus deriving from the material benefits of market relationships. The third was pressure. If the enterprise acted entirely in isolation from market competition—if there was no competitive pressure among producers—there could be no competitive pressure among consumers. This pressure of competition is essential in promoting production, improving quality, and lowering costs.

Dissociating enterprises from the marketplace had several unwanted results. Production became highly subjective and willful—and thus unable to satisfy society's demands for an abundance of high-quality goods. The distribution and application of goods was very irrational. And enterprises developed so sluggishly that technological progress and the development of new products were greatly hindered. Not only did productivity and economic returns not improve quickly, they tended to decline.

At the test sites for reform of the economic system over the last few years, including the twenty enterprises we surveyed, planning regulation and market regulation have been integrated to expand the autonomy of enterprises. In addition, a series of corresponding measures has been taken, including the setting of plans according to market demand for final products. For example, to encourage competition among enterprises, those that meet their planned assignments are allowed to market some of their own products. All reform measures of this type undoubtedly represent a significant advance in the area of integrating planning and markets. Marketing requires decentralization, and decentralization, in turn, promotes marketing.

But the relationship between planning regulation and market regulation has not been understood by some economists in our country—with less-than-ideal practical or theoretical results. The main problem is that regulation through planning is simply regulation through administrative procedure, whereas market regulation is primarily the self-activating regulation of the law of value in a free market. In other words, planning regulation refers to the part of production that is in accord with mandatory plans, whereas market regulation refers to the part of production that the enterprise is allowed to market itself. The two parts are treated as components of socioeconomic life that do not interfere with one another; they are lumped together only artificially and mechanically.

After practical experience and theoretical investigations in reform over the last few years, economists in China have finally abandoned the traditional concept that planning regulation and market regulation are antithetical and incompatible. In the historical stage of socialism, there still remain internal contradictions in economic interests, including those among individuals, between individuals and the collective, among collectives, and between the collective and the state. It has been objectively determined that we must distribute individual consumer goods according to labor while preserving the commodity-currency relationship. Thus the market is the same as distribution according to labor, a necessary economic mode adopted to resolve the internal contradictions in socialist economic life.

In the past, the people's understanding of the socialist economy was overly simple. The socialist economy was a planned economy, with all labor being directly socialist, with no contradictions between individual labor and labor needed by society, and with all products going immediately and directly into consumption. There was thus no need to use the commodity-currency relationship to resolve conflicts of interests among people. Nor was there any need for a market to solve the problem of making products. So long as a socialist economy depended entirely on planning directives, it could move ahead without considering the effect of the marketplace.

The simplicity went so far as to attribute planning mistakes to insufficiently modernized measures, as if increasing the number of computers would solve the problems of planning. In reality, the use of modern methods in planning can make planning more scientific, but conflicts of interest among people cannot be resolved solely through the use of mathematical methods. Economic methods must be used to solve conflicts through an adjustment in production relationships. Practical experience in China and other socialist countries has shown that this understanding of socialism, and the measures that went along with it, would bring about a slowdown in socialist economic development and a decline in economic productivity.

A socialist economy is a planned commodity economy. Planning regulation and market regulation meld into one, so that a socialist economy cannot be clearly divided into one part regulated through planning and another regulated through the market. A socialist economy is an organic whole. Every part of it operates under the effects of two types of regulating mechanisms, planning and market. A socialist economic mechanism comprising a planning mechanism and a market mechanism is complete. When we say "planned economy," we are referring to society's (or the state's) intentional regulation of all socioeconomic activities to ensure, regularly and consciously, the planned, proportional development of the society and the economy. If we go so far as to speak of what form of regulating mechanism to use to achieve this planned, proportional development, we should start from the reality of the socialist economy, mingling both the planning and the market regulating mechanisms. We cannot, for ideological reasons, reject the use of the market mechanism, treating it as some capitalist model that will lead to an anarchic state of affairs and bring on an economic crisis.

Treating the planning mechanism and the market mechanism as regulating mechanisms will make it possible to integrate them into the regulation of socialist economic development. Moreover, only by combining the two can we more effectively promote development of the socialist economy. With this approach we will be able to avoid the faults of excessively leaden economic control and getting sidetracked from consumption. It will also be possible to avoid the anarchic state of affairs that may arise when control over economic activities is lost as a result of the exclusive use of the market mechanism. On the one hand, even if we rely primarily on administrative measures and compulsory plans in our economic life, we must also give full consideration to the requirements of the law of value and use the market mechanism, so that planning accords with the realities of market demand. On the other hand, that portion of the economy under the system of ownership by the whole people that is controlled entirely by market regulation must also be controlled and influenced by economic planning, so that it becomes a component part of a planned, commodity economy. It cannot be entirely at the mercy of the self-activating market regulator.

It is also possible to use market information to measure and rectify mistakes in planning. Experience has shown that the commodity-currency relationship has a positive effect in socioeconomic life, that it is a forceful lever promoting economic development. Steel, for example, is an important product for the nation and for people's livelihood, and thus it is subject to mandatory plans. Nonetheless, a number of steel enterprises, because of the irrationally small price difference between rolled steel and steel ingots, are willing to take orders only for steel ingots, not for rolled steel. Anshan Iron and Steel produces nineteen-millimeter round steel and eighteen-millimeter round steel. The manufacturing procedure is the same and the costs are similar, yet the contract price of the former is much higher than the latter. Thus very little nineteen-millimeter rolled steel is produced, and it is impossible to ensure that society's demands for it will be met. The authorities have tried to counteract this situation, with meager results. Ultimately it will be necessary to widen the price difference between rolled steel and steel ingots so that order assignments for rolled steel can be met.

We must make use of administrative methods and economic methods, properly handling the relationship between the two. Under China's previous economic system, people were accustomed to using administrative methods to control economic operations. Moreover, it was emphasized that using administrative methods to manage the economy was an inherent requirement and manifestation of a socialist economy, the worry being that economic methods might change the nature of the socialist economy. Management, control, and guidance must be exercised over socialist economic activities at all times and under all circumstances because socialist construction is unable to proceed on its own. If all socioeconomic activity is to undergo planned, proportional development, the state's administrative organs must be used to formulate and promulgate compulsory laws, decrees, plans, and directives that will be passed down level by level through the various subordinate relationships. At the same time, contradictions persisting in the interests of the state, collective bodies, and individuals must under certain circumstances be handled by the state through administrative methods.

There are limits, however, to the use of administrative methods in the management of the economy. The administrative approach cannot be made the primary method of economic management for three reasons. First, the administrative approach can easily lead to bureaucracy. Second, it can create structural duplication, with an increase in turnover and a decline in economic efficiency, which results in missed economic opportunities. Third, it can create artificial economic divisions and economic blockages, hindering the development of commodity production and circulation.

For these reasons, ths use of administrative methods should gradually be reduced in favor of economic methods. "Economic methods" refers to the use of economic organization, economic levers, and the people's concern for their own material interests to control, influence, and guide people's economic activities to achieve the anticipated results. A socialist economy is a commodity economy, and the use of economic methods to manage the economy is not determined by people's subjective desires but by the objective requirements of economic laws. China's economic reforms in recent years, as well as economic reforms in other socialist countries, have shown that the economic approach in managing a socialist economy cannot only change the nature of that socialist economy but it can promote its development, strengthening and consolidating the path a socialist economy must take.

The specific methods to be used in managing the economy, and the extent and degree to which they are to be used, are related to the nature of the economy. Basically, however, methods of economic management are neutral. It cannot be said that administrative methods are proper to a socialist economy while economic methods are proper to a capitalist one. In the social sphere, a capitalist economy is self-developing. But the capitalist economies, to overcome the severe difficulties they are facing, are resorting more and more to administrative methods to manage and intervene in their economies. This approach cannot change the nature of a capitalist economy. In the same way, a socialist economy is basically able to achieve planned, proportional development. But to achieve plan targets, it must use economic methods in conjunction with administrative methods as much as possible. And this approach cannot change the nature of a socialist economy.

Under the present conditions in China—when the changeover from a sellers' market to a buyers' market has not yet been realized and when reforms of the price system are far from complete—a perfect combination of planning mechanism and market mechanism cannot be achieved. But that should not deter us from adopting, to the extent possible, some measures that need to be adopted or from removing the abuses that have arisen from the past separation of planning and the market. Nor should it deter us from exploring further the ways to combine planning and the market more effectively.

Forms of Planning

In the past, China's state-operated industrial enterprises were all subject to mandatory plans. The main characteristic of this form of planning is that it is compulsory; the mandatory planning assignments sent down by the state have the effect of law for the enterprise and must be implemented. The purpose of this mandatory form of planning is to use the strength built by the upper levels of the state to ensure the planned, proportional development of the national economy. During the socialist economy's development, this form of planning has been used to concentrate human, material, and financial resources in key sectors selected by the state in order to solve the most pressing economic problems. It has had a positive effect, accelerating socialist industrialization and consolidating national defense.

But the use of mandatory plans unavoidably leads to abuses. The state wishes to use mandatory plans to manage state industrial enterprises and all of their production operations and activities directly. The state cannot do this, however, since the state cannot have all the information necessary for the enterprises' production activities. The planning orders it sends down to the enterprises more often than not are at odds with reality and are derived from subjective wants. This type of mandatory plan is, of course, without any scientific foundation, and if mandatory plans are unscientific, there is no point in discussing their seriousness or legality.

All twenty of the enterprises we surveyed were subject to mandatory plans, and one of the following two situations was present in all of them. First, the enterprise implemented the plans according to regulations and its obligations to the state. Doing so may have created imbalances in production, supply, and marketing and conflicts between production and demand—thereby lowering economic returns. Second, the enterprise clearly understood that the plans were unattainable. The enterprise formally accepted them and then proceeded to point out how the plan would not work, thus requiring the state to make revisions. Under most circumstances the state ultimately had to accede to the enterprise's views. The situation just described prevailed at almost all the enterprises we surveyed. The production plans of the Chongqing Clock and Watch Company for alarm clocks were adjusted downward from 1,150,000 to 520,000. The Shenyang Smelting Plant sought a downward adjustment in its profit plans so as to coordinate them with the output value and production plans, and the state ultimately gave in. Such situations demonstrate that the various mandatory plans sent down by the state to the enterprises in the past were formal documents devoid of meaning.

In the light of problems brought about by mandatory plans, the reform of plans has become an important aspect of the reform of the economic system. The focus is on two problems: the position of mandatory plans in socialist planning, and the future evolutionary trends in mandatory plans.

The traditional concept was that all socialist planning had to be mandatory in China. There has been some retreat from this position in recent years, but some economists still stress that mandatory plans are the main form of socialist planning. The theoretical basis for such a view is primarily as follows. The use of mandatory plans is determined by the system of public ownership of the means of production. Under the system of ownership by the whole people, it is impossible to separate ownership from operating authority. And if the state does not directly guide the enterprise's production activities, there will be no way to ensure that social production will be carried out according to the interests of all the people. Therefore, the requirements of socialized production and the system of ownership by the whole people cannot be realized economically. Furthermore, some comrades assert that China's national situation is also the basis for the use of mandatory plans. Since China is a large country with a huge population, scarce resources per capita, a low standard of living, and uneven economic development from one region to another, it is necessary to adopt the mandatory form of planning to concentrate funds on key construction targets, to distribute the productive forces rationally, to take full advantage of all resources, and to provide a planned, gradual improvement in the people's lives.

Theoretically, however, the system of public ownership of the means of production does not predestine the state to guide and manage the enterprises directly. Proprietary rights and operating authority can here be separated in the same way. It is not, as some have said, that separation of ownership and operating authority can occur only between two private owners, not between the state and the enterprise as the same owner. In reality, the separation of ownership and operating authority is a phenomenon that occurs everywhere as economic activities are carried out. It occurs not only between two private owners; it may also occur with a single owner. "Owner" here may be either a private owner, as with a capitalist, or it may be a public owner, such as a socialist state.

A socialist state is the representative of all the people; it is the owner of state-operated enterprises. Yet it cannot directly manage an infinite number of enterprises; it must delegate management authority to representatives. Thus there is a separation of ownership and operating authority. The inference that a separation of the two may change the nature of the state-operated enterprise requires some debate. Undoubtedly there is a mutually controlling relationship between ownership and operating authority, and in this sense it may be said that the separation of ownership and operating authority is not absolute and unconditional.

Even if enterprise autonomy is expanded, and the enterprise handles its own operations and takes responsibility for its profits and losses, it still must obey the relevant laws and decrees of the state and operate in accordance with economic policies. The enterprise does not and cannot operate freely, completely dissociating itself from the state's control. At the same time, there may be other modes of control in addition to ownership and operating authority. For example, control may take the form of rents, taxation, and other types of benefits. Even if ownership and operating authority are separated, the owner may still employ other methods, such as levying taxes or raising various kinds of funds, to exercise his own proprietary rights.

Therefore it cannot be held that separating ownership and operating authority changes the nature of state enterprises. In fact, "state ownership" and "state operation" were originally two distinct concepts, but over a long period of time they became confused with one another, so that "state-operated enterprise" became another way of saying "an enterprise under the system of ownership by the whole people." Following tradition, I have also used this concept of state-operated enterprise in this chapter. But for the sake of accuracy, when conditions are ripe we shall have to correct this usage and replace "state-operated enterprise" with "state-owned enterprise."

As to the assertion that China's national situation requires the use of mandatory plans, some concrete analysis is required here too. China's national situation has determined that it is necessary to give priority to solving a number of key problems—for which compulsory, mandatory plans are necessary. But because of its vast territory, huge population, and uneven development, China's economic activity differs greatly from that in other socialist countries. It requires more flexibility and variety in the area of plan control. It also requires the use of guideline plans that provide indirect regulation rather than mandatory plans that provide direct control.

In a planned commodity economy that uses administrative and economic approaches to management, mandatory planning is rarely used alone. Aside from some mandatory plans still maintained, guideline plans have generally been adopted for enterprises. Some enterprises are now being allowed to operate completely freely. In its use of guideline plans, the state must still send down assignments for production operations in accord with the requirements of national economic development. But these assignments are not binding on the enterprises. Instead, by applying various economic levers, the state guides the enterprise's production operations onto the general track of the national plans. Experience has shown that, because of the intimate relationship between guidance plans and the market, guidance plans are drafted on the basis of more ample, complete, and accurate information. They thus accord better with reality; assist in linking up production, supply, and marketing; and promote a balance between production and demand.

At the same time, the state's guidance plans prompt the enterprise to be concerned with meeting planning assignments for its own economic interests, and thus full advantage is taken of the enterprise's initiative and enthusiasm. Therefore, correcting the notion that mandatory plans are the only form of planning will not hurt the planned economy. It will, on the contrary, greatly improve planning effectiveness and exploit the superiority of the planned economy.

The second problem, that of the future evolutionary trends for mandatory plans, has always evoked two diametrically opposed views. The first view holds that the scope of mandatory plans will in the near future have to be cut back but that with the development of the socialist economy and improvements in economic management levels the scope will once again be expanded. The other view holds that the scope of mandatory plans will continue to diminish, both in the near and distant future, and that this trend cannot and should not be countered. To shed light on this issue we must analyze the dynamics of all factors involved in determining and applying mandatory plans.

Usually there are two factors that determine whether or not mandatory plans are applied to enterprises. The first is the importance of the enterprise and its products in national economic life; generally speaking, large, mainstay enterprises, whose production affects national plans and the people's livelihood, must be subjected to mandatory plans. The second is the product's supply-and-demand situation: products whose supply does not meet demand must normally be subjected to mandatory plans. Also to be taken into account is the possibility of applying mandatory plans if conditions are right for accurately forecasting the relevant economic movements. Such conditions, in turn, are determined by the availability and processing of information and the ability to make forecasts. In general, if it is possible to have more or less complete and accurate information on the relevant production, supply, and marketing links for a product, it will also be possible to use this information to forecast changes in economic movements accurately, so that mandatory plans can be applied to its production and distribution.

In the present economic situation, the two factors do not exist independently. They must be considered comprehensively, after which a judgment can be made as to whether it is necessary and possible to apply mandatory plans. For example, it cannot be said that all products of large, mainstay enterprises must without exception be subjected to mandatory plans. Nor are such enterprises' products that are in short supply necessarily subject to mandatory plans. Nor can mandatory plans be applied if there is no way of getting the necessary economic information to make an accurate forecast. Only economic methods can guide the production of these products to meet the demands of national economic development.

Now we can analyze future evolutionary trends in mandatory plans. First, large, mainstay industries whose production affects national plans and the people's livelihood will not undergo any basic changes in the foreseeable future. Neither will there be any clear differences in the future range of products affecting national plans and the people's livelihood. The firms considered part of large, mainstay industries are always relative. As modernization proceeds, there may be an increase in large, mainstay industries. But the experience of a number of countries has shown that as modern technology advances in quick leaps in a commodity economy, enterprises tend to become smaller. At the same time, measured by future standards, some of today's large, mainstay industries will decline in scale to become ordinary enterprises. Therefore it is not possible to draw any conclusions about whether the scope of mandatory plans will expand or shrink.

Next is the supply and demand of products. During modernization, commodities in short supply will become even scarcer, owing to the growth of production and the development of foreign trade. Mandatory plans for several products have now been lifted, because the tight supply has been eliminated or alleviated. Preparations are under way to lift the mandatory plans of other products. Naturally, there are always new products, the supply of which nearly always falls short of demand, and mandatory plans will still have to be applied to handle their production and distribution. Thus, mandatory plans cannot be entirely eliminated. But the trend is toward a steady decline in commodities whose supply does not meet demand, and the scope of mandatory plans will undergo a corresponding reduction.

Finally, technological advances will lead to more economic information and more accurate forecasting, enabling the state to make better use of mandatory plans. National economic planning and statistical agencies will be using computers and other modern methods more and more, and the information gathered will be more complete and timely. Forecasting capabilities will improve as experience accumulates. On the other hand, as socioeconomic life develops, it will become more complex and multifaceted, which may limit the information that people can obtain. As conditions change, people's understanding of socioeconomic production will also change. Hence, there may be differences in the degree of completeness of the information they obtain, and not all aspects of economic activities will be able to be accurately forecast. This situation will also limit expansion of the state's application of mandatory plans. It is thus hard to tell whether more economic information and better forecasts will increase or decrease the use of mandatory plans.

Two points emerge from the foregoing discussion. First, mandatory plans cannot be eliminated and will persist primarily because there will always be commodities whose supply does not meet demand. Second, the scope of mandatory plans will steadily decline because commodities whose supply does not meet demand will continue to decrease in number. China's economic life in recent years has provided forceful proof of this. As time goes on, the range of activities in which the socialist state applies mandatory plans to exercise direct control over the economy will steadily diminish, and the influence and guiding effects of such economic measures as prices, credit, taxation, and exchange rates will gradually increase.

Organization of Planning

The organization of planning under China's original economic system has two chief characteristics. The first is a hierarchical organizational structure with many levels; the second is a scattered organizational structure with multiple leadership.

The agencies that formulate, promulgate, control, and examine plans are multitiered. Although the number of levels in the hierarchical planning organization is influenced by the scale of the enterprise, generally speaking state-operated industrial enterprises, regardless of their size, all have such an organization guiding them.

A "scattered organizational structure with multiple leadership" refers to several structures that lead and organize the implementation of enterprise plans. In addition to the corresponding professional agencies responsible for the enterprises, a series of related specialized economic organs and comprehensive economic bodies participate in providing planning leadership. This "multiple" and "scattered" feature is also manifested in the fact that the party and government systems also provide leadership for enterprises in their planning production operations. If the various structures that lead, manage, and assess enterprise planning are taken into account, leadership in the planned economy is unfortunately even more "multiple" and "scattered." The planning systems of the twenty enterprises we surveyed show that the multilevel, multiple leadership of the organizational structure for planning creates a series of conflicts and difficulties for enterprise operations and activities.

First, plan targets conflict with one another. Government structures at all levels and in all areas have the authority to send down one or more plan targets to enterprises, according to their own needs, although there has been no prior centralized study and coordination. Thus, the plan targets sent down to the enterprise more often than not contradict one another, leaving the enterprise unsure of which target to follow. In general, the professional agency responsible for the enterprise sends down plans for output, variety, and quality. The economic organs of the enterprise's municipality or county send down plans for output value and profit. There is normally no way of matching and coordinating the two types of targets. Under ordinary circumstances, the output targets for value and profit are too high, so that even if the output plans sent down by the responsible agency are met, it is not possible to meet the plans sent down by the local authorities. For example, in 1982 and 1983 Jiao County in Shandong Province sent down targets for output value to the Qingdao Forging Machinery Plant of Y19 million and Y18 million, respectively. But the output value of the targets for variety and quality sent down by the Qingdao Machine Industry Office was only Y13 million and Y16 million. As a result, the Qingdao Machine Industry Office expressed satisfaction with the plant's having met the production plan and commended it. But Jiao County treated this plant as a backward unit for failing to meet its plans for output value and criticized it.

Second, enterprise production has been isolated from supply and marketing activities. An enterprise's production activity, materials supply, and product marketing are three links that form an organic, interrelated whole. But under the original planning organization, the enterprise's plans for production, supply, and marketing are sent down by different agencies at different levels. As a result the targets for output, variety, quality, and other materials are often sent down by the professional agencies responsible for the enterprise at the central or local level. Profit and other financial targets are sent down by the planning commission, economic committee, or other economic leadership organ of the enterprise's locale. The plans to supply materials are the responsibility of the various agencies at the central, provincial, municipal, or county levels. The drafting and implementing of plans for marketing for some products are the direct responsibility of the central government or the concerned central agency—and for other products are the responsibility of the provincial or municipal trade agency, the county trade structure, or the enterprise.

The main problem is that the agencies sending down production assignments are not concerned with materials supply, which must be handled through a separate channel. Thus materials supply is often dissociated from production requirements. It regularly happens that the supply of materials cannot satisfy the demands of production plans. Generally the enterprise has been required to send a report to the state every July or August on the types and quantities of raw and processed materials and equipment it needs for the coming year. After a comprehensive balancing by the corresponding agency, depending on the type of materials, an annual plan target for materials supply is sent down to the enterprise. Finally, in accord with the state's supply of materials, an ordering meeting is called, and enterprises sign contracts among themselves for goods orders; the contracts include varieties, specifications, quantities, and delivery times. But the concerned agencies cannot send down the production planning assignments until February or March of the plan year. In some cases, planning assignments have been delayed until June or even later. This situation unavoidably leads to a lack of coordination between plans for production and materials supply. For commodities in great demand, the marketing plans more often than not have larger targets than the production plans and much larger targets than the supply plans. Trade agencies often reject outdated, slow-selling commodities, pushing them off on the enterprises so they will market them themselves. Furthermore, when the marketing plans for some products are drafted and implemented, there are still conflicts between domestic commerce and foreign trade in such areas as pricing and resources.

Third, plans for the distribution of the labor force do not accord with enterprise needs. The recruitment and distribution of the labor force has been handled entirely by the labor department of the area where the enterprise is located. The enterprise annually sends its request for labor to the responsible professional agency. The agency then compiles the needs of all the enterprises under it and reports its labor demand plans to the labor agency, including such information as numbers of personnel, male-female ratio, educational levels, and health status. But the labor agency nonetheless drafts and sends down its distribution plans primarily according to local labor resources and employment demand.

With China's abundant labor resources, the labor force distributed to the enterprises generally exceeds demand, and all the enterprise can do is accept its political assignment as a job provider. The male-female ratio often fails to correspond to the enterprise's characteristics and requirements. In the enterprises we surveyed, although the proportion of female workers assigned by the labor agencies was always higher than the enterprise's demands, the enterprise always had to accept the assignment. The enterprises also ask for more university and secondary vocational school graduates, requests usually unmet. Well-educated workers are usually siphoned off at higher levels. Small and medium-size enterprises in small and medium-size cities and counties sometimes go for years without being assigned a university or secondary vocational school graduate. Moreover, the labor agencies sometimes assign old or incapacitated workers, and the enterprises must accept them.

To overcome these problems, the planning organization, with its multiple levels, needs to be reformed. If we are to achieve planned, proportional development of the socialist economy, we must establish a natural organizational structure for planning. But what sort of structure should we establish? And should we take full advantage of it so that we may assist rather than hinder socialist economic development?

The socialist economy is an economic organism created on the basis of socialized production and public ownership. It contains many complex interrelationships, which require the creation of a corresponding planning organization that relies on the economy's internal relationships and coordinates all these relationships. At the same time, the socialist economy's internal relationships can be further divided into relationships in the macroeconomic realm of society and in the microeconomic realm of the enterprise. The relationships in the macroeconomic realm can be divided into relationships within the country, within one region, between sectors, and within a sector. Coordinating these various internal relationships requires that we set up an organizational system for planning that corresponds to them—including a central planning organization, a regional planning organization, an overall planning organization, a sectoral planning organization, and an enterprise planning organization.

For a socialist country, the divisions of the planning organizations listed above will take on the outward appearance of a hierarchical organizational structure, with vertical subordinate relationships. Originally, the distinctions among the various organizational structures for planning lay only in the extent to which they coordinated the relationships of economic activities. That is, the distinctions were in the division of labor. But these planning organizations soon became identical to the state's political structures. Such planning organizations are generally hierarchical systems composed of central planning structures, local planning structures at all levels, and enterprise planning structures, with subordinate authority relationships existing among the different levels. Planning organizations having the characteristics of a hierarchical structure are still useful, inasmuch as it is possible to make use of administrative directives to coordinate all aspects of economic relationships. This use of administrative directives helps ensure that society and economy follow the direction of development set by the state.

But a hierarchical structure in planning organization unavoidably brings with it certain defects and conceals the risk of political abuse of power in economic work. The higher-level planning organs often take on the responsibilities of others, substituting themselves for the lower-level planning organs in setting policy and thereby becoming subjective and bureaucratic. Such a situation may also lead to meddling in lower-level planning, which carries the danger of putting the leadership for plans onto two or more tracks having mutual conflicts and restraints that prevent the effective execution of that leadership.

The reform of the economic system must therefore be accompanied by the reform of the hierarchical structure of planning organization, which cannot be eliminated, since the state still exists. Thus the necessary reform measures can deal only with the questions of how rationally to divide up the policymaking authority of the upper and lower levels of planning and of how to coordinate leadership relationships among the various levels. In pursuing answers to these questions three main factors must be considered.

The first is the availability of information. Planning organizations at all levels can make decisions only in realms in which they can obtain and master information. If they do not have information or cannot master it, they will necessarily make errors.

The second factor is the nature of policy targets. The availability of information is not and should not be the sole basis for dividing up policymaking authority, whereby the policy targets of upper-level and lower-level planning organs sometimes duplicate or overlap each other. Policymaking authority must be divided among higher and lower planning organizations on the basis of whether targets are ordinary or special and whether they are long-term or short-term.

The third factor is the relationship between planning authority and economic interests. The division of planning authority among the various levels of planning institutions is closely linked with the interests of the managers and the managed. In dividing the decisionmaking power among the different levels of planning institutions, the following principle should be maintained: the division of power should encourage the planning organizations to appropriately link the interests of their own institutions or those of the regions under their administration with the interests of society as a whole, so that in pursuing their own interests, they would simultaneously promote the maximization of the interests of society as a whole.

To reform multiple leadership, then, it is necessary to understand clearly that a planning system led by several mothers-in-law is not good—and that a planning system which has gone from several mothers-in-law to just one is not any better. The real problem lies not in having several mothers-in-law or just one to lead enterprise planning but in just what the higher authorities are leading and how they are implementing that leadership. If the higher authorities think constantly about controlling every aspect of enterprise planning and handling all matters great and small, the planning leadership system will still have to be reformed, even if one mother-in-law replaces several. Therefore changing several mothers-in-law to one should not be the objective of the reform of the planning system for enterprises. The crux of the matter lies in correctly exploiting the leadership of planning organizations at all levels—reforming them from the ground up. The higher planning organs must no longer intervene in the enterprise's everyday business of drafting and implementing production, supply, and marketing plans. The focus of their work should be to provide guidance, coordination, oversight, and service for the enterprise's production operations and activities.

China is now proposing to establish an economic network of the central cities to exploit their diversified functions. Except for a few special, large, mainstay enterprises (mainly those in petrochemical, nonferrous, or military-industrial production), all enterprises directly managed by the central government and the provinces will be turned over to the central cities. These cities were a product of the development of the commodity economy, and they now are centers of activity in the commodity economy. Turning the enterprises over to them should thus help to break down the segmented and compartmentalized management system. (But some comrades are concerned that the enterprises, when turned over to the cities, would have yet another mother-in-law to listen to.)

After the enterprises are turned over to the cities, however, the cities must not be allowed to become new mothers-in-law of the enterprises. They can be prevented from doing so if the cities' functions are reformed, and rather than intervening in everyday enterprise affairs they exert indirect control—primarily through economic measures—so as to provide guidance and service to the enterprises. After setting up this new system, no planning structure will directly intervene in the enterprise's everyday plans for production, supply, and marketing. Trade centers will be established, money markets will be opened to take advantage of the banks' usefulness, and the taxation system will be completed to enable the use of such economic levers as prices, credit, taxation, and exchange rates to create a suitable economic environment for enterprises and to guide their productive activities.

Horizons of Planning

What form of planning is most appropriate for long-term, medium-term, and short-term plans? In China, no national economic development plans for longer than ten years have been formulated and implemented. Only relatively long-range proposals outlining economic and social development have been put forth. For example, the Twelfth Party Congress of the Chinese Communist party proposed the quadrupling of industrial and agricultural output by the end of the century. Science, education, energy, and communications are to be the strategic development focuses for this twenty-year period. During the 1980s China is to lay the foundation for vitalizing the economy during the 1990s.

Making clear the strategic goals undoubtedly helps in guiding the development of China's economy. But this does not mean there is a long-term development plan for the national economy. China primarily formulates five-year plans, which serve as medium-range plans, and annual plans, which serve as short-term plans. The state sends enterprises annual plans, which serve as the basis for assessing their activities. In the past, these annual plans helped to ensure the construction of key national projects and to achieve the planned, proportional development of the national economy. But such annual plans were often dissociated from the market, drafted without a full understanding of the enterprise's situation, and divorced from reality.

Planning assignments given to the enterprises either exceeded or fell short of market demand, which resulted in overstocking or in products being sold out.

At the beginning of the year, the state would send down planning assignments to nearly all the enterprises we surveyed. In mid-year, the enterprise would demand that the state revise them, and at year's end the state would once again send down the planning assignments. While the final version of the plans retained the outward appearance of the state plans, it nearly always embodied the enterprise's proposals. The state accepted these proposals not because the enterprise had any special planning ability, but because the enterprise could not meet the state's planning assignments. The state could not justify why the enterprise had to meet the planning assignments. Although this type of plan was supposed to be legally mandatory, in reality it was no plan at all. It could not be effectively realized; it did not even influence or guide the enterprise's production activities.

Mandatory plans naturally require a short time limit and concrete content. It is not possible to have as the main form of planning medium- or long-term plans expressing only intentions. In the enterprises we surveyed, annual plans predominated. But there were also examples of monthly plans as the planning focus. In Qingyuan County, Guangdong Province, the economic commission focuses on sending down monthly plans and assessing the ten or so enterprises under it on that basis. In their view, annual plans deal with a major direction, quarterly plans provide an outline, and monthly plans provide a concrete administrative program for organizing the enterprises' economic activities.

In future reform of the planning system, as the scope of mandatory plans is gradually cut back and the proportion of guidance plans gradually increases, there will be a need to shift the focus of national plans from the short term to the medium and long term. After the focus of planning has shifted to formulating and sending down medium- and long-term plans, enterprises will have to program their long-term development direction in order to realize medium- and long-term planning targets. The enterprises can then handle their everyday production activities according to market demand and the requirements of meeting those targets. The relevant state agencies will no longer intervene by sending down short-term plans (whether annual, quarterly, or monthly). Thus the enterprises will have long-range development goals and will also be able to take full advantage of their own initiative and enthusiasm. This will mean a basic transformation of the past situation, in which the enterprises had no long-range development direction and their hands were tied.

Planning requires a focus on the medium and long terms because the shorter the planning time, the more specific the task and the more conflicts requiring resolution. In socialist modernization, none of the tasks of social, economic, and technological development can be completed in a short time. Nor is it likely that socioeconomic conflicts can be resolved in a short time.

The drafting of plans for the medium and especially the long term means determining the basic direction of economic, technological, and social development. The experience of a number of countries shows that such plans are relatively stable and that they can effectively guide economic practice. But they should not be all-encompassing, a list of instructions for the enterprise's everyday production activities. Such plans cannot have the required stability and cannot effectively control, set, and influence the direction of socioeconomic development.

Assessments of Performance

In China, the system of norms for assessing enterprises has already changed. During the first five-year plan, there were twenty norms, including total output value, output of main products, types of new products, trial manufacture of products, important technological and economic quotas, cost reduction rate and amount, total number of staff and workers, number of workers arriving by year's end, total wages, average wages, productivity, and profit. In 1957 the number was reduced to four: output of main products, total number of staff and workers, total wages, and profit. Later, the number of norms was adjusted to eight categories: output, product types, quality, consumption, productivity, cost, profit, and occupation of circulating funds. Although there have been changes in the planning norms sent down by the agencies to the enterprises we surveyed, these eight categories constitute the main basis for assessment.

Under the past planning system, there were two main problems in the state's planning assessment of the enterprises: too many norms, and norms centering on the value of total output. Using total output value as the primary norm for assessing the production activities of enterprises has created many problems. To meet planning assignments, enterprises are willing to produce only high-value commodities that consume a high proportion of energy and raw materials, without considering whether the commodity is socially needed. This approach leads to a dissociation of production and demand, a waste of raw materials and energy, and lower economic returns. Under such circumstances, the stronger the oversight and the stricter the assessment of how enterprises meet the plans, the more lopsided the enterprises' pursuit of output value at the expense of economic returns.

For example, an assessment norm of wages per hundred yuan of output value was applied in recent years to accelerate the rate of construction, reduce the idleness of funds, and increase the construction industry's economic returns. But this norm had just the opposite result: although the rate of construction did speed up, quality often declined while costs rose; economic returns thus actually declined.

The problem of "whipping the fast ox" is also associated with planning assessment. The annual plan targets sent down by the state to the enterprises often take as their base the planning assignments completed by the enterprise during the previous year. This raises the enterprise's planning assignments year after year. The better the enterprise fulfills its plans, the heavier its planning assignment will be next year. Since the fast ox gets the worst of it and the slow ox gets off lightly, the enterprises often hold back, making no effort to exploit their potential. And as year's end approaches, many enterprises deliberately slow down their operations. Censuring the enterprises for this behavior cannot resolve the problem. Only through correcting the approach of whipping the fast ox will it be possible to mobilize the enthusiasm of enterprises for autonomous operation and self-development.

A third problem is how to reform the assessment of planning. Sending down annual planning targets to assess enterprises has many drawbacks and few advantages. It often makes plans a mere formality, fails to promote full mobilization of the enterprise's enthusiasm and initiative, and leads to an emphasis on quantity at the expense of economic returns. State planning organs should now concentrate on drafting medium- and long-term plans, gradually shifting from assessing the everyday production activities of enterprises to forecasting economic development. The state should determine only the overall direction of these activities, while studying and solving the problem of comprehensive balance in the national economy.

Rationalizing Enterprise Behavior

Production, supply, and marketing relationships among enterprises have long been handled through consultations among agencies, regions, and enterprises. What are playfully called "fast-horse conventions" are frequently convened to solve some of the problems of interenterprise production through fierce price negotiating and bargaining. As society and the economy develop and there is an ever-greater division of labor in society, these relationships will become closer and more complex—and their proper handling will become more difficult. The fast-horse conventions will become larger and more frequent, but they will still not resolve many problems in interenterprise relationships or resolve them well. The main problems are that, for various reasons, contracts between enterprises are ineffective, supplies are regularly short, some product types have no market, and goods are not delivered on time.

The basic method of resolving horizontal relationships between enterprises is to use market mechanisms fully. The enterprises should be allowed to market their own products and to purchase the equipment and materials they need on the market. By allowing the market mechanism to take effect, the enterprise will be concerned more with its material interests. Given this internal motivation, the enterprise can develop production, increase product variety, and raise quality in accord with market demand. These developments will provide the basis for a satisfactory resolution of horizontal relationships between enterprises. Enterprises can follow the principle of voluntary mutual benefit in accord with market demand and in the framework of the macroeconomic development plans that the state sets. The signing of contracts will stabilize these mutual relationships, so that interenterprise activities conform to the laws of movement in a commodity economy and are on the same track as the national economy.

In the reform of the planning system, we must see to it that the state no longer sends down annual planning assignments to the enterprises. The enterprises must set their own annual plans according to the medium- and long-term plans promulgated by the state. Taking into consideration market demand, the enterprises must be able to formulate their own concrete quarterly, monthly, semimonthly, and daily plans. Their annual plans should be reported to the appropriate state agency only for recording, not for approval. To fulfill its planning assignments, the enterprise must establish a production responsibility system for the offices, shops, teams, groups, and even individuals at all levels. From the various sections of the plant offices down to each shop, from each group and team down to each staff member and worker, all must clearly understand their production responsibilities, and each must be given the authority needed to exercise that responsibility. Moreover, material benefits must be set, as long as production responsibilities are met. China's practical experience in economic reform shows that this sort of system—integrating responsibility, authority, and benefit—is highly effective in mobilizing the initiative and enthusiasm of the various production organizations, staff, and workers. It is also useful in improving the productive and operational activities of enterprises.

The planning system—including the sort of planning targets, the method to carry out assessments, and the sort of rewards and penalties—thus directly influences enterprise behavior. Although such factors as ideological and political education and the quality of the staff and workers affect enterprise behavior, the primary determinant of this behavior is the economic environment.

To see what basic enterprise behavior was like under China's original planning system, we need first to study enterprise behavior in relation to enterprise goals. In 1979, before the key test sites for reform of the economic system were chosen, the only goal of enterprises was to meet the planning assignments sent down by the state. But because of central control over income and expenditure, there was no relationship between plan fulfillment and an enterprise's material interests. If the enterprise fulfilled its planning assignments, it would be considered advanced, its leadership would have greater opportunities for promotion, and its staff and workers would enjoy the glorious reputation of being part of an advanced enterprise. Though spurring managers, such motivation did not have much effect in encouraging the plant's staff and workers to meet the plans.

In recent years, as the autonomy of some enterprises has been expanded, the state first implemented a profit-retention scheme and then a system of replacing profits with taxes. In this situation, how well an enterprise meets state planning assignments is directly related to how much profit it withholds or has left after taxes, and the amount of retained profit in turn directly influences how much the enterprise applies to its bonus fund and welfare fund. The struggle to retain more profit or have more left over after taxes, and thereby more bonus and welfare funds, has thus become a goal of the enterprise, and a motivation to fulfill enthusiastically the planning assignments sent down by the state.

Whether enterprises strive to fulfill plans for political glory or to retain more profits, they have developed the attitude that the lower the state plan targets sent down the better. And the more human, material, and financial resources distributed to them the better. But the state, starting from the demands of economic development, still thinks that the plan targets it sends should be higher and that the human, material, and financial resources it distributes to the enterprises should be lower. Thus, haggling regularly occurs between the state and the enterprises over how high the targets should be and how much human, material, and financial resources should be provided. Under these circumstances, the enterprise, to reduce the difficulty of meeting its assignments, often conceals its production potential, seeking more materials and funds from the state. This necessarily means that the information the enterprise provides to the state is to some extent false. And since the state cannot be completely familiar with the enterprise's situation (in addition to being unable to obtain truthful information from the enterprise, the concerned state organs are physically removed from the scene), the assignments sent down are usually dissociated from reality and sometimes degenerate into blind, subjective bureaucratic directives.

The various types of negative behavior generated by the constraints of these enterprise goals demonstrate that it is not worthwhile for the state directly to send down planning assignments. To mobilize the enterprises fully and at the same time to control socioeconomic activity more effectively, the original planning system must be changed.

Is it necessary to apply rewards and penalties to enterprises according to their fulfillment of plans? If so, by what means should these rewards and penalties be implemented, and what effect will they produce on enterprise behavior? Under the past system of planning assessment, whether the enterprise fulfilled its plans or how well it did so was unrelated to the enterprise's material interests. The enterprise thus had little or no motivation to improve its operations. But since planning assignments are now linked to how much profit enterprises could retain, enterprises have been exceeding state stipulations, even vying for production development funds and wildly issuing bonuses and material benefits—thus placing enterprise interests above national interests.

To counter this behavior, the state is using administrative directives to impose financial discipline and to control the enterprises' disbursement of wages and bonuses. But we cannot be content to control enterprise behavior merely through administrative measures, because such measures alone cannot solve the problem of rationalizing enterprise behavior. Whether the enterprises have little or no enthusiasm and initiative, or whether they forsake national interests, we shall ultimately redress the problems through the reform of the planning system, gradually guiding enterprises to patterns of rational behavior. We must synthesize the experience of economic reforms here and elsewhere—and study, design, and establish a planning system to renew economic mechanisms and control and to influence and change enterprise behavior. With enterprises placing themselves in the midst of this new planning system, they will be able to integrate their interests with the state's.

Finally, the urgency of reforming the planning system for China's state-operated industrial enterprises must be emphasized once again. China's economic development is moving from an extensive stage to an intensive stage. In the extensive stage of socialist economic development, a planning system is dissociated from the market, featuring a predominance of administrative measures and central authority. This situation is appropriate in a stage where relationships are relatively simple and an emphasis is placed on quantitative development. But the intensive stage of socialist economic development is incompatible with such a planning system. In this stage, the socioeconomic structure becomes more complex and economic relationships more intimate. The organization of socioeconomic activities requires that economic information be obtained more quickly, more completely, more systematically. At the same time, the intensive stage of development places more emphasis on improving the quality of production elements. Improved productivity requires greater exploitation of the initiative and enthusiasm of the enterprises and the laborers.

The planning system is a concrete form of production relationships. The type of system to be adopted is ultimately determined by the objective requirements of economic development. But in a certain stage and to a certain extent, people's subjective activity is useful. Given the same objective economic conditions, people can make different choices. We must strive to make the optimum choice to benefit economic development. At present, the reform of China's economic system is proceeding well. The party's Central Committee has set the overall path for the reform of the economic system. We—China's economic theoreticians—must closely synthesize the reality of economic reform, summarizing new experiences and studying new problems. Through debates on economic theory, we must promote rather than hinder the historical process of economic reform.

8

Planning and Supply

Gene Tidrick

China is a developing country onto which was grafted a Soviet-type central planning and material supply allocation system. Underdevelopment was bound to affect the extent to which the alien system took root. China's own traditions, along with thirty-five years of episodic change—including extensive reforms since 1979—have also imparted a unique character to the Chinese system.

Although China's planning and supply system is a recognizable variant of the Soviet model, it differs from that in other socialist countries in several ways. First, the scope of Chinese central planning is limited. Local rather than central authorities partly control the production of many key materials, which results in separate planning and allocation subsystems. Second, plans are often ill-defined, with slack or negotiable targets. Third, an increasing proportion of China's industrial output is allocated through the market rather than the plan. Enterprises are often allowed (or forced) to sell some of their output on the market. Although supplies are deliberately underallocated, output is not constrained, because they are readily available through a variety of market or quasi-market means. Fourth, multiple channels of supply give rise to multiple prices for the same product—one of the most unusual features of the Chinese system.

Main Features of the Chinese Planning System

Like the U.S.S.R., China has three categories of producer goods.[1] Category I goods have unified distribution and are subject to balancing by the State Planning Commission and to mandatory allocation through the State Material Supply Bureau. Category II goods are specialized products allocated by the central industrial ministries responsible for their production. These two categories, along with manufactured consumer goods allocated by the Ministry of Commerce, constitute the centrally planned industrial production. Category III goods include less important goods that are subject to allocation by local governments.

Scope of Central Planning

China allocates fewer goods centrally than the U.S.S.R. In 1981 there were 837 category I and II products,[2] compared with about 65,000 in the U.S.S.R. (of which about 50,000 were balanced and allocated by ministries).[3] Some of this difference is due to the broader categories the Chinese use. For example, steel, coal, timber, and cement were listed among the 210 products under unified distribution in 1979. Only steel products were further subdivided.[4] Soviet and Chinese planning may cover similar proportions of industrial output, but Soviet planning is nearly a hundred times more detailed and is correspondingly more comprehensive and complex.

The scope of Chinese central planning is even narrower than the above comparison implies, because not all goods in categories I and II are allocated by central planners or ministries. There are two other allocative channels: local planning and the market.

For historical reasons—mainly the strategy of "walking on two legs" and periodic attempts to attain regional self-sufficiency—locally controlled enterprises also produce goods in categories I and II. Because ownership or administrative control of an enterprise normally confers the right to allocate its output,[5] local governments in 1980 allocated the following shares of category I products: coal, 46 percent; steel, 42 percent; nonferrous metals, 36 percent; lumber, 18 percent; and cement, 71 percent (Li 1982, cited in Koziara and Yan 1983, p. 699). China thus deviates markedly from the ideal central planning model, in which all production in categories I and II is under central control and output would be allocated in blocks to local governments for distribution to their category III producers. In the ideal model, production responsibility and material allocation are hierarchical. In China, there is a contrasting cellular model (Donnithorne 1972) of separate, almost self-contained industrial systems at several levels. In this cellular model, centrally planned enterprises supply other centrally planned enterprises, provincial enterprises supply all goods to other provincial enterprises, and municipal and other enterprises do the same. The Chinese system is an amalgam of hierarchical planning, cellular planning, and markets.

Both the hierarchical and cellular models have a built-in tendency toward autarky. In the hierarchical system, ministries strive for self-sufficiency; in the cellular system, each geographical planning unit tries to be self-contained. Ministerial self-sufficiency, or departmentalism, is a feature of most socialist economies, but regionalism to this degree appears to be a distinctively Chinese phenomenon.[6]

Increasing use of the market has also narrowed the scope of central planning in China. The number of centrally allocated products peaked around 1980 at 837. Before then, the number of products expanded and contracted with cycles of centralization and decentralization, but contractions were due to administrative decentralization of planning to lower levels of government.[7] Beginning with the period of adjustment and reform, many products subject to central allocation were allocated through market sales by enterprises (self-marketing). Most machinery products (157 of category I goods and 200 of category II goods in 1979) were allocated largely through self-marketing by 1980.[8] Almost all the enterprises in our sample engaged in some self-marketing during 1980–82 (see table 10-2). This was a consequence of adjustment rather than reform. Although self-marketing was consistent with the reformers' emphasis on greater autonomy and market use, the reduction in central allocation was a practical response to excess supply after adjustment policies slowed the growth of heavy industry and expanded investment in light industry. Market transactions existed before the reform period as well. Many links between the different self-contained systems were market or quasi-market transactions rather than planned allocation. For example, provinces traded products, and centrally planned enterprises bought coal from locally controlled mines. The extent of market allocation has expanded significantly in recent years, however, changing an already complicated planning and supply system.

An unusual feature of China's allocation system is multiple prices for the same product. The State Price Bureau sets the price of centrally planned production, whereas a local price bureau normally controls locally allocated output. Prices are usually set to cover the production cost of most plants, but since many small plants have high production costs, the price of locally controlled output is higher. For example, the centrally controlled price of cement is Y47 per ton, whereas the price of lower-quality cement from locally controlled enterprises is as much as Y92. Self-marketing by state enterprises is supposed to take place at controlled prices, but there have been numerous complaints of added service charges. (Small collectives have been freer to sell some output at negotiated prices.) In May 1984 a State Council decision authorized state enterprises to charge a floating price within 20 percent of the controlled price for self-marketing. Thus, each of the three main channels of supply (central allocation, local allocation, and market) can set a different price for the same item. In practice, pricing is even more complex (see the section below, "Mechanisms for Obtaining Above-Quota Supplies").

Enterprise Targets

In its ideal form the Chinese planning cycle is a "two-up, two-down" process that delivers a final binding plan before the beginning of the plan year. In practice, often just the final plan is handed down, after long informal bargaining. In 1982, of nine of the sample enterprises, only two received the final output plan in the planned year's first quarter, two received it in the second, two in the third, and three in the fourth. Allocations of material supply are badly coordinated. Initial supply allocations are given in October or November of the year before the plan period, before any initial production targets have come down. Enterprises frequently complain that the variety and total allocation of supplies bear little relation to production targets. Although a second adjustment conference for supply allocations is held in May, this is only a partial corrective, especially for enterprises receiving final output plans later.

The number of plan targets handed down has been reduced. Before the reform, enterprises frequently had lists of eight or ten binding targets. But in cases of conflict, the gross value of industrial output and the physical output targets were the most important. Most enterprises now receive four types of target: gross value of industrial output, physical output of main varieties, quality, and profits. Targets for exports, cost reduction, or financial targets, such as the amount of circulating capital, sometimes supplement them. A few enterprises still have long lists of targets,[9] but most claim to have fewer targets than before reform.

Variety targets are given for only a few major products or broad categories. The Chongqing Clock and Watch Company receives targets only for clocks and watches, not individual grades or styles. For the Anshan Iron and Steel Corporation, the procedure is more elaborate. Anshan receives targets for fourteen categories of rolled steel in its production plan. These categories are further disaggregated into 300 to 400 targets given through a sales-resource plan. From an engineering point of view, however, there are as many as 60,000 varieties and specifications of rolled steel. It is left to individual contracts, signed between Anshan and buyers at an ordering conference, to specify the exact product. For other enterprises, contracts serve the same purpose. Contracts are supposed to be enforceable by law, and enterprises are required to fulfill all contracts within the plan to be eligible for bonuses. The extent to which variety targets and contracts determine product mix is discussed in a later section.

The introduction of self-marketing reduced the importance of variety targets. Many enterprises facing a buyers' market now plan in accord with sales. One spokesman for a textile mill summed up the difference as follows: "Before 1980, the mill's production capacity was the basis of sales plans. Since then, market demand has been decisive in making production plans." The effect on the formal planning system, however, is barely perceptible. For some enterprises that plan in accord with sales, mandatory targets for variety are no longer given (the Qingdao Forging Machinery Plant, for example). But most enterprises still receive variety targets, and all twenty of our sample enterprises still receive targets for gross value of industrial output and for profit. Variety targets ostensibly provide a basis for supply allocations. In view of the lack of coordination in timing between supply and production planning and the supply gaps discussed below, however, it is difficult to see what real purpose variety targets have for enterprises that plan in accord with sales. When production decisions are driven by demand, variety targets are an anomaly.

Self-marketing has also given rise to a distinction between mandatory and guidance plans. "Guidance planning" was initially another term for planning in accord with sales. Most enterprises now have both mandatory and guidance plans, however, including enterprises that face sellers' markets (such as Anshan and the No. 2 Automobile Plant). The only enterprises in our sample still totally subject to mandatory planning are the North China Petroleum Administration and the Chengdu Locomotive and Rolling Stock Factory.

Guidance plans appear to mean different things to different enterprises. To the Sanchazi Forestry Bureau, for example, the guidance plan is said to be for minor products that have no variety targets but are included in the target for gross value. To most enterprises, however, the guidance plan covers the portion of output for which the enterprise must arrange both supply and sales. It is, in effect, the enterprise's own plan. Whether a guidance plan is a benefit or a burden, therefore, depends on market conditions for inputs and outputs. In 1984, for example, the No. 2 Automobile Plant was allowed to self-market output in excess of its mandatory plan at a floating price. No. 2 Auto also had to arrange its own material supply, including scarce rolled steel, for self-marketed output (30 percent of total output). Trucks are in such short supply, however, that the plant was able to obtain rolled steel from customers, many of whom represent provinces with their own supplies of steel. No. 2 Auto sought to reduce its mandatory output quotas, whereas the Material Supply Bureau has tried to increase it. At the opposite extreme, the Jiangmen Nanfang Foodstuff Factory faces a buyers' market for its candy products, but its raw material, sugar, is scarce. Sugar is supplied at a low price for the portion of candy output allocated by the mandatory plan and at a higher negotiated price for the portion that is self-marketed or allocated by the guidance plan. The factory therefore wishes to expand its mandatory plan while the supply and marketing company tries to reduce it.

A new incentive system, based on retained profits and bonus payments, has had major implications for the significance of plan targets. Details of the schemes, as well as profit retention or tax rates, vary for each enterprise, but a common feature is a proportion of retained profits that can be used for bonuses. The right to pay bonuses has usually been linked to fulfillment of plan targets. Failure to reach target lowers the average allowable bonus by a specified percentage. The importance of the plan is greatly increased by giving workers and managers a direct material stake in fulfilling plan targets.

In practice, however, bargaining has weakened the link between plan fulfillment and bonus payments. Internal management reforms have also stressed the link between plan and bonus. One of these reforms, introduced by Capital Iron and Steel and widely copied, has been to link bonuses to plan targets disaggregated to the plant, workshop, group, or even the individual.[10]

The new incentive system reinforces the importance of profits and profit targets. The right to pay the full bonus depends on reaching the threshold of 100-percent plan fulfillment for output value, variety, quality, or cost targets. Enterprises do not benefit from overfulfillment, but every increase in profits increases the bonus fund, as well as the welfare and production development funds. In some schemes, there has also been a higher retention rate (or lower tax rate) for above-plan profits. Thus the new system created an incentive to maximize profits and to overfulfill the profit target rather than simply to reach a threshold.

Multiple Leadership

Many state-owned industrial enterprises are under dual or multiple leadership of agencies at different levels of government. Several key enterprises were put under local control during cycles of decentralization, then they were partly restored to central or provincial control when local governments could not guarantee supplies or arrange marketing. Under the Ministry of Metallurgy and Liaoning Province since 1969, Anshan Iron and Steel, the country's largest steel plant, exemplifies the dual leadership. Because Anshan is nationally important, its production targets are set by the State Planning Commission, and its main materials and sales are handled by the ministry. Yet its financial targets come from Anshan Municipality, based on block profit targets handed down from the Ministry of Finance to the province, to the city, and to Anshan.

Some enterprises have multiple leadership that is even more complicated. For example, until it was recentralized in late 1983, Shenyang Smelting Plant was under the Ministry of Metallurgy for raw materials and distribution of output, the province for electricity and other subsidiary materials; and the municipality for labor and finance. Financial targets came from the Municipal Metallurgy Bureau, and output targets came from both the Ministry and the municipal bureau. Qingdao Forging Machinery Plant has an equally complicated three-layered leadership (Chen and others, 1984). No wonder Chinese enterprises regularly complain of too many mothers-in-law.

These tangled lines of responsibility have led to several problems, the most serious being an inconsistency between plan targets. Almost all enterprises face some inconsistency between targets for output and for profit, even if they are nominally under unified leadership, because the two sets of targets originate in different ministerial hierarchies. Output targets come from the industrial ministry, profit targets from the Ministry of Finance.[11] Output targets are based on material balances, or even on individual enterprise sales projections; profit targets are disaggregated from block profit targets handed down from level to level. There is little coordination between the two sets of plans. For example, when the prices of Nanning Silk and Linen Textile Mill's products were cut in 1982, there was no change in the profit target. Most enterprises faced a similar problem in the readjustment period, when demand (output or prices) fell but profit targets kept rising.

Inconsistencies between targets are worse, however, for enterprises under multiple leadership. Lower levels of government have considerable autonomy, and no single economic commission has the authority to resolve conflicts between levels. Moreover, some large enterprises dwarf the low-level government units that supposedly share responsibility for their supervision. This means that the local government is dependent on the enterprise for meeting block targets handed down from higher levels. It also means that the local government regards the enterprise as a resource to be tapped rather than as a subordinate to be managed.

This exploitative attitude leads lower-level governments to assign additional production targets to enterprises, even though output targets are supposedly the responsibility of the industrial ministry. In 1984, for example, the Provincial Building Materials Bureau raised the output target of the Xiangxiang Cement Plant from the 890,000 tons set by the State Building Materials Administration to 1 million tons. It also required the allocation of 30,000 tons of the added production to Hunan Province. For Shenyang Smelting, the Municipal Metallurgy Bureau often set electrolytic copper output targets more than twice as high as those given by the ministry. Moreover, the bureau did not provide material supply allocations for the additional production targets, and it set a profit target that in 1983 was 30 percent higher than its own inflated output target.[12]

Multiple leadership also complicates supply allocations, which may be as inconsistent as plan targets. Shenyang Smelting was victimized by all its superior organizations. Local authorities diverted Shenyang's allocations; central authorities may have withheld ore supplies; and after recentralization in 1983, municipal authorities balked over the supply of construction materials.

Despite these problems, the elimination of multiple leadership is not a panacea. Although Shenyang Smelting faced less conflict between plan targets after being subordinated to a national nonferrous metals corporation, the municipality would no longer overlook its severe pollution once the plant was out from under municipal control. Other enterprises under higher level control also find that local governments can make life difficult. Some local governments extort materials or output from large enterprises outside their control.[13] One central government official even suggested that because localities always allocate such important inputs as electricity and food for workers, shared control over large enterprises might be desirable. Otherwise, the local authority would not have "the enthusiasm to provide what the enterprises need." This view may be too fatalistic. It should be possible to mitigate local obstructionism by giving local governments a limited financial stake without giving them control over the enterprises in their locales. As long as the present system of planning and allocation exists, however, enterprises may be caught in disputes between different levels of government over allocation of inputs or output.

Tautness and Firmness

The inconsistency of plan targets creates a problem for Chinese enterprises, especially since the incentive system links bonus payments to fulfillment of all major plan targets. How do enterprises decide which conflicting target to give priority to?

For most enterprises, this is an academic question, because plans are not taut.[14] Unlike the U.S.S.R., where plan targets are ambitious and input coefficients often reduced to achieve overall material balance, Chinese output targets are generally set below production capacity. Chinese enterprises have considerable room for maneuver. Although Chinese production targets may be taut with respect to material allocations, the supply channels outside the central plan usually enable enterprises to obtain enough supplies to meet their targets. With slack plans, enterprises are rarely forced to choose between targets—they simply fulfill the highest one. If plans are insufficiently slack to do this, plan revisions become a second line of defense. In brief, Chinese plans are neither taut nor firm.[15]

The consistent overfulfillment of plans suggests that the "ratchet effect" (of overfulfillment leading to a higher quota next year) does not operate in China. Enterprises such as the Qinghe Woolen Textile Mill in Beijing have accused their superiors of "whipping the fast ox" and claim that they must "hold back a trick or two." But it is difficult to take this at face value because the mill overfulfilled output targets for its two main products by an average of 10 percent in each year from 1979 to 1982.

A ratchet effect does appear to operate for two exceptional sample enterprises, the Shanghai High-Pressure Oil Pump Plant and the Shanghai No. 17 Cotton Mill. Both claimed that their superior organizations did not want overfulfillment, a claim substantiated by plan fulfillment in 1982 (but not before then) within 0.5 percent of all targets for which data are given. To prevent targets from being raised the following year, production is restricted near the end of the year. This pattern appears to be a recent development, limited to Shanghai.

Although planning authorities generally refrain from jacking up targets to remove slack from the plan, some new incentive schemes induce a ratchet effect. The Jiangmen Foodstuff Factory was put under a "chain comparison," which permitted wage increases for 30 percent of its workers each year if it surpassed the previous year's profit level. As soon as the factory earned more profits than in the previous year, it would slacken its efforts. The Xiangxiang Cement Plant has a similar system. If profits handed over to the state increase, bonuses may increase by 13 percent of the above-quota portion. If profits handed over decrease, the bonus is cut proportionately. This system creates a perverse incentive to reduce profits to create an easy base for future increases. Xiangxiang has spurned this approach, in part because it would lose "its honored place as an advanced unit."

The other reason that inconsistent plan targets create few problems for enterprises is the frequency and ease of plan revision. Plan targets are the subject of protracted negotiations, but enterprises know that in the end they can always change unreasonable targets. Such targets have been changed even in the last week of December. Sometimes, they have been eliminated altogether.[16]

Bargaining over plan targets is not completely one-sided. Targets are sometimes raised. No. 2 Auto was given a 10 percent increase in its truck target in the third quarter of 1982, and a similar increase in the second quarter of 1983. Targets may also be raised in the last few days of the year, usually to offset a shortfall by another enterprise. In such a case, the enterprise understands that it is doing its superior organization a favor to be reciprocated in the future. Higher authorities have limited flexibility because of their own targets. The Nanning Finance Bureau, for example, was willing to slash the profit target for the Nanning Textile Mill to Y3.0 million in 1983 (compared with realized profits of Y13.5 million in 1981) when the mill faced severe marketing problems. But the bureau was unwilling to lower the target to Y1.6 million as suggested by the mill. Consequently, the mill was forced to introduce new products and undertake strenuous sales efforts to meet the Y3.0 million target. Failure to have met the target would have meant ineligibility for a wage increase.

Thus there is enough uncertainty about the target revision to force firms to make a good faith effort to reach targets. But as far as we could determine, no firm in our sample ever had its bonus reduced for failing to meet a plan target, even when the plan target was not revised and the enterprise failed to meet it. The Mindong Electrical Machinery Corporation failed to meet its cost target in 1982, but no bonus deduction was levied because the failure was due to outside conditions. This does not mean that no enterprise in China has ever had its bonus deducted for failing to meet a plan target, but neither is this simply an artifact of our sample of advanced enterprises. Mindong's leading authority, the Fujian Machinery Bureau, noted that "for the nine enterprises previously under our direct jurisdiction, objective conditions are taken into account in setting their plan targets, so targets are generally achieved." The bureau could not recall an example of failure to meet a target which was the fault of any subordinate enterprise rather than due to factors beyond its control.

A minimum level of bonus payments has been virtually incorporated into the basic wage. The standard varies by enterprise and region, but it is equivalent to at least two months of basic wages. There is considerable resistance to any lowering of a previously attained bonus level. The notion is spreading that the regular bonus should be guaranteed and that fulfilling a particularly difficult target deserves a superbonus.

The link between profits and bonuses is only somewhat stronger than that between plan fulfillment and bonuses. Some enterprises have multiyear profit-retention rates that automatically link retained profits and bonuses to overall profitability. For most enterprises, the profit-retention rate is negotiable each year, as is the new adjustment tax rate. When profits fall, retention rates are usually adjusted to protect bonuses and collective welfare payments. When profits rise, enterprises generally share in the windfall.[17]

In summary, despite the formal links with bonuses, plan targets have little effect on enterprise incentives because plans are neither taut nor firm. Profits have a slight effect because increased profits usually mean higher retained profits and higher bonuses and welfare payments—up to a maximum limit. Still, the incentive is asymmetrical. Except for a few schemes in which the retention rate is not negotiable, retained profits will be partially shielded from falling profits. The result is that bonus and welfare payments determine profit retention and plan targets, not the reverse.

Main Features of the Chinese Supply System

China's supply system has several features which distinguish it from that in other countries: allocation through three channels, the deliberate underallocation of supplies, a relative absence of supply constraints, and numerous mechanisms for obtaining more than the quota of supplies.

Multichannel Allocation

The interaction of three distinct supply channels—central allocation, local allocation, and market (including quasi-market)—has several important consequences. Each level of authority (central, provincial, municipal) and each ministry or bureau strives to reduce dependence on other authorities as much as possible. This leads to compartmentalized allocations of materials. Enterprises under the control of a central ministry, for example, are supplied as far as possible by other enterprises under that ministry, and enterprises under a province are linked with other provincially controlled enterprises. Because no system can ever be completely self-contained, enterprises are partly dependent on supplies produced outside the control of their authority.[18] At the same time, the diversity of supply channels also creates opportunities that do not exist in a more conventional planning system.

An extreme example of the problems of coordinating supply allocations from multiple planning authorities is the case of six Nanjing enterprises, including an oil refinery, a large nitrogen fertilizer plant, three petrochemical plants, and a plastics factory. These plants, some of them key national producers, were all within seven kilometers of each other and were closely linked in supply use and allocation (nineteen pipelines linked the plants). But they were under the jurisdiction of three levels of government (national, Jiangsu Province, and Nanjing Municipality) and three ministries (petroleum, chemicals, and light industry).

The problems that administrative barriers created were manifold. Administrators reported disputes over scheduling and quotas that led to reduced outputs. By-products that could have been used by other plants were wasted. One chemical plant had to buy part of its liquid chlorine from Shanghai while another plant half a kilometer away sold chlorine to Anhui Province. Some plants undertook the synthesis of raw materials that they could have obtained in better quality from nearby plants. Moreover, the duplication (and consequent underuse) of support and transportation facilities was widespread. The situation was well summed up by the remark of one plant official, "Pipelines link the plants, but the valve switch is controlled in Beijing."

The solution was a merger of the six plants in 1982 into the Jinling Petrochemical General Corporation. Jinling was originally placed under provincial leadership, and later, in July 1983, it was put under the new National Petrochemical Corporation. The merger solved some of the most blatant problems of coordination and led to growth of profit and output of 8 to 9 percent in each of the first two years. It did not solve all supply problems, however. Because individual plants were still independent accounting units, none was willing to give up its support or transportation facilities. Disputes over prices of some materials continued.

Now that Nanjing Municipality is no longer the leading authority (and recipient of profit remittances) of some plants, material supply allocations from the city have been reduced. Informal barter links with local enterprises have become more difficult. Similarly, now that Jinling is controlled by the national corporation, chemical supplies to the province have been reduced. Although it represents an improvement over the fragmented planning and supply system, the merger illustrates the limits of administrative reorganization in solving these problems.

Another side to the complex administrative system, one that illustrates its flexibility, is the case of the No. 2 Automobile Plant. No. 2 Auto originally was provincially controlled and was obliged to obtain all its components—such as glass, tires, and bearings—from enterprises in its home province, Hubei. Many of the supply operations were set up to supply No. 2 Auto. In

1981, however, the plant was placed under the control of a national ministry (the Ministry of Machine Building) and was allowed to engage in joint ventures and loose associations with other automobile plants and component suppliers under the Dongfeng Automobile Corporation. These relationships allowed it to obtain up to 30 percent of its components from out-of-province suppliers.

No. 2 Auto still obtains 70 to 80 percent of its components from eighteen nearby plants set up to supply it. But now it has diversified its sources of supply to more than one hundred other factories in nineteen provinces. Originally, the eighteen designated suppliers charged prices above the state price on the ground that they were producing trial products. Competition with other sources, however, led them to reduce their prices and to improve quality. No. 2 Auto still has occasional problems with component supply. It must compensate occasionally for provincial underallocations to its local suppliers by arranging their supplies itself. But generally the enterprise has little difficulty in obtaining components from its diverse sources. Two points about No. 2 Auto's situation should be noted. First, unlike the administratively imposed merger of Jinling, the associations under Dongfeng are voluntary. Second, unlike raw materials for petrochemicals, which remained in short supply, components for vehicles often moved into excess supply.

Part of the success of No. 2 Auto is also due, no doubt, to its national importance. The national ministerial planning authority facilitates supply, even when it is arranged locally by the plant. But other enterprises have diversified their supply sources as well, although usually outside their plan allocations. Thus, for many enterprises, the benefits of obtaining supplies outside the plan have more than offset the burdens of contending with multiple levels of administrative authority.

Underallocations of Supply

In the ideal central-planning model, the allocation of material supplies is just enough to meet output targets, and all output is allocated through the plan: allocated supply = output target = allocated output. In China, this equation does not hold. With the introduction of self-marketing, enterprises may be given production targets with no guarantee that their output will be allocated through the plan. And materials supplied through plan allocations may fall far short. Underallocation occurs in the U.S.S.R. and Eastern Europe but usually as a result of taut planning and deficiencies in material balancing. The extent and pervasiveness of underallocation in China is far greater than in the U.S.S.R.—it is deliberate.

Underallocation to enterprises in the sample is substantial. Supplies obtained outside plan allocations are often more than 50 percent for inputs like coal. In one extreme case, the Sanchazi Forestry Bureau stated that "the amounts of nationally allocated materials included in 1983 and 1984 were, respectively, 50 percent and 54 percent of our annual consumption, but the amounts the Bureau of Forestry received were only 85 percent of the 50 percent figure and 63 percent of the 54 percent figure." In other words, Sanchazi obtained about two-thirds of all its category I and II inputs outside the plan in 1984.

The Qingdao Forging Machinery Plant claims that underallocation of inputs was significant before 1978, and there are other references to underallocation in the prereform literature. But most enterprises in our sample link the beginning of underallocation to the change in market conditions after 1978. The Mindong Electrical Machinery Plant, for example, stated that from 1979 to mid-1982 enterprises had to market their own output and purchase supplies on the market. After mid-1982 "many products were brought under unified distribution and we began to have problems with supplies." The reduction in allocation of material supplies through the plan is thus closely linked to market conditions. As a spokesman for Jinling put it, the authorities in charge of allocation "tighten control when there is a shortage and relax control when there is a surplus."

The gap between total needs and supplies obtained through the plan is not due entirely to deliberate underallocation. Part of the shortfall is due to the poorly synchronized planning cycle, in which supplies are allocated before production plans are given. Many enterprises complain that making blind supply applications is tricky if the product mix turns out differently. The process leads to both overstocking and gaps, which are partially remedied by trading with other enterprises. Because enterprises treat supplies obtained through barter as "outside the plan," the net underallocation for all enterprises is less than the gross underallocation reported by any single enterprise. Enterprises often have problems obtaining the variety of inputs needed and are forced to go outside the plan to obtain the correct variety or else make do with what they are given. Trading with other enterprises only partly remedies the problem, however, because the correct variety may be in short supply. Thus, the North China Petroleum Administration had stocks of unwanted materials equivalent to 15 percent of total stocks but was forced to obtain needed varieties through purchase at negotiated prices.

Enterprises may also have to go outside the plan to obtain the right quality. The No. 2 Automobile Plant obtains half its pig iron outside the plan, even though it is allocated a full 100 percent. The quality of half its allocation is simply unacceptable. Similarly, the Baoji Nitrogen Fertilizer Plant can use only 60 percent of the coal allocation it receives. Moreover, Baoji receives only 70 percent of what it is allocated, so that it is forced to purchase more than half its coal at high cost. Failure of designated suppliers to deliver on time, or at all, is another reason enterprises go outside the plan.

Finally, enterprises go outside the plan to obtain supplies for above-plan or guidance-plan production, or when they establish collective enterprises to employ their workers' dependents. Especially in the northeast, where collective employment is large, enterprises need materials for these subordinate firms. Collectives account for 10 to 15 percent of the category I and II supply needs of the Sanchazi Forestry Bureau. Anshan used about 4 percent of its self-marketed output (0.4 percent of total output) in 1983 to supply collectives employing 160,000 dependents of workers. This probably understates their importance, however, because Anshan also supplies them with scrap steel.

A substantial part of the shortfall in allocated supplies, however, is due to deliberate underallocation. For some enterprises (such as the Jiangmen Foodstuff Factory) the underallocation corresponds to its self-marketed, guidance-plan output. For others, there is underallocation even for mandatory output targets. The North China Petroleum Administration, totally subject to mandatory planning, receives insufficient allocation of supplies, including, ironically, diesel fuel and gasoline.

The Fujian Machinery Bureau acknowledged that it underallocated supplies to Mindong. It provides even less steel to a bearing plant because that plant can obtain extra steel in exchange for bearings. Underallocation bears little discernible relationship to the importance of the enterprise. Anshan receives only 70 percent of the steel scrap and ferro alloys needed to meet mandatory plan targets. No. 2 Auto received only 70 percent of its steel and 40 percent of its tin through the plan in 1982, compared with self-marketed output of 10 percent. Only two patterns are apparent. First, textile mills and Shanghai enterprises are not subject to deliberate underallocations of main raw materials. Second, underallocation is usually greater for the investment plan than for the production plan.

Supply Constraints

Obtaining some material supplies outside the plan does not necessarily mean that the plan supply is secondary. A shortage of any essential nonsubstitutable input will hurt production. If critical inputs are not available outside the plan, or are available only in limited quantities, planned allocations will be the determinant of resource allocation. One way to test the importance of supply and planning is to analyze what limits production and what determines product mix. In a market economy, production is limited by demand, and product mix is determined by profitability and demand. In the short run, production may be limited by capacity, but investment will quickly expand capacity so that production is again limited by demand and profitability. In a fully planned economy, production is limited by capacity or by supply of material inputs. Product mix is similarly limited by plan targets and supply allocations. To what extent does supply constrain production or determine product mix in China today?

Table 8-1. *Constraints on the Production of the Twenty Sample Enterprises*

Constraint and enterprise	*Secondary constraint and comments*
Demand	
Mindong Electrical Machinery	Leading authority also limits production through plan
Qingdao Forging Machinery	
Shanghai Oil Pump	
Chongqing Clock and Watch	Short-term supply constraint for main raw material (ramie) because of demand shift.
Jiangmen Foodstuff	
Nanning Textile	Minor electricity shortages
Northwest Cotton	
Qinghe Woolen Textile	Exports constrained by shortage of imported wool. Minor electricity shortages
Shanghai Cotton	Leading authority also limits production through plan
Tianjin Textile	
Capacity	
North China Petroleum	Raw material reserves also constrain
Sanchazi Forestry	Raw material reserves also constrain
Anshan Iron and Steel	
Baoji Nitrogen Fertilizer	
Jinling Petrochemical	
Xiangxiang Cement	Minor electricity shortages
No. 2 Automobile	
Chengdu Locomotive	Minor electricity shortages
Supply	
Shenyang Smelting	Shortage of copper blister and scrap for unrefined copper smelting and of electricity for zinc smelting. Other products capacity-constrained
Qingyuan County Economic Commission	Electricity shortage since mid-1983

Constraints on output. For the most part, plan targets and the allocation of supplies do not constrain Chinese industrial output in the sample enterprises. The main constraints are demand and capacity (see table 8-1). Of course, production capacity to some extent limits output, and supply allocations control investment—determining output in the long run. But as Byrd and Tidrick argue in chapter 4, central control over capital allocation is also limited. Our sample may be unrepresentative, however, since it contains mostly model enterprises.

The supply of electricity is a special case because it is almost entirely allocated, cannot be stored or traded, and is seldom self-generated. Electricity shortages are said to be responsible for the loss of as much as 20 percent of the gross value of China's industrial output. In the sample, two enterprises have been seriously affected by electricity shortages. Since late 1983, the seventeen small-scale enterprises under Qingyuan County restricted work to five days a week because of power cuts. Shenyang Smelting has been forced to operate at 80 to 90 percent of capacity because too little electricity was allocated.

Several other enterprises faced occasional power cuts, but they rearranged production so as not to reduce annual output. The Qingdao Forging Machinery Plant, for example, uses its foundry only at night. Anshan sometimes has to shut down ancillary operations or limit electricity to collective enterprises to keep its central steel-making facilities operating continuously. The Qinghe Textile Mill had to protest repeatedly to schedule its three or four monthly power cuts at times when they would be less disruptive. And Shenyang Smelting employs two people full time to cajole the provincial economic commission and power authorities into keeping the electricity flowing.

There is little doubt that our sample of enterprises (other than Qingyuan) are favored in the allocation of electricity. Anshan recently received permission, after appealing to the premier, to take over and expand a municipal power plant. Both Shenyang Smelting and the Nanning Textile Mill have received allocations, whereas those of electricity-intensive aluminum smelting plants were cut.[19] If they had not been favored, our enterprises probably would have faced greater electricity constraints.

Supplies of raw materials generally were not a constraint. The Nanning Textile Mill was one exception when ramie was in short supply due to the shift in world demand for ramie products and the short-term inelasticity of raw ramie supply. The major exception to adequate raw material supplies is Shenyang Smelting. Shenyang manages to obtain enough copper ore to utilize fully its capacity for converting ore into copper, but its additional capacity for smelting copper blister or scrap is not always utilized. The reasons are instructive. Shenyang receives an allocation of imported copper blister but generally not enough. It has no foreign exchange of its own, and it cannot obtain domestic copper scrap, which is sold almost entirely on a free market. Small-scale refiners whose output price is not controlled bid up the price of scrap to nearly the price of above-quota refined copper (20 percent above the state price). Shenyang cannot compete for this scrap because it would take losses even if the refined copper could be sold at the maximum allowable premium of 20 percent. Moreover, Shenyang is prohibited from producing more profitable downstream copper products, such as cable and alloys, because the State Material Supply Bureau allocates its supply of pure metals and because user ministries control the production of most alloys. Thus, Shenyang cannot obtain inputs outside the plan because its output price is controlled, and its products are subject to plan allocation. In this case, the market for an input works against the enterprise and creates a supply constraint.

Product mix. Product mix can be determined by supply constraints, plan (variety) targets, profitability, or marketability of products. Left to their own devices, managers of Chinese enterprises will normally try to produce the most profitable products, assuming they are marketable, or those that are marketable when higher-profit products are difficult to sell. But supply allocations or variety targets sometimes frustrate managers' intentions. Many textile mills delayed efforts to shift their product mix in early 1983 when the controlled prices of cotton textiles were raised and those of synthetic textiles were lowered. Short-term difficulty in rearranging supplies was expected, but most authorities threw the burden of adjustment onto enterprises. Some authorities even imposed rigid planning procedures to obstruct adjustment.

For example, the Northwest No. 1 Cotton Mill wanted to reduce its output of cotton textiles and shift toward the faster selling synthetics and blends. But it was instructed to continue to produce the types of cotton in its plans, even though such types were unpopular. At the same time, the Commercial Department canceled orders for cotton textiles, and the mill was forced to market the slow-moving varieties itself. To do so, the mill contracted for printing and dyeing with a plant outside Shaanxi Province, but Shaanxi provincial authorities then insisted that the mill do all printing and dyeing in Shaanxi. Northwest Cotton has been refused permission to invest in its own finishing facilities owing to an excess of finishing capacity in Shaanxi.[20] This restriction reduced sales and profits because of low-quality finishing by local producers. Finally, the provincial authority opposed the mill's attempts to obtain more chemical fibers. Chemical fiber plants were willing to supply the mill, but higher authorities would not approve requests before delivery and would demand a "fair share" of any unauthorized deliveries. In brief, Northwest Cotton faced an inflexible planning system designed to maximize provincial textile output. By 1984 the planning system adjusted to shifts in market demand by changing product-mix targets and supply allocations, but the suboptimal and self-defeating policy of provincial autarky remained in place.

Plan targets sometimes restrict product mix independently of supply allocations. Profit rates on steel vary widely, yet Anshan Iron and Steel is constrained by contracts based on its sales-resources plan targets for both low- and high-profit varieties. Above-plan production, however, is limited almost entirely to high-profit varieties. The Qinghe Woolen Textile Mill was also forced to forgo profitable production for the domestic market in 1983 in order to meet export plan targets.

These cases illustrate a key point about the relationship between variety targets and market conditions. In a sellers' market, such as that for steel or woolen textiles in 1983, variety targets will be necessary to ensure the needed product mix unless prices can be set to equalize profits for different products. But in a buyers' market, variety targets may lead to the production of unwanted goods.

In a sellers' market the lack of detailed variety targets often leads to quality improvements that may not serve national economic interests. Shenyang Smelting is given a target for production of first- or second-grade zinc. Because first-grade zinc is more profitable and zinc is scarce, Shenyang can insist that customers accept first-grade zinc. Similarly, Xiangxiang Cement gradually upgraded the average quality of its output. Production of the most profitable types of cement has grown almost fivefold, whereas low-grade (and low-profit) varieties are no longer produced.

In a buyers' market, variety targets are either redundant or pernicious. Without targets, enterprises will adjust production to demand and normally will make strenuous efforts to expand sales through new product development and other means. The Chongqing Clock and Watch Company developed new products, shifted its product mix toward the lower-grade watches desired by consumers, and surreptitiously raised the quality (and lowered the price) of other watches (see Byrd and Tidrick 1984, pp. 52–55). For the most part, planning authorities have recognized the need to eliminate variety targets when buyers' markets have emerged. Equally important, they have begun to recognize the importance of using price reform as a substitute for variety targets.

In a buyers' market, freely negotiated flexible or floating prices will balance supply and demand and give appropriate incentives for production and investment decisions. In a sellers' market, floating prices do not eliminate the need for variety targets unless prices can rise high enough to eliminate excess demand. The 20 percent band of floating prices introduced in 1984, for example, did not change Anshan Iron and Steel's above-plan decisions for its product mix because all above-plan steel prices rose 20 percent, thus leaving relative profitability unchanged. In a sellers' market, relative administered prices have to be changed so that the rate of profit on each product is equalized before variety targets can be removed.[21] In practice, however, the calculation is likely to be beyond the capacity of central planners. It is better to work toward elimination of the sellers' market.

Mechanisms for Obtaining Above-Quota Supplies

China has made several innovations to the centrally planned allocation of supplies. One of the best known, the conference for ordering materials, was introduced in the 1960s to balance within-quota allocations and disaggregate quotas and output targets. These conferences helped create a basis for widespread marketlike developments because they provided the framework for trading and direct contact. China has also introduced trade fairs, self-marketing, and materials-adjustment conferences (to exchange surplus materials), which facilitate the flow of supplies outside the plan.[22]

Market purchases. Perhaps the most common way to obtain above-quota supplies is to purchase them from the self-marketed output of state enterprises or collectives. This method is common for the three main construction materials (steel, timber, and cement) and for coal. But not all materials can be obtained in this way, and one major disadvantage of purchasing on the market is that market prices are often higher than the allocated prices.[23] Qingdao Forging Machinery estimated that purchases of materials at negotiated prices cost an additional Y400,000 in 1982; this was less than 3 percent of production costs but about 25 percent of administrative profits (Chen and others, 1984, p. 89). The Northwest No. 1 Cotton Mill has had to leave buildings unpainted and improperly roofed because the price of above-plan construction materials depleted its investment funds. For many self-financed investment projects, no materials are allocated, making the high prices of construction material particularly burdensome. Even if enterprises can and will pay high negotiated prices, the state objects because the practice reduces profits and state revenue. (This is only true, of course, if profits of sellers are taxed more lightly than those of buyers, or if sellers understate their revenues—a likely occurrence.) The authorities have tried to prevent both sellers and buyers from exceeding negotiated price limits in excess of 20 percent above the controlled price. But many enterprises in our sample have paid a much higher premium.[24]

Barter. Many enterprises get most of their above-plan inputs by trading some of their output for scarce inputs. The transaction normally consists of mutual sales between firms. State prices are supposed to be used, but the mutual sales need not be balanced. If cement is scarcer than steel, the steel factory may have to sell more than it buys from the cement factory. It helps, of course, if an enterprise has self-marketing rights, but the main requisite for barter is that the output is scarce. The Sanchazi Forestry Bureau, which has no self-marketing rights, secured approval from higher authorities to barter timber for road construction by the People's Liberation Army. The Mindong Electrical Machinery Plant, though marketing its own output, has to rely on other means to obtain above-quota inputs.

Control over the allocation of a scarce output gives enterprises flexibility in obtaining scarce inputs. Shenyang Smelting can market a large share of its production of sulphuric acid and retain some for its own use. It sells part of its allocation to rural areas in exchange for rice for the plant's employees. Part of the marketed output in 1983 was used to obtain steel from Anshan in a tied sale. The bulk of above-quota output goes to Liaoning Province in implicit exchange for an allocation of 3,000 tons of fuel oil per year at state prices.

Although the exchange of output for inputs is conducted on a large scale, it is far from straightforward. The No. 2 Automobile Plant, for example, manufactured 2,895 trucks in 1983 in return for the following material from customers: 22,100 tons of rolled steel, 20 tons of tin, 969 tons of zinc, and 19,000 tons of coal. In 1982, however, No. 2 Auto was forced to turn over some trucks promised to material suppliers to the State Material Supply Bureau after a dispute over allocation. In that year, some of the designated buyers of No. 2 Auto's mandatory output were unable to purchase trucks because of a lack of funds. No. 2 Auto therefore arranged to sell these trucks to other customers that had funds but no allocation. The buyers that had been allocated trucks in the 1982 plan obtained funds in 1983 and insisted on receiving their trucks. Because No. 2 Auto had received an allocation of materials for these trucks, the Material Supply Bureau ruled that the enterprise owed the output to the original buyers. Some of the customers who had provided No. 2 Auto with materials in 1983 did not receive their trucks.[25] Agreement with the bureau over the distribution of trucks and materials was finally reached in October 1983.

In some circumstances, enterprises may derive little benefit from the exchange of output for inputs. Shenyang Smelting receives an insufficient allocation of copper ore and scrap for its smelting capacity, but because the plant cannot market above-plan output owing to price controls and restrictions on product diversification, inputs are as scarce as outputs. The only way Shenyang can obtain copper ore or scrap is to agree to resell the output to the supplier. In effect, this is nothing more than a processing agreement, for Shenyang receives neither financial benefits nor extra supplies from it.

Not all enterprises can exchange their output for supplies from leading state enterprises. Above-plan supplies may be available only from local enterprises, and protectionism can compound the problem. The Sanchazi Forestry Bureau is required to get all its spare machinery parts in Jilin Province, which produces inferior quality. Locally supplied inputs such as cement and coal not only may have higher official prices than centrally controlled output, but the price controls are laxer than those placed on prominent firms.

Compensation trade. In recent years enterprises have started providing investment funds in return for raw materials. For the enterprise providing the financing, this method has the advantage of securing a long-term contract for supplies, which is usually unobtainable through market purchases or barter of products. For the recipient, it breaks the bottleneck for investment funds common in such low-profit activities as mining.

The No. 2 Automobile Plant has been one of the most active enterprises in arranging such compensation trade. It has given an interest-free loan to Yunnan Province to expand tin production with repayment in tin, thus solving No. 2 Auto's biggest raw material problem. (In 1983, No. 2 Auto was allocated only 20 to 30 percent of its tin requirements.) No. 2 Auto has also invested in the development of sand production for its casting molds and has helped to establish a nearby commune factory to produce steel balls used in manufacturing trucks. By investing in the commune factory, No. 2 Auto circumvented the difficulty of obtaining extra land to set up its own factory or of having to provide employment for displaced commune workers from such land.

Most enterprises are not as flush with self-retained investment funds as No. 2 Auto. Shenyang Smelting had to use its circulating capital to provide a fifteen-year interest-free loan of Y1.7 million to a county-controlled cement plant in return for an annual supply of 10,000 tons of cement at the provincially controlled price of Y92 a ton. It is not clear whether this use of circulating capital, which was shown as an increase in receivables, was approved by the bank or local authorities.[26]

Investment does not always guarantee supply. The Chemical Fertilizer Plant under Qingyuan County invested in a phosphate mine in Yunnan Province to obtain raw materials, but so far no phosphate has materialized, because the province failed to meet its central quota. Sometimes, too, the compensation trade appears to be closer to extortion by suppliers than to a mutually beneficial agreement. The North China Petroleum Administration had to provide Y5 million to help renovate and expand provincial cement factories that suddenly stopped supplying cement in mid-1983. North China supplied the funds by paying an additional Y16.7 a ton for 300,900 tons of cement over a three-year period. It is not clear whether this was a loan to be repaid or simply a price increase.[27]

Mergers and backward integration. Because long-term supply contracts under compensation trade are uncertain, many enterprises prefer to invest in production under their direct control. As in all planned economies, Chinese enterprises have long exhibited a strong drive toward self-sufficiency. This autarkic tendency exists mainly because allocated supplies are difficult to obtain and their delivery is uncertain. Nearly all enterprises in the sample (and probably most Chinese enterprises) have manufactured some of their own equipment, and many have machine shops that are badly underutilized.

The attempt to secure captive supplies has been held in check by the dangers of trespassing bureaucratic, especially ministerial, boundaries. Anshan, for example, recently had to turn over its petroleum refinery to the new National Petrochemical Corporation. It refrained from investing in the expansion of a cement plant placed under its control in the early 1970s, in part because it feared that it would lose control of the plant and not be compensated for its investment.

Since 1979, the tendency toward self-sufficiency in individual factories has declined, partly because of the relative ease of obtaining some supplies from other enterprises.[28] Both the Chongqing Clock and Watch Company and the

Qingdao Forging Machinery Plant have recently replaced self-manufactured equipment with purchased equipment. Another reason for the decline in factory self-sufficiency is the possibility open to enterprises of channeling the drive for captive supplies into new forms of industrial organization: mergers, associations, joint ventures, and collective enterprises employing dependents of workers. Mergers into corporations, such as those for Chongqing and Jinling, and the development of associations, such as the Dongfeng Automobile Corporation, have afforded many opportunities for gaining greater control over supplies in a single organization.

Although mergers have been formed for many reasons, the better coordination of supply has been an important motive.[29] For the most part, mergers and associations have led to specialization or rationalization of production among member factories, allowing economies of scale and lower production costs.

Miscellaneous sources. There are other minor ways to fill gaps in material allocations. Three of the most common include using inventories, substituting materials, and trading inputs with or borrowing from other firms. In any period, total supplies obtained in this way may be fairly substantial, but since they are forms of borrowing that must be repaid, their net contribution to supply is small. Enterprises also sometimes borrow from next year's quota to fill the current year's gap. Like short-term loans that are rolled over, this borrowing may never have to be repaid. As a spokesman for the Mindong Electrical Machinery Corporation said, "From the enterprise's point of view, it is rather like a son borrowing from his father. If things go well, the son may repay. If not, it may not be necessary to repay."

One final means of obtaining above-plan supplies is to import them, using foreign-exchange-retention quotas. A few firms in the sample had rights to retain some foreign exchange, but only the No. 2 Automobile Plant appears to have used them. And some firms borrowed foreign exchange from the China International Trade and Investment Corporation to import materials.[30]

Evaluation of the Planning and Supply System

The Chinese planning and supply system exhibits many of the same strengths and weaknesses as Soviet-type central planning. The strengths include the ability to mobilize high rates of surplus, to direct resources to priority sectors, and to generate a high rate of industrial growth. Some of the weaknesses include problems of administrative coordination, low efficiency of resource use, and a bias against innovation.

- Poor administrative coordination. Plan targets are delivered late, and output plans are not synchronized with supply allocations. Financial and physical output targets are often inconsistent. This inconsistency is aggravated by multiple leadership—a source of administrative inefficiency that may be unique to China. Also, ministerial and regional lines of authority often cut across each other. China thus suffers not only from the endemic departmentalism of other planned economies but also from regionalism.

- Inefficient resource use. The drive for self-sufficiency leads to duplication of facilities and prevents specialization. Fragmentation along administrative lines leads to long cross-hauls of products and inefficient use of transport. It also further encourages enterprises to be as self-sufficient as possible, and thus they hoard supplies and tie up large amounts of resources in working capital.

- Bias against innovation. The classic explanation for slow innovation and diffusion of technology in socialist economies stresses overemphasis on quantity targets, taut planning, lack of price incentives for quality improvements, and difficulty in obtaining supplies for new products (Berliner 1976). Chinese experience suggests that the pervasive influence of sellers' markets may be the most potent inhibition against innovation. The lack of innovation and of diffusion of best-practice technology and management is reflected in the decline of total factor productivity in Chinese industry from 1957 to 1982. Net output grew more slowly than the weighted average of capital and labor during this period (Tidrick 1986 and World Bank 1985).

But there are also major differences between China and other planned economies. Some of these differences have existed since China introduced its system of planning and supply. Others have emerged only since 1978 as a result of the adjustment and reform. The differences have had a big impact, good and bad, on Chinese industrial performance. Five of the most distinctive features of the Chinese planning and supply system are evaluated below: links between plans and incentives, bargaining with authorities, multiple sources of supply, multiple prices, and the existence of buyers' markets.

Links between Planning and Incentives

China has avoided some of the most severe motivational problems of the Soviet economy. The ratchet effect, which induces firms to disguise their true production capacity and expend less effort, has not been a serious problem in China. China has also largely avoided the partial indicator problem, which leads firms to try to fulfill inconsistent or overly aggregated plan targets with an output mix that does not satisfy user requirements. These problems typically arise in planned economies, because plan targets are taut and poorly specified and because managerial incentives are closely linked to their fulfillment. In China, plan targets are also poorly specified. Indeed, inconsistency or excessive aggregation of targets is inevitable in a complex industrial economy, especially when prices are rigid. But targets in China usually are not taut—and if they are, they can be easily revised if they cannot be met. Moreover, although worker and manager bonuses theoretically have been tied to fulfillment of plan targets, this link has never been tightly enforced. The experience of other socialist countries and the inevitability of poor specification of plan targets suggest that the links between bonuses and plan targets should probably be severed rather than enforced.[31]

The Bargaining Economy

Another notable feature of the Chinese system is that everything is negotiable. It is wrong to think that plan targets, supply allocations, and profit-retention rates are imposed from above. They are all outcomes of prolonged and complex bargaining. Moreover, the notion that everything is, or ought to be, negotiable is deeply rooted. Bargaining reflects the grip of customary allocation and distribution principles (some of which may only have been developed during the Cultural Revolution), with their emphasis on egalitarianism and security. Responsibility is acceptable for profit but not for loss, and it is wrong to penalize enterprises and their workers for shortcomings outside their control. Bargaining also reflects the considerable power of lower levels of government. Local governments cannot simply be ordered to provide electricity and water to enterprises run by higher levels, and enterprises cannot take for granted the allocation of such services. They must always offer something in return. The frequent characterization of China as a command economy could not be further from the truth.

Bargaining is the main reason plans are neither taut nor firm. It has also reduced the potentially distorting effect of changes in incentives and thus thwarts attempts to link incentives to poorly specified plan targets or to profits reflecting distorted prices. But bargaining also has several disadvantages. It is likely to limit any attempt to strengthen incentives or to improve financial discipline. In other words, it leads to a soft budget constraint with all that implies (Kornai 1980 and chapter 13 in this volume).

It also perpetuates the pernicious use of made-to-measure incentives, a practice that in many less-developed countries has had serious consequences of resource misallocation, corruption, and inequality. In China, the treatment of every enterprise and problem as a special case leads to collusion between local governments and enterprises, with the local governments often acting as patrons rather than regulators. The lack of universally applicable rules diverts the energies of enterprises to bargaining from improving efficiency and product quality. Enterprises seek rents rather than profits.[32] They look for ways to manipulate the rules to their financial advantage rather than taking the rules as given.

Multiple Sources of Supply

Perhaps the most distinctive feature of China's system of material allocation is the availability of most key producer goods outside the central plan. Enterprises are able—indeed, they are forced by underallocations—to obtain such goods as steel and coal through channels other than central allocation. These other channels are fed from two sources—the production of local enterprises outside the central system, and the self-marketed output of state enterprises within the system. The first channel—production of centrally allocated goods (categories I and II) by enterprises ranging down to the commune and brigade—is a long-standing feature of the Chinese system. The second—widespread self-marketing by state enterprises—is relatively recent.

The main advantage of having multiple sources of supply is increased flexibility. The system helps to correct planning errors and to reduce the mismatch between supply and demand. Absolute supply constraints, or even supply-determined product-mix constraints, are uncommon. The corollary is that, because many key producer goods are available outside the central plan, that plan plays a far smaller role in resource allocation. Enterprises are less constrained by plan targets and supply allocations, and they consequently have greater autonomy to pursue profits, expansion, or whatever else they please.[33] Allocation of producer goods through the plan affects the distribution of profit (because allocated goods are cheaper) more than it affects overall resource allocation. China is far from being a market economy, but it is significant that attempts to curb aggregate self-financed investment since 1980 have had to rely mostly on indirect financial levers (such as compulsory purchase of government bonds and a transport and energy tax) or outright bans on investment in surplus goods such as cigarettes. Control over the allocation of construction materials was ineffective, and most machinery is no longer allocated.

Multiple Prices

Although prices and profits now play a greater role than planning in allocating resources, the existing pricing system is a poor guide. The desirability of moving away from the distorted structure of controlled prices is widely recognized, but there is less agreement about the desirability of keeping multiple prices for the same goods.

Multiple pricing is an inherent feature of the multiple sources of supply. For most key producer goods, there are several prices (usually in ascending order): the centrally controlled allocation price, the floating price for self-marketed output, the locally controlled allocation price, and the negotiated price in markets of varying legality. This system of multiple prices has some obvious advantages. Higher prices for locally controlled production and above-plan output provide an incentive to expand production of goods in short supply. The system also enables enterprises that have failed to obtain enough materials because of mistakes in allocation to buy critical inputs. The existence of a market for some production thus increases the flexibility of the overall system and increases total output. If the price for residual marketed production is market clearing, it also ensures that at least some output will be allocated to users with the greatest need, as reflected by ability to pay.[34]

Some argue that it would be even more beneficial if all output were allocated through the market—that multiple pricing is a first step to full market allocation. Others argue that a multiple-price system is itself ideal. It confines price changes (and hence inflation) to a small part of total production; it permits resources to be allocated according to plan while providing flexibility; and it concentrates incentives on the margin, thus avoiding big shifts in income distribution that would result from letting inframarginal prices change as well.

Although the multiple-price system has advantages, it also has defects that make it particularly unsuitable as a permanent system. First, multiple prices create a strong incentive to divert goods from low-priced allocations to higher-priced market sales. There are reports that this diversion is beginning in China. In the first half of 1985, Anshan fulfilled only 23 percent of its contracted sales quota for pig iron because negotiated market prices were higher.[35] Black markets in such goods as cement have also been reported. The danger is that conflicting incentives created by multiple prices will lead to corruption or other forms of behavior that may discredit reforms or harm long-term development.

Second, multiple prices reinforce the effects of compartmentalized allocations by encouraging uneconomic long-distance hauls. Enterprises will prefer low-priced allocated goods from distant sources to high-priced goods from nearby sources, even though the cost to the economy would be far less if they purchased them locally. Centrally allocated cement delivered by rail for more than 2,500 kilometers costs less than locally allocated cement delivered by road from only 50 kilometers away (World Bank 1985).

Third, total demand under multiple prices may be greater than it would be either under unified market-clearing prices or strict quantity rationing. This shortcoming is highly relevant to the conservation of energy and raw materials. If enterprises have to pay high prices for only a fraction of their coal, for example, they have less incentive to invest in more efficient boilers because savings on the low-priced, allocated portion will be small.

Fourth, and perhaps most serious, China's multiple-pricing system leads to high-cost production by small, inefficient producers. In Liaoning Province, more than thirty small copper smelters recycle scrap. Their copper losses in production range up to 20 percent, but they receive a far higher price for their output than Shenyang Smelting. These inefficient but highly profitable small smelters can thus outbid the more efficient but less profitable Shenyang Smelting for inputs.[36] The system of multiple prices and multiple sources of supply has created a protective umbrella for inefficient local producers in numerous other industries in China while discouraging expansion of more efficient, centrally controlled enterprises that must charge lower prices.[37]

In summary, the Chinese system of multiple prices and multiple sources of supply has enhanced the flexibility of supply, but at a high cost. It has also increased enterprise autonomy and weakened central control over resource allocation—without, however, providing an effective alternative market-control mechanism. To improve efficiency, China will have to move toward greater price unification. Unifying within-plan prices for goods produced by centrally and locally controlled governments would be the first step. The second should be to allow a single market-determined above-plan price applicable to all producers to emerge. Establishing the same price at the margin for all producers would reduce the most serious distortion of the present system—the incentive for setting up higher-cost production units. Finally, the share of production subject to allocation at controlled prices should be gradually reduced until, finally, allocation and fully unified prices are abolished.

Buyers' Markets

The emergence of buyers' markets in 1980 had more far-reaching effects than any conscious reform, except possibly the retention of profits. These buyers' markets were the unintended consequence of adjustment policies that favored light industry and decentralized investment decisionmaking and that led to an excess supply of machinery—enabling several consumer-goods industries to expand rapidly.

Buyers' markets had a large impact on the mechanics and scope of planning. They are associated with self-marketing, planning by sales, guidance planning, and to a less extent the practice of underallocating inputs. More important, buyer's markets have had a consistently favorable effect on economic performance. The ratio of input inventory to sales declined between 1979 and 1980–82 for thirteen of eighteen enterprises for which data are available (see tables 2-17 and 2-21). It is difficult to determine how much of this improvement was due to profit retention, which made enterprises sensitive to costs, and how much to easier access to inputs resulting from market changes. But the fact that all five of the enterprises whose ratios did not decline depend heavily on allocated inputs suggests that buyers' markets were important.[38]

The most significant changes brought about by buyers' markets were due to the intensive response to sales difficulties (see chapter 10). The buyers' market for inputs typically enabled users to obtain better quality, prices, delivery, and service. Almost all the enterprises in the sample that faced a buyers' market for their products improved quality and introduced new products and variations. And the more efficient firms expanded their market shares, thus further improving economic efficiency. These changes were due not to self-marketing but to the change in market conditions. The Chongqing Clock and Watch Company began to introduce new products only when faced with difficulties in self-sales, and pressures for variety changes and quality improvement were transmitted to the Nanning Textile Mill by the Commercial and Foreign Trade Departments.

Principles to Guide the Reform

This concluding section draws on the preceding analysis to outline three basic principles that should guide reform efforts. The first principle is that administrative solutions to planning and supply problems are a dead end. The second is that withdrawing from unsatisfactory relations (exit) is better than complaining about them (voice). The third is that all other solutions will fail without price reform.

Administrative Solutions Are a Dead End

Although eliminating such glaring contradictions as multiple leadership can improve the system, neither the centralization nor the decentralization of planning and allocation go to the heart of existing problems. The experience of the Jinling Petrochemical Corporation shows the limits of administrative reorganization. New supply problems emerged almost immediately because the input-output table is inherently at odds with clear-cut administrative lines of responsibility. There are always important linkages that cannot be brought within the confines of a single enterprise. If they are, the enterprise is unwieldy. Very large enterprises simply replicate economywide problems. Both Jinling and North China Petroleum have been unable to prevent their subordinate units from hoarding repair facilities and supplies. Shenyang Smelting provides another example of the limits of administrative solutions. Recentralization under a national Nonferrous Metals Corporation reduced the inconsistencies of plan targets, but it failed to solve Shenyang's basic supply constraints and created new conflicts with the province and municipality. Where new administrative organization has improved supply and planning—as it has with the formation of the Dongfeng Automobile Corporation—the association has been voluntary rather than mandatory, and the improvement has come from changed market conditions.

In brief, administrative reorganization does not remove the incentive to develop captive, high-cost sources of supply. Nor does it give the enterprise greater room to maneuver. It simply shifts the area of bargaining.

Exit Is Superior to Voice

Exit and voice are alternative responses to deterioration in the quality of goods and services provided by an enterprise.[39] The exit option is to withdraw from relations with the unsatisfactory organization—to take one's business elsewhere. The voice option is to complain to the organization or higher authority in order to correct the shortcoming in quality. In a planned economy, voice is usually the only option open because all participants are locked into a closed system with no choice of supplier, product mix, or customer. But even the voice of complaint cannot be raised if power is unequal. In China, for example, supply contracts are governed by law, and the fulfillment of contracts is a precondition for paying bonuses. Yet, as one enterprise manager stated, "The plant dares not complain about poor quality because the new shipments will be worse if it does."

In China, voice is typically used, but the ensuing bargaining leads to an antisocial outcome. The limits of voice are illustrated by the experience of Anshan Iron and Steel Corporation with its magnesium supply. Until 1980, Anshan had its own magnesium mine and facilities for manufacturing refractory bricks for furnace linings, but the captive supplier was handed over to a newly formed specialized magnesium company in order to rationalize production and to tap the area's rich potential for exports and higher-quality production. The new company was placed under the Ministry of Metallurgy (also Anshan's leading authority for planning and supply), and part of its output of bricks was allocated to Anshan by the ministry, which controls this category II product. The reorganization realized its objectives. Product quality improved and exports increased under the specialized enterprise. In 1982, however, the magnesium company failed to supply enough bricks for a new steel plant being constructed by Anshan. It is not clear whether this was because of the higher price for exports or because of a failure by the ministry to allocate enough bricks for Anshan's investment project, which had been approved by the State Council. Whatever the reason, the magnesium company used its monopoly position to extort better terms for its above-plan supply of bricks. It demanded from Anshan a fifteen-year, interest-free loan of Y3 million and from the ministry an annual supply of 2,000 tons of crude oil and a one-time allocation of construction materials. Anshan countered with a request to import bricks or ore (at the international price if necessary) to manufacture bricks itself if the magnesium company would not guarantee supply. After several months of negotiation, the ministry approved all of the magnesium company's demands (except that it reduced the term of the loan to three years) and granted Anshan the right to import bricks if the magnesium company failed to supply enough bricks.

This case illustrates again that an administrative solution (formation of a magnesium company) often creates a new problem. It also illustrates the ineffectiveness of voice in resolving problems sensibly and expeditiously, even when both parties to the dispute are under control of a single ministry.

A system favoring exit implies greater enterprise autonomy. For the enterprise, two essential elements are the right to choose its suppliers and the right to choose its product mix. If the Northwest No. 1 Cotton Mill had been able to contract freely for printing and dyeing outside the province or to install its own finishing facilities, the mill, the province, and China would have been better off. A credible threat of exit would have created pressure on the finishing plants to improve quality, as it did for the No. 2 Automobile Plant's suppliers.[40] And the choice of product mix, including the right to produce new products, can permit the specialization and expansion of more efficient producers. Shenyang Smelting could produce copper alloys more efficiently than the many small alloy producers in existence, but it is prevented from making alloys.

Price Reform Is Essential

Giving enterprises the right to determine what products they produce will be beneficial only if it is coordinated with price reform. Shenyang still could not compete with small alloy producers as long as they receive copper at the state-controlled price and Shenyang is forced to purchase copper scrap at market prices. Similarly, giving Anshan the right to regularly import or to produce its own magnesium bricks might have been preferable to the cumbersome solution eventually devised, but the best solution would have been to give Anshan these rights *and* to bring domestic and world prices into line. Then the magnesium company would not have had an incentive to export materials that clearly had a higher value to the economy if used to complete a key national investment project, and Anshan would not have had an incentive to produce its own bricks at higher cost. Anshan and the magnesium company could have negotiated a price which would have benefited both of them and the national economy.

The experience of our enterprises has shown that economic performance has improved in response to a buyer's market and that this has posed a threat to enterprise and worker benefits. An increase in enterprise exit options—the right to choose suppliers and to enter new fields of production—will promote competition that can eliminate sellers' markets. Similarly, elimination of made-to-measure incentives will restrict the scope for voice to determine enterprise rewards and divert enterprise energies from bargaining into more productive channels of improving product quality and production efficiency. But in both cases these changes must go hand-in-hand with rationalization of prices to ensure that they reflect social costs and benefits. If China moves in these directions, it can also continue to move away from detailed production planning and supply allocation, with even better results than those obtained in the past several years.

Notes

1. Standard Western sources on Soviet planning and supply include Berliner 1976, Granick 1954, and Levine 1959.

2. This number included 256 in category I and 581 in category II. See Byrd 1983, Wong 1986, and table 9.1 in this volume.

3. From Soviet sources cited by Wong (1986), the total includes material balances for 2,000 products prepared by Gosplan. See also Kushnirsky 1982, p. 112, and chapter 5, note 1, this volume.

4. *Zhongguo Shehui* 1983, appendix 4. Steel was divided into twenty categories, such as large, medium, and small section steel; steel plate of medium thickness; and silicon steel. Counting subcategories of steel and other products (mostly rare metals), there were 276 products in category I in 1979.

5. Except for enterprises under dual or multiple leadership, discussed below. See also Wong (1985).

6. Regionalism also emerged during the Soviet experiment with local economic regions beginning in 1957, but the experiment was short-lived and regionalism did not become entrenched as it did in China.

7. During the early 1970s the number of centrally allocated products fell to 217 from a previous high of 532 in 1957. See table 9-1 in this volume.

8. Of the 256 category I products in 1980, 78 semifinished metal products, 2 chemicals, and 144 machinery products were "freed from restrictions." See Li Kaixin 1982.

9. The Qinghe Woolen Textile Mill has ten evaluation targets and another ten relative targets that are used in comparison with other textile mills to determine which are worthy of being ranked as first category mills.

10. The Xiangxiang Cement Plant, for example, has an elaborate system of five fixed quotas, two contracts, and one reward linking bonuses to disaggregated targets.

11. Inconsistencies may arise even under a single supervisory agency because the profit target comes from a separate financial department.

12. For more details on Shenyang's problems of multiple leadership, see Byrd 1985.

13. An extreme case in our sample was a provincially controlled enterprise that refused to accede to a local request to provide construction materials. The municipal engineering department then destroyed the plant's water pipeline on the pretext that it did not meet the municipal construction code.

14. A taut plan is one in which the targets are difficult to achieve. Plans may be taut with respect either to production capacity or to supply allocation. A firm plan is one in which targets are set early and not revised.

15. Evidence from our sample of enterprises confirms that plans are not taut. For 1979–82, 50 percent of the annual output targets and 61 percent of the profit targets

for which data are available were overfulfilled by more than 10 percent. Only 6 percent of the output targets and 8 percent of the profit targets were underfulfilled; of those, no target was underfulfilled by more than 2 percent. For more details, see tables 5-1 and 5-2.

16. A key target was changed for the Chengdu Locomotive Factory in the last week of December, and Chongqing Clock and Watch was allowed to eliminate its output targets during a clock market crisis. For more details, see Byrd and Tidrick (1984, p. 26).

17. This pattern is evident in the results of regression analysis of percentage change of retained profits as a function of percentage change of total profits for three years (1979–80, 1980–81, 1981–82) for our sample of twenty enterprises. When total profits were falling, there was little correlation ($r = 0.15$) between change in retained profits and change in total profits. The low correlation suggests that a fall in retained profits is subject to intense negotiations. There was, however, a relatively high correlation ($r = 0.66$) when profits were rising, with retained profits increasing 2.4 percent for every 1 percent increase in total profits. The high correlation shows that there is generally little ratchet effect when profits are rising.

18. For examples of similar problems from other enterprises, see Liu and Wang 1984.

19. This decision, of course, is probably a sensible one when power is short, though it might be more sensible to shut down very energy-intensive production altogether and import the products.

20. William Byrd discusses this example of internal protectionism (chapter 10 in this volume).

21. In a buyers' market it is not sufficient to set administered prices to equalize profitability. If there is excess capacity for, say, clocks, the price of clocks may need to fall far enough to eliminate profit temporarily to balance supply and demand and signal that producers should switch to more profitable products.

22. For a discussion of reform of the material-supply system, see Byrd (1983).

23. The market price is distinct from the difference between centrally allocated and locally allocated prices of commodities, such as coal and cement. The locally allocated price is invariably higher than the centrally allocated price. In some cases, the price premium cited by enterprises is for locally allocated materials.

24. All claim never to have sold any output at illegal prices, and this may be largely true, since they are mostly large, model enterprises that are easy to monitor and that have much to lose from such irregularities.

25. One of the frustrated customers was Guangdong Province, which had used its self-retained foreign exchange to import materials in exchange for 1,030 trucks.

26. See Byrd 1985, p. 76. A similar use of circulating capital by the Chongqing Clock and Watch Company to finance investment in an associated enterprise was allowed to go through when discovered by its local bank, but Chongqing had to pay a penalty for the increase in borrowed funds. See Byrd and Tidrick 1984.

27. Anshan was also forced to enter a disadvantageous compensation trade agreement to secure supplies of magnesium. I discussed this case later in the chapter.

28. This change should not be overstated. As noted earlier, Anshan successfully lobbied to gain control of a municipal power plant, and the individual factories of Jinling Petroleum have refused to integrate their repair shops.

29. The main motive for establishing collectives for dependents of workers has been to provide employment, but many of these collectives provide supplies to the parent enterprise.

30. Most enterprises prefer to spend their modest amounts of retained foreign exchange for capital expenses rather than recurrent expenses. They fear, in part, that if they were ever to start down the path of using retained exchange to fill supply gaps, the higher authorities might institutionalize the gap, just as appears to have happened when domestic supplies became readily available outside the plan.

31. Granick (1975) has argued that the German Democratic Republic has benefited from a system in which plan targets are not overly taut, are meant to be neither overfulfilled nor underfulfilled, and are not closely linked to managerial bonuses.

32. See Krueger 1974 for an account of the problems that rent-seeking can cause in less-developed countries.

33. For a discussion of enterprise objectives, see chapter 4 in this volume.

34. The extent to which there is a market-clearing price for residual production depends on the product. Effective price controls on above-plan production and restrictions on resale will prevent establishment of market-clearing prices, for example. For most products, it appears that administrative controls and the unavailability of transport lead to fragmented markets. Thus, there may be a separate market-clearing price for the same product in each of several markets. This fragmentation greatly reduces the extent to which even residual output is allocated to users with the greatest need.

35. Xinhua, quoted in BBC, *Summary of World Broadcasts*, FE/8029/BII/11 (August 14, 1985).

36. As noted above, Shenyang could also produce copper alloys and fabricated products more efficiently than many of the actual producers. For these products, inefficient production arises because Shenyang is prohibited from diversifying production. In the case of refined copper, the inefficiency arises from a partially reformed price system. This situation illustrates the general theory of second best: fulfillment of one of the conditions for Pareto optimality (allowing the price for copper scrap to be determined in the market) may reduce social welfare if all other conditions (including a free market for refined copper) are not met.

37. Small producers are not always less efficient. Moreover, some small producers may also have low profits due to high input prices but still produce because of other systemic features (supply shortages and multichannel allocation). Despite these qualifications, it seems clear that multiple pricing has encouraged inefficient production and that there would be large efficiency gains from permitting all enterprises to compete equally.

38. A sharp break between ratios in 1978 and 1979 was probably due to a campaign to write off inventories of unusable supplies in 1979.

39. The concepts are those of Hirschman (1970). Hirschman argues (p. 120), however, that voice may be superior to exit in many circumstances—or, more generally, that there is an "elusive optimal mix of exit and voice." The argument here is simply that Chinese inclinations are so tilted in favor of voice that almost any increase in exit options will help.

40. The right to choose equipment suppliers is especially important in ensuring that special user needs are met and in reducing the incentive for inefficient self-manufacture of equipment (see Tidrick 1986, chap. 5).

References

Berliner, Joseph S. 1976. *The Innovation Decision in Soviet Industry.* Cambridge, Mass.: MIT Press.

Byrd, William. 1983. "Reform of the Material Supply System." Washington, D.C.: World Bank. Processed.

———. 1985. "China's Nonferrous Metals Industry: Reforms and Recent Developments in the Shenyang Smeltery." Washington, D.C.: World Bank. Processed.

Byrd, William, and Gene Tidrick. 1984. "Adjustment and Reform in the Chongqing Clock and Watch Company." In *Recent Chinese Economic Reforms: Studies of Two Industrial Enterprises.* World Bank Staff Working Paper 652. Washington, D.C.

Chen Jiyuan, Xu Lu, Tang Zongkun, and Chen Lantong. 1984. "Management and Reform in the Qingdao Forging Machinery Plant." In *Recent Chinese Economic Reforms: Studies of Two Indusrial Enterprises.* World Bank Staff Working Paper 652. Washington, D.C.

Donnithorne, Audrey. 1972. "China's Cellular Economy: Some Economic Trends since the Cultural Revolution." *China Quarterly* 52 (October/December):605–19.

Granick, David. 1954. *Management of the Industrial Firm in the USSR.* New York: Columbia University Press.

———. 1975. *Enterprise Guidance in Eastern Europe.* Princeton, N.J.: Princeton University Press.

Hirschman, Albert O. 1970. *Exit, Voice, and Loyalty: Response to Decline in Firms, Organizations and States.* Cambridge, Mass.: Harvard University Press.

Kornai, Janos. 1980. *Economics of Shortage.* 2 vols. Amsterdam: North-Holland.

Koziara, Edward Clifford, and Yan Chiou-Shuang. 1983. "The Distribution System for Producers' Goods in China." *China Quarterly* 96 (December):689–702.

Krueger, Anne O. 1974. "The Political Economy of Rent-Seeking Society." *American Economic Review* 64 (June): 291–303.

Kushnirsky, Fyodor I. 1982. *Soviet Economic Planning, 1965–80.* Boulder, Colo.: Westview Press.

Levine, Herbert S. 1959. "The Centralized Planning of Supply in the Soviet Union". In U.S. Congress, Joint Economic Committee, Subcommittee on Economic Statistics, *Comparisons of the United States and Soviet Economies.* Washington, D.C.: Government Printing Office.

Li Kaixin. 1982. "How China Manages Its Supplies." *1981 Zhongguo Jingli Niankian* (1981 Chinese economic almanac). Hong Kong: Modern Cultural Company.

Liu Guoguang and Wang Ruisun. 1984. "Restructuring of the Economy." In Yu Guangyuan, ed., *China's Socialist Modernization.* Beijing: Foreign Languages Press.

Ma Hong, ed. 1982. *Xiandai Zhongguo Jingji Shidian* (Contemporary handbook of Chinese economic affairs). Beijing: Social Sciences Publishing House.

Tidrick, Gene. 1986. *Productivity Growth and Technological Change in Chinese Industry.* World Bank Staff Working Paper 761. Washington, D.C.

Wong, Christine. 1985. "Material Allocation and Decentralization: Impact of the Local Sector on Industrial Reform". In Elizabeth J. Perry and Christine Wong, eds., *The Political Economy of Reform in Post-Mao China.* Cambridge, Mass.: Harvard University Press.

———. 1986. "Ownership and Control in Chinese Industry: The Maoist Legacy and Prospects for the 1980s." In U.S. Congress, Joint Economic Committee, *China in the 1980s.* Washington, D.C.: Government Printing Office.

World Bank. 1985. *China: Long-Term Issues and Options.* Baltimore, Md.: Johns Hopkins University Press.

Zhongguo Shehui Zhuyi Wuzi Guanli Tizhi Shilue (Socialist material management system in China). 1983. Beijing: Materials Publishing House.

9

Supply and Marketing

Tang Zongkun

Two systems administer the supply and marketing of producer goods and products for state industrial enterprises in China. The state manages the supply and marketing of manufactured producer goods, and the commercial system deals with agricultural raw materials and manufactured consumer goods.

Manufactured producer goods are divided into three categories, according to the division of responsibility for them. The most important goods are those that have a bearing on the national economy and people's livelihood. Called nationally allocated goods, they are allocated by the State Planning Commission and distributed by the State Material Supply Bureau. The important specialized goods come under the jurisdiction of the relevant industrial ministries and are called ministerially controlled goods. The remaining manufactured producer goods form the third category, and their production and marketing are arranged by agencies at provincial, municipal, and autonomous region levels, or left with the enterprises.

Agricultural raw materials and manufactured consumer goods also fall into three categories, according to the division of administrative responsibility. The control of goods in the first category is centralized and the State Planning Commission allocates procurement, marketing, distribution, stocking, and import-export quotas. In the second category, the State Planning Commission is responsible for overall balance, but the control of most items is delegated to the various agencies and only a small portion remains centrally administered; interregional flows are arranged to make up the supply gap. The third category of goods is basically controlled by local agencies.

Material supply agencies are established according to the tiers in the state administrative system. At each level of government, there is a material supply bureau. Under the State Material Supply Bureau are a number of specialized national corporations dealing with nationally allocated goods, including metals, machinery and electrical equipment, industrial chemicals, timber, and building materials. These corporations have set up purchasing and supply stations (called first-level stations, for short) in each major administrative area to organize supplies. Industrial ministries have their own supply and marketing units to organize the marketing of products and material supply for enterprises under their jurisdiction. Material supply bureaus at provincial, municipal, and autonomous region levels also set up specialized companies and supply stations.

Enterprises individually submit requisitions for raw materials, equipment, fuel, and other items required for production and capital construction to the relevant agencies according to the relation of subordination. For nationally and ministerially controlled goods, supply contracts are usually signed between the producers and users at a national ordering conference held twice a year in accord with the state-allocated quotas. For large allocations, contracts are signed directly between the producer and user. For small allocations, the relevant administrative agencies or the local material supply units combine the allocations and sign contracts with producers.

The state wholesale network consists of three levels. In major cities where commodities originate, first-level purchasing and supply stations are set up directly under the various specialized national corporations of the Commerce Ministry. In other major or medium-size cities, there are second-level purchasing and supply stations. These stations are subordinate to the specialized companies under the commerce departments or bureaus at the provincial, municipal, and autonomous region levels. At the county level, there are third-level wholesale outlets. The specialized companies exercise administrative responsibilities. Within the state trading system, the distribution of commodities starts with the first-level purchasing and supply stations, then moves to the second level and the third level before reaching the retailers. Manufactured goods that are produced by state industrial enterprises and marketed through the state trading channels are purchased from the producers by the first- and second-level purchasing and supply stations.

As I explained earlier, producer goods are allocated according to administrative divisions. But an industrial enterprise sometimes requires goods concurrently involving three categories for production and capital construction. So it must submit requisitions to multiple administrative agencies for the allocation of goods in the first and second categories and for the procurement of goods in the third category. According to the survey of twenty state industrial enterprises by the Chinese Academy of Social Sciences and the World Bank, all enterprises face complex arrangements for material supply, despite differences in their operations. Some examples from the survey are spelled out in the following section.

Examples of Arrangements for the Supply of Materials

The No. 2 Automobile Plant is a large, centrally controlled enterprise. The automobiles it makes are allocated by the State Material Supply Bureau, while the allocations of steel and other important materials to the factory are determined by the State Planning Commission. Supplies are organized by the State Material Supply Bureau. The factory has designated suppliers of intermediate goods (fourteen groups altogether). Since these suppliers come under the jurisdiction of the ministries of machine building, the electronics industry, the chemical industry, light industry, and the building materials industry, the factory has to submit requisitions to many agencies each year.

The Baoji Nitrogen Fertilizer Plant, a medium-size, provincially controlled enterprise, is recognized as the priority fertilizer enterprise in Baoji Province. For feedstock coal, fuel coal, and specialized chemical equipment, the plant prepares and submits requisitions to the Ministry of the Chemical Industry through the chemical fertilizer company under the Shaanxi Provincial Petrochemicals Bureau and various other agencies. Allocations approved by the Ministry of the Chemical Industry are communicated back to the various supply agencies. Requisitions for standard machinery and electrical equipment, industrial chemicals, cement, timber, and steel are submitted to the Shaanxi Provincial Material Supply Bureau, and the various specialized companies under the same bureau are responsible for these supplies. Through its own initiative the plant procures packing materials, metal products, electrical appliances, paint, and indigenous building materials (bricks, sand, gravel). The agricultural producer-goods company under the control of the Shaanxi Provincial Commerce Department purchases and markets the whole of the plant's output.

The Qingdao Forging Machinery Factory is a medium-size enterprise under the control of Qingdao, the provincial municipality. The factory is in Jiaoxian County in the suburbs of Qingdao, and the jurisdiction over the factory has switched several times between the higher and lower levels. The changes of jurisdiction have resulted in unusually complicated arrangements for material supply. For key materials (steel, pig iron, nonferrous metals, timber, coke, and refractories), the factory submits its requisition to the Shandong Provincial Machine-Building Industry Bureau, which allocates quotas to the factory within its overall allotment from the Provincial Material Supply Bureau. After the allocation has been determined, the factory signs contracts with supplying enterprises designated by the Provincial Material Supply Bureau. For raw coal, the factory submits its requisition to the Qingdao Municipal Material Supply Bureau, and the supply is organized by the fuel company under the same bureau. Petrol, diesel fuel, and lubricants are allocated and supplied by the petroleum supply station under the Jiaoxian commerce bureau. From city- or county-controlled trading companies, the factory buys other auxiliary materials such as caustic soda, sodium carbonate, paint, calcium carbide, plastic products, and low-value consumables. And it purchases indigenous building materials from neighboring communes and production brigades.

The material supply arrangements for textile enterprises have their own features. Assisted by the Ministry of the Textile Industry, the commercial departments distribute cotton and raw flax and ramie in accord with the national allocation plan. The Ministry of the Textile Industry allocates wood and controls the production and allocation of textile machinery and equipment and synthetic fibers. Imports of fibers and dyes are organized by foreign trade departments, but the allocation of imports is controlled by the Ministry of the Textile Industry. Quotas are assigned to textile industry departments and bureaus at provincial, municipal, and autonomous region levels.

Enterprises individually submit requisitions to the relevant departments and bureaus. The Northwest No. 1 Cotton Mill, for example, submits its requisition for cotton to the supply and marketing company under the Shaanxi Provincial Textile Industry Bureau (now called Shaanxi Textile Industry Corporation). It receives cotton from the Shaanxi Provincial Cotton and Flax Company, which belongs to the system of supply and marketing cooperatives. The Nanning Silk and Linen Textile Mill applies for the allocation of ramie to the supply and marketing company under the control of the Textile Industry Bureau of the Guangxi Zhuang Nationality Autonomous Region. It receives ramie from the Leping County supply and marketing cooperative—a supply base of ramie in Guangxi. The Tianjin Color Textile Corporation applies for yarn to the Tianjin Municipal Textile Industry Bureau. The allocation is channeled through the Cotton Textile Industry Corporation under the same bureau. The Qinghe Woolen Textile Mill submits its requisition for sliver and cashmere to the Wool, Linen, and Silk Textile Corporation under the Beijing Municipal Textile Industry Bureau.

For synthetic fibers, enterprises submit their requests every year to the relevant administrative departments and bureaus. They sign contracts with producers designated by the Ministry of the Textile Industry after the allocation is determined. For enterprises that produce export goods, the foreign trade departments provide a certain amount of synthetic fibers. For instance, for the export of every 10,000 meters of dacron-ramie fabrics through Guangdong, the Nanning Silk and Linen Textile Mill obtains one ton of dacron sliver from the foreign trade departments concerned. For the supply of imported dyes and chemicals, the Qinghe Woolen Textile Mill must submit a plan twice a year, in early February and August, to the Dyes Section of the Supply Division of the Beijing Municipal Textile Industry Bureau through the Materials Section of the Wool, Linen, and Silk Textile

Corporation. For dyes and chemicals of domestic origin, the enterprise submits its requisition to the Industrial Chemicals Company under the Beijing Municipal Commerce Bureau. For textile equipment, the enterprise places orders once a year with suppliers after the allocation is drawn up by the Textile Machinery Company under the Beijing Municipal Textile Industry Bureau. For steel, timber, and cement, the Beijing Municipal Material Supply Bureau allocates a quota to the Beijing Municipal Textile Industry Bureau, which in turn allocates its allotment among all the textile enterprises under its jurisdiction through subordinate companies. The actual supplies to individual enterprises are channeled through the Beijing Municipal Metal Products Company, the Beijing Municipal Timber Company, and the Beijing Municipal Building Materials Company in accord with assigned quotas.

Among the state industrial enterprises, there is a group of directly supplied enterprises under the relevant industrial ministries. The reason for this is that the local supply agencies could not meet the needs of these enterprises after the jurisdiction over these enterprises was transferred from ministries to the local authorities. Anshan Iron and Steel Corporation, for example, is a giant enterprise and the backbone of the steel sector. Its products cater to the national market, but it depends heavily on various parts of the country for material inputs, fuel, and equipment. Before 1969 Anshan was under the direct control of the Ministry of Metallurgy. In 1969 Liaoning Province was given administrative authority over it. The province authorized the city of Anshan to undertake administrative responsibility. As authority was decentralized, supplies from the ministry to Liaoning Province decreased. But the province could not ensure supplies for Anshan Iron and Steel. Nor did the province have the authority or the capability to control the national allocation of the company's products. So supplies of essential goods to the company have since been directly administered by the ministry. In other words, the ministry has been responsible for the allocation, distribution, and supply of the nationally and ministerially allocated goods that the company requires. The ministry is also responsible for drawing up plans for the company's production and capital construction.

Anshan now is nominally under the dual jurisdiction of the Ministry of Metallurgy and Liaoning Province, with the province taking greater responsibility. The ministry, however, sets targets for the quality and quantity of output and for technical renovation tasks. The ministry also administers the supply of raw materials, coal, heavy oil, and major equipment to the company. Among the 791 types of nationally and ministerially allocated goods the company requires, the Liaoning provincial supply agencies are responsible for about 30 items, including power and natural gas. The supply in the third category is organized by the Anshan city supply agencies. The company can procure supplies on its own whenever it has to.

Shenyang Smelting is also a directly supplied enterprise of the Ministry of Metallurgy. Previously, it was under the direct control of that ministry. Authority over the plant was transferred to the city of Shenyang, but the ministry retained control of essential material supplies, such as copper and lead concentrates and primary zinc. The plant submits requisitions to the ministry and signs contracts with ministry-designated supplying mines after the allocations are finalized. Supplies of fuel, steel, timber, cement, caustic soda, and so on are transferred through the Liaoning Provincial Metallurgical Industry Department, which signs contracts with supplying enterprises in accord with the quota approved by the ministry. The plant submits requisitions for a portion of the ministerially allocated goods to the Metallurgical Industry Bureau of the city of Shenyang, which signs contracts with producers on behalf of the plant.

Xiangxiang Cement Plant is a large cement producer under the control of Hunan Province. It is also a directly supplied enterprise of the State Building Materials Bureau. The bureau draws up the plant's plans for production and capital construction. The plant output is subject to national allocation. The bureau administers and allocates supplies of major raw materials and equipment to the plant (limestone is supplied by a captive mine). The Hunan Provincial Building Materials Bureau raises, by a certain margin, the output quota of the plant as set by the state bureau. It provides a certain amount of material inputs in exchange for a small share of the plant's output for allocation in the province.

In sum, China's supply and marketing system for state industrial enterprises has five main features. First, the division of allocation and administrative responsibility is based on the impact of each type of good or product on the national economy and on its scarcity. Second, according to the hierarchical administrative structure, requisitions for producer goods flow upward and allocation commands downward; production plans come from above and output allocation decisions are centralized; and responsibilities are divided among several agencies in the categories discussed earlier. Third, goods are allocated to enterprises primarily according to the relationship of subordination. The directly supplied enterprises are the products of compromise when the devolution of authority over these key enterprises inevitably conflicts with the central control of material resources. This means that the relevant ministries regain control over these enterprises. Fourth, the requisitions for and allocations of producer goods are processed up and down the vertical chain of the administrative system. The horizontal links between producers and users are merely a complementary and passive means to execute the administrative commands. Fifth, for the flow of goods, accounts are settled at administratively fixed prices (prices fixed by the State Prices Bureau, ministries, provinces, cities, and autonomous regions). But those prices have only a passive allocative role. In short, the present supply and marketing system substitutes decisions about administrative allocations for economically efficient exchanges of commodities.

Deficiencies of Administrative Decisions

A system that relies on administrative decisions to mobilize and allocate material resources played a positive role in the early stages of socialist construction. The system mobilized limited material resources, ensured the construction of high-priority projects, guaranteed a basic level of consumption for the people, and laid down the foundation for socialist industrialization. During that period, economic links between the economy's sectors and subsectors were relatively simple, and the system worked reasonably well. But even then, supply shortages and discrepancies between supply and demand were common. As socialist construction and production became more specialized, the economic links became more complex. Eventually, the incompatibility between the system and further economic development became apparent.

The original system was designed to avoid the trial and error of market forces, mobilize and allocate material resources in a planned way, match supply and demand through relatively simple procedures, ensure the rational and efficient use of material resources, and promote the planned and coordinated growth of the national economy. But the operating efficiency of the system over much of the past several decades indicates that things do not always turn out as planned. And the performance of the twenty state industrial enterprises in our survey suggests that the system needs to be reformed.

Gaps between Requirements and Allocations

The use of administrative decisions to mobilize and allocate material resources is an integral part of a centralized economic system based on public ownership of the means of production. Under this system, the state ultimately assumes all investment risks, and ministries, local authorities, and enterprises need to bear none. But their interests are linked with the resources they obtain from the state. The more investment funds and material resources an organization can gain, the easier it can fulfill its annual plan and improve the welfare of its employees. Therefore, investment requirements are often exaggerated. Excessive investments drive up the demands for material inputs, resulting in supply shortages that ministries, local agencies, and enterprises responsible for the production of goods in short supply in turn use to justify their demands for more investment funds and material inputs. The available material resources controlled by the state constantly face excessive demands. Moreover, the allocation priorities of state agencies are influenced by cries for help from all parts of the country. Indeed, it is very difficult to achieve rational allocation of resources under this system. As a result, many justifiable demands have not been met.

For essential raw materials, fuel, and power, almost all enterprises in the survey report gaps between the official allocations and the figures in the annual plans of the enterprises.[1] In 1983, for example, the allocations of steel, pig iron, and tin to the No. 2 Automobile Plant respectively accounted for 90 percent, 54 percent, and 20 percent of the factory's demand in the annual plan. For the Mindong Electrical Machinery Plant, only 60 to 75 percent of the company's demands for essential materials are met by the official allocation calculated on the basis of output value target set by the Fujian Provincial Machine Building Industry Department. At the Shanghai No. 17 Cotton Mill, the allocation of steel meets only 60 percent of the mill's demand, and supplies of suitable varieties account for only 70 percent of the allocation quota. For the Sanchazi Forestry Bureau, allocations of nationally allocated goods in recent years averaged only about 60 percent of its total needs. In 1983, steel allocation made up 70 percent of total demand; cement, 50 percent; and coal, 40 percent. For the Northwest No. 1 Cotton Mill, allocations of steel, timber, and cement earmarked for production maintenance can satisfy only 20 percent of the demand, and the allocation of sulfuric acid and caustic soda for producing viscose also falls short of demand. Economists have been making appeals to planners "not to leave gaps in plans." But gaps exist not only because of defects in the planning methodology. They also originate from the economic system, since the state assumes all investment risks.

Nationally and ministerially controlled goods are allocated by broadly defined groups, not by particular types and specifications. Indeed, not much can be done as long as goods are allocated downward along the administrative chain. For example, there are more than 1,000 different types of domestically produced steel with more than 20,000 specifications. Individual users require steel for different purposes, and administrative allocation cannot cater to the particular requirements of each user. After the allocation quota has been determined, big users such as the No. 2 Automobile Plant can negotiate directly and sign contracts with supplying enterprises through national ordering conferences in an attempt to match types and specifications of supply with those of demand. But because the State Material Supply Bureau designates suppliers, the types and specification of products the suppliers can or are willing to make do not necessarily coincide with what the factory needs. For No. 2 Auto the deliveries of suitable types and specifications account for about 85 percent of the allocation quotas, better than usual.

Small users place orders with suppliers through the relevant administrative agency or local material supply bureaus. They have even less assurance that supply will match demand. The State Building Materials Bureau allocates a timber quota to the Xiangxiang Cement Plant for capital construction purposes. The quota refers only to quantity, not variety. The actual supply the plant receives is organized by a provincial material supply bureau. Only 20 percent of the material supply is China fir and the remainder is indigenous pine, which cannot be used for permanent structures because of its tendency to warp. Qinghe Woolen Textile Mill needs steel primarily for the maintenance of equipment used in the manufacture of some parts and components. Hence, it needs small pieces of steel weighing about ten kilograms each. But the mill is supplied with pieces weighing more than one hundred kilograms each and which the woolen mill has to saw. Civil works require steel rods by length, but the allocation is made by tons. The steel rods supplied to the Northwest No. 1 Cotton Mill for expansion work were so thick that they were discounted 80 percent when passed over to the construction unit, resulting in a bigger supply gap and the increase of unit construction cost. As a result of mediation by the responsible person at the provincial administrative agency, the responsible person at the provincial material supply bureau agreed to allocate 1,000 tons of steel to Baoji Nitrogen Fertilizer Plant for capital construction purposes. But when the plant was informed by the provincial metals company that only flat steel and bearing steel were available, it was at a loss, not knowing how to use flat steel and bearing steel in construction work.

For the supplies of dyes and raw materials to textile mills, there is no guarantee regarding type, specifications, and quality. Enterprises have no choice over sources of raw materials and are obliged to organize production according to the supplies they are given. For instance, after substantial price cuts for synthetic textiles in early 1983, the Qinghe Woolen Textile Mill knew there was a good market for sliver-dyed blend fabrics. But due to raw material constraints, the mill had to continue to produce roll-dyed pure wool fabrics, slow sellers at that time. Nor do cotton supply agencies take into account the blending requirements of the cotton mills. Mills that plan to produce coarse yarn are supplied with high-quality cotton, increasing their production costs. In 1983, hearing that some other agency outside Shanghai had a stock of low-quality cotton and was willing to exchange it for high-quality cotton, the parent company of the Shanghai No. 17 Cotton Mill took the initiative and arranged a barter deal with the other party. Despite the good economic results from the exchange, Shanghai Cotton was criticized by the department concerned because the exchange undermined the national allocation plan for cotton. The company was warned that no such exchange would be allowed in the future. The supply agencies cannot allocate materials to suit the needs of individual enterprises. Nevertheless, they insist that enterprises stick to convention at the expense of efficiency.

Ordering problems. The discrepancies between supply and demand are aggravated by a sequence in which enterprises submit requisitions to relevant agencies before the state assigns production plans to individual enterprises. Although they operate in a rapidly changing economic environment, producers and users can rely only on semiannual ordering conferences to match supply with demand. The first such conference, called a preparatory ordering conference, is usually held in the fourth quarter of the year before the plan year. The second conference, called the annual ordering conference, is usually held in the second quarter of the plan year. Generally, the state issues enterprise production plans for the plan year in February or March. The state is unable to issue enterprise production plans before the preparatory ordering conference because the state planners depend on the conference to collect information from central and local agencies about the availability of and demand for material inputs. Otherwise, the plans would be without foundation.

Before the state completes and issues production plans to enterprises, the enterprises have to submit requisitions. They do this for the plan year in the third quarter of the year before the plan year and place orders at the preparatory ordering conference held in the fourth quarter of that year. In preparing requisitions and placing orders, enterprises can only make estimates about their needs on the basis of empirical data or draft production plan. Enterprises that do not place an order at a preparatory ordering conference will not get supplies during the first half of the plan year. Enterprises that do place orders do so at the risk of facing a shortage or an overstock of materials if the state-assigned production plans differ from the enterprise's estimates. Enterprises consider this "planned blindness" a real headache. All the enterprises covered by our investigations complained strongly about it.

Here are two examples. The Qinghe Woolen Textile Mill has to submit its requisition for imported dyes and chemicals before making final decisions on the colors for its products; otherwise the mill will not be able to get supplies during the first half of the coming plan year. Once the requisition is submitted, no changes can be made. Moreover, payments have to be made on delivery, and each shipment is worth between one hundred thousand and several hundred thousand yuan. If the decisions on colors of the products turn out to be different from initial estimates, the imports are stocked, and the mill has to find other ways to get the dyes and chemicals it needs.

The Chengdu Locomotive and Rolling Stock Factory undertakes repair work of Dongfeng diesel locomotives for the whole country. Because railway conditions vary in different parts of the country, so does the wear and tear on locomotives. In the mountainous southwest region, the rims of wheels wear fast. In the northwest, the internal parts of diesel engines and transmissions wear rapidly because of wind and dust. Locomotives used in the northeast require good heating and insulation. Because locomotives also differ by model, service time, and history of reconditioning, they require various types and quantities of spare parts. Before completing its annual plan, the factory has to submit its requisition and orders for spare parts. But the factory's management cannot be sure that the spare parts ordered will suit its needs.

For Jinling Petrochemical General Corporation, some capital construction projects were submitted for approval ahead of the annual ordering conference so that supplies could be obtained in the year concerned, even though preparations for the projects were not complete. Had this not been done, the projects would have waited at least another year for material allocations. But once the projects were submitted, the materials were allocated before the construction plans were drawn up. To produce any type of producer goods, a producing enterprise uses products of many other enterprises as inputs, while its product in turn becomes an input for other enterprises. From raw materials to final product, many links form an input chain. Under the present system, when requisitions and purchase orders are based on estimates, the subplan of each link in the input chain contains uncertainty. As a result, plans do not conform to reality.

Delivery problems. Not only have the allocations to enterprises fallen short of what has been requested, but also there has been no guarantee of deliveries. Although the provisions in supply contracts specify the economic liabilities the party in default should bear, even a big user has no alternative if its supplier fails to deliver the contracted amount, for it still depends on the supplier when supply falls short of demand. Of 6,600 contracts between the North China Petroleum Administration and various suppliers of oilfield equipment, more than 30 percent were unexecuted or only partly executed, because suppliers could not fulfill their own plans or because subsuppliers failed to deliver. Deliveries of coke to Shenyang Smelting accounted for only 20 percent of the amount contracted for in some years.

The material supply performance of upstream links in an input chain also affects the execution of a supply contract. For example, the Nankou Rolling Stock Plant's failure to deliver locomotive wheels under contract nearly forced the Chengdu Locomotive and Rolling Stock Plant to shut down in the first half of 1983. Nankou's default was caused by the failure of the Manshan Iron and Steel Company to supply it with blanks for gears because the state did not assign allocation quotas to Manshan for molybdenum iron. Under the present system of allocating goods through administrative procedures, the discrepancy between the supply and demand for one link can thus have repercussions throughout the whole chain.

Inadequate transport capacity and its irrational allocation contribute to the low compliance rate of supply contracts. For rail transport, capacity is allocated by the number of wagons, irrespective of whether their capacity is thirty tons or fifty tons. Moreover, the allocation quota for raw materials becomes invalid if supplies are not delivered by the end of the year or—for quotas subdivided into monthly allotments, as they are for raw coal—by the end of the specified month. For the North China Petroleum Administration, deliveries of cement reach only 90 percent of the allocation, those of raw coal only 75 to 85 percent, owing to transport constraints. In 1982 the iron ore delivered to Anshan Iron and Steel from Hebei Province reached only 30 percent of the contract amount because of bottlenecks in rail transportation. And at Anshan's rolling mill, large inventories of urgently needed steel often accumulate because of the lack of rail wagons.

The Xiangxiang Cement Plant was forced to shut down for a while in 1982 because poor transport was causing the plant to run out of coal. In 1983 the delivery of slag to the plant was 16,000 tons short of the contracted amount as a result of transport problems. And the plant often cannot fulfill its own contractual deliveries, again because of transport problems. In the first and third quarters of 1983, the plant's cement storehouse was fully loaded because there were not enough rail wagons. The plant management had to ask city and county authorities in the province to organize trucking. In exchange, the province got an extra supply of cement outside the official allocation, but this made it more difficult for the plant to fulfill its obligations under the supply contracts. Managers at the No. 2 Automobile Plant feel that transport arrangements for intermediate goods do not suit the needs of balanced production. Once the factory wanted nylon film air-freighted to Shanghai, but the consignment sat idle at the airport for more than twenty days. Transport departments do not participate when producers and users sign supply contracts. And they do not bear economic liabilities for transport delays and damages.

According to the No. 2 Automobile Plant, the domestic transshipment of imported materials takes too much time. When damages are found upon receipt, it takes weeks before the rail authorities account for the damage. This delay results in delays in claims against foreign suppliers. The rail authorities are even more irresponsible about damages and losses during transit. In a shipment of 8,000 pieces of glass, 500 pieces were damaged (with a total value of more than Y300,000). This situation badly hinders the further specialization of industrial production.

Inventory problems. Excessive inventories are common in supply systems that rely on administrative decisions to allocate goods.[2] Central material supply agencies, industrial ministries, subordinate units at lower levels, and enterprises all keep inventories, which results in the slow circulation of goods. For example, between 1953 and 1981 (excluding 1958–60 for which accurate data are not available) the stockpiles of steel products were more than half the production in all twenty-six years and more than the total production in ten years. Inventories of steel products in short supply were especially excessive (see Zhou and others 1984, p. 351). Who was holding them at the end of 1981? Supply units of administative agencies accounted for 20 percent of the total, individual enterprises 54 percent. Local material supply bureaus, which cater to consumers at large, accounted for only 22 percent. The producers' inventories of final steel products made up the remaining 4 percent. From this example, it can be seen that most of the inventories are out of circulation.

When signing contracts, suppliers often choose the delivery time that best suits their production scheduling and ignore the needs of the other party. They take advantage of supply shortages to impose their wishes on users. For example, the consumption of cement at the Sanchazi Forestry Bureau, peaks in the second and third quarters of the year because of weather conditions. But large quantities of cement always arrive during the first quarter of the year, thus tying up a lot of funds. Specialized textile supplies are delivered to the Qinghe Woolen Textile Mill once a year, so the enterprise has to stockpile at least one year's consumption. Supplies to the Chengdu Locomotive and Rolling Stock Plant, which originate outside the province, are also delivered once a year. Some items (such as bearings) have many different specifications. The enterprise cannot afford not to keep each in stock, otherwise they will be unavailable when needed, even though the enterprise is taking the risk of overstocking. The Shanghai High-Pressure Oil Pump Factory consumes about one ton of seamless tubing every month. But the minimum order is five tons, so each delivery lasts at least five months. For many reasons, then—gaps between allocations and needs, long delivery cycles, unsatisfactory performance by suppliers, and transport constraints—enterprises always attempt to stockpile materials to prepare for any contingency. The smaller the production volume of an item, the more it is wanted. Some enterprises even buy and stock items that they do not need in their operations, hoping to arrange informal barter deals with other enterprises for needed goods. These perverse purchases increase the dispersion and excessive stocking of inventories.

Administrative Partitions

The administrative system erects partitions that restrict the flow of material resources. The plants that now make up the Jinling Petrochemical Corporation were previously under the direct control of the central, provincial, and municipal governments. And they were administered by the Ministry of the Petroleum Industry, the Ministry of the Chemical Industry, and the Ministry of Light Industry. This led to the partitioning of petrochemical technology and the irrational use of material resources. For example, the Nanjing Oil Refinery and the Qixiashan Chemical Fertilizer Plant are only half a kilometer apart, and they share six interlinking pipelines. But Nanjing was administered by the Ministry of the Petroleum Industry, Qixiashan by the Ministry of the Chemical Industry. Any materials above the monthly quota that Qixiashan needed from Nanjing required the approval of higher authorities.

Because goods are allocated according to administrative divisions, there is considerable transshipment and circuitous routing. The Anshan Iron and Steel Corporation used to have its own oil refinery. But the diesel fuel that refinery produced had to be shipped out according to state plans and be allocated nationally. So Anshan had to meet its needs with shipments from Fushun. (The refinery is now affiliated with the Jinling Petrochemical Corporation.)

Ministries and local authorities naturally compete with each other for material resources. There are 1.3 million tons of slag available each year in Hunan Province. But the slag from the Xiangtan Iron and Steel Mill is allocated by the Ministry of Metallurgy, that from the Lianyuan Iron and Steel Mill is allocated by the Hunan Provincial Building Materials Bureau. The Xiangxiang Cement Plant is a directly supplied enterprise of the State Building Materials Bureau, and its output is subject to national allocation. But Xiangxiang's slag supply is allocated by the Hunan Provincial Building Materials Bureau, which allocates most of the slag under its control to small, provincially controlled cement plants (because it allocates the output of these plants). The State Building Materials Bureau allocates only 200,000 tons of slag to the directly supplied enterprises in Hunan Province each year. In 1983 the Xiangxiang Cement Plant needed 260,000 tons of slag, but received 135,000 tons.

Administrative partitions lead to other sectoral and regional barriers to the flow of goods as well. For the purchase of passenger cars and trucks, the Anshan Iron and Steel Corporation has to ask the Liaoning provincial authority (via the Anshan municipal authority) for approval. Since passenger cars are scarce, the request is often turned down. Only those trucks made in Liaoning Province are available, and Anshan is not allowed to buy outside the province. The miscellaneous rubber items required by the Chengdu Locomotive and Rolling Stock Plant belong to the third category, and supply is plentiful in Chengdu. But the administrative authority of the higher level has stipulated that the plant has to place orders with supplying enterprises under the Ministry of Railways, even though the plant has to pay higher prices. The Sanchazi Forestry Bureau does not want to use the spare parts made by the machine building plants under the Jilin Provincial Forestry Department because of their poor quality. But the material supply company under the Jilin Provincial Forestry Department imposes a quota on Sanchazi Forestry Bureau and does not allow the bureau to seek supplies outside the province. The textile supplies made in Shaanxi Province are low in quality but high in price. For example, out of every ten fine-yarn spindles made in the province, only three to five are usable. And the price of each spindle is two yuan higher than the same kind made in Shanghai. The supply and marketing company under the Shaanxi Provincial Textile Industry Bureau had been imposing allocations of such spindles upon provincially controlled textile mills, and only recently was the province forced to discontinue the production of spindles, owing to an increase in the supply of spindles outside the province and the reluctance on the part of textile mills to buy the Shaanxi spindles. Another example is the Northwest No. 1 Cotton Mill, which has been allowed to dispose of 10 percent of its output on its own since 1982. The mill has no printing and dyeing facilities and is able to produce only blank cloth, so it contracted to have blank cloth printed and dyed outside the province, in Nantong and Changzhou. The cloth sold out quickly. But in 1983 the Shaanxi Provincial Textile Industry Bureau prohibited the mill from seeking printing and dyeing services outside the province and insisted that local processors be used instead. Because the local processors have fewer patterns to offer and charge higher rates, Northwest Cotton is forced to sell gray cloth.

With the central control of material allocation, users have no choices, and supplying enterprises need not worry about marketing their products. As a result, there has been little competition and little incentive to innovate in product design and technology. The textile machinery manufacturing industry is a typical ministry-controlled monopoly. The national allocation and supply of textile machinery is centrally administered by the National Textile Machinery Corporation, under the Ministry of the Textile Industry. This administrative system helps the ministry standardize the technical specifications of textile machinery, match the production of textile machinery with sales, serialize the product range nationally, and form manufacturing capabilities quickly.

To what avail? In old China, all textile machinery and equipment was imported, whereas in the early 1950s the then newly built Northwest No. 1 Cotton Mill was equipped with the first complete cotton-spinning plant made in the country. Now, the textile machinery manufacturing industry not only can make various types of complete sets of equipment for the domestic textile industry but can also offer a complete textile plant for export. But because of the lack of innovation in product design and technological progress, textile mills now face a common problem of "new equipment of old design" when they replace existing equipment or expand production capacity.

The Shanghai No. 17 Cotton Mill has been replacing old looms with new domestic looms since the 1960s, but the basic design of the new looms is from the 1930s. Some new equipment is not as good as the original equipment, which has been renovated several times. Thus the new equipment has to be modified before it can be put into use. In 1983, Shanghai Cotton procured 240 wide looms. More than 60,000 parts and components were changed during installation and commissioning—at a cost of Y110,000, which averages Y458 per loom and accounts for 25 percent of the loom price. In a similar experience, the Qinghe Woolen Textile Mill was allocated new woolen looms for a recent expansion. But the modifications that were needed to bring these new looms up to basic operating requirements took nine months. The mill received a batch of new spinning frames of 1970s design, but they were inferior to those of the 1960s, could not run during commissioning, and needed many modifications before they were put into use.

Circumventing the partitions through barter. Because the administrative allocation and official supply cannot fully meet the needs for production and construction, a parallel market for nationally allocated and ministerially controlled goods has come into being. In existence since the introduction of the centralized allocation system, the parallel market enables exchanges of scarce goods. In the past, barter deals were considered "illegal" and "to be strictly banned." In an attempt to replace such deals, the planning and supply agencies at the center and in the provinces, municipalities, and autonomous regions once organized exchanges of surplus inventories among enterprises and their respective administrative agencies. But because such exchanges were still subject to administrative application and approval, involved cumbersome procedures, and were unable to suit actual needs, they could not replace and eliminate barter deals.

An example shows how primitive the barter deals can be. In 1977 the Materials Bureau of Wuxi County (Jiangsu Province) exchanged AC electric motors produced over and above the fixed quota for 2,160 tons of silicon steel sheets in the following way. First, the electric motors were exchanged for pig iron and steel billets from such provinces as Hebei, Yunnan, Sichuan, Henan, Gansu, Guizhou, and Shanxi. Then these steel goods were shipped out in exchange for silicon steel. The bureau exchanged 1,000 tons of pig iron for 500 tons of small silicon steel sheets from the Shanghai Handicrafts Administrative Bureau. Through the Shanghai Metallurgical Industry Bureau it sent steel billets to some steel works to be processed into rolled steel, 8 percent of which was silicon steel. It exchanged some rolled steel for 570 tons of silicon steel sheets from the Metals Companies under the Qinghai and Shanghai materials bureaus, the General Materials Plant under the Shanghai Railway Bureau, and the Class 1 Station of the Shanghai Transport and Power Systems. It also exchanged 250 tons of rolled steel for 500 tons of silicon iron from the Heavy Industries Bureau of Nanjing Municipality and used the iron to provide 200 tons of silicon steel sheets. Then, at the metals reallocation meeting organized by the State Materials Bureau, the rolled steel was exchanged for 540 tons of silicon steel sheets from the metals companies under the Fujian, Shaanxi, and Jiangxi Provincial Materials Bureaus and from the Tianjin Municipal Purchasing and Supply Station.

With the reform of the economic system beginning in 1979, the ban against barter deals between enterprises was lifted and other moves were made toward giving producers greater autonomy. To get needed producer goods, industrial enterprises have also been allowed to sell or exchange a part of their above-quota production as well as their production that uses raw materials and fuels procured outside the official allocation channel. Such exchanges are common, particularly among enterprises producing scarce goods. For example, Anshan Iron and Steel's captive mines supply about 85 percent of its demand for mineral ores. Supplies from other domestic sources and imports make up the remaining 15 percent. In 1984 the corporation had to trade 40 percent of the steel for iron ore from domestic sources. For another example, the State Building Materials Bureau set the output quota of Xiangxiang Cement Plant at 890,000 tons, of which 50,000 tons were at the plant's disposal. Of the above-quota production, 30,000 tons of cement were subject to allocation by the Hunan Provincial Building Materials Bureau, 10,000 tons were subject to allocation by the Xiangtan Municipal Material Supply Bureau, and the plant was to have 100,000 tons at its disposal. It exchanged 25,000 tons for raw coal, 4,000 tons for power, 5,000 tons for wrapping paper, 4,500 tons for iron powder, and 5,000 tons for spare parts. In addition, it earmarked 3,000 tons of cement for the railway authorities in exchange for better transport arrangements.

Over time, the terms of exchange for various goods have been set in physical units, with prices settled separately. One ton of cement, for example, can be traded for one ton of coal, one and a quarter tons of slag, or a sixth of a ton of wrapping paper. Shenyang Smelting exchanges three tons of sulfuric acid for one ton of steel from the Anshan Iron and Steel Corporation. The No. 2 Automobile Plant exchanges one five-ton truck for ten to thirty tons of steel. These terms of exchange refer only to physical units. Moreover, the terms of exchange vary for different times, locales, and goods. And if one party to the exchange is dissatisfied, it might delay delivery considerably.

Circumventing the partitions in other ways. In addition to barter deals, enterprises seek goods in short supply through other channels outside the official allocation system.

- Providing materials for processing in exchange for finished products. During 1981 and 1982, Guangdong Province and other localities provided steel to the No. 2 Automobile Plant in exchange for automobiles under contracts.
- Importing materials with self-raised foreign exchange. The No. 2 Automobile Plant once imported steel with foreign exchange provided by the China Trust and Investment Corporation and assumed sole responsibility for

the profits or losses of its foreign transactions. Such imports have to be handled by China National Metals and Minerals Import and Export Corporation following the state import quota. The Mindong Electrical Machinery Plant has also been given some autonomy in foreign trade in recent years and has imported equipment and materials with its retained foreign exchange earnings (about 15 percent of its export earnings). But such use of retained foreign exchange is subject to the approval of the provincial planning commission.

• Applying for related goods and exchanging them for needed goods. In the first half of 1983 the Mindong Electrical Machinery Plant badly needed enamel-insulated wire, but the provincial material supply bureau ran out of stock. So the company applied for copper instead and exchanged five tons of copper for ten tons of enamel-insulated wire from the Shanghai Electrical Appliances Factory. It also exchanged fifteen tons of copper for twenty tons of enamel-insulated wire from a wire factory in Zhejiang Province.

• Purchasing directly from enterprises exempt from the allocation system. For such goods as coal, acid, cement, sheet glass, and caustic soda, the prices for the output of large and medium-size enterprises are set by ministries or departments. But for the output of small enterprises, the prices are set by price bureaus of provincial municipalities and autonomous regions. Although the quality of products from small, locally controlled enterprises is lower than that of products from large and medium-size enterprises, the prices are higher. In 1982, for example, the national benchmark price of raw coal was Y26 per ton. But the Qingdao Forging Machinery Plant paid Y40 per ton for coal from local mines, including transport costs.

Restrictions on the transport of materials purchased outside official channels made the burden even heavier. For transporting coke, railway authorities will provide wagons only with the clearance of provincial metallurgical industry departments. In 1982 Qingdao Forging Machinery Plant consumed 1,175 tons of coke. Purchases outside official channels accounted for nearly the total consumption, since the allocated amount was only 88 tons. But because the factory did not get clearance for the purchases from the provincial department, rail transport was not available, and the supply of coke had to be trucked 400 kilometers to the factory. That pushed the cost of the coke to more than Y50 per ton, twice the national benchmark price. During 1981 and 1982 the Baoji Nitrogen Fertilizer Plant met about half its demand for lump anthracite through purchases from small local coal mines in Shaanxi Province. Since the Shaanxi provincial authority stipulates that coal from local mines can be moved by road only within the provincial boundary, the coal bought by the Baoji Nitrogen Fertilizer Plant was trucked all the way to Hancheng in Shaanxi Province and then shipped by rail to Baoji. The cost of transport alone was Y53 per ton.

• Purchasing above-quota supplies. Enterprises can purchase above-quota goods from the sales outlets under the control of material supply agencies. But the prices of these goods include charges for administration, service, unloading, and storage. So they are higher, by varying degrees, than those of within-quota supplies.

• Investing in exchange for output. The No. 2 Automobile Plant provided an interest-free loan for the development of a tin mine with the understanding that the mine would supply its output to No. 2 Auto in lieu of cash repayment. Shenyang Smelting converted a scrapped rotary kiln, originally used for making zinc white, into a cement kiln—and then provided the kiln, along with a concessional loan and technical assistance, to the Benxi County Cement Plant in exchange for priority in getting cement. Another form of investment is a grant. Supported by the Ministry of the Petroleum Industry, the North China Petroleum Administration provided a Y5 million grant to Hebei Province for the expansion and rehabilitation of existing cement plants. For its part, Hebei Province is committed to supplying 300,000 tons of cement to the oilfields between 1983 and 1989. The investment cost (excluding interest) comes to Y16.7 per ton.

The examples show that administratively controlled allocation of materials and supplies cannot ignore market forces and that those forces have an irreplaceable role in a socialist economy.

Inadequate Information and Communication

A centralized allocation system requires the centralization of information. In other words, accurate and timely data from individual enterprises need to be continuously collected and transmitted to the decisionmaking bodies responsible for the allocation of all material resources. Such decisionmaking bodies should not only have information in hand about the aggregate supply and demand for each type of goods under their jurisdiction. They should also have such information for the model and quality of each product, as well as for delivery times and transport arrangements. They therefore need the details of production, supply, and marketing for each enterprise and each product.

Even if it were possible to collect such a vast amount of data, the efficiency of doing so is doubtful. The opportunity cost would be high, and the time required for collecting, transmitting, and processing the data would render the information obsolete before it could be used.[3] Moreover, the centralized allocation system itself creates obstacles for the centralization of information. Information flows mainly in a vertical direction between higher and lower levels of the administrative structure, and thus the horizontal sharing of information between enterprises is discouraged. But the vertical information channel is too narrow to accommodate the stream of data needed for

Table 9-1. *The Number of Nationally Allocated and Ministerially Controlled Goods in Selected Years*

Year	*Number of nationally allocated goods*	*Number of ministerially controlled goods*	*Total*
1950	8	—	8
1952	55	—	55
1953	112	115	227
1957	231	301	532
1959	67	218	285
1963	256	260	516
1965	370	222	592
1972	49	168	217
1978	53	636	689
1982	256	581	837

Note: Dashes indicate that data are not applicable.
Source: Zhou and others 1984, p. 519.

centralized material allocation. And to avoid being inundated by the data stream, planning and supply agencies have to combine products and inputs into a few hundred broadly defined groups, omitting needed information about the attributes of products and inputs (see table 9-1).

The simplification of data—and the fact that material allocation agencies designate links between producers and users—blocks communication between enterprises and creates microeconomic discrepancies in production, supply, and marketing. Besides, even the vertical flow of information must, from source to terminal, pass through numerous administrative institutions. The resulting long transmission aggravates the time lags between production, supply, and marketing—and increases the possibility of leaks and distortions during transmission of the information, thereby affecting its accuracy.

The allocation system also constrains the behavior of the parties to economic activities. Under the system, interactions between superior and subordinate institutions focus on the formulation and execution of plans. But the decisionmaking bodies are too far from enterprises to know the actual production capacity and the attainable consumption coefficients for inputs. And to help in material balancing, the decisionmaking bodies tend to ask enterprises to produce more scarce outputs and to minimize the consumption of inputs. Enterprises, on the other hand, tend to place priority on the production of products that can meet the physical and financial targets set by higher authorities. They also try to maintain high input-consumption coefficients to maximize their share of material allocation. Either way, the possibilities for distorting information through manipulation are great.

The centralized material allocation system does not guide economic activities according to economic principles. Instead, it relies on administrative commands to achieve its centrally formulated objectives. Therefore, it often conflicts with the vested economic interest of parties concerned at various levels. When such obstacles confront the centralization of information, the central government must decentralize its control of material allocation, relinquishing part of it to ministries and local governments. Such partial decentralization, however, creates new conflicts. Partial decentralization involves not devolution of economic decisionmaking but the devolution of administrative authority. Now that they are vested with decisionmaking powers, ministries and local governments can use administrative commands to implement their own decisions. But the objective functions of ministries and local governments are not necessarily in line with that of the central government. Therefore, the ministry-controlled monopoly and regional blockade come one after another, resulting in the partition of material resources by administrative boundaries. This partition impedes the rational utilization of resources. An enterprise's task consists of receiving commands and executing plans. Since enterprises lack decisionmaking power, they do not bear economic liability nor are they economically motivated toward the rational utilization of resources. An enterprise's concern is to get what it needs to fulfill annual production plans. In order to deal with the uncertainties surrounding the supply of inputs, enterprises resort to all kinds of methods to increase their access to goods. Goods not directly used as inputs are stocked as means of exchange. When overstocked goods become obsolete and useless, they are discarded and written off the balance sheet (whether they are financed by the bank or by the Ministry of Finance), and nobody is asked to bear the responsibility. Hence, although the state made several attempts to reduce inventories, the problem remains unsolved.

The administratively controlled system of material allocation also disregards market forces and downgrades the basic function of prices to a means of accounting. The system does not allow prices to respond to supply and demand—and thus stifles the function of prices in signaling the scarcity of resources. Neither do prices tell producers what products are most needed and how to produce them most economically. Nor do they show where material resources can be put to best use. The system thus lacks an objective yardstick for determining how resources should rationally be used—and gives enterprises the wrong signals. Distorted prices, together with the enterprises' preoccupation with output value and profit targets, often induce enterprises to produce overpriced and highly profitable goods, regardless of the market. They also induce the use of cheap raw materials and fuels, regardless of their scarcity. So, surpluses get larger and larger, while scarce goods become scarcer. The outcomes are disguised price increases, backdoor deals, misuses of power, and purchases and resales of scarce goods for exorbitant profits.

Progress with the Reforms

In 1980 the main mode of purchasing and marketing industrial consumer products—centralized allocation by departments of commerce—was augmented by three other modes: planned purchases, purchases through purchase orders, and selective purchases through departments of commerce.[4] And it is stipulated that industrial enterprises will have some right to market on their own. Later, some other modes were developed with departments of commerce acting as purchasing and marketing agents, and purchasing and marketing done jointly by industrial and commercial departments. Within the departments of commerce, the system for product allocation into first-class, second-class, and third-class wholesale centers began to be broken too. Since 1983, cities have, one after another, established trading centers to trade industrial products free from regional, departmental, and ownership restrictions.

Improving Supply

Measures have been taken to reduce the planned allocation of the means of production and to improve the material supply. While the planned allocation and transfer are maintained for the means of production that are important and in short supply, the state permits industrial enterprises to market what the operating units of the material supply departments retain after they fulfill the assigned quota. Users who have a demand for specific materials that is greater than their assigned quota will continue to apply for their allocation directly through their supervisory organizations. Other enterprises will no longer apply directly for their allocations. Instead, their local authorities will submit a joint application, and the supply will be organized and effected through the operating network of the material supply departments (supply centers, retail departments, and marketing centers for the means of production).

The methods for ordering some types of commonly used goods and materials have also started to change somewhat. The circulation of physical goods will be separated from the quota allocation (a change similar to separating the circulation of commodities from that of goods and materials). In other words, the quotas for the allocation of goods and materials will be assigned through the administrative system and transferred to the departments of goods and materials of the cities where the enterprises are located. Then these departments of goods and materials will organize the supply of physical goods and materials locally.

Big quantities of goods and materials that enterprises need will increasingly be supplied directly by designated centers. But smaller quantities will be supplied through transfer centers of the departments of goods and materials in cities—centers that will organize wholesale purchase and retail sales. The nodes of the operating network will use open-ended supply, allocated supply according to needs, supply by certificates or coupons, supply through contracts to form a complete set, and various other methods of supply according to the situation for different resources and uses. Service companies established for adjusting the supply of goods and materials will further develop their services for the means of production, principally acting as the purchasing agent, marketing agent, processing agent, consigning agent, and also regulating and exchanging. In recent years, the departments of goods and materials started to establish trading centers for goods and materials in large cities. But the goods and materials that currently enter the trading centers are still not those on the list of planned allocations.

The foregoing reforms, though in the early stages, have shaken the closed and rigid system of supply and marketing for state industrial enterprises. They have also played a positive role in enlarging the decisionmaking authority of enterprises and in promoting the transformation of enterprises from mere producers into marketers. The reforms have also addressed the need to improve the methods of supply under the original system of planned allocation, but these methods are secondary to the problems of planned allocation. The basic framework of the original supply and marketing system for state industrial enterprises has fundamentally remained intact. The reform of the sales system for enterprises that manufacture industrial consumer goods has progressed faster than that of the supply system. But the equal relationship of enterprises and commercial departments in a commodity economy has not yet been genuinely developed.

Improving Marketing

The scope of marketing by producers of industrial consumer goods is restricted to surpluses of commodities of unified purchase and marketing (centralized allocation) and planned purchase, as well as the surplus left from the purchase orders of commercial departments. The scope of marketing by the manufacturers of the means of production is restricted to the surplus of the planned allocation. This surplus includes goods and materials remaining after the manufacturer fulfills the purchase contracts of the departments of goods and materials; items not listed in the planned allocation or priority purchase order; products manufactured with the raw materials and energy that enterprises procure themselves; and new trial products.

In practice the enterprise's rights of marketing are unstable and tend to change with supply and demand. When supply easily meets demand, enterprises are allowed broader marketing rights. When it does not, the rights are restricted. For example, the proportion of steel production that enterprises marketed was 4 percent in 1979, 11 percent in 1980, 20 percent in 1981, 14 percent in 1982, and 4 percent in 1983. When the adjustment of the national economy started during 1979 and 1980 and experimental reforms were tried, the proportion of marketed steel products increased. As the economic adjustment continued in 1981, capital construction was greatly reduced, and the supply of steel products was ample—giving enterprises the highest proportion of steel for marketing since the experiment began. But in the second half of 1982, the demand for steel increased again, and consumers had to order steel products according to their allocated quotas—reducing the proportion that enterprises marketed to 2 percent. The proportion in 1983 was even a little lower than in 1979. When the state ceased centralized allocation of the long-line steel products in the latter half of 1979, the Anshan Iron and Steel Corporation was forced to promote sales and it sold the overstocked long-line types of steel products in combination with the short-line types. It also started to study the requirements of customers, organize production in light of supply and demand, increase the varieties of products, and reduce lot quantities. During those two years, the proportion of marketing reached 15 percent. But after a drastic reduction in 1982, when the Anshan Iron and Steel Corporation again set out to study the needs of the customers, the enthusiasm for such market research was dimmed because customers' lack of supply quotas made the research meaningless.

The experience of the auto industry was much the same. Before 1980 the state allocated all manufactured automobiles, and auto manufacturers could not sell even one on their own. In 1981 the auto market suddenly became sluggish because the state tightened the money supply and reduced investments in capital construction. Units originally qualified to apply for the allocation did not have the money to buy automobiles, and units and individuals originally disqualified from applying for the allocation could not buy them even if they had had money. The No. 2 Automobile Plant had an assigned production target of 35,000 automobiles for 1981, but only 16,000 of them were ordered at the meeting for placing orders. The state departments of goods and materials could not buy the unordered vehicles because they had no funds. But they were also not willing to market them for No. 2 Auto, so the plant was forced to study the market. It sent people to various places to promote sales and accept orders to make autos with materials supplied by customers. The autos would then be sold on credit, through the buyer's bank, and endorsed by the state. No. 2 Auto sold more than 20,000 autos, thereby surpassing its production plans for the year.

In 1982 No. 2 Auto's target was 50,000 automobiles. But when the meeting for placing orders was held at the end of 1981, the departments of goods and materials were willing to take only 8,000 of the 20,000 autos that they originally planned to market. Once again, the plant organized itself to market and accept orders on its own. But the demand for automobiles started to pick up in February and March of 1982, and the State Bureau of Goods and Materials required the plant to turn over all of its planned production for the year for centralized allocation. This request caused the plant to fall short in fulfilling purchase orders gained from its own marketing effort.

As long as the basic system of centralized supply and marketing is kept intact, the higher administrative departments can withdraw the partial delegation of marketing rights at any time. Moreover, the inevitable conflicts with the centralized system restrict the efficiency of marketing by enterprises. Such delegation of marketing rights can, however, be regarded as only transitional. The eventual goal is to switch fully to a planned commodity economy. The relationship between the departments and industrial enterprises will then no longer involve administrative instructions. Instead, supply and marketing will be based on the principles of commerce. Supply and demand will be designated not by administrative departments but by free choice, with regard to the economic benefits.

Added Requirements for Commodity Circulation

To establish equitable commodity trading, the departments of industry, commerce, and goods and materials should first separate their administrative duties from those of enterprises. This separation would enable enterprises to carry out their economic activities as independent producers and operators. The enterprises should manage production, supply, and marketing themselves. The government departments should develop industrial strategies and technological policies to serve the enterprises and to exercise necessary and effective control over them. But they should not try to ensure the coordinated and proportional development of the national economy—for that tends to create confusion in production, supply, and marketing.

For macroeconomic control, the state should seek to balance aggregate supply and demand through national income policies. It should also use its economic leverage to coordinate enterprises' decisions in production, supply, and marketing with state objectives.

Reform should enable the means of production to enter the market, and it should enable the administrative allocation of commodities to be replaced by the circulation of commodities. The mere improvement of supply methods will not overcome the defects of the administrative allocation of goods and materials. Only by replacing the system of administrative allocation with commodity circulation can the segmentation of the departments of goods and materials and the regional administrations be broken. The unified socialist market will then be established, with prices indicating the scarcity of resources. And enterprises will then be encouraged to select their inputs rationally and use their resources economically—to achieve the rational distribution of resources. The supply of scarce goods and materials needed for key state construction projects may have to be guaranteed through government or priority purchase orders. But that should account for only a small part of the supply of all inputs.

Reforming the allocation system boils down to solving the problem of the "circulation of commodities." Once that is solved, it will be easier to solve the problem of "circulation of materials." In light of the current situation in China, the most feasible solution is to bring primitive modes of barter trade onto the track of normal commodity circulation—and to reduce the scope of administrative allocation step by step. In addition, the controls on the prices of the means of production that enter the market will be relaxed with respect to the differences in competitive environments for the various goods and materials. In this way the market price that reflects supply and demand can be established gradually. With the gradual realization of market prices, list prices will be drawn closer to market prices. And with the further relaxation of the price system, the circulation of commodities will determine the flows of goods and materials originally allocated through administrative measures.

Notes

1. Exceptions include a few items, such as cashmere, cotton wool, and dacron and acrylic sliver, at the Qinghe Woolen Textile Mill. The items are ensured in quantity, but problems still exist for variety and specifications.
2. Consider a quotation from the Czechoslovak newspaper *Red Right* in Sik 1985: "Inventories in Czechoslovakia totaled 230 billion korun as of the end of 1973, equivalent to two-thirds of national income. By the end of 1976, the value of inventories increased to 315 million korun, or 84 percent of the national income. Inventories in Poland equal 87 percent of the national income."
3. A famous airplane designer in the U.S.S.R., Antonov, said in his book (1965), "According to the calculations of mathematicians in Kiev, it would take all the people in the world to work 10 million years to compile a precise and very complete annual plan for the supply of material and technology just for the Ukraine" (p. 23).
4. The commodities of unified state purchase and marketing (centralized allocation) are purchased and managed by the departments of commerce in a unified way. For the commodities of planned purchase, purchase plans are made by the state. Industrial enterprises are required to turn over commodities according to plan, whereas departments of commerce make the purchase according to plan. The overfulfilled part in excess of the plan can be marketed by industrial enterprises themselves. The production and marketing of commodities will be coordinated by the industry and commerce together. The industrial department will assign production targets, and the industry and commerce will sign contracts through negotiations. For the commodities of selective purchase, they can either be purchased selectively by the departments of commerce or marketed by the industrial enterprises on their own.

References

Antonov, Oleg Konstantinovich. 1965. *For Everyone and for Oneself* [English translation of the Russian title]. Moscow.

Sik, Ota. 1985. *For a Humane Economic Democracy.* Fred Eidlin and William Graf, trans. New York: Praeger Special Studies.

Zhou Taihe, ed. 1984. *Dangdai Zhongguo de Jingji Tizhi Gaige* (Economic system reform in contemporary China). Beijing: Zhongguo Shehui Kexue Chubanshe.

10

The Role and Impact of Markets

William Byrd

THE ROLE OF THE MARKET mechanism in the distribution of industrial products in China has expanded greatly since 1978, whereas that of administrative directives and controls (including planning) has correspondingly diminished.[1] For consumer goods, direct retail sales by industrial enterprises accounted for more than 17 percent of the value of retail sales of nonagricultural commodities in 1983, compared with 14 percent in 1980, under 11 percent in 1979, and considerably less in earlier years.[2] Just as important, many of the commercial system's purchases of industrial consumer goods are becoming voluntary and are occurring outside the framework of command planning. The share of such voluntary transactions between industrial enterprises and commercial units reportedly was about 40 percent in 1981 and 48 percent in 1982 (Liu 1982, p. 8; Zhou 1984, p. 488).

For producer goods, the share of output distributed outside the framework of directive planning and administrative allocation has also increased sharply. The direct marketing of machinery and electrical equipment by producers became common in 1979–80 as orders for many types of machinery through the state plan declined sharply. In 1980, direct sales outside the state plan accounted for 46 percent of total sales by enterprises under the First Ministry of Machine Building (compared with only 13 percent in 1979) and 33 percent of sales by all machinery producers.[3] Many enterprises in this industry, including some in the sample, have become responsible for almost all their sales. Direct marketing of rolled steel outside the plan accounted for only 4 percent of total national production in 1979, but it accounted for 11 percent in 1980 and hit a peak of 20 percent in 1981 (Zhou 1984, p. 357).

Nascent market institutions of various kinds have sprung up in China's state-owned industrial and commercial system. "Markets for the means of production" have been established in Shanghai and other large cities (see

Byrd 1985a). More recently, wholesale markets for industrial consumer goods have been set up in Chongqing and elsewhere. Advertising, virtually prohibited during the Cultural Revolution, has become a major means of sales promotion. In addition, some enterprises hold "ordering conferences" (often in scenic spots) for the same purpose. Retail outlets established by state, collective, and individual commerce, as well as by industrial enterprises, have also proliferated.

Just as striking as the expanding role of the market mechanism is the emergence of buyers' markets (excess supply) for many commodities, in sharp contrast with the chronic shortages and sellers' markets (excess demand) typically found in centrally planned economies. Ordinary machinery has been in excess supply since the late 1970s. Some consumer durables and many other consumer goods have also shifted from a sellers' market to a buyers' market. With continuing shortages of raw materials, energy, and some basic living necessities, the Chinese economy is now characterized by great diversity in market conditions as well as by variation across commodities in the relative importance of the market mechanism and administrative allocation.

There are four central questions about markets in China's state-owned economic system. What caused the shift from a sellers' market to a buyers' market for many commodities? What is the relationship between the emergence of buyers' markets and the increase in the share of market transactions (which occurred more or less simultaneously)? How sustainable are China's buyers' markets? How well do markets work in an environment in which administrative decrees previously were the predominant mode of resource allocation and remain important? Related questions concern the impact of market forces on Chinese state-owned industrial enterprises, government response to changing market conditions, dynamic patterns and trends during the past half decade, and implications for the future.

Markets, Competition, and Equilibrium

In analyzing the evolving role of the market mechanism in Chinese industry, it is crucial to understand how markets work in industrial capitalist countries and how they achieve the benefits commonly attributed to them. This topic is vast and controversial. The following comments draw on a line of analysis developed by Schumpeter (1950, especially chap. 7), which can be traced to Marx.[4] This approach emphasizes the role of competition and views the capitalist economy as advancing through an uneven yet highly dynamic process of "creative destruction." Existing capital values are eroded by new innovations, which earn those who bring them into the marketplace temporary "monopoly profits" before other firms catch up and the process of erosion gets under way again. In this situation, there is no long-term equilibrium in any meaningful sense of the word, and the definition of "competition" is something akin to the layman's understanding of the word ("conscious rivalry"). It is far removed from the neoclassical definition of "perfect competition" (in which the numerous firms in an industry are too small to have an impact on the market and therefore take market prices as given).

Market forces can affect enterprise behavior and stimulate improved performance in many ways. An obvious but important one is cost reduction. Facing an effectively functioning market for their outputs, firms are under strong pressure to reduce costs and use the most efficient technology available. High-cost producers are likely to be forced out of business over the long run. Similarly, market pressures may prevent firms from charging excessively high prices, and eventually (with free entry) there may be a tendency to eliminate economic profits. Other dimensions involve a more dynamic and long-term impact. These areas include product differentiation (a response to demand); advertising and other forms of sales promotion (which provide useful information to customers but may also manipulate the demand curve for a product directly by altering or developing tastes); and most important, the development and diffusion of technological innovations of various kinds. Enterprises facing competitive markets also have a strong incentive to meet customer needs by improving marketing and distribution and by providing warranties and after-sales service. Market competition may also generate strong incentives to improve or maintain product quality. Finally, by widening markets and breaking down barriers to trade, enterprises can increase overall efficiency significantly.

Enterprises relying on the market mechanism cannot reap its benefits unless they have meaningful discretionary authority in their operations. Two other prerequisites are appropriate motivation and incentives for enterprises and effective competition among producers. For incentives to work, enterprises must be concerned about profits, but they do not have to be pure profit maximizers. Various other objective functions of enterprises are consistent with striving to increase profits: sales maximization (subject to a profitability constraint); growth maximization (particularly when the firm must rely mainly on reinvestment of retained profits to finance expansion); maximization of the value of the company as measured by the stock market; and even "satisficing" (for example, achieving enough profits to keep shareholders happy and avoid the threat of takeover).[5]

Similarly, perfect competition is not a prerequisite for realizing the potential advantages of the market mechanism. Indeed, perfect competition may not permit enterprises to expend resources in such crucial areas as research and development. At the other extreme, the adverse impact of monopolistic or collusive oligopolistic arrangements on efficiency—on technical efficiency or X-efficiency even more than allocative efficiency—is well recognized.[6] Between these extremes, vigorous price and nonprice competition among firms whose actions can and do affect market conditions may well be the best arrangement from a dynamic perspective. The optimal degree and form of competition probably varies considerably across products, technologies, time, and so on. And the threat of competition from possible entrants to an industry can be crucial.

A buyers' market tends to foster effective competition among sellers (producers). In the industrial market economies, enterprises often deliberately operate with some excess capacity and ample inventories, which allows them to meet unexpected surges in demand without turning away customers.[7] At the same time, it generates a stable situation in which a buyers' market prevails. On the other hand, a sellers' market (excess demand, whether actual or perceived) generates competition among buyers striving to obtain a share of the limited supply of goods available. In such a market, there is little hope for effective competition among producers, because they can always sell their output to eager buyers (see Kornai 1980). In particular, sellers will not respond to nonquantitative aspects of demand (they may expand output as much as possible for various reasons), and buyers scrambling for supplies will not be in a position to make their preferences felt.

Market conditions (particularly chronic shortages) can have a major impact on enterprises even when most goods are at least nominally subject to administrative allocation through mandatory plans. Shortages can have a strong influence on enterprises that must obtain part of their supplies outside the plan—as can excess supply, on producers responsible for some marketing (even though most of their output may be subject to allocation by plan). In either case, the importance of market conditions tends to be magnified by their impact on enterprises' marginal decisions. Even if all outputs and inputs are subject to mandatory plans, shortages can manifest themselves as underfulfillment of enterprises' input supply quotas. Moreover, a secondary market in which enterprises can trade goods almost invariably arises, even if the plan determines the initial distribution. Administrative allocation can also generate and preserve "artificial" shortages. Even though ample supplies of a good may be available nationally, enterprises wanting to buy them may be hindered by administrative barriers and procedural requirements.

Distinctions must be made among the different terms and classifications used (sometimes casually) to describe market conditions: "equilibrium" versus "disequilibrium," "buyers' market" versus "sellers' market," and "excess supply" versus "excess demand." "Static equilibrium" is a clear concept: demand and supply are equal at the equilibrium price. "Disequilibrium," then, by definition implies that prices are not at the equilibrium level (perhaps because of administrative controls). In this context, "excess supply" means that prices are too high and "excess demand" means that prices are too low.

The concepts of buyers' and sellers' markets, on the other hand, do not rely on the existence of market-clearing prices. At the extreme—in a situation of chronic shortages—it is possible that no feasible price change will clear the market. Economic behavior and even institutions become adapted to the situation, which can then be strongly self-reinforcing. Nevertheless, there are invariably strong upward pressures on prices (even if substantial price increases would not dampen demand significantly). In a buyers' market, producers act "as if" there is excess supply—that is, they do not take demand for granted, but they compete for and respond to the market. This does not mean that price reductions would occur, much less that in some meaningful sense they would "clear the market." Hence, in a stable buyers' market, there may be equilibrium in the sense that no producer has an incentive to offer a lower price (except for temporary sales or discounts to tap certain segments of the market), and purchasers are free to buy all of any good they want at the going price. This means that there may not be strong downward price pressures in a mature buyers' market.

The crucial role of exit and what Schumpeter calls the "erosion of capital values" in the dynamic process of market competition must also be stressed. Technological advance and the development of new products mean that older products and technologies become obsolete, that capital designed for them loses value much faster than physical depreciation occurs, and that some enterprises lose their competitiveness and exit from the scene. Protective measures by large corporations may make exit less likely for them, but this does not prevent the erosion of capital values and the need to replace older technologies and products with new ones. All that is changed is that such adjustments are more likely to occur in a single organization.

This brief excursion into the theoretical aspects of markets suggests some important questions to guide empirical analysis in China. Perhaps most important, under what conditions will the response of state enterprises to market forces in a socialist economy be similar to that of private corporations in a capitalist economy? If it turns out that the response will be similar only in a buyers' market, what are the conditions under which a buyers' market can emerge and become entrenched in an economy like China's? Even if the response of enterprises in a socialist economy turns out to be similar to that in a capitalist system under appropriate conditions, are there any systematic differences in the actions of the government or in other factors that would cause a divergence in industrywide and medium-term or long-term developments? Before tackling the broader questions, I will look for empirical patterns in the information from the sample of twenty enterprises.

Enterprise Responses to Market Forces

Sellers' Markets

The responses of enterprises to a sellers' market can be divided into four main types, in ascending order of difficulty and economic benefits. The first is the "passive response"—taking advantage of the secure market position to avoid any exertion, even that required just to expand output to the limit of capacity. Naturally, there is no responsiveness to nonquantitative aspects of demand (such as quality or user specifications), since the enterprise is not even responding to the strong quantity signals of a sellers' market. Enterprises with some motivation (or prodding from supervisory agencies) will generally act more positively in the face of a sellers' market. It is not surprising, then, that few enterprises in the sample exhibit this response even temporarily.[8]

A second type of behavior is the "expansion response." Here, the enterprise vigorously increases output until it meets a constraint it cannot overcome or a change in market conditions. But it makes no attempt to cut costs, develop new products, meet customer needs, or otherwise respond to nonquantitative aspects of demand. It is even possible that performance in these areas will deteriorate as a result of the rush to increase output as rapidly as possible. A premier example of this kind of response is the Chongqing Clock and Watch Company in 1979–81.[9]

A third response can be characterized as a "technical response." It is often related to engineering priorities and solutions.[10] It may involve a focus on quality improvement, even beyond customer needs; acquisition and use of the most advanced modern technology, again disregarding costs and customer needs; an attempt to introduce new, more technologically advanced products; or, more rarely, cost reduction. The key point is that these actions are undertaken without regard for what is actually needed or preferred on the demand side. Hence, despite the often considerable effort involved, the benefits are limited. Most of the enterprises in the sample facing a sellers' market for their output end up in this mode, particularly if they are constrained by supply or capacity rather than by finance.

The fourth response to a sellers' market could be termed the "market-oriented response." It is rare, even among the enterprises in our sample. Sometimes it occurs in enterprises that have developed habits in buyers' markets—habits that persist when market conditions revert to excess demand. It may also be related to an enterprise's desire to increase its prestige, perhaps through demonstrating the ability to export. And it may be related to financial incentives that promote exports, to a focus on long-term expansion, or to an effort to increase domestic market share by enticing customers away from other producers. The most notable example of an enterprise that used this response is the No. 2 Automobile Plant, which became more responsive to customers during a period of excess supply on the market in 1981 but then continued this pattern even when the market tightened again in 1982–83. No. 2 Auto is striving to increase its market share (it is already one of the two largest truck producers in China), to develop exports, and to expand into regional markets previously served by the No. 1 Automobile Plant.

Buyers' Markets

The first response of an enterprise to a weak market for its output tends to be *neglect and disbelief*. The enterprise usually is slow to recognize that market conditions have changed. It may maintain an inward technical orientation similar to the technical response to a sellers' market, or it may continue rapid expansion. But once the enterprise realizes the new situation, its reaction may be one of *despair and passive dependency*. Seeing no way of coping on its own, the enterprise relies on help from authorities (subsidies or protection from outside competition) to stay in business. The enterprise usually hopes that commercial units will continue to buy its products even if they are unsalable on the market. Well-managed enterprises are unlikely to maintain this posture for long, and supervisory agencies in China have often proved unwilling to allow them the luxury of this option for more than a short time. Thus it usually is not a stable long-term response.[11]

A second response involves vigorous *sales promotion*. The enterprise increases its sales staff, sends out people to drum up business, engages in some advertising, and so on. Price reductions also may form part of this strategy. But there is no effort to cut costs, raise quality standards, improve products or develop new ones, or otherwise respond to demand. For enterprises producing high-quality goods (like most of those in the sample), this response can be at least temporarily effective in opening new markets and stimulating sales. Nearly all the enterprises in the sample that face a buyers' market engage in sales promotion, but most of them have taken other actions as well.

This second response to a buyers' market is naturally supplemented by a third, the *intensive response*. This response is a genuine attempt to meet customer needs by an appropriate combination of shifting product mix, improving quality, developing new products or varieties, cutting prices directly or by selling a better product for the same price, and providing better warranties and postsale service. Price reductions may generate pressures for cost reductions, but in many cases it appears that enterprises can shift most of the burden of lower revenues onto the government (by lowering profit remittances). Thus the pressures for cost reduction may remain relatively weak. Otherwise, the benefits of this type of behavior in terms of generating goods better suited to demand, at least at the microlevel, are obvious. A key distinction between the second and third types of response is that the former does not involve the sphere of production, whereas the latter takes place primarily in this area.

One more radical response to a buyers' market is that of *exit* into new lines of products. This positive, active response involves a wholesale change of orientation. There are no examples of enterprises that completely change their lines of products or that simply exit from the scene in the sample, but some are on the verge of exit from producing one of their main products (clocks at Chongqing Clock and Watch). Others strive to develop completely new types of products to use underutilized factors of production (usually labor but sometimes also land or facilities).

Market Conditions and Enterprise Responses

The crucial impact of market conditions on enterprise response is readily apparent from table 10-1. Of the eight enterprises in the sample that produce goods in excess demand,[12] at least four appear to have ended up in the third (technical) response, not very responsive to purchasers' needs. Only one exhibits the market-oriented response. Perhaps more important, there appears to be no dynamic force in the confines of a sellers' market that leads enterprises to more positive and economically efficient actions. At most, there may be an evolution from the second response (expansion) to the third response. Enterprises facing a capacity constraint in a sellers' market will invest heavily in expansion if given the opportunity. If they then meet a raw material constraint, they may turn to focus on quality, technology, and so on.

The response to a sellers' market may, however, depend a great deal on the cause of the shortage. If the primary constraint is insufficient capacity in the industry, producers, if given access to financial resources, will tend to engage in the expansion response. This leads naturally to a shift from excess demand to excess supply. If the main constraint is a key material input (or energy, for energy-intensive industries), enterprises are likely to move to a technical response, since scope for output expansion is limited. Finally, if input and output prices that make production unprofitable are the primary cause of a persistent sellers' market, producers will generally try to exit to the extent that they are allowed to do so and that attractive alternatives are available.[13] Firms unable to exit (for example, those engaged in mining) will in any case not be able to expand with internally generated funds, and low profits may also dissuade organizations with funds available (banks, local governments) from providing them.

A buyers' market, on the other hand, generates strong pressures for enterprises to respond in ways that benefit buyers. Of the enterprises in the sample that face a buyers' market, most have moved into the intensive response. The negative responses (the first and the second) tend to be, at most, temporary stages in a natural sequence that leads to more positive actions. As long as production remains profitable, the cause of the buyers' market does not appear to have a great effect on enterprise response. In particular, makers of producer goods that face a buyers' market because of a government-mandated cutback in investment respond similarly to producers of high-priced consumer durables in excess supply due to industrywide overexpansion.

Table 10-1. *Product Characteristics, Technology, and Market Conditions, 1982–83*

Market conditions and enterprise	*Enterprise response*[a]	*Nature of product*[b]	*Type of product*[c]	*Production technology*[d]	*Market conditions for main inputs*
Sellers' market					
North China Petroleum	1–2	HOM	RAW MAT	EXTR	—[e]
Sanchazi	1–2	HOM	RAW MAT	EXTR	—[e]
Anshan	3	HOM/DIF[f]	INTERM	CONT	Shortage[g]
Baoji	2[h]	HOM	INTERM	CONT	Shortage
Jinling	3	HOM	INTERM	CONT	Shortage
Shenyang	3	HOM	INTERM	CONT	Shortage
Xiangxiang	3	HOM	INTERM	CONT	Shortage[g]
No. 2 Auto	4	DIF	INVSTMT	ENG	Shortage
Buyers' market					
Mindong	7	DIF	INT/INV	ENG	Shortage
Qingdao	7	DIF	INVSTMT	ENG	Shortage
Shanghai Oil Pump	6(3)	DIF	INTERM	ENG	Shortage
Chongqing	7	DIF	CONSM	ENG	Surplus
Jiangmen	7	HOM/DIF	CONSM	ENG	Shortage
Nanning	7	DIF	INT/COM	TEX	Surplus
Northwest Cotton	6–7	HOM	INTERM	TEX	Shortage
Qinghe	7	DIF	INTERM	TEX	Shortage
Shanghai Cotton	5(3)	HOM	INTERM	TEX	Shortage
Tianjin	7	DIF	INT/COM	TEX	Surplus(?)
Other					
Chengdu	3	DIF	SERVICE	ENG	n.a.
Qingyuan	7	n.a.	n.a.	n.a.	n.a.

n.a. = not available.

a. 1: passive response; 2: expansion response; 3: technical response; 4: market-oriented response; 5: neglect/dependency; 6: sales promotion; 7: intensive response.

b. HOM: homogeneous product; DIF: differentiated product; HOM/DIF: enterprise produces both.

c. RAW MAT: raw material; INTERM: intermediate good; INVSTMT: investment good; CONSM: consumption good; INT/INV: enterprise produces both intermediate products and investment goods; INT/CON: enterprise produces both intermediate products and consumption goods; SERVICE: service activity.

d. EXTR: extractive; CONT: continuous process; ENG: engineering industry (including assembly line operations); TEX: textile industry.

e. These enterprises in extractive industries are their own source of inputs. Both petroleum reserves and forestry resources, however, are in very short supply in China.

f. Rolled steel can be considered a differentiated product with many varieties, whereas pig iron and unprocessed steel can be considered homogeneous products, but this distinction is somewhat arbitrary.

g. These factories "own" mines producing their main material input and are therefore to a large extent sheltered from the general shortage situation.

h. It was very difficult to ascertain this enterprise's response from the information provided.

Other Factors Influencing Enterprise Responses

Product characteristics and production technology. Technical aspects can influence the enterprise's response to market forces and influence market conditions themselves. There are a number of dimensions, as can be seen from table 10-1. Broadly speaking, most producers of homogeneous goods in the sample face sellers' markets, whereas most producers of differentiated products face buyers' markets. The relationship between market conditions and the classification of goods—as raw materials, intermediate products, investment goods, or consumer goods—is more complex. The only producer of final goods facing a sellers' market is the No. 2 Automobile Plant. Enterprises facing a buyers' market, on the other hand, include producers of both intermediate and final goods, though most of the latter are consumer goods.

All of the firms that face a sellers' market use continuous-process technology, except for the two enterprises in extractive industries and the No. 2 Automobile Plant. But all the enterprises that face a buyers' market use batch production techniques, except for the textile plants (whose classification in this schema is somewhat fuzzy anyway). From another angle, only one of the enterprises that face a sellers' market (No. 2 Auto) is in an engineering industry. The rest are in extractive or processing industries.

Some of the superficially strong associations in our sample are probably misleading. For example, the linkage between product homogeneity and a sellers' market most likely does not result from direct causation between the former and the latter. Similarly, the lack of producers of final goods that face a sellers' market is in part illusory. Cement, timber, and much steel are direct inputs into the construction industry (which creates investment goods in the form of civil construction), and hence they do not differ as greatly from machinery (which must be installed before it unambiguously becomes a final good) as this classification would suggest.

Technology and product characteristics, aside from the direct or indirect effect they may have on market conditions, in many ways constrain an enterprise's behavior and its response to market forces. For homogeneous products, the scope for new product development is limited, and new products may have only a small effect in stimulating demand anyway. The fixity of the capital stock required for many continuous-process technologies often makes exit difficult and uneconomical. Moreover, it may be very costly to slow or stop production. Thus, enterprises that produce homogeneous products with continuous-process technologies will find it hard to respond in quantitative or qualitative ways to the demands of a buyers' market, which means that price changes have to take up most or all of the burden of adjustment. Price-inelastic demand may be a problem. But more important in China, price controls may hinder even downward adjustments in prices. Still, all the enterprises in the sample that produce homogeneous products with continuous-process technologies face a sellers' market and thus do not have to make difficult adjustments to a buyers' market in the absence of price flexibility.

Another important factor is the ease with which product mix can be altered. This factor is particularly relevant for multiproduct enterprises facing different market conditions for different goods. At one extreme, the Shenyang Smelting Plant has almost no control over the amount of various kinds of by-products it recovers from ores during smelting. The main determinant is the mineral composition of the ores it receives. Reducing production of by-products is not a viable alternative, because it would increase pollution. This restriction makes it impossible for the enterprise to respond to excess supply by cutting production. The homogeneity of its products (pure nonferrous metals) makes other responses ineffective as well. In the end, Shenyang dealt with severe excess supply of cadmium by tying sales of it to those of zinc, one of its main products for which demand is strong.[14] The Chongqing Clock and Watch Company presents both an intermediate case and the opposite extreme. Although workers can be shifted to some extent from clock production to watchmaking, the scope for shifting equipment is much more restricted. Thus the room for maneuver in shifting the composition of output between clocks and watches is limited without significant new investment. On the other hand, the company can alter the grade of its watches merely by redesigning the face and changing the brand name.[15]

Direct marketing and exports. The share in total sales of direct marketing (or self-marketing) done by enterprises predictably varies with changing market conditions (table 10-2).[16] Except for the No. 2 Automobile Plant and Anshan Iron and Steel (both faced excess supply in 1981), none of the sample enterprises facing a sellers' market freely sold more than 10 percent of its output in 1980–82. But some of the enterprises facing a buyers' market had to sell most of their output on their own. Available fragmentary information at the national level supports the hypothesis that a buyers' market is a precondition, though not necessarily a sufficient condition, for a high share of direct marketing.

The qualitative role of direct marketing also varies systematically with market conditions. In a strong sellers' market, the right to self-market some output is a valued privilege, conferred on producers often over strenuous objections from commercial organizations or supervisory agencies. In these circumstances, self-marketing is generally closely tied to enterprise-specific reform packages or even special favors granted to enterprises. The benefits for the producer from direct sales in a strong market include exchanging products for other goods the enterprise needs; capturing part or all of the commercial

Table 10-2. *Direct Marketing and Exports, 1980–82*
(percent)

Market and enterprise	*Share of self-marketing in total sales*[a]	*Share of exports in total sales*[b]	*Share of direct exports in total exports*[c]
Sellers' market			
North China Petroleum	0.2[d]	n.a.	0
Sanchazi	0[e]	0.3	0
Anshan	12.0[d]	1.1	45.4
Baoji	Very small[f]	0	0
Jinling[g]	Very small[f]	15.3	0.1[h]
Shenyang	1.8[i]	n.a.	0
Xiangxiang	8.6[j]	0	0
No. 2 Auto	41.6[d]	0.4	92.7
Buyers' market			
Mindong	82.5[k]	31.3	74.0[k]
Qingdao	90[l]	1.7	0
Shanghai Oil Pump	n.a.	39.2[m]	0
Chongqing	30[n]	3.1	0
Jiangmen	39.3[o]	8.3	0
Nanning	26.6[p]	28.1	0
Northwest Cotton	12.6[q]	23.2	0
Qinghe	3.9[r]	36.8	0
Shanghai Cotton	Very small[f]	10.7	0
Tianjin	10.5[s]	47.0[t]	0
Other			
Chengdu	0	0	0
Qingyuan	High	Low	Low

n.a. = not available.

a. Ratio of revenues from products sold on a voluntary basis outside of mandatory plans to total sales revenue, unless otherwise indicated.

b. Share of revenues from sales for export (including sales to foreign trade departments and direct exports) in total sales revenue, unless otherwise indicated. Export sales are valued at prices actually received by the producer. Note that exports and self-sales do not overlap, except in the case of direct exports.

c. Direct exports are defined as those undertaken by the enterprise on its own account, as opposed to sales to foreign trade departments.

d. Share of physical output that was self-sales (crude oil in the case of the North China Petroleum Administration, rolled steel in the case of the Anshan Iron and Steel Corporation, and trucks in the case of the No. 2 Automobile Plant).

e. Before 1980, the enterprise had some self-marketing rights, which were taken away in that year. Now all sales outside the plan apparently must be approved by the Jilin Provincial Forestry Bureau. Some timber is exchanged with units of the People's Liberation Army in return for road construction services, while some is also provided to "owners" of some of the afforested land and to units which tend forests under contract.

f. Precise figures were not given, but the enterprises indicated that they were very small.

(Notes continue on the following page.)

margin through sales at the wholesale or even the retail price, rather than the factory price; manipulating the product mix and self-marketing the most profitable goods and varieties; and, where permitted, increasing profits by charging a higher price. Of these four benefits, the ability to exchange products for other goods is probably the most important, because it allows the enterprise to obtain needed inputs for production and consumer goods for employees.

Not surprisingly, self-marketing in a sellers' market is an issue of contention. Implementation is likely to be restricted by the within-plan distribution agency, and bargaining over the exact share of self-marketed output may be lengthy and difficult. An example is the Baoji Nitrogen Fertilizer Plant, where the right to self-market 10 percent of its output was formally granted only in 1982 and was not implemented. Self-marketing can also be eroded by the pressuring of enterprises by various authorities to sell goods to them (or to designated customers) outside the plan. In the Xiangxiang Cement Plant, the share of self-marketing has crept upward year by year, rising from 7 percent in 1981 to 10 percent in 1984. But a considerable share of self-marketed output is allocated by government agencies or virtually "requisitioned" by such powerful organizations as the railways and power bureaus. Given the chronic and worsening shortage of cement in China, the rise in the share of self-marketing at Xiangxiang indicates the independent impact of reforms, but perhaps even more, it shows how enterprises consciously use

---

(Notes to table 10-2, continued)

g. 1981–82 only.

h. Rough estimate based on ratio of tonnage of direct exports to tonnage of total exports.

i. Not including self-sales of the main nonferrous metals produced (copper, lead, zinc), which reportedly were relatively small.

j. Quantity of self-sold cement divided by total sales of cement in 1981–83.

k. Since 1981, all production has been marketed by the enterprise itself and all exports have consisted of direct exports.

l. Rough estimate.

m. Ratio of exports to output of plunger pumps (value of plunger pump production accounts for about 98 percent of gross industrial output value of the factory).

n. Share of self-sales of watches in 1982.

o. Share of output of candy and noodles sold to units other than the two "official" commercial intermediaries (the Jiangmen Municipal Candy Company and Jiangmen Municipal Foodstuffs Company). Even sales to these organizations have been largely on a voluntary basis, determined by their provision of raw materials.

p. Share of self-sales was 18 percent in 1981, 49 percent in 1982, and 82 percent in 1983.

q. Share of total physical output of cloth sold directly by the enterprise in the second half of 1982 and in 1983, not including cloth sold to commercial departments but on a voluntary basis.

r. Share of self-sales rose from 0.8 percent in 1981 to 7.7 percent in 1982.

s. Very rough estimate of the share of self-sales of cloth in total physical output of cloth.

t. Share of cloth exports in total cloth output.

self-marketing of goods in short supply in order to obtain needed inputs above their plan allocations.

On the other hand, self-marketing in a buyers' market is a burden on the enterprise, which therefore may resist increases in the share of self-marketing, at least at first. For the sample enterprises, however, such resistance has not worked. There is often a considerable lag while perceptions of market conditions change and bargaining goes on. But in the end, most enterprises have been forced to take on substantial marketing responsibilities. Because self-marketing makes producers feel the impact of market forces directly, the mechanism by which a buyers' market tends to be associated with a large share of self-marketing is very important. If most or all of an enterprise's output continues to be allocated by plan or administrative directives even when there is excess supply, the pressure on enterprises to become more responsive to customer needs will be much weaker or even absent. From the experience of the sample enterprises and from other evidence, it is clear that the rise in the share of self-marketing is the direct result of the responses of commercial units and government agencies to the emergence of a buyers' market.

There also is a superficially close relationship between market conditions and the share of exports in total sales (table 10-2). Except for the Jinling Petrochemical General Corporation, enterprises facing a sellers' market export only a very small proportion of their production. But export shares for firms facing excess supply domestically range as high as nearly 50 percent. For some of these enterprises, the link between the buyers' market and high exports is at least partly causal. One obvious response to a weak domestic market for enterprises with the capability to do so is to expand exports. Several producers have followed this strategy—for example, the Jiangmen Nanfang Foodstuff Factory, whose share of exports in sales rose from 3 percent in 1978 to 11 percent in 1982. Another example is the Mindong Electrical Machinery Plant, whose export share rose from virtually nil before 1976 to 38 percent in 1978, and thereafter rose and fell around an average of over 30 percent, partly in line with changes in domestic market conditions. A final case is the Nanning Silk and Linen Textile Mill, whose export share jumped from 22 percent in 1983 to 45 percent in the first 10 months of 1984. But the relationship between market conditions and the average levels of exports is largely spurious. Many enterprises now facing a buyers' market also had relatively high export shares when in an environment of chronic excess demand. Moreover, the export shares for some enterprises that face a buyers' market, notably the Qingdao Forging Machinery Plant, decreased rather than increased. On average, the share of self-marketed exports in total exports is higher for enterprises that face excess demand than for those that face excess supply—a paradox that raises further doubts about the relationship between market conditions and self-marketed exports.[17]

Exports may be very important in providing enterprises with experience in competitive international market conditions. The Mindong Electrical Machinery Plant, for instance, captured the Singapore market for small electrical generators from a Japanese firm in the late 1970s by successively matching price reductions. After the competitor exited, Mindong was able to raise prices somewhat. Even more important, there is almost no difference in quality standards between Mindong's domestic products and its exports, to the obvious benefit of domestic users. The authority to export directly and to have direct contacts with foreign customers is crucial here. For most of the other enterprises in the sample, there is considerable insulation between domestic and export production, due at least in part to their lack of authority to export directly.

Financial considerations. As can be seen from table 10-3, all the enterprises in the sample are profitable, though profit rates vary widely. There are no systematic differences in the profit rate on sales between enterprises facing a sellers' market and those facing a buyers' market. The average profit rate on capital for the former enterprises is 21 percent, compared with 51 percent for the latter, however.[18] The five textile enterprises, whose average profit rate on capital is 74 percent, cause most of this difference. The modest difference in indirect tax rates between the two groups is entirely explained by higher tax rates for consumer goods (14 percent) than for other goods (6 percent). Perhaps more important than the lack of any systematic relationship between market conditions and profitability is the apparent failure of profitability to have an influence on enterprise response, at least in the short run.

For individual enterprises, the onset of a buyers' market tends to reduce profitability. In only one enterprise, the Jiangmen Foodstuff Factory, was there a sustained rise in the profit rate on sales during a period when the firm was facing a buyers' market. In other factories, the deterioration in profitability attributable to a buyers' market was sometimes spectacular. At the Nanning Silk and Linen Textile Mill, the profit rate on sales dropped from 31 percent in 1981 to 17 percent in 1982 and to about 10 percent in 1983. In sixteen of twenty-three "observations" (years in which enterprises faced a buyers' market), profitability dropped. These declines are only partly due to falling prices. Costs also tend to rise, sometimes owing to reduced production (which means higher overhead costs per unit of output) but also to increased spending on the sales promotion, quality improvements, and product differentiation needed in the new market situation.

Input and output markets. There is a clear relationship between the market conditions for outputs and those for main material inputs (see table 10-1). All the enterprises facing sellers' markets for their output use raw materials that are also in short supply. Four of the eight, however, have their own source of

Table 10-3. *Financial Indicators, 1980–82*

Market and enterprise	*Profit-sales ratio*[a]	*Profit-capital ratio*[b]	*Tax rate on sales*[c]
Sellers' market			
North China Petroleum	0.377	0.264	0.061
Sanchazi	0.243	0.154	0.060
Anshan	0.351	0.207	0.069
Baoji	0.195	0.114	0.030
Jinling	0.197[d]	0.275[e]	0.108[d]
Shenyang	0.092	0.302	0.057
Xiangxiang	0.358	0.253	0.132
No. 2 Auto	0.189	0.111	0.050
Average	0.250	0.210	0.071
Buyers' market			
Mindong	0.113	0.212	0.052
Qingdao	0.108	0.092	0.040
Shanghai Oil Pump	0.514	0.821	0.051
Chongqing	0.234	0.287	0.272
Jiangmen	0.055	0.038	0.052
Nanning	0.265	0.469	0.153
Northwest Cotton	0.241	0.581	0.150
Qinghe	0.302	0.645	0.179
Shanghai Cotton	0.218	1.016	0.146
Tianjin	0.278	0.977	0.049
Average	0.233	0.514	0.114
Other			
Chengdu	0.302	0.270	0.050
Qingyuan	0.148	0.179	0.102

a. Ratio of administrative profits to sales revenue.

b. Ratio of administrative profits to total value of fixed assets valued at original purchase prices.

c. Ratio of indirect taxes to sales revenues.

d. 1981–82 only, since the Jinling Petrochemical General Corporation was set up in 1981.

e. 1982 only; the assets of two large plants under Jinling were only "certified" and included in the inventory of fixed assets in that year, despite already being in operation in 1981. This distorts the figure for 1981.

raw materials and are therefore somewhat insulated from the sellers' markets for their inputs.[19] Most enterprises facing buyers' markets for their output were in the unenviable position of facing a sellers' market for their inputs (at least in 1982–83). Thus, a sellers' market for output appears to be invariably associated with a sellers' market for main inputs, but a shift to a buyers' market does not necessarily mean that a corresponding change will occur immediately for inputs.

Part of the explanation for this seemingly paradoxical phenomenon lies in administrative obstacles: enterprises may still be forced to buy inputs through the customary administrative channels, which may be slow to reflect changes in market conditions. In some cases, there may be lags, so that a buyers' market for inputs emerges only after a buyers' market for output has been established for a while. The relative price structure in China, where profits at each stage of processing a given raw material tend to be higher than at the previous stage, may also contribute to overinvestment in the downstream stages of processing (and to excess supply) but to underinvestment in upstream stages (and hence to shortages of inputs). This pattern would make the number of enterprises facing a buyers' market for their output and a sellers' marker for inputs more numerous than if prices were randomly determined.

But the main explanation for a continuing sellers' market for inputs in the face of a buyers' market for output is that many material inputs have several uses. Therefore, if there is heavy demand by some users of an input, they will take up any slack caused by the reduction of orders from other users, and a shortage for everyone will thus be preserved. The metal products that are the main material inputs at the Mindong Electrical Machinery Plant, the Qingdao Forging Machinery Plant, and the Shanghai High-Pressure Oil Pump Factory can also be used for other purposes (at least with certain adjustments by their producers). The sugar used by the Jiangmen Nanfang Foodstuff Factory can be consumed directly as well as used in producing candies, soft drinks, and the like.

Market conditions for inputs do not appear to affect the response of enterprises to a buyers' market. Shortages of inputs certainly make the producer's task more difficult and may divert attention to arranging supplies or constrain response in other important ways. And to the extent that the prices of material inputs determine production costs, a sellers' market for inputs makes it more difficult to reduce costs. None of these factors, however, prevents enterprises from engaging in the intensive response to a buyers' market.

Government Responses to Market Forces

The responses of government authorities to market forces and changing market conditions can crucially affect their impact on enterprises, enterprise responses, and dynamic trends. Government actions can take a variety of forms, ranging from budgetary investments in different industries to controls over the production and investment decisions of enterprises and to attempts to affect the market directly. Much analytical work has already been done on government responses to a sellers' market—or on how shortage signals in a centrally planned economy affect government actions and controls (see, in particular, Kornai 1980). But government responses to a buyers' market have not been analyzed extensively.

Sellers' Markets

The Chinese government has usually tried to avoid price increases for the entire supply of a good for which there is a persistent sellers' market, particularly if producer profitability is already adequate. But parallel markets with higher, flexible prices have emerged in recent years for goods not subject to planned distribution. Dual-price systems have become prevalent as a result. Increasing imports (or decreasing exports) is a relatively simple short-term response to severe shortage of an important good. In China, however, this response has been notably lacking in a number of instances, such as the maintenance of coal and petroleum exports in the face of an increasingly severe energy shortage. Increasing funds for investment may improve the supply situation over the long run. But in China, investment appears to be responsive to profitability, which means underinvestment in low-profit industries (the most obvious example in the past has been coal). The decentralization of control over a large share of investment in recent years has probably increased this responsiveness of investment to profitability (see chapter 4 in this volume). Another problem in China is that the budgeting process makes it difficult to change investment shares of different sectors drastically.

An almost universal response of governments to shortage is an attempt to impose orderly rationing that ensures adequate supplies for high-priority users (from the government's perspective). In China, there was widespread rationing of consumer goods before the changes in market conditions in the late 1970s. Producer goods are rationed through the mandatory allocation plan, but coverage is uneven and incomplete for many commodities. Moreover, rationing through the state material supply plan in China appears to be sticky: the shares of different sectors are hard to change in the light of changing government priorities or changing relative shortages. This rigidity makes rationing an unsatisfactory tool for improving economic efficiency through ensuring adequate supplies for priority users.

Buyers' Markets

Government responses to buyers' markets in China have been most striking in marketing. The government planning and distribution systems have essentially abdicated responsibility for procuring enterprise output, forcing producers to fend for themselves on the open market, with responsibility for sales of their own products (at least at the margin). This response is a crucial link in the chain of causation leading from a buyers' market to a beneficial enterprise response. It appears to be missing in the U.S.S.R., where at least temporary surpluses of some consumer goods are not unknown.[20] The process for this passive (but arguably very beneficial) government response differs somewhat for consumer goods and producer goods, but the end result is much the same.

For consumer goods, the impact of a buyers' market is first felt as a buildup of inventories in the warehouses of commercial units buying goods from industrial producers.[21] The commercial units may continue to purchase the goods concerned for a while, perhaps thinking that the situation is only temporary. As commercial inventories grow to immense proportions, the pressure for a change in policy increases. This pressure may be due to the heavy financial cost of carrying large inventories or to the limits on warehouse space. An interim response might involve storing some goods at the factory or directly imposing production ceilings (with the commercial system still purchasing all output). But eventually the burden of marketing almost invariably is put on the producer, which then becomes responsible for joint decisions on production and sales, with sales supposedly determining production. It is not surprising that Chinese commercial enterprises would want to stop buying consumer goods when sales are slow and inventories are accumulating. What is interesting is that they have been able to do so, at least to a considerable extent. Such action must have involved government approval or passive acquiescence.

If there are no other changes, the refusal of commercial units to purchase an enterprise's output makes the enterprise responsible for its sales and subjects it to the direct impact of market forces. This in turn largely removes the whole area of marketing from government control and stimulates competition among producers and between producers and commercial units (which still have large inventories to sell off). One reason the government allows this loss of control to occur may be that forcing enterprises (particularly large, otherwise successful ones) to cut production would be contentious and difficult. Forcing enterprises to make joint decisions on production and sales in response to market forces, which are more impersonal than production ceilings imposed by the government case-by-case, may be politically easier. There may also be some link with reforms promoting direct marketing, but reforms in the commercial system, encouraging more profit-oriented behavior and control over inventories, probably are a more important factor.[22]

For producer goods, the effect of excess supply on marketing can be even more immediate, since so many transactions take place directly between producers and users.[23] When users have their production or investment plans cut, they simply make no new plan-based orders and even cancel existing contracts if necessary, leaving the producer facing the full brunt of a buyers' market almost at once. Indeed, machinery producers were the first major group of enterprises in China to feel the impact of a buyers' market, when, in 1979–80, material supply organs refused to continue buying ordinary products in excess supply.

Government responses in pricing also appear to be rather passive. But in some cases they intensify enterprise responses by preventing price adjustments that might narrow the gap between supply and demand. Letting prices float freely downward has rarely been the response chosen, except for some commodities considered less important and not subject to strict price controls all along. Downward adjustments in administratively set prices are common, but they invariably are too late and too small to restore equilibrium. Sometimes limited downward flotation of prices at the initiative of producers is permitted.

The difficulty of directly imposing ceilings on the production of individual factories and regions has already been alluded to. Ceilings have been imposed in the textile industry but not in any other industries covered by the sample. The central government tried to restrict investments in capacity expansion for several kinds of consumer durables like watches with only limited success. Controls do not cover all investment in the industries concerned, particularly that by small factories "outside the state plan." Moreover, existing enterprises can increase production by using slack capacity or improving efficiency, which may also permit some disguised capacity-increasing investment. Investment controls may even encourage preemptive investment by enterprises and localities to increase their long-term market share.[24]

Another possible government response is to force some producers to exit. Those under pressure to leave the industry almost invariably are small, rural collective enterprises, not large or medium-size state enterprises like those in the sample. A policy of forced exit can be applied for numerous reasons other than market conditions, including concerns about efficiency, energy consumption, and financial considerations. When strictly applied, as in small cigarette plants, this response appears to prevent further entry by small producers even if it does not greatly reduce the number of existing producers. Success in other industries has been more mixed. In any case, closure does not affect large state enterprises directly, and it appears only to ameliorate a buyers' market trend, not reverse it.

Internal Protectionism

Another form of government response to a weak market is local government protection of producers from outside competition, which goes against national policy. This protection is most commonly imposed by ordering local users and commercial enterprises to buy only from designated local producers, even if the local producers cannot meet competition in terms of price or quality. The enterprises in the sample appear to have benefited little from this kind of protection. But in several cases they have suffered from protectionist behavior by local governments, their own or others. The Mindong Electrical Machinery Plant faced severe difficulties in trying to expand its sales network to other provinces or even to other parts of its home province of Fujian. The

No. 2 Automobile Plant faced resistance of some local governments to mergers it proposed with smaller local truck factories. In addition to being pressured to buy spindles and other textile equipment from local sources, the Northwest No. 1 Cotton Mill for a time was ordered not to ship any gray cloth outside Shaanxi Province; this action was an effort by provincial authorities to assure that local printing and dyeing plants would be able to run at close to capacity.

Internal protectionism thus places obstacles in the path of dynamic, expanding enterprises trying to move into regional markets outside their traditional area. It also holds back enterprises in backward areas by forcing them to buy high-priced, poor-quality locally made inputs and capital goods. Another problem, not evident in the sample but undoubtedly of great importance, is that protectionism insulates backward enterprises from competition that would force them to make improvements to survive and develop. More generally, protectionism results in highly fragmented markets with a consequent loss of potential efficiency gains from free trade and economies of scale. And it undoubtedly slows adjustment to market forces and impedes the exit of inefficient producers.

All in all, government intervention has not succeeded in transforming a buyers' market into a sellers' market. In some respects, government responses have intensified the situation (for example, slow and insufficient price adjustments). In others, they have dampened the impact (production or investment controls, protectionism). One action, however, may be able to reverse a buyers' market immediately. A sharp increase in government-financed investment or in government approvals of investment projects (where these had been restricted) can cause a buyers' market for investment goods (and intermediate inputs into investment goods) to be eliminated fairly rapidly and to be replaced by a brisk sellers' market. This change happened in China in 1982 and especially in 1983–84. But government-mandated increases in investment activity are not a direct response to the buyers' market. There is some link, but it is rather tenuous: the government may see the buyers' market as evidence that the economy can absorb some increase in investment without overheating or, less likely, that investment may be increased partly as a means of easing the difficulties of producers hard-hit by the buyers' market situation.

Patterns of Market Competition and Price Adjustments

Competition is normally broken down into two main categories: price competition and nonprice competition. The first category can be further subdivided according to the mode of price determination. The second can involve a whole range of competitive instruments, including product quality, product differentiation, innovation and new product development, distribution and marketing networks, warranties and after-sales service, and advertising and other forms of sales promotion. For many goods in China, external price controls restrict overt price competition, even though price competition in a buyers' market tends to exert downward pressure on prices. Price discrimination based on demand characteristics also appears to be taboo, though price differentiation based on supply considerations (such as the cost of production and within-plan versus above-plan output) is often permitted.

In other countries, price competition for differentiated products is often limited even in the absence of price controls. For homogeneous goods with numerous producers, something close to perfect competition may be prevalent, with each firm taking the market price as given and having no competitive price strategy other than meeting that price. If there are significant economies of scale and relatively few large producers, unfettered price competition can be severe. Business firms in the United States and other countries have gradually learned to avoid the worst excesses of price competition. Sometimes they have done so through overtly collusive price fixing but more often by tacit or informal arrangements (for instance, following the lead of a dominant or more visible firm in setting prices). Moreover, nonprice competition has become a substitute for vicious price competition. For homogeneous products, this type of competition may lead to artificial product differentiation through brand names and advertising.

Chinese enterprises are increasingly unrestricted in the types of nonprice competition they can undertake, and nonprice competition can be very beneficial in improving the efficiency and flexibility of the economic system. There are many examples in the sample enterprises of substantial improvements by enterprises responding through nonprice-competitive measures to the exigencies of a buyers' market. But some of the negative aspects of nonprice competition in other countries are also likely to emerge, including artificial product differentiation and excessive advertising.

Parallels with Competition in International Trade

Interregional competition (either between established producers or between established producers and new entrants) may be the most important form of competition in Chinese state-owned industry. Local competition between major enterprises is likely to be relatively weak. A local government probably would not set up more than one producer of the same type of good in a small area. If there are several producers, they are likely to be under different government agencies, which means that their distribution channels are probably compartmentalized and largely insulated from each other. And even if they are all under the same jurisdiction, the government (say, at the provincial level) could intervene to limit competition by dividing the market. The strength of competition between established state enterprises and small, local, nonstate enterprises (which may not be sponsored or protected by the local government) depends greatly on how suitable the technical and other conditions are for small-scale production.

A second major feature of the landscape is that local and provincial governments maintain considerable control over industry and trade in their jurisdictions. Moreover, their objectives include fostering local or regional industry and increasing revenues.[25] To further these goals, they have often attempted to protect their industry from outside competition. Thus, interregional competition in Chinese industry may be more akin to competition in international trade than to competition in well-integrated national markets. This conclusion, if valid, has some interesting implications.

In the first place, at least in the short run, barriers to interregional trade erected by local and provincial governments may be the most serious obstacle to the development of competition—and to such resulting benefits as improved efficiency and increased regional specialization. The danger of collusive anticompetitive arrangements by enterprises is probably relatively small. This danger could increase over time, as internal trade barriers are relaxed and governments play a smaller role in day-to-day economic management. But the central government's vigilance against internal protectionism appears to be warranted in the current situation.

Another parallel with international trade is the importance of establishing distribution networks in "foreign" markets, particularly for differentiated products. This seems to have been a prerequisite for the Mindong Electrical Machinery Plant to expand sales in other provinces and even in other parts of its home province of Fujian. Mindong's retail outlets in different parts of the country typically involved a joint venture or association of some sort with a commercial unit in the market being penetrated. Local governments in these areas understood what was happening and often tried to disrupt Mindong's establishment of sales outlets. Other kinds of joint ventures and associations, including those involving production, often have the objective of gaining footholds in new markets or maintaining position in existing markets.[26]

Another possible parallel with international trade is the difficulty of exiting from industries in which the country or region suffers from a comparative disadvantage. It may be that the exit from an entire industry as a result of international competition is more strongly resisted than the exit of some firms from an industry as a result of domestic competition. Chinese competition may follow the international pattern in this respect because of fears about supply shortages and also because of revenue considerations.[27]

The parallels between competition in Chinese industry and competition in international trade lead in many respects to pessimistic conclusions. But they also give grounds for hope in that growing international intraindustry trade involving competition in differentiated products leads to changing niches and market shares rather than widespread specialization by industry. This kind of competition has important benefits and would appear to be feasible in China. Of course it is more appropriate for some products than for others, and it cannot work for commodities for which different regional resource endowments play an important role (for example, coal mining or nonferrous metals production). Finally, the analogy with international competition suggests that mutual action in lowering barriers to interregional trade is important—and that there may be room for gradual coordinated lowering of barriers to allow local and regional adjustments.

Price Pressures and Adjustments

The interactions between market forces, price determination, and enterprise responses are crucial. One issue is the responsiveness of state-owned industrial enterprises to changing prices for outputs and inputs. By and large, the enterprises in the sample facing a sellers' market are very responsive to relative profitability in their decisions on product mix (to the extent that they are not constrained by product-mix targets).[28] Reforms emphasizing the importance of profits and weakening external controls over product mix have undoubtedly strengthened this tendency. For example, the Xiangxiang Cement Plant no longer produces lower grades of cement, which were less profitable. The Shenyang Smelting Plant, given the freedom to produce either grade one or grade two electrolytic zinc, now produces only the former, because its price is higher and its unit costs are about the same. In other cases, insufficient price differentiation by quality leads enterprises to avoid producing better-quality goods. A lack of responsiveness to input prices also is evident. Although many enterprises complain bitterly about price increases for key inputs obtained outside plan allocations, they appear not to be easily deterred from such transactions. Because of distorted prices, production may be profitable even with higher prices for inputs. Moreover, enterprises can often avoid paying higher prices by exchanging their products for needed inputs, valuing both at low state-set prices.

When market conditions shift from excess demand to excess supply, enterprises become much more responsive to quantity signals for their output. But at the same time they remain sensitive to relative profitability. Indeed, because reform implementation and an increased emphasis on profits have come at roughly the same time as the emergence of buyers' markets, the responsiveness of enterprise to both price and quantity signals for their output may have increased. When these two signals conflict (when the products in demand are the less profitable ones), the degree to which enterprises give priority to profitability depends greatly on the tautness and firmness of their profit targets—on whether those targets are to be strictly enforced and on whether they are unlikely to change. Thus the Nanning Textile Mill was forced to shift production sharply toward more profitable varieties only in 1983, when its profit target became very firm after two successive sharp yearly declines in realized profits. For inputs, if there is continuing shortage, responsiveness to prices may remain weak, as long as production remains profitable at the margin. If the market for inputs has turned soft, however, enterprises naturally strive to obtain lower prices. The Chongqing Clock and Watch Company, for example, intended to force suppliers of components for its products to accept lower prices, hoping to increase its own profits.

The extent and speed with which government authorities adjust prices in response to changing market conditions is an important factor. The experience of enterprises in the sample suggests that there is some responsiveness of administratively set prices to market conditions. But this occurs only with a lag, sometimes a very long lag. Thus watch prices were reduced several times during 1980–84, but the reductions were too late and too small to prevent a growing excess supply, at least nationally. The textile price adjustment of early 1983, which appears to have ameliorated severe imbalances in the supply and demand for different textile products, occurred at least a year after industrywide problems with excess supply had become apparent. Instituting official price increases for goods in excess demand is even more difficult. Prices of many "basic goods" are held down, and examples of administrative price increases that clear the market are rare indeed. Resistance to price reductions appears to be based mainly on fears about the effect on profits and revenues to the government. Resistance to price increases is based on similar fears of users (for producer goods) and concerns about inflation (for consumer goods or inputs into consumer goods).

Most enterprises in the sample produce goods subject to a considerable degree of price control, yet most of them formally or informally have some role in setting prices.[29] But enterprise pricing decisions, even when ostensibly made freely, can be a source of rigidity. Willingness to lower prices appears to depend to a large extent on the perceived ability to have targets for profit remittances lowered to compensate for the loss of revenues. Often enterprises lower their prices first, if they are allowed to do so, and worry about adjusting their targets for profit remittance later. But some enterprises have not raised prices or have not raised them by the full amount allowed even in a strong sellers' market. This may be due in part to a desire to maintain their reputation or to avoid criticism for price gouging (a motivation that may be stronger among enterprises in the sample than in Chinese industry generally).

There is a basic asymmetry between a buyers' market and a sellers' market in price pressures and price adjustments. When there is excess supply, buyers exert downward pressure on the price of the total supply of the good. They can almost always refuse to buy goods if they consider the price too high, particularly if they can get them at a lower price from another source. This tactic is obvious for consumer goods. But even for producer goods, enterprises for the most part can refuse to purchase items they do not need (which can often be a cover for refusal on the grounds of excessively high price).[30] On the supply side, as we have seen, producers are often willing to cut prices to meet competition and sell their products, provided that they can also reduce their profit remittances to the government, thereby preserving their net after-tax financial position.

Price pressures under excess demand are felt somewhat differently. There is no pressure from buyers with access to supplies to raise prices. In fact, they would strongly prefer prices to be held down. On the other hand, would-be purchasers without access to supplies at the (low) controlled price are willing to pay market-determined prices, which is better than doing without the good. Hence, buyers do not mind a dual-price system when there is excess demand, though there will be conflicts over which ones obtain the benefits of assured supply at the controlled price. Producers obviously prefer the price of total supply to be raised. Nevertheless, they find a dual-price system better than being forced to sell all their output at the low price. (They may, of course, try to divert output from low-priced, within-plan channels to sales outside the plan at higher prices.) In this situation, a two-tiered pricing system has tended to emerge for most goods chronically in short supply.

Thus, upward pressures on prices can be partially accommodated by maintaining low within-quota prices and higher (often virtually market-determined) prices at the margin. But downward pressures can usually be relieved only by a general price reduction. Indeed, in the sample there are no examples of differentiation between within-quota and above-quota prices for goods in excess supply, whereas even before 1984, nearly all the enterprises facing a sellers' market were in industries where multiple pricing was prevalent. It may have been common, however, for larger enterprises to be forced to sell all their output at the low state price, and for smaller plants to be able to get a higher price for all their output based on their higher production costs.

Dynamic Adjustments and Performance

Consumer Goods

The Chinese watch industry and the Chongqing Clock and Watch Company in particular exemplify one kind of dynamic adjustment. In a highly profitable industry that has been given priority access to investment resources and for which raw material constraints are relatively unimportant, producers (supported by local supervisory agencies) will engage in the expansion response. In addition, when it is technically feasible, many new producers will enter the industry. As a result, supply will grow rapidly, and in a fairly short period it will meet and then surpass demand. Even when material inputs are in short supply, as in the case of grain and sugar for the Jiangmen Foodstuff Factory, their diversion from alternative uses may permit the expansion response to occur.

Much depends on the government's response to the emerging buyers' market. For watches, despite some lagged downward adjustments, prices remained too high to stimulate demand sharply or to discourage producers. Attempts to impose investment ceilings also were only partly successful. Most important, producers were not insulated from the market. Commercial units were not required to procure all watches produced, which burdened producers with the task of making sales, at least at the margin. Under these conditions, industrial enterprises became very responsive to customer needs, and competition became heated. It included price competition (largely disguised) and various kinds of nonprice competition (involving quality, styling, warranties, and after-sales service). Many of China's consumer-durables industries seem to have followed this pattern, though perhaps not in as extreme a form as for watches. These industries are now characterized by incipient or actual oversupply for ordinary, low-quality brands and by continuing severe shortages for a few of the best national brands and for imports. In terms of quantities, the bulk of domestic production faces a buyers' market.

Dynamic adjustment in the textile industry has followed a broadly similar route. The prices of synthetic textiles at the outset were extremely high. Moreover, the textile industry received priority allocations of resources as a result of national adjustment policies promoting growth of consumption. In 1982 a nationwide buyers' market emerged, and its effects were felt in varying degrees by all the textile enterprises in the sample. In certain respects, the government response to the buyers' market in textiles was similar to that for watches and other consumer durables. After building enormous inventories, commercial units were allowed to refuse to purchase all or part of factory output, forcing producers to feel the impact of market forces directly. Attempts to impose production ceilings on different locales and factories appear to have been more successful, but they did not eliminate the buyers' market. In early 1983, the prices of textiles and textile raw materials were comprehensively adjusted. The adjustment appears to have eliminated much of the great difference in prices and profitability between synthetics and cotton. It also may have had a considerable influence on product-mix decisions by individual factories. Nevertheless, there continues to be a buyers' market for most textiles, with increasingly discriminating consumers choosing on the basis of quality, color, styling, and other similar attributes rather than simply purchasing whatever is available, or even what is cheapest.

These examples suggest that adequate profitability and access to financial resources may be prerequisites for the emergence of a buyers' market in consumer goods. The impact of market conditions for material inputs is harder to gauge. For textiles, chemical fiber production was also relatively profitable, and large imports were permitted. Large imports of cotton also were allowed, and just as important, cotton prices were raised sharply in the late 1970s to stimulate domestic production, though government subsidies held down the prices that factories paid. But the textile factories in the sample had difficulties in obtaining raw materials of the appropriate quality and specifications, in part because of continuing administrative control over supplies of cotton and synthetic fiber. These difficulties did not prevent textile factories from moving into an intensive response to the market situation. The Jiangmen Foodstuff Factory, which relied on sugar (which was in very short supply), is an even more clear-cut example.

Investment Goods

The transition to a buyers' market for investment goods (and intermediate inputs into investment goods) resulted from a reduction in investment demand first caused by a cutback in government-financed investment. This reduction in turn caused a decline in orders for capital goods from users with plan allocations and from the material supply system. If anything, the impact of a buyers' market for producer goods has been felt more quickly than that for consumer goods. This is particularly true of the sharp cutback in central government investment in 1981, which temporarily generated an excess supply of goods chronically in short supply before and since, such as copper and trucks.

The first response of the government to the buyers' market is the same as that for consumer goods: producers are largely left to fend for themselves. Many machinery factories, like the Qingdao Forging Machinery Plant, had to sell most of their output directly. The Mindong Electrical Machinery Plant also is now responsible for most sales. Even the Anshan Iron and Steel Corporation had to sell 14 percent of its output directly in 1981 (the average for the steel industry as a whole was nearly 20 percent). For producer goods, there may be somewhat greater willingness on the part of the government to let prices float downward in response to market conditions. Lower prices do not mean automatic revenue losses for the government, because if sales go to other state enterprises, lower profits for producers should be offset by higher profits for users or lower costs of investment goods (paid for by the budget). But perhaps sensing that demand is fairly price-inelastic anyway, enterprises are reluctant to cut prices to stimulate demand in a weak market. In any case, if the cause of the buyers' market is a cutback in government-financed investment demand, price reductions are unlikely to clear the market.

A major factor in market trends for intermediate goods and investment goods is the emergence of new sources of demand that partly offset the decline in budget-financed investment. Starting in 1980–81, collective enterprises were for the first time allowed to take part in ordering conferences for producer goods. The dynamic rural collectives had a particularly large appetite for investment goods as they expanded rapidly in the late 1970s and early 1980s. These sources of demand may have been more discriminating than those they replaced. Moreover, the products that collective enterprises needed usually had different specifications from those previously sold to state enterprises, so producers often faced excess supply for their old products and had to adjust their product mix to produce goods in demand.

The staying power of the buyers' market for investment goods and intermediate goods depends greatly on central government investment demand and on money and credit policies. Capital construction investment started to revive in late 1981, as decentralized investment by enterprises and local authorities continued to increase rapidly. Budget-financed investment rose sharply in 1983, which more than offset the stabilization of decentralized investment through administrative controls. In 1984, decentralized investment again boomed and was the main source of sharply increased aggregate investment demand. The revival of investment demand had an almost immediate effect on market conditions for certain basic intermediate goods produced by process industries, which had suffered briefly from excess supply in 1981. The sellers' market for rolled steel had returned in full force by 1983, and copper from the Shenyang Smelting Plant suffered from a problem of excess supply for only a few months in 1981.

In the engineering industries, experience has been more varied. The sellers' market for trucks returned quickly in 1982, but the machinery producers in the sample still faced a rather weak market in 1983. Apparently the number of producers of ordinary types of machinery remains very large, so even a sharp increase in demand can be accommodated. Relative prices that allow higher profits on machinery and equipment than on many basic process industries may also partly explain the difference between the two. Another factor may be the gradual liberalization of policies on the importing of machinery and equipment. Users often prefer to buy imported equipment because of its superior quality and reliability, even though the price is usually much higher.[31]

Conditions for Sustaining a Buyers' Market

Under what conditions does a buyers' market emerge? Under what conditions is it sustainable over the long run? The emergence of a buyers' market seems to require that production be reasonably profitable and that resources be made available for expansion (which happened in consumer durables) or that demand be cut back sharply enough to match or fall short of supply (intermediate goods in 1981) or a combination of both (possibly machinery). The ability to sustain a buyers' market does not appear to be a serious problem for consumer goods, partly because demand is inherently limited by consumers' characteristics and preferences. Moreover, in China, consumer goods continue to receive some priority in resource allocation, and profits remain high enough to attract new entrants. Yet a revival in investment demand can very quickly cause a reversion to a sellers' market for investment goods and intermediate inputs into investment goods.

Thus a buyers' market for investment goods and intermediate inputs is much more fragile than a buyers' market for consumer goods. In the sample there is no clear-cut case of a buyers' market for consumer goods reverting to chronic excess demand. But this happened for two producers of intermediate goods (Shenyang Smelting and Anshan Iron and Steel) and one producer of investment goods (No. 2 Auto). Sharp cutbacks in investment are likely to be only temporary, part of cyclical swings. Nevertheless, it may be possible for a buyers' market to "stick," particularly if many producers have slack capacity (which may be the case for ordinary types of machinery).

Did enterprises learn beneficial behavior patterns when there was a buyers' market for their products and stay with them even when conditions reverted to excess demand? And did the government sustain the new institutional arrangements, particularly direct marketing by producers? Though scant, the evidence on the second question is more clear-cut than that on the first.

When market conditions revert to excess demand, commercial agencies or material supply authorities try to retake control over product sales and to prevent enterprises from freely selling goods on their own. Their justification for this action is the perceived need to allocate now-scarce commodities to priority uses. Enterprises try to resist this tendency, since direct marketing in a sellers' market confers important benefits. Because of general inertia and the enterprises' high share of self-marketing (and possibly because of reform rhetoric about increasing enterprise decisionmaking), enterprises are in a much better position to retain sales control when market conditions revert from excess supply to excess demand than they were in trying to expand direct marketing in the original sellers' market. Anshan Iron and Steel's share of self-marketed sales dropped only from 14 percent in 1981 to 10 percent in 1983. No. 2 Auto kept the right to market directly about 17 percent of its total truck output in 1983, despite bitter disputes with the State Material Supply Bureau. This pattern may be typical of Chinese industry as a whole, though Anshan and No. 2 Auto, as large, centrally run enterprises, probably were better able to withstand pressures.

Changed sources of demand may also enable an enterprise to maintain a high share of self-marketed sales after the market situation has reverted to excess demand. The Qingdao Forging Machinery Plant, for example, continued to sell most of its output directly, even after demand strengthened in 1982–83, because most of its customers were collective enterprises, which do not get plan allocations for investment goods anyway. Perhaps because of their obsolete technology and high energy consumption, Qingdao's friction presses may not be in great demand from users with access to more suitable equipment through state plan allocations. If this surmise is correct, Qingdao's presses face different conditions in two different parts of an administratively segmented market.

It is much more difficult to ascertain whether there has been continuity in enterprise behavior patterns during a reversion from a buyers' market to a sellers' market. No. 2 Auto appears to have continued to exhibit customer-oriented behavior since 1982, and it has aggressively engaged in associations with other enterprises as a means of increasing its market share.[32] But No. 2 Auto is among the most entrepreneurial enterprises in the sample and is atypical of Chinese state-owned industrial enterprises. Anshan, in contrast, may have exhibited more typical behavior in closing its "retail shop," at which steel had been sold in small quantities, primarily to rural collectives. Anshan also became less aggressive in promoting product sales, even though it had sent people all over the country to find buyers in 1981.

To hold down investment demand (and preserve the buyers' market for investment goods and intermediate inputs into investment goods), central planners must show great self-discipline. They must limit their approvals of large new capital construction projects, restrict budgetary spending on investment, and control aggregate investment by lower levels in the economic system. To a considerable degree, Chinese central planners began the shift in orientation from production and growth to efficiency and consumption in 1979. National production and investment plans have generally been slack and have been overfulfilled by large margins in recent years. There have also been strong forces limiting budget-financed investment.[33] The limited budgetary resources for investment have led to concerns about the price and availability of investment goods (because this has a direct effect on the "real" investment from budgetary funds). Those concerns have led to the imposition of direct controls over investment financed by local governments and enterprises. The net result was to maintain a buyers' market for many types of investment goods (notably machinery) at least through 1982. On the other hand, the boom in housing construction has generated a strong sellers' market for building materials throughout the period since the reforms began.

Since 1983, however, budget-financed investment has again boomed, as subsidies were brought under control and revenue constraints were eased by the imposition of a 10 percent levy (later 15 percent) on the extrabudgetary incomes of enterprises and government organizations. The extremely rapid growth of industrial production in 1983–84 undoubtedly has further tightened market conditions for intermediate goods and investment goods. As a result of these developments, the three producer-goods enterprises in the sample that faced a buyers' market at the time of the interviews may now face a sellers' market. Another serious problem is that the cost of capital to enterprises remains very low despite attempts to raise it (see chapter 4 in this volume). As a result, enterprises have no incentive to economize on their use of capital, and their latent demand for investment is restrained only by the availability of funds.

Even if strong at the outset, the self-discipline of central planners and investment allocators is likely to be eroded over time, particularly in China, where an investment boom by local governments and enterprises may nullify self-discipline and tight control of budget-financed investment. But in China the "suction effect" (whereby excess demand for investment goods pulls resources away from production of consumer goods, exacerbating shortages) so far has been limited. The buyers' market for many consumer goods appears robust despite strong investment demand.[34]

Socialist Markets and Economic Performance

How important is the socialist buyers' market in improving economic efficiency and performance? What obstacles may impede such markets from fully playing the role ascribed to well-functioning markets in a capitalist economy? The problems of measuring the efficiency of enterprises are formidable. Linking changes in performance to possible explanatory factors is nearly impossible. Moreover, the relationship between enterprise performance and industrywide or economywide performance is ambiguous. An added complication is that measured performance is likely to deteriorate when an enterprise faces a buyers' market, even though it takes strenuous measures to respond to demand and to maintain sales. Prices may be soft in a buyers' market, but in any case the enterprise's efforts to promote sales, alter product mix, develop new products, and improve quality will almost certainly raise costs. The burgeoning of inventories as producers take on commercial roles (or simply as production lags behind adjustments in demand) also causes deterioration in performance.

So it is not surprising that profitability declined for most enterprises that faced a buyers' market. Fragmentary data on other indicators of efficiency do not show that trends in performance are better for enterprises facing a buyers' market than for those in a sellers' market. But quantitative indicators do not tell the whole story. The strong measures taken by many enterprises facing a buyers' market to respond to nonquantitative aspects of demand must weigh heavily in any evaluation. The difference from the behavior of most enterprises facing a sellers' market (and even the same enterprises during times of a sellers' market) is often striking. Undoubtedly the benefits to consumers and users are far greater in a buyers' market—ready availability, improved quality, a closer match of customer needs with precise grades and specifications, better warranties and after-sales service, and downward pressures on prices.

Set against these advantages are some costs. The most obvious one is that of excess capacity and forgone production. This cost is exacerbated in China by the slow (even perverse) adjustment of the production structure to a weak market: the exit of enterprises is impeded, and profitability continues to attract new entrants who may not be aware of the situation or who hope to operate in protected local markets. Nevertheless, the excess capacity in industries facing a weak market does free up supplies of intermediate inputs in short supply (steel and electricity) for use in the production of other goods that enjoy a sellers' market. Thus the situation in a socialist economy facing uneven market conditions (widespread surpluses and shortages for different goods) differs from that in a capitalist economy suffering from inadequate aggregate effective demand and unemployment.

The problem of excess capacity may be symptomatic of potentially more serious difficulties with medium-term industrywide adjustment to a buyers' market. Capitalist firms in an industrial market economy typically maintain some excess capacity as part of a competitive strategy that puts a high priority on the ability to meet customer demand. In China's buyers' markets, in contrast, industrywide excess capacity is mostly the unintended result of numerous investment decisions by investment-hungry investors. In this context, the excess capacity in some industries in China may be a sign of slow, inefficient adjustments to market conditions—not a "normal" level of inventories which better allows an industry to meet unexpected surges in demand.

Several obstacles hinder the full impact of a buyers' market in a socialist economic system. The extreme difficulty of closing down state-owned enterprises is an obvious one. This near-inability of the system to allow widespread exit as a means of adjusting to a weak market damages efficiency and economic performance. But even more harmful is the government behavior this inability may engender: government-sponsored cartel-like arrangements for market sharing or investment control, or internal protectionism instigated by local governments, which fragments the market and generates the well-known inefficiencies associated with barriers to trade.

Another common feature is the lack of pressure on enterprises to reduce costs, even in a buyers' market characterized by vigorous competition in other areas (including price cutting). This feature is most probably due to the weak financial discipline of enterprises: the burden of declining profitability (in a weak market) can usually be passed on to the government budget by means of reduced profit remittances. A squeeze on profits therefore may not generate much pressure to reduce costs, and a major benefit attributed to well-functioning markets in a capitalist economy is lost.[35] This possibility suggests that a combination of buyers' markets and relatively firm enterprise profit targets may generate stronger incentives to reduce costs than the present situation (for many industries) of weak markets and slack and manipulable profit targets.

Finally, lags in price changes may have rather heavy costs in terms of inhibiting industrywide adjustment to a buyers' market, even though these lags may intensify the responses of the enterprises. Assuming that output prices are sufficiently high for enterprises to earn substantial profits, in a sellers' market both price and quantity signals to enterprises will be consistent in calling for increases in production. But if a buyers' market emerges and prices are not adjusted downward substantially, price and quantity signals will be contradictory. Existing enterprises will be encouraged to expand, and new entrants will be attracted to the industry by high prices and profits. Quantity signals, in contrast, will accurately reflect the weak market (once indiscriminate purchasing by commercial intermediaries is stopped). In this situation, industrywide adjustment will be uneven, slow, and perhaps even perverse (if new entrants flock to the industry).

A general picture of what occurs in socialist buyers' markets can be drawn from the experience of Chinese industry and the enterprises in the sample. In most respects, the situation is unambiguously better than the chronic sellers' market characteristic of a traditional centrally planned economy. But some features of the institutional environment present obstacles that prevent many of the advantages of well-functioning markets from being fully realized, even if the buyers' market can be preserved long enough to have an impact. The very survival of buyers' markets is in doubt for investment goods and intermediate inputs.

Notes

1. The term "market mechanism" refers in this chapter to the allocation of goods and services by voluntary exchange (barter) for each other, for money, or for a combination of both (tied transactions). Neither the opposite party in a transaction nor the quantity or specifications are determined by directives from supervisory authorities in a hierarchy. Price controls are not ruled out, however.

2. These ratios were calculated by subtracting retail sales of agricultural products and revenues of the catering trade from the total value of retail sales and then dividing the value of retail sales by industrial enterprises by the resulting figure. See "China Economic Yearbook" Editorial Committee 1981, pp. IV-121, IV-122; State Statistical Bureau 1982, pp. 331, 332; and State Statistical Bureau 1984, pp. 348, 350, 351.

3. "China Economic Yearbook" Editorial Committee 1981, pp. III-39, IV-125; Ma 1980, p. 2. The latter figure may include some consumer goods produced by the engineering industries, such as radios, watches, and sewing machines.

4. For an interesting comparison of the ideas of Marx and Schumpeter on economic development, see Sylos-Labini 1984, chap. 2.

5. For a discussion of the objective function of Chinese state-owned industrial enterprises, see chapter 4 in this volume.

6. Leibenstein (1966) coined the term "X-efficiency." It refers to the efficiency with which a given set of factor and nonfactor inputs are transformed into outputs, as opposed to "allocative efficiency," which refers to the efficient allocation of inputs among different possible uses.

7. Being forced to turn away a customer because of a lack of goods in stock can be very costly to a capitalist enterprise. Many customers are "repeaters," who stick with the same firm once a relationship has been established. Thus, if an enterprise does not have enough stock or capacity, it runs the risk of losing customers permanently. Where investments are "lumpy," it is often advantageous to create initial excess capacity in anticipation of later growth in demand. Investments in excess capacity may also be made on strategic grounds to deter entry by new competitors.

8. The failure of the Sanchazi Forestry Bureau to expand output is due to concern about maintaining the long-term production potential of forestry reserves. Similarly, falling output at the North China Petroleum Administration masks great efforts to maintain production from declining oil fields.

9. See Byrd and Tidrick 1984, pp. 38–44. This kind of response differs little from what would happen in a traditional centrally planned economic system when an enterprise is given priority access to resources and a mandate to expand output.

10. This response to a sellers' market is intimately related to the "engineering motive" in the discussion of the enterprise objective function in chapter 4 in this volume.

11. A good example of this brief stage of hopelessness is the Qingdao Forging Machinery Plant's initial reaction to the sharp fall in demand resulting from the investment cutbacks of 1979–80. See Chen and others 1984, p. 80. Indeed, Qingdao went through the first three responses to a buyers' market in succession.

12. Output market conditions are those faced by the industry concerned as a whole in 1982–83. Moreover, they refer to the supply-demand situation at official, government-set prices, leaving open the question of whether prices for above-quota output cleared the market (if such a market existed). In most cases the enterprises made it clear in the interviews whether they (and their industry) were facing a sellers' market or a buyers' market, but for a few, such as the Shanghai High-Pressure Oil Pump Plant, market conditions had to be inferred indirectly from enterprise statements about sales promotion, competition, and so on. Some factories in our sample are in industries that faced excess supply in 1982–83, but because of superior quality, a tighter administrative supervisory system, or simply lags in the impact of the buyers' market, they were largely unaffected at the time that interviews were conducted. This situation applies to both of the Shanghai enterprises in our sample and also to some of the other textile plants.

13. The constraint of profitability may also affect downstream products, since a low price for a material input can result in a supply constraint for enterprises that use the particular good in production.

14. Before Shenyang instituted such tied sales, the price of cadmium on the open market had dropped by as much as 50 percent without eliminating excess supply. Supply obviously is largely price-inelastic, since nearly all cadmium is produced as a by-product in zinc smelting. Demand for the metal in China was sharply reduced after

the discovery that using cadmium as an additive in plastic sheets for agricultural use was contaminating food supplies. See Byrd 1985b, pp. 55–56.

15. Parts and components for all grades of men's watches produced by Chongqing are basically the same. They differ only in the quality standards they meet in postproduction testing (see Byrd and Tidrick 1984, p. 55).

16. "Direct marketing" refers to the share of sales arranged by the enterprise itself on a voluntary basis with customers (including sales for money and exchanges for other goods), as opposed to sales arranged through mandatory production or distribution plans or goods that the enterprise is required to sell to the "official" commercial agency in charge of its products.

17. Only three enterprises in the sample are allowed to engage in large-scale direct exporting. Two of them are large, centrally run enterprises for which exports account for only a small proportion of total sales. The third, the Mindong Electrical Machinery Plant, was one of the first enterprises given direct export authority as part of China's economic reform program.

18. Asset valuation is distorted because of low depreciation rates and the lack of revaluation of existing assets, which means that older enterprises have artificially high profit rates on capital. The Shanghai enterprises and the Shenyang Smelting Plant are examples.

19. Anshan Iron and Steel Corporation is only 85 percent self-sufficient in iron ore, and Xiangxiang Cement Plant relies heavily on coal it must buy from outside. The North China Petroleum Administration operates declining oil fields. Although the Sanchazi Forestry Bureau has ample forest reserves, there are limits on the amount of timber cut to preserve long-term exploitation potential. Thus, none of these enterprises escapes problems of raw materials.

20. Government response in China can be contrasted with the plausible alternative of "planned" adjustment to a weak market, in which the planning and distribution systems continue to take responsibility for the procurement of all output but administrative pressure is brought to bear on enterprises to adjust product mix, improve quality, and so on.

21. Retail units selling to the public apparently do not keep very large inventories. When demand falls, they cut down their orders from wholesale commercial enterprises.

22. In this context, it is interesting to note that a policy of "selective purchase" by commercial enterprises (where they are allowed to refuse to buy poor-quality or unmarketable goods) had been tried out in China on two separate occasions before the late 1970s, once in 1956–57 and once in 1961–63. The first trial was interrupted by the Great Leap Forward, and the second appears to have been limited and was in any case wiped out by the political currents that led to the Cultural Revolution. See Solinger 1984, pp. 220–230. Wiles 1962 has singled out selective purchase as a potentially important Chinese policy innovation. Though this tradition did give Chinese reformers a historical basis and an intellectual underpinning for releasing control over procurement of industrial goods by the commercial system, the driving force has been strong buyers' markets. Designation of goods for selective purchase (and the variant form "purchase by order") has often lagged behind actual developments, merely validating rather than determining changes in commercial procurement practices.

23. Users may build up large inventories of producer goods, but scope for this appears to be limited. Many capital goods are purchased for specific investment projects and would not be bought if the project is rejected or cancelled. Moreover, preexisting inventories of many types of producer goods were very large due to hoarding. In any case, producers sooner or later realize that they no longer need blindly to purchase all supplies that become available.

24. See Byrd and Tidrick 1984, pp. 44–45 and 68–69, for a discussion of the imposition of investment controls in the watch industry and problems with watch factories "outside the plan."

25. Wong 1985, pp. 268–75, has argued that local governments in China increasingly act like "economic agents" striving to maximize revenues. The orientation toward regional and local industrialization is an enduring legacy of the Cultural Revolution (see Wong 1986, pp. 78–80).

26. The Chongqing Clock and Watch Company's joint ventures with small watch producers in backward Yunnan and Guizhou provinces appear to have been motivated primarily by the desire to maintain dominance over the watch market in these provinces (see Byrd and Tidrick 1984, p. 20).

27. If some but not all local producers are shut down, there may be no loss of local government revenue if the remaining producers take up the slack. But shutting down the only local producer means the "export" of the local government revenues earned by it, particularly since local governments have little authority in setting tax rates.

28. This supports the assertion that enterprises in a centrally planned economy are sensitive to price signals but not to quantity signals on the output side and the reverse on the input side (see Kornai 1980, pp. 340–41).

29. A good example is the No. 2 Automobile Plant, which reduced the price of its trucks by 28 percent in three stages in 1980–82. Though approval of the State Price Bureau was required, the reductions occurred at the initiative of No. 2 Auto. Prices were cut because of a drastic decline in costs as production grew rapidly and because of the need to match the lower prices charged by the No. 1 Automobile Plant.

30. There are a few exceptions in the sample: enterprises under tight administrative control, particularly if their supervisory agency also has jurisdiction over suppliers of the goods concerned. For the Chengdu Locomotive and Rolling Stock Factory, lower-priced goods were available locally, but the enterprise was forced to buy from distant, high-priced suppliers under the Ministry of Railways. The Northwest No. 1 Cotton Mill wanted to acquire spindles of better quality at a lower price from distant suppliers but was ordered to buy locally, which it refused to do.

31. Of course, this preference for imported capital goods may be irrational, particularly because investors may not be very cost-conscious.

32. One manifestation of No. 2 Auto's customer-oriented behavior was its loyalty to customers who ordered trucks during the period of excess supply in 1981–82 but were squeezed by the revival of within-plan demand. Although some of these customers had to endure delays, No. 2 Auto fought for its case against the State Material Supply Bureau. In the end it was allowed to fill most of their orders despite large demand by sectors that planning authorities deemed to be of higher priority.

33. In particular, the commitment to increase consumption has been implemented to a large extent by the use of wage increases (which reduce state enterprises' profit remittances to the budget) and subsidies (which in effect constitute a prior claim on

budgetary resources). Combined with a great aversion to budgetary instability (manifested by sharp reductions in expenditures and budget deficits in 1980–81), this has meant that there have been strong built-in controls over budgetary investment, at least through 1982.

34. Aside from the continuing priority that central authorities give to expanding the production of consumer goods, the high profitability of many consumer goods and the orientation of enterprises toward promoting workers' interests may in part explain this phenomenon. Another important factor is inherent limitations on demand for many varieties of consumer goods.

35. The contrast with American corporations, whose first response to a weak market and falling profits tends to be cost cutting, is striking. See Williamson 1964, pp. 94–121, for some interesting case studies.

References

Byrd, William. 1985a. "The Shanghai Market for the Means of Production: A Case Study of Reform in China's Material Supply System." *Comparative Economic Studies* 27, no. 4 (Winter):1–29.

———. 1985b. *The Shenyang Smelter: A Case Study of Problems and Reforms in China's Nonferrous Metals Industry.* World Bank Staff Working Paper 766. Washington, D.C.

Byrd, William, and Gene Tidrick. 1984. "Adjustment and Reform in the Chongqing Clock and Watch Company." In *Recent Chinese Economic Reforms: Studies of Two Industrial Enterprises.* World Bank Staff Working Paper 652. Washington, D.C.

Chen Jiyuan, Xu Lu, Tang Zongkun, and Chen Lantong. 1984. "Management and Reform in the Qingdao Forging Machinery Plant." In *Recent Chinese Economic Reforms: Studies of Two Industrial Enterprises*. World Bank Staff Working Paper 652. Washington, D.C.

"China Economic Yearbook" Editorial Committee. 1981. *Zhongguo Jingji Nianjian 1981* (1981 China economic yearbook). Beijing: Jingji Guanli Zazhishe.

Kornai, Janos. 1980. *Economics of Shortage.* 2 vols. Amsterdam: North-Holland.

Leibenstein, Harvey. 1966. "Allocative Efficiency versus 'X Efficiency.' " *American Economic Review* 56, no. 3 (June):392–415.

Liu Yi. 1982. "Shangye Shichang Huoyue Fanrong Wending" (Commercial markets are brisk, flourishing, and stable). *Caimao Jingji* (Finance and trade economics), no. 10 (October):7–9.

Ma Hong. 1980. "Jingji Kexue Yao Jiaqiang Dui Shengchan Ziliao Liutong Wenti de Yanjiu" (Economic science should strengthen research on questions relating to the circulation of means of production). *Jingji Guanli* (Economic management), no. 5 (May):2–3.

Schumpeter, Joseph A. 1950. *Capitalism, Socialism and Democracy.* 3d ed. New York: Harper and Row.

Solinger, Dorothy J. 1984. *Chinese Business under Socialism: The Politics of Domestic Commerce, 1949–1980.* Berkeley, Calif.: University of California Press.

State Statistical Bureau. 1982. *Statistical Yearbook of China, 1982.* Hong Kong: Economic Information Agency.

———. 1984. *Statistical Yearbook of China, 1984.* Hong Kong: Economic Information Agency.

Sylos-Labini, Paolo. 1984. *The Forces of Economic Growth and Decline.* Cambridge, Mass.: MIT Press.

Wiles, P. J. D. 1962. *The Political Economy of Communism.* Cambridge, Mass.: Harvard University Press.

Williamson, Oliver E. 1964. *The Economics of Discretionary Behavior: Managerial Objectives in a Theory of the Firm.* Englewood Cliffs, N.J.: Prentice-Hall.

Wong, Christine. 1985. "Material Allocation and Decentralization: Impact of the Local Sector on Industrial Reform." In Elizabeth J. Perry, and Christine Wong, eds., *The Political Economy of Reform in Post-Mao China.* Cambridge, Mass.: Harvard University Press.

———. 1986. "Ownership and Control in Chinese Industry: The Maoist Legacy and Prospects for the 1980s." In U.S. Congress, Joint Economic Committee, *China in the 1980s.* Washington, D.C.: Government Printing Office.

Zhou Taihe, ed. 1984. *Dangdai Zhongguo de Jingji Tizhi Gaige* (Economic system reform in contemporary China). Beijing: Zhongguo Shehui Kexue Chubanshe.

PART THREE

Enterprise Organization

In chapter 11 Xu Lu examines the role of corporations and other forms of association in Chinese industry. Chinese corporations are normally formed by merging several small independent enterprises. These corporations can be specialized (horizontally integrated) or integrated (vertically integrated). And they can be economic, with independent accounting units at least nominally responsible for profit and loss, or administrative, with the corporation acting as the lowest-level administrative unit under an industrial bureau and sharing the profits of several factories that are independent accounting units. Chinese enterprises also form associations in which they contract to undertake joint activities for, say, production or marketing while retaining their identity as independent accounting units.

Xu traces the development of corporations since 1949 and distinguishes four phases. The first is the postliberation period, when the government nationalized large private corporations and established some new state-owned integrated corporations such as the Anshan Iron and Steel Corporation. The second phase started in 1956, when the government nationalized small private enterprises and grouped them under specialized administrative corporations. The third phase began in 1963, when specialized industrywide "trusts" were established, only to be dismantled during the Cultural Revolution. The fourth phase is the post-1978 reform period, during which a large share of the state industrial sector has been organized into corporations. Encompassing only a sixth of the state enterprises above the county level, these industrial corporations accounted for more than half the national industrial output value and more than three-fifths of taxes and profits.

Based on the experiences of six corporations in the sample, Xu draws three general conclusions. First, there is no universally applicable model. Not all corporations or associations should be organized the same way, nor should all enterprises participate in a corporation. Second, all corporations should be organized on voluntary principles. Enterprises should freely join and have the right to withdraw from any corporation or association. Third, economic benefit should be the measure of success, for only with mutual economic benefits can associations endure.

Xu argues that segmentation of administrative authority into functional "lines" (organized vertically under specialized industrial ministries) and regional "blocks" (organized horizontally under provincial or local governments) is one of the most serious problems of China's enterprise management system. Corporations can play an important role in breaking down these administrative barriers. But creating corporations does not automatically solve problems. Creating a corporation across different lines or blocks merely pulls the problem of cooperation inside the corporation. It also raises difficult internal management issues about which decisions to centralize at the corporate level and which to decentralize to the factory level.

Xu notes that several corporations in the sample have found it difficult to strike the right balance. He offers three guidelines for organizing corporations so that they will be more effective in breaking down administrative barriers. First, corporations should be economic rather than administrative units. Many of the administrative corporations dealing with enterprises in our sample merely interfered in day-to-day production decisions and charged fees for unwanted services. Second, national corporations such as the China Automobile Corporation should not be given monopoly power over production and marketing because such power would eliminate the competition's motivation to improve. Finally, integration across administrative boundaries has worked well when based on leadership of relatively technically advanced enterprises.

In chapter 12 Zheng Guangliang surveys the evolution of the leadership system in state enterprises and evaluates the system's consistency with broader reforms of enterprise management. As with other aspects of enterprise management, there have been numerous changes and reversals in the leadership system since liberation. Equally striking, however, has been the continuity of themes and forms in the attempt to achieve a balance between the party and the technicians. Of the five modes that Zheng distinguishes, the most important was the tripartite system of plant-director responsibility, staff-and-worker assembly, and party committee leadership. As early as 1956 this system replaced the one-director system modeled on the U.S.S.R. During the Cultural Revolution, the balance swung further toward party dominance (after a brief period when revolutionary committees eclipsed even the party leadership) with a unified leadership system in which the party secretary was also the plant director. But after the downfall of the Gang of Four in 1976 the tripartite system was gradually restored. More recently there have been two significant changes. One is the campaign to bring in younger, better-educated, and more technically competent managers. The other is the experimentation with a new plant-director responsibility system in pilot enterprises.

In the evolution of China's leadership system, the key problem to be solved, according to Zheng, is the proper balance of three interests: production, party, and workers. Zheng argues that the present tripartite system, although better than anything that has gone before, still has many shortcomings. Multiple and overlapping external leadership often makes it difficult to organize a coherent internal system. In many enterprises, the party committee's continuing involvement in such day-to-day administrative matters as wage adjustment and housing allocations weakens both production administration and the party's political role. Many members of the party committee do not understand the technology of their enterprises but must approve major production decisions. The staff-and-worker assembly is often dormant or merely formalistic in carrying out its functions. But since both the party committee and the assembly (where it exists) must approve major decisions, it is difficult to make timely decisions or fix responsibility. This is a severe handicap for enterprises producing for the market. Nor is the present system suitable for joint ventures, especially those with foreign capital.

Zheng nevertheless feels that the new responsibility system under trial implementation in a few enterprises has the potential to solve most of these problems. Under the new system the enterprise director has full authority over daily production decisions and internal plant organization. He also proposes long-term plans, major investments, and appointments of all his subordinates. The party committee performs a supervisory role, "enthusiastically supporting the plant director's functions and duties," and is responsible for ideological and political work. The staff-and-worker assembly has the authority to deliberate on major production decisions, approve major rules and regulations, make decisions about worker welfare questions, and criticize and supervise enterprise management. In small enterprises it may appoint plant directors. Although this new system is obviously intended to enhance the role and accountability of the enterprise director, Zheng argues that it does not and should not restore the one-man director system. Instead, it represents a new division of responsibility and functions among the director, the party, and the workers.

Zheng concludes with a discussion of the system for appointing managers. Normally the party committee of the enterprise's superior governmental unit appoints enterprise directors. In recent years, however, there have been a few experiments with staff-and-worker assemblies' electing or hiring managers. One such experiment was dropped, and it appears that there is disenchantment with the national experiment. The reasons are not entirely clear, but one factor appears to have been that enterprises with elected managers proved to have too strong a family orientation. Zheng alludes to this issue by asking how the interests of the state are to be represented and how excessive bonuses are to be prevented in enterprises with elected managers. Zheng also considers how the system of managerial appointments might be adapted to interregional, intersectoral, and foreign joint ventures. He proposes that a board of directors representing all interested parties appoint the plant directors. More generally, he suggests that a board of directors may be appropriate for all large enterprises, with the board deciding major issues, including the appointment of the plant director.

11

Industrial Corporations

Xu Lu

China's state-owned industrial enterprises have recently set up some specialized (horizontally integrated) and integrated (vertically integrated) corporations that are national or regional in scope. Most of these corporations were formed by putting together several factories, mines, and other economic units that are closely related in their production and operations. Formed according to the principle of cooperation based on specialization, these corporations are under unified management and run on economic principles to suit the needs of socialist industrialization.

The formation of the industrial corporation, inevitable in the development of modern industry, can be done legally with the government's approval. The industrial corporation has, in general, four features. First, it is set up by two or more shareholders. Second, it is managed on the principle of economic methods, with the shareholders assuming financial responsibility (limited or unlimited). Third, it exists for the sole purpose of making profits, and the profits are distributed in proportion to the investment each shareholder has contributed (dividends are drawn in proportion to the number of shares held). Fourth, it is legally a person, having certain legal rights and being bound by certain obligations. Some of China's state-owned industrial enterprises have adopted the organizational form of a corporation. These corporations, as relatively independent economic entities, possess the four features just mentioned, except that their purpose is not quite the same owing to their socialist nature.

The formation of an industrial corporation can bring many advantages. It can streamline the administrative structure and staff; raise efficiency; break down the barriers between regions or departments; develop specialized cooperation and integration in production; make a comprehensive utilization of resources; speed up the improvement of techniques; use manpower, materials, and financial resources rationally; raise the economic results; and put into full play the advantages of socialized mass production and the superiority of the socialist system. In the restructuring of the Chinese economy, the industrial corporation was born at an opportune time. We will continue to aid in its establishment and development, based on the needs of the economy and the mutual needs of enterprises. Needless to say, the newly formed industrial corporations, whether national or regional, should all be economic enterprises in nature. They should no longer be administrative corporations.

In addition to the state-owned industrial corporations, there have also appeared, along with the reform of China's economic management system, a whole batch of integrated economic associations that are structurally loose but stable. Those industrial enterprises involved in integrated economic associations maintain their own accounting and assume sole responsibility for their profits and losses. And on the principle of compensatory payment for deficiency in the course of equivalent exchange, production management activities are carried on among the member enterprises to achieve set-completion of products. They cooperate in using productive, material, and financial resources—and in the transfer of technology. The nature of integration is confirmed by contracts. But the integration will not affect the ownership of each enterprise or its status and financial relations with others.

The Development of Corporations since 1949

Before 1949, China was very backward in industrial production. There were very few industrial corporations. Since the founding of the People's Republic of China, two categories of corporations have appeared. The first includes enterprises confiscated from the bureaucratic capitalists in the early years after liberation. These enterprises retained their organizational form, which is corporate. Besides this category, China also built, in a planned way, a few large and medium-size industrial corporations, such as the Anshan Iron and Steel Corporation. Between the first five-year plan and today, there have been three large-scale nationwide readjustments of industrial corporations in conjunction with the reform of the economic management system.

The first readjustment was in 1956, when the socialist transformation of privately owned industrial enterprises took place. In big cities, where most industrial enterprises were concentrated, some industrial corporations were established, according to the nature of trade and products, as joint state-private industrial enterprises. All these corporations were administrative. Still, they played a positive role in adjusting the structure of industry, of products, and of enterprise organizations. These adjustments strengthened enterprise management, developed specialized cooperation, promoted production, and improved techniques.

The second readjustment started in 1963, with four objectives: to change the administrative approach in enterprise management, to reform the industrial management system, to improve the managerial organization, and to learn how to organize "trusts" (based on industries or major products).[1] Twelve industrial corporations—all of them trusts—were set up on a trial basis throughout the country. Among other things, these corporations produced automobiles, tractor engines, cigarettes, and pharmaceuticals. They merged individual industrial enterprises and economic organizations into a specialized industrial corporation.

The advantages of unified management and administration soon became evident. After the Auto Industrial Corporation of China was formed (with branches in Changchun, Nanjing, Jinan, and Beijing), China's auto production became more specialized. All the enterprises shared the work, thus promoting the development of China's auto industry. And with the establishment of the Tobacco Industrial Corporation, the number of cigarette factories throughout the country was reduced from 107 to 65. Fifteen of the big cigarette factories produced 61 percent of the cigarettes for the whole country. Moreover, 470 inferior brands of cigarettes were eliminated and the number of staff members and workers was reduced by 13,000. Production capacity, meanwhile, was raised from 3.8 million to 4.3 million cartons a year—a 35 percent increase in production. And total production costs were reduced by 21 percent. Great efforts were made in coordination with the Ministry of Agriculture to produce high-quality tobacco leaf and cigarettes through unified management and in purchasing, re-flue-curing, allocating, and grading the leaf tobacco. In a word, these trusts, established on a trial basis, not only promoted production and construction but also improved the management of enterprises. But during the Great Cultural Revolution, launched in 1966, the industrial corporations that resembled trusts were indiscriminately eliminated. Some of the twelve industrial corporations were broken up, whereas others ceased to exist except in name. To keep them going was out of the question.

The third readjustment began after the smashing of the Gang of Four. New industrial corporations of various forms were gradually organized in the central and local industrial sectors on the principle of cooperation among specialized units. In September 1979 the state selected thirty-five industrial corporations as experimental units to carry out readjustments. They were under seven departments—the First Ministry of Machinery Engineering, the Ministry of Agricultural Machinery, the Fourth Ministry of Machinery Engineering, the Metallurgical Ministry, the Textile Ministry, the Ministry of Light Industry, and the Pharmaceutical Ministry—in six cities and provinces (Beijing, Tianjin, Shanghai, Liaoning Province, Jiangsu Province, and Sichuan Province). Of the thirty-five industrial corporations selected for the pilot projects, eleven were under direct state administration and twenty-four were under local administration.

By the end of 1983, according to incomplete statistics, there were 2,240 corporations and general factories under the administration of the departments of industry and communications and affiliated organizations. Of these, 135 were under central administration. Large corporations are found in such industrial sectors as shipping, petrochemicals, automobiles, nonferrous metal, and tobacco. More than 19,000 enterprises are incorporated into the new industrial corporations. They account for 17 percent of the state industrial and communications enterprises at the county level and above, 55 percent of the national industrial output, and 63 percent of taxes and profits turned over to the state.

Corporations have thus developed rapidly. But many are administrative and are undergoing reorganization and consolidation. Corporations such as Anshan Iron and Steel, the No. 2 Automobile Plant, and the Jinling Petrochemical General Corporation are being required to restructure and improve their internal management—and to grant more decisionmaking power to their subordinate enterprises. At the same time, work on the further expansion of horizontal economic ties must also be put on the agenda. For example, impetus must be given to economic cooperation between the coastal areas and the hinterland.

To summarize, since the founding of the People's Republic—and particularly during the economic restructuring and reforms of the last few years—we have gained practical experience in merging state industrial enterprises. The road has been tortuous, but the experience is valuable. The merging of industrial enterprises into industrial corporations has very broad prospects for development under the socialist system. Such corporations are a natural product of large-scale socialized production. They will also play a key role in economic readjustment and in the reform of economic management. In merging and organizing these industrial corporations, we should learn from other countries and do what is best for us—advancing down the road of reform while adhering to the socialist orientation.

Examples from the Survey Sample

Of the twenty industrial units in the survey, some are factories, like the Qingdao Forging Machinery Plant, and others are government administrative departments, like the Qingyuan County Economic Commission of Guangdong Province. Still others are industrial corporations, such as the Anshan Iron and Steel Corporation, the Mindong Electrical Machinery Plant, and Jinling Petrochemical. Some are integrated economic entities, such as the Chongqing Clock and Watch Company and Dongfeng Automobile Corporation, which has the No. 2 Automobile Plant as its main body.

As stipulated, I will deal only with some (integrated and specialized) enterprise-type corporations and some integrated economic entities. In the discussion of integrated corporations, I will focus on Anshan Iron and Steel and Jinling Petrochemical. In the discussion of specialized corporations, I will focus on Mindong Electrical Machinery and the Tianjin Color Textile Corporation. And in the discussion of integrated economic entities (associations), I will focus on Chongqing and Dongfeng. I will not discuss factories, administrative units, or industrial corporations that are administrative.

Integrated Industrial Corporations

Anshan Iron and Steel Corporation. A large integrated enterprise, Anshan is basically constructed after a model of an independent corporation having its own organizational structure in the early years following the founding of the People's Republic of China. This integrated corporation engages in the whole production process, from the production of raw materials to product processing. The main productive enterprises subordinate to this corporation are five mines, four ore-dressing plants, five nonmetal mines, four sintering plants, nine blast furnaces, seventeen coking furnaces, three steel mills, and fourteen rolling mills.

Anshan's production activities have three features. The first is continuity: the whole process from mining to sintering, iron smelting, steel making, cogging, and finished product is continuous. The second feature is interdependence: basic production, subsidiary production, and affiliated production are interdependent—as are the power network and the transportation network. The third is the unanimity of the goal of different links of the production chain: the main goal of production in iron smelting, steel making, steel rolling, refractory manufacturing, coking, machine maintenance, and so on is one and the same—to produce steel products up to the standard the state requires.

We learned from the administrative personnel at Anshan that it would be inadvisable to change the management system there. The corporation should remain as a legal and economic entity, which directs both production and management affairs. Anshan should not be dismembered into several independent, self-managed enterprises. Besides employing the system of unified management and administration, Anshan should adopt the system of multilevel administration. It should also introduce the responsibility system in its subordinate enterprises and see to it that these enterprises enjoy decisionmaking powers.

Jinling Petrochemical General Corporation. A regional corporation characterized by specialized trade, Jinling is subordinate to the China Petrochemical Industrial Corporation. It was formed by integrating six petrochemical enterprises: the Nanjing Refinery, the Qixiasham Chemical Fertilizer Plant, the Nanjing Alkyl-Benzene Plant, the Changjiang Petrochemical Plant, the Zhongshan Chemical Plant, and the Nanjing Plastic Factory. The general corporation is an economic entity that appraises how much profit each plant will retain and delivers the profits from subordinate enterprises to the state. The general corporation is also charged with laying down internal prices for raw materials (such as liquid hydrocarbon, pure benzol, and ethylbenzene) needed for complete-set production. The corporation ensures that any price deficiency is made up by raising the base for profits to be retained for the plants producing the intermediate products for use in complete-set production. Moreover, the general corporation helps the affiliated enterprises share material resources. Plants extend credit to each other to help regulate the surplus and lack of funds, and each plant is granted the power to manage its own funds. As one corporation official remarked, these methods ensure "that each of the subordinate plants has a share in the benefits, that each feels satisfied with the other, and that production develops and the state benefits as a result."

The general corporation's unified leadership helps the subordinate plants maintain a proper balance in production. It also creates favorable conditions for expanding production, creating products, strengthening technical superiority, and speeding the pace of technical transformation. And through the adjustment of production facilities, the economic results have been markedly improved.

Jinling's administrative personnel said that the most pressing issue to be solved is for the industrial corporation to delegate more decisionmaking powers to the Jinling company. Old established practices still prevail in planning, distribution, finance, and personnel. This situation prompts an urgent need for reform and for the delegation of more decisionmaking powers to the subordinate enterprises. Moreover, there is no strict legal protection for the economic benefits of the general company, which still has too many restrictions imposed on it. The petrochemical industry is known as "a big chunk of meat."[2] Everybody is very eager, for various reasons, to take a big bite beyond that stipulated by the state.

Specialized Industrial Corporations

Mindong Electrical Machinery Corporation. A specialized industrial corporation based in the city of Fuzhou, Mindong includes eight plants with various types of ownership. Mindong is transregional, comprising several different trades. It is characterized by "three integrations." One is the integration of industry with commerce, which means the corporation has self-marketing rights. The second is the integration of imports with exports, which means the corporation markets its own exports and has some right to retain a portion of foreign exchange earnings. The third is the integration of scientific research with production. Mindong also has "centralized management for personnel, finance, raw materials, production, supply, and marketing.

The corporation's eight plants are located in Ningde and Jinjiang districts and in the city of Fuzhou in Fujian Province. There are three types of ownership in these plants: the ownership of the whole people, the collective ownership, and the ownership of the whole people attached with the collective ownership. Of the eight subordinate plants, plants No. 5 and No. 8 are jointly managed, because these plants used to be under the management of the neighborhood committee and the city government.

After their merging as an industrial corporation, the enterprises formed a leading body comprising personnel from all sides. This body signed an agreement on the production of electrical machinery and on profit sharing with the corporation. Except for Plant No. 6 (a big, collectively owned plant in Fuzhou), the plants are enterprises owned by the whole people. But two of the plants also have collective ownership attached to the ownership by the whole people. The reason for this is that some dependents of the staff and workers also join in the plant's production activities. Despite belonging to the category of workers under the neighborhood committee, which is collective ownership, they enjoy the same treatment as the staff and workers under the ownership by the whole people. They also enjoy the same wages, material benefits, and right to promotion. That explains the third type of ownership—the ownership by the whole people, with collective ownership as its appendage.

In 1981 the Mindong Electrical Machinery Corporation, the Beijing Electric Machinery Plant, the Jiamusi Electrical Machinery Plant, the Xian Electric Motor and Appliances Factory, the Xiangtan Electrical Machinery Plant, the Chongqing Electrical Machinery Plant, and others formed the China Electrical Appliances Joint Exports Corporation. Later, the electrical machinery plants from Shanghai, Guangzhou, and other places were incorporated into the joint exports corporation, a loosely organized integrated economic entity that specializes in export activities.

Mindong has a marketing network with fifteen branches in various cities, including Beijing, Shanghai, Guangzhou, Wuhan, Xiamen, Fuzhou, Qingdao, and Xinxiang. The network is classified into three types. The first is the Handling Department, managed solely by Mindong. The second is the Joint-Management Department, which promotes the sale of Mindong's products. The sales location is provided by the buyer. It is managed by personnel appointed by both sides, with the understanding that each party will get benefits through profit sharing in proportion to the value of their contribution to the Joint-Management Department. The third type is called the Agency. Its responsibility is to sell the products, and in return it gets a commission of 3 to 5 percent on the products sold.

Since its founding the production in Mindong has been normal owing to centralized management, under which each plant produces its specialized products and complete-set products. Under centralized management the practice of specialized production has been strengthened, and the pace of creating new products quickened. In 1982 alone the corporation produced and trial-produced 391 product series in sixty-five specifications. The same year, to expand the sale of its products, this corporation held a Goods Ordering Fair on three occasions. As a result, sales increased by 59 percent over that of the previous year.

Some problems nevertheless cropped up after the corporation was formed. First, too much power went to the corporate level, with very little decisionmaking power granted to the subordinate plants. This defused initiative and enthusiasm in the plants. Second, the state should have treated the corporation as an enterprise, imposing a value-added tax only on the affiliated plants, not a product tax at each level. This product tax increased the burden of the enterprises. Third, as a result of the first two problems, economic results dropped slightly despite the growth in production. To improve the situation, the corporation decided to grant more decisionmaking powers to the lower level and to implement a two-level accounting system. Since then, the corporation has examined the safety, profit, and quality and variety of products of its subordinate plants and awarded prizes to the best performers. Moreover, it grants each plant the right to open accounts in the bank and to purchase certain spare parts and components and some other low-cost, easily consumed materials.

Tianjin Color Textile Corporation. A regional specialized corporation, Tianjin is one of the twenty-four corporations formed as experimental units and approved by the State Economic Commission in 1979. By 1983 Tianjin had twenty subordinate units—fourteen weaving mills, two dyeing mills, one fabric finishing mill, one Supply and Marketing Handling Department, one small-sized garment factory, and one workers' training school.

Since its establishment the corporation has, by means of unified management, set for itself the following tasks: to determine the amount of profits to be retained, to deliver to the state the profits from its subordinate units, to make arrangements for the use of production funds, and to handle applications and repayments for bank loans. In financial matters, the corporation and its subordinate units practice a two-level accounting system. Tianjin follows the principle of having "the factory turn out specialized products and the whole corporation produce a complete variety of products," so that each unit manufactures only one or two kinds of major products. Another rational adjustment has been made to divide work among factories producing goods for exports and for the domestic market. In the past, the plants arranged such matters as production, the supply of raw materials, marketing, technical transformation, and living quarters and dwellings for the workers and staff. The results were not satsifactory, and in fact, some problems could not be resolved at all. But the situation has gradually improved since the formation of the corporation. Under the unified management of the corporation, issues that used to be difficult to solve have become manageable, and the workers and staff of the subordinate plants are fairly happy with the way their problems have been settled.

Integrated Economic Entities (Associations)

Since 1979, various forms of associations have gradually emerged in the industrial sector. The reason for the associations is the integration of the production, scientific research, technology, equipment, manpower, materials, and marketing of enterprises belonging to the same economic entity. They should do so voluntarily, under the guidance of the state and on the basis of equality and mutual benefit, with stress on economic efficiency. In the meantime, each association member is an independent accounting unit and assumes sole responsibility for its profits and losses. The production of complete-set products, the supply of materials, and the transfer of technology are carried out among the members of the association by following the principle of compensatory payment for equivalent exchange. Among the twenty industrial units we surveyed, there were two such integrated industrial economic entities. One is the Dongfeng Automobile Corporation, which has as its main body the No. 2 Automobile Plant. The other is an association organized by the Chongqing Clock and Watch Company.

Dongfeng Automobile Corporation. Dongfeng is a successful association. Its members adhere to the principle of acting voluntarily in organizing multilevel integrated economic entities of various forms. The association has twenty-seven subordinate specialized factories under its direct management, with the general factory serving as the general headquarters. Four closely integrated enterprises handle such affairs as material supply, production, marketing, personnel, and property under the centralized management of their associations. But each retains its status as a legal entity. Fifteen semiloosely integrated enterprises carry out "Three No Changes": no change in the form of ownership, no change in its status of subordination with other units, and no change in financial channels. These fifteen enterprises also have "Four Unifications": a unified product series, a unified transformation program, a unified production plan, and a unified management approach. Production management is conducted under the unified administration of the integrated economic entity, but the factories are still granted the right to produce some other products to meet the needs of their localities. Eighty-three loosely integrated enterprises produce only part of the series products for the Dongfeng Automobile Corporation. They also produce some other series products according to their own plans. The joint company exercises its leadership only on the production of the Dongfeng brand of series products and does not interfere in the other production activities of its subordinate factories.

The members of the association adhere to the principle of mutual benefit and employ different ways of profit sharing. In the closely integrated enterprises, the ratio of profit sharing between the association and the enterprise is 2:8 before taxes, or 1.5:8.5 after taxes. Instead of siphoning off the profits, the company leaves them as a fund for technical transformation in the enterprise. This fund automatically becomes the additional investment by the joint company in the subordinate enterprise. In the loosely integrated enterprises, the principle of equivalent exchange is followed in handling profits, and the business relationship between the joint company and its subordinate enterprises is defined in a contract arrived at through negotiation.

In its various activities, the integrated economic entity plays both the role of the backbone and the role of a handlebar (determining the direction and orientation). The enterprises participating in the integrated economic entity can get high-quality spare parts and components from the No. 2 Automobile Plant to assemble or refit high-quality vehicles. Moreover, No. 2 Auto has helped transform these enterprises by giving them technical assistance in overcoming some of their problems. As a result, they have been able to establish an advanced production and management system. No. 2 Auto has also helped train technicians and managers for these enterprises. Under the unified leadership of the integrated economic entity, a division of labor based on specialization has been achieved by taking into consideration the special features and strong points of each enterprise. Since 1984, some joint factories, by using No. 2 Auto as their handlebar, have started the joint design and development of new products. This has speeded up the remodeling of products and has helped strengthen the technical force of the enterprises participating in the integrated economic entity.

Association of the Chongqing Clock and Watch Company. This association, which has no name, is based in Chongqing City under the leadership of the Chongqing Clock and Watch Company, which was itself formed by a merger between the Chongqing Clock and Watch Factory and other factories in the city. The association engages in production, supply, and marketing in southwestern China, encompassing Yunnan, Guizhou, and Sichuan provinces. The original subordinate relationship with other units and the form of ownership of the enterprises participating in the association remain unchanged. We learned from the survey that the enterprises in the integrated economic entity can be classified into three types—jointly managed enterprises, back-to-original-trade enterprises, and enterprises directly affiliated with the company.

The jointly managed enterprises (or joint ventures) in the association are owned by the whole people and located outside Chongqing. Among these enterprises are the Kunming Watch Factory of Yunnan Province, the Guiyang Watch Factory of Guizhou Province, and the Chengdu Watch Factory. Their relationship with the Chongqing Clock and Watch Company is fairly loose. Chongqing takes on the responsibility of coordinating the production plans of these factories. It also supplies key components, supervises the output, quality, and variety of products, and extends its technical and financial support to the factories. These factories produce their own brands and market mostly in their own province. Chongqing delegates its personnel to the administrative committee of each factory, but it does not interfere in the daily production routine. The profit that Chongqing gets from profit sharing is used as its additional investment in the associated factory and is not to be withdrawn for a specified number of years.

The back-to-original-trade enterprises in the association are state-run and collectively owned industrial enterprises. They have a close relationship with Chongqing and are under the dual leadership of the company and the local department responsible for industrial management. The company is responsible for arranging the production, supply, and marketing for these enterprises. It must also issue production plans and supply raw and semifinished materials to them. And it must approve any purchase of piecemeal fixed assets of more than Y200 or any applications for a bank loan by these enterprises.

Eleven enterprises are directly affiliated with the company. Their general affairs—related to production, supply, marketing, personnel, finance, and materials—are under the company's unified management. They are incomplete legal entities because the company holds some of their rights. For example, these enterprises may open bank accounts, but only for deposits, not for withdrawals. So the revenue they gain through marketing must go into the company's bank account. And their spending must be covered by financial allocations from the company. The same holds true for paying taxes, turning in profits, and applying for bank loans. All are under the centralized management of the company.

In addition, the company has under its management one research institute, three workers' training schools, and two technological home bases. It also has forty marketing branches throughout southwestern China.

The company's subordinate factories divide the work. Some specialize in producing spare parts and components for watches and clocks, and others specialize in assembling them. The marketing and service network promotes the sale of clocks and watches and gives maintenance service. Besides producing its main products—clocks and watches—the company manufactures some special-purpose machine tools for use in clock and watch production, such as gems and timers.

General Considerations

In merging enterprises and organizing industrial corporations, it does not do to pursue formalism, or to try to launch a campaign. Nor is it right to set up one model and ask everybody to conform. There can be loose mergers, tight mergers, or mergers that become increasingly tight-knit. There can also be comprehensive mergers, with the merging units becoming one, or partial mergers, involving no change in the affiliation of the merging parties. Because we want to promote only rational and scientific production, not all plants and enterprises should be required to participate in a corporation. For example, the No. 2 Automobile Plant deliberately did not include a number of parts-and-fittings plants in the Dongfeng Automobile Corporation. Instead, it let them carry on as cooperative plants—to encourage them to compete with each other, to raise product quality, to lower cost, and to reduce prices. And they have obtained very good results. But some corporations have stressed form only, aiming at largeness and comprehensiveness. They wanted too many plants under their corporation, even when they were not ready. Their results have not been good.

Horizontal integration should be promoted on the basis of mutual needs and voluntarism. Since the enterprise-type of corporation is to be an independent economic entity—a work unit that engages in the production of commodities and that has unified operations and independent accounting—it is inevitable that a part of the authority enjoyed by its affiliates should be centralized. Under such circumstances, no matter if the corporation is liberal-minded or not, it necessarily becomes a "mother-in-law" to the merging enterprises. Because it does so, the principle of voluntarism must be adhered to when organizing corporations. The parties must feel that they have mutual needs, so that the staff and workers in the enterprises joining the corporation can enjoy its advantages.

At the same time, there must be an equitable company charter to protect the legitimate rights of all participating parties. This will help all parties realize that while making a greater contribution to the nation they can enjoy benefits and increase economic results. On the other hand, the participating factories are not mere "daughters-in-law." They must be equal partners in the corporation, being free to join and free to withdraw. Only under such terms can the corporation do well and develop stably.

In the actual work of organizing a corporation, attention must be given to integration within the region. The enterprises in the province and prefecture must be classified, and then a plan for reorganization must be worked out whereby corporations are merged by the specialization of products, the manufacture of parts, and their use of technology. But horizontal integration should also be pursued and corporations merged that cover different regions and industries, such as Dongfeng and Chongqing. Industrial corporations involving regional and vertical integration are necessary, because they help expand specialized production and cooperation. But horizontal integration is even more urgently needed for economic development, because it can help end the separation of the "lines" from the "blocks" and serve a mutually complementary role for the enterprises in terms of capital, technology, management, and resources. This aspect of our work should be strengthened.

It is also crucial to strengthen management and to enhance real economic benefits. Whether the industrial corporation, once it is set up, can be solidified and developed depends primarily on whether its advantages can be brought into play. How can such advantages be measured? The only criterion is the degree to which economic benefits have been raised. Administrative types of corporations are ineffective because they are formalistic and do not raise economic benefits. That is why the enterprises have discarded them. The enterprise-type corporation, on the other hand, is an economic entity. It is a product of reform with substantive content. Therefore, it has certain advantages, but the advantages are not sent from heaven.

Once a corporation is organized, it takes decisionmaking skills (based on the corporation's strength in the marketplace) and sound management to increase production and economic benefits. One example is the Mindong Electrical Machinery Plant. When first formed, the factory's strategic objective to gain a place in Fuzhou was successful. But the corporation exercised too much authority over its affiliates' affairs, hurting their initiative and sense of responsibility. And the economic benefits decreased. Subsequently, the corporation became aware of the situation, and authority was appropriately decentralized and management improved. As a result, there was a resurgence of staff enthusiasm, and productivity began to rise again. The corporation was revitalized. Another example is the Jinling Petrochemical General Corporation, which underwent Mindong's experience not long after it was founded. Only by bringing into play the advantages of a corporation can it be solidified and developed. The economic productivity increased through advances in technical and managerial know-how.

One serious problem in the system of enterprise management has been its breaking into lines and blocks, thus cutting off many horizontal links between enterprises. (Here "lines" refer to the enterprises from higher levels down to the grass roots, whereas "blocks" refer to several enterprises on the same level bound together.) The lines and blocks are all trying to be independent firms with their own systems, which results not only in the overlapped construction of various enterprises but also in a situation of "big and complete" or "small and complete" in quite a few enterprises. Moreover, the government organs in charge of these "lines" and "blocks" have mixed the responsibilities of government administration with those of enterprise. They have interfered in the normal daily economic activities of the enterprises and deprived them of their decisionmaking power and vitality. This interference is harmful to industrial management and economic productivity. And it does not help the development of large-scale socialist production. Hence the demand for reform. It is against this background that, in recent years, many corporations have sprung up and developed.

From the survey we can see that the newly formed enterprise-type corporations are correct in their directions, although some are better than others. There are three main criteria for the success of such corporations.

The first criterion is that the corporations be economic entities. Not long ago the General Administration of Industry and Commerce clarified the definition of a corporation in its *Tentative Provisions for Corporation Registration*: By corporation is meant an economic entity that engages in productive operations or services with independently owned property and self-directed operations, assuming all economic responsibilities as required by law and being responsible for its own gain or loss. The corporation is a legal entity.

The problem is that China still has a number of the old, administrative-type industrial agencies, or enterprises, that are called corporations. But they constitute a level or layer of an administrative bureau. And to the affiliates, they are yet one more layer of administration, and thus a possible extra burden. For instance, they might impose certain fees in proportion to enterprise revenues; they might collect a portion of the enterprise's depreciation fund; they might transmit a portion of the profit; they might tell the enterprises what they can and cannot do in productive operations while serving no useful role with respect to the enterprise's operations and management and the expansion of its activities. Such corporations are what we call administrative-type corporations. The Beijing Municipal Wool, Linen, and Silk Textile Corporation, for example, oversees the Qinghe Woolen Textile Mill. The China Automobile Corporation, which supervises No. 2 Automobile Plant, is a similar company.

Such corporations are being reformed and reorganized. Some will be eliminated, others will be reorganized. Most of the following approaches have been adopted. Some of these administrative units have called themselves corporations, but they do not assume real economic responsibility, and they are still fulfilling their functions as government organs. For such corporations, the first step is to transfer their powers to the enterprises, which should rightly have them. Some of them will be eliminated, some will be merged with other organizations, some will be changed into service companies that are allowed to charge a fee for the services they render, and some will be restored to their old status as administrative units, pending approval by their supervising departments. But their responsibilities must be clearly defined, and they should no longer intervene in the day-to-day affairs of the enterprises. And the name "corporation" should be renounced.

There is another type of corporation that plays the dual role of an enterprise and an administrative unit. These have taken on several names. To such organizations, the principle of "separating government from enterprise" and "simplifying administration and decentralizing the powers" should be applied. They should be reorganized and broken up. One organization should not simultaneously assume several names. In other words, a government administrative organization should exercise only its administrative functions, whereas a corporation must be an economic entity.

The second criterion is that national corporations should not monopolize the production and marketing of their products, for such a monopoly would hurt the incentive to improve. National corporations, such as the China Automobile Corporation, should not have too much control over their subordinate factories. Instead, they should let their large subordinate enterprises, such as the No. 2 Automobile Plant, exercise more authority in management. In fact, a major economic entity such as No. 1 Auto or No. 2 Auto should be a large enterprise, not a national corporation that has a monopoly over its field or product.

The third criterion is horizontal integration. At present, with the city as the center and big enterprises as the foundation, greater attention must be paid to the development of horizontal ties among some enterprises to achieve various forms of integration. Economic integration that transcends districts, departments, and trades has enabled enterprises to take advantage of their technical personnel and equipment. Integration has also helped enterprises bring new products into mass production, increase the variety of products, and expand production. Integration has also greatly helped these enterprises develop in size and production capability. Furthermore, economic integration has helped enterprises solve problems brought about by the lack of coordination among "lines" and "blocks." And it has promoted the development of the industry of the nation. Big enterprises as well as advanced enterprises should do more in this regard, and the departments responsible for the work should try to develop horizontal ties.

If China is to solve the problems of industrial management, it must develop industrial cooperation and economic associations. It must also pay attention to the comprehensive application of economic forces in economic management. A socialist planned commodity economy will flourish once the separation of power and responsibilities of the authorities and its subordinate enterprises is achieved, once horizontal economic ties are developed, and once the long-standing problems brought about by the lack of coordination among "lines" and "blocks" have been solved.

Notes

1. A "trust" can be defined as a combination of enterprises producing a particular product within a designated geographical area.

2. This phrase refers to plants that produce petrochemicals. Normally, such plants have a high rate of profit and consequently a higher proportion of retained profit. As a result, local government agencies, organizations, and institutions come up with all kinds of excuses to try to share in those profits. These excuses include proposals to run joint ventures and requests for a donation to benefit public causes. Although such "extortion" is illegal, the petrochemical plant, in order not to damage its relationship with those units, often feels compelled to oblige.

12

The Leadership System

Zheng Guangliang

As the decision regarding the reform of the economic system by the Central Committee of the Chinese Communist party clearly pointed out, increasing industrial vitality, and in particular the vitality of large and mid-size enterprises under the system of ownership by the whole people, is the central link in overall economic system reform concentrating on the cities.[1] The committee went on to say that in focusing on this link, we should establish a correct relationship between the state and the enterprises under the system of ownership by the whole people. This relationship would expand enterprise autonomy. We should also establish a correct relationship between the workers and their enterprises, ensuring the position of laborers as masters of their enterprises. Thus, the party has determined the direction we should take in reforming the enterprise system. The reform of China's urban economic system is now proceeding gradually. In every region and sector, the masses of enterprise staff and workers are working vigorously to increase the vitality of enterprises. For this reason, we must now consider how to reform the leadership system in state-owned industrial enterprises and how gradually to establish a Chinese system of enterprise management for socialist modernization.

Historical Review

Subjected to many reforms, the leadership system of China's state industrial enterprises has gone through a repetitious and tortuous process of creation and development. Such enterprises as the Anshan Iron and Steel Corporation, the Shenyang Smelting Plant, and the Shanghai No. 17 Cotton Mill depended on foreign capital before the founding of the People's Republic. Those such as the No. 2 Automobile Plant, the Jinling Petrochemical

General Corporation, the North China Petroleum Administration, and the Mindong Electrical Machinery Plant were organized after the Cultural Revolution. Still others, such as the Chongqing Clock and Watch Company and the Chengdu Locomotive and Rolling Stock Factory, were established at various times after the founding of the People's Republic.

The creation of the leadership system in China's industrial enterprises had already begun during China's second revolutionary war. At that time, the public enterprises in the revolutionary base area used a three-man team, with the plant director, the party branch secretary, and the union committee chairman constituting the leadership core. The three-man team addressed major problems arising in plant production, and if the three could not agree with each other, the plant director had the authority to make the decision. This system played a key role in supporting the revolutionary war at that time. But it was very incomplete, and there subsequently arose disagreements with the administration, the party branch, and the union, each handling different matters. In the latter period of the War of Resistance against Japan, the governments of the border provinces of Shaanxi, Gansu, and Ningxia replaced the three-man team with a plant affairs conference. Under the leadership of a higher-level party committee, the plants implemented a centralized system of plant management, with leadership centered on a plant director. Production was the joint responsibility of the plant, the party, and the government—with the plant director representing the government and concentrating management within the plant. In some enterprises, the plant director was responsible for everything. This tended to cripple the independent work of the party branch and the union.

When the entire country was liberated, many bureaucrat-capitalist enterprises were turned into state enterprises. Large and mid-size enterprises such as Anshan Iron and Steel, Shenyang Smelting, and Shanghai Cotton were taken over. There were also many joint state-private firms whose leadership and management systems had to undergo a series of production and democratic reforms. To meet the demands of the situation and strengthen enterprise leadership, a joint management committee was established in state-owned enterprises by the administration and the union. The management committee comprised the plant director as chairman, the union chairman, the deputy plant director, the chief engineers, others responsible for production, and a corresponding number of union representatives. The committee served as the unified leadership organ of the plant (in some cases called the administrative organization). At the same time, the unions set up a staff-and-worker assembly to hear and discuss reports by the plant director and management committee and to examine, criticize, or offer proposals on administrative work. Such plant management committees and staff-and-worker assemblies meant a new development for the enterprise leadership system.

In 1953 China entered a phase of large-scale construction. To overcome problems of enterprise management, the party Central Committee approved the implementation of a "production administration plant-director responsibility system" (called the "one-director system" for short) in a series of enterprises in northern and northeastern China. The state asked plant directors to introduce a system of production administration under which they would take full responsibility for state plans, for enterprise administration and management, and for production technology and finance work. Within the enterprises, the party took responsibility for political and ideological leadership in plants and mines. A plant management committee was also established under the leadership of the plant director and with the participation of staff and worker representatives in production management.

The strict one-director system established more effective economic and work procedures. In our survey, the original director of the Shenyang Smelting Plant, Chen Chuntai, noted that the one-director system led to rapid plant development. The system was highly efficient and responsibilities were clearly defined. Moreover, the system conformed to the laws of economic development. In many enterprises, however, the administrative and leadership personnel dogmatically copied the Soviet approach to the administrative process, neglecting ideological and political work and democratic management. As a result, the one-director system was later subjected to criticism.

In 1956 the Eighth Party Congress decided that enterprises were to terminate the one-director system. The congress called for the universal implementation of a plant-director responsibility system under the leadership of the party committee. That system would combine collective leadership and individual responsibility with the party at its core. All major problems of the enterprise were to be discussed collectively by the enterprise party committee and decided by common accord. Day-to-day work would be the responsibility of specially assigned personnel.

In 1957 the party Central Committee decided that at the same time as the plant-director responsibility system under the leadership of the party committee was implemented, mass supervision under party committee leadership was to be implemented and strengthened. The enterprise was enthusiastically to implement, on a trial basis, a permanent staff-and-worker assembly system to serve as the organ of power for mass participation in enterprise management, supervision, and administration. But during the Great Leap Forward in 1958, the emphasis on the "party secretary taking command" meant that this leadership system, combining collective leadership and individual responsibility, had not been thoroughly implemented. In 1961, as the policy of "adjustment, consolidation, replenishment, and improvement" was being implemented, the party Central Committee issued its "Work Regulations for State-owned Industrial Enterprises (Draft)" (also known as the Seventeen

Industrial Regulations). These regulations reaffirmed that enterprises must implement a plant-director responsibility system and a staff-and-worker assembly under the leadership of the party committee.

During the Cultural Revolution, the enterprise leadership system suffered severe damage. The party organization was paralyzed, with the "rebel faction" replacing the party organization. Anarchy reigned, and the effective system of rules and regulations was destroyed. The administrative command of the plant director was eliminated, and production management was in chaos. The plant was governed by a revolutionary committee established by military representatives, leadership cadres, and mass organizations.

Toward the end of the Cultural Revolution, party committees were restored in the enterprises, with a unity of party and administration. The party secretary also served as the head of the revolutionary committee. Party and administration authority was concentrated in the party secretary and revolutionary committee head. This created an irregular situation in the enterprises, with the party committee handling all matters great and small. After the smashing of the Gang of Four, the revolutionary committees were abolished. The "Seventeen Industry Regulations" stipulated that the plant manager division-of-labor responsibility system and the staff-and-worker assembly system, under the leadership of the party committee, were to be restored. But the guiding ideology of the Left could not be corrected. With no distinction between the party and the administration, the party replaced government in the enterprises.

In 1978, after the Third Plenary Session of the Central Committee of the Eleventh Party Congress, the Central Committee adopted a series of reforms rectifying the Left's mistakes in guiding the ideology for economic work. There were reform-oriented inquiries into the enterprise leadership system. But there was no adjustment in the relationship between the enterprise, the administration, and the masses. As the economic system was reformed, this type of leadership system was considered more and more unsuitable. In 1984, after the Third Plenary Session of the Central Committee of the Twelfth Party Congress, regions, sectors, and enterprises also instituted a separation of government and enterprise, in keeping with the spirit of the Central Committee's decision. Administration was given less authority while the enterprises' administrative and management powers were expanded. A number of enterprises were also selected to test a plant-director system—a move that was well received by the staff and workers. The reform of the enterprise leadership system is attracting more and more attention.

Thus, the industrial enterprise leadership system in China can be divided into six phases and five modes: the three-man team in the revolutionary bases during the revolutionary war period; the plant management committee and staff-and-worker assembly system, implemented around the time of liberation; the one-director system, during the first five-year plan; the plant-director responsibility system and staff-and-worker assembly under the leadership of the party committee decided on by the Eighth Party Congress in 1956 and reaffirmed in the Seventeen Industrial Regulations; the unified leadership system in the Cultural Revolution; the restored plant-director responsibility system; and the staff-and-worker assembly system under the leadership of the party committee after the Third Plenary Session of the Central Committee of the Eleventh Party Congress.

This history reveals the three key points. First, China's enterprise leadership system must fulfill the central mission of the enterprise, which is to realize its strategic production and operating goals. It must also establish the respective position and purposes of the party committee, the administration, and the staff and workers in the enterprise. The functions and authority of each must be properly divided. Socialist publicly owned enterprises must retain the interconnecting and mutually restricting relationships between the party, the administration, and the masses. A good leadership system must harmonize all three. Though they share the same goal, each must have its own functions and responsibilities. The system should take full advantage of each and strengthen the work of all three. The leadership system must not deviate from the strategic operational and production goals of the enterprise. Nor can it violate the internal relationships among the three or set them off against each other. Historically, practice has shown that the three independent authorities cannot go their own ways. There must be a separation between the party and the administration, with neither party arrogating all powers to itself. That would only scatter the forces and fail to mobilize the enthusiasm of all sides, thus affecting production and construction.

Second, a complete, effective system of enterprise leadership must combine both centralized leadership and democratic management. An enterprise leadership system belongs to the category of superstructures and reflects social productive forces. Leadership systems, especially in large or mid-size state industrial enterprises, must reflect the objectives of socialized production. It is necessary to establish a unified, powerful, highly efficient production command system, as well as administration and management systems. Complex production processes and various operational activities must be effectively organized with a unified will—centralized and coordinated to ensure that production operations proceed smoothly. When a socialist enterprise employs a system of public ownership of the means of production, the masses of staff and workers become the masters of the state and the enterprise. They participate in enterprise management and exercise authority as masters in their own home. This is the basic distinction between a capitalist enterprise and a socialist enterprise. A socialist enterprise must have a highly centralized leadership with unified command, as well as a high degree of democracy. The two must be combined. Emphasizing centralization while ignoring democracy may cut one off from the masses and reality, fostering bureaucracy. Emphasizing democracy while ignoring centralization may bring on anarchy and produce chaos. Therefore, centralization and unity must be established democratically to take advantage of the pooled wisdom and efforts of everyone and to prevent individuals from making arbitrary decisions. Only when the leadership and the masses are combined, with both sides working together, can the enterprise be vital and well run.

Third, a good system of enterprise leadership must also have leadership cadres that correctly implement the system and constitute a good leadership team. This is the key to good leadership in an enterprise. If the system is good, the leaders can be fully exploited and errors avoided or reduced. If the system is poor, it checks the spirit of the leaders, or covers over their mistakes, and leads to arbitrary decisions. But the system is not omnipotent. A good leadership system without good leadership cadres will not work. The leadership system relies on the cadres' ideological awareness and professional and organizational skills. The Four Izations of cadres (revolutionization, youthization, intellectualization, and specialization) must be followed in selecting the primary leadership cadres of an enterprise in order to provide a fully vital, harmoniously united, and rationally combined enterprise leadership team. Only in this way can the enterprise's masses of staff and workers be led to do good production and construction work.

The System of Enterprise Leadership

The two leadership systems now used in China's state industrial enterprises are the plant-director responsibility system and the staff-and-worker assembly system, both under the leadership of the party committee. These are the enterprise leadership systems that have lasted the longest since the founding of the People's Republic. Moreover, they are universally in force throughout China. It is appropriate to use a management system featuring authority concentrated in the central government, with enterprises having regularly to engage in political movements. It makes leadership and management less chaotic and promotes production and construction.

In September 1961 the Central Committee issued "Work Regulations for State-Owned Industrial Enterprises." In those regulations, the committee said that "a plant-director responsibility system under the leadership of the party committee shall be implemented" and that "the enterprise staff-and-worker assembly system encourages the masses of staff and workers to participate in enterprise management, supervision, and administration." The regulations also pointed out, "Administratively, each enterprise may only be managed by one responsible organ; multiple leadership is unacceptable. The enterprise's party committee should place survey and research work as well as proper ideological and political work first. It should not replace the plant director and handle all administrative matters. Moreover, it must properly lead and support the entire administrative command system of the enterprise, headed by the plant director, in exercising its functions." The promulgation and implementation of these regulations have controlled chaos, established order, and helped overcome the corrupt practices of the three-year Great Leap Forward. At that time, with the guiding ideology of the Left reigning supreme, enterprise production and construction focused on stirring up mass movements, with high targets and blind commands. These commands lacked any substance, however, any detailed division of labor and responsibility. The new regulations established the necessary rules in enterprises and restored normal, orderly production. But after the Cultural Revolution these achievements were severely set back.

After the Gang of Four was smashed, and since the Third Plenary Session of the Central Committee of the Eleventh Party Congress, a number of needed reforms have been carried out in the leadership system for state industrial enterprises in China. With the reorganization and comprehensive reform of the enterprises, the Central Committee has put forth a few basic principles: Collective leadership by the party committee; democratic management by the staff and workers; and administrative command by the plant director. The focus has been on bringing order to the enterprise's internal relationships. This approach has had a positive effect on enterprise reorganization, on the improvement of the management system, on the enthusiasm of the leading cadres as well as the masses, and on the enhancement of economic benefits. Moreover, results have been achieved, primarily in three areas. The party committees have begun to distinguish between the party and the administration in attempting to handle all administrative matters. The production technology and operational command system, which is headed by the director, has been strengthened. And there have been new developments in democratic enterprise management.

The enterprise leadership system now in effect is still subject to severe abuse, however. In particular, after shifts in key national work sites, construction under the Four Modernizations was accelerated and economic reform began, expanding the autonomy of the enterprise. Enterprises and markets, production, and consumption are being more closely associated with one another. Enterprises are changing from production models to operational development models. The current enterprise leadership system is clearly becoming even more poorly adapted. The abuses of the system show up clearly in five main areas.

First, the use of multiple leadership by higher-level organs with no coordination presents enterprises with difficulties on all sides. Under China's current economic management system, there is no unified leadership for the enterprises' production operations. Production, supply, and purchasing are all independent, separate segments. Consider the Qingdao Forging Machinery Plant, one of the twenty state industrial enterprises in the survey. The responsible organs are the Qingdao Machine Industry Office and the Qingdao Jiao County Committee, where the plant is located. The office handles plant production matters, while the committee handles party affairs at the plant. But the office handles only output and product variety, not output value, which is included in the county plans for output value plans. Material supplies are handled by the national Ministry of the Machine Industry, the Qingdao Materials Board, and Jiao County. There are two separate systems for dealing with workers and cadres. The one handling workers does not deal with cadres; and the one handling personnel transfers does not deal with hiring and firing cadres. This multitiered, segmented leadership system causes all sorts of conflicts for the enterprise. Targets sent down from above frequently contradict one another. No one unit handles the enterprise's production, supply, and marketing. The relevant county agencies demand personnel and supplies from the plant as the county needs them, and generally the plant must comply. All these things have an impact on the enterprise's production management and put the enterprise in a difficult position.

Second, the leadership of the party committee in enterprises is total. The party and the administration are not separated. The party replaces the administration, the political organization, and the economic organization combined. The party committee addresses all major problems regarding production operations in the enterprise. Its mission is to implement policy—a role that usurps many functions of the enterprise's administrative structure. The party committee is primarily composed of political cadres, who understand less than a third of the technology involved. Thus, accurate policymaking through the party committee could be difficult indeed. The party tends to get bogged down in everyday administrative matters. Such thorny procedural matters as wage adjustments, housing allocation, employment for the children of workers, and so on, all require that the secretary be sought out or that they be added to the party committee's agenda. Immersed in all these administrative matters, the party committee is necessarily unable to handle its own construction and ideological political work. The party cannot exploit its own strength or the value of its members, so the effects of its leadership are weakened.

Third, the plant director has little authority and a burdensome mission. Everything he does must pass through three separate channels: a plant affairs conference, the party committee, and the staff-and-worker assembly. As a result, things simply do not get done. Thus, decisionmaking for the enterprise's production operations, administration, and management is slow and inefficient. The plant director must carry out decisions reached collectively by the party committee, but he has no corresponding authority over personnel, finances, production, administration, or management. So, while the party committee nominally provides collective leadership and takes collective responsibility, no one is or can be responsible, and matters ultimately are settled by leaving them unsettled.

Fourth, democratic management is inadequate. The staff-and-worker assembly has not yet been established in many enterprises. In units where it has been established, it is to some extent a mere formality. In some enterprises, the convening of the assembly remains unsystematic and without procedures. If the staff and workers want to assemble, they do; if they don't, they don't. An assembly is held when a problem arises, but none is held if things are running smoothly. Some units hold noisy and raucous assemblies at which the plant director gives a long report, which the assembly votes to approve. After the meeting, things quiet down and everyone leaves. But the staff and workers' supervisory authority means little. The party committee must deal with major enterprise issues, which are in turn discussed and approved by the assembly. The plant director often feels that this method is too procedural. Staff and workers also believe that it is mere formalism. This system of enterprise leadership has thus not achieved its purpose of the democratic management of staff and workers.

Fifth, the system is ill-suited to the new situation. To implement the Central Committee's program of opening doors to the outside world and its policy of making the domestic economy more dynamic, all regions, sectors, and enterprises must exploit their strengths. The last few years have seen the creation of various types of joint economic entities. These jointly owned enterprises can make decisions only through joint operating committees or boards of directors. These entities include representatives of all sides, inasmuch as they have broken down the barriers of region, sector, and ownership. It would be difficult to handle many new problems if they continue to use a plant-director responsibility system under the leadership of the party committee and if they are led by the local party committee. Furthermore, the inflow of foreign capital means that a number of Sino-foreign joint enterprises have been set up. Regulations stipulate that these leadership enterprises must be headed by a board of directors or management committee composed of both the joint-capital parties. In such enterprises, the current enterprise leadership system may not be continued.

At the same time, the expansion of enterprise autonomy, economic responsibility, management jurisdiction, and economic benefits have been integrated. Responsibilities of enterprise leaders, therefore, have become more weighty, requiring a unity of authority and responsibility with clearly defined functions. Modernized production requires leadership that is centralized, unified, and highly efficient. Moreover, complete democratic management is required, and all aspects of supervision must be strengthened. In particular, as domestic and international market competition develops, enterprise leaders will have to be skilled at operational decisionmaking. The present enterprise leadership system clearly is ill-suited for this new situation.

In short, a long period of practical experience has demonstrated that the current system of enterprise leadership is not conducive to the modernization of enterprise management, to the reform of the industrial management system, and to strengthening party work in the plants. Reforming the system of enterprise leadership is now more urgent than ever.

Trial Implementation of the Plant-Director Responsibility System

Since the Third Plenary Session of the Central Committee's Eleventh Party Congress decided to focus on socialist modernization, the stress has been on reform. The party has firmly implemented the program and policies of opening to the outside and stimulating the domestic economy. Enterprises have been switching from turning over profits to paying taxes and gradually expanding their operating autonomy. Various forms of economic responsibility, based primarily on contracts, have been established, and egalitarianism in distribution has been broken. The labor force has been assured of its role as master of the enterprises. These major adjustments by the state in enterprises have created excellent conditions for the enterprises to reform the leadership system.

It is essential that enterprises promote the plant-director responsibility system. China's state industrial enterprises now face competition in foreign and domestic markets and an intense struggle in the world technological revolution. To meet these challenges, the enterprises must closely integrate production and operation as well as sales and marketing—and break through the old management modes concerned solely with production. They must move toward an operational development mode, testing markets and consumers, overcoming the various abuses in the current system of enterprise leadership, and strengthening enterprise vitality.

Last year, the Central Committee and the State Council summarized the historical experience of China's system of enterprise leadership. The summary focused on the period since the founding of the People's Republic. China's state enterprises, it was found, continually suffer from the fact that no one takes responsibility or has authority. That is why it is necessary to reform China's leadership system for state enterprises and implement a plant-director responsibility system in production, operations, administration, and management. At the same time, relationships between state and enterprise must be resolved, and enterprise autonomy should be expanded. The scientific summary of China's enterprise leadership system by the Central Committee and the State Council presents the requirements for further reform.

First, the plant-director responsibility system embodies the goals of socialist production. Modern enterprises feature detailed divisions of labor; production is highly continuous, with rigid technical requirements; their cooperative relationships are complex. It is necessary to establish a unified, strong, highly efficient system of production command and administrative management—to unify thinking, to coordinate work, to ensure that production proceeds smoothly, and to continue to develop. This requirement can be met solely through the plant-director responsibility system.

Second, the nature of the enterprise determines the implementation of the plant-director responsibility system. State industrial enterprises are independent economic entities under the socialist system of ownership by the whole people. They are producers of and dealers in socialist commodities. They operate autonomously and take responsibility for profit and loss. They should have the capacity for self-transformation and self-development and become legal entities with certain powers and duties. As market competition grows more fierce, and as new technologies develop, the situation will change. Enterprises will be producers of and dealers in commodities, which means that they will have to make decisions on production, technology, economic information, and operating modes. They cannot afford to leave any problems unresolved or any opportunities missed. Only the plant-director responsibility system can meet these requirements.

Third, the plant-director responsibility system must be implemented if enterprises want to improve administration and management and raise economic benefits. Once the state makes decisions about enterprise ownership and operating authority, the economic system will become less rigid. The direct administration and management of enterprises by state organs and local agencies will be changed. Instead, the enterprise and the administration will be separated. Management modes will be dominated by economic measures. And after the conversion from paying profits to paying taxes has been made, enterprise autonomy will expand. This greater autonomy will require enterprises to combine their decisionmaking authority in production and operation with their command authority. It will also help them deal with the phenomenon of no one's accepting responsibility. Overcoming the segmented situation of the past will encourage horizontal associations and the rational division of labor among the enterprises. It will also promote the creation and development of a unified socialist market, improve enterprise management, and raise economic benefits.

Fourth, the plant-director responsibility system must be used to improve and strengthen the party's leadership. The party leads enterprises primarily through programs, policies, and plans—and through targets, provisions, and plans set by state organs. But the party organization in the enterprise should not have as much authority as the government and the enterprise in administrative work or production commands. Nor should it replace the enterprise in handling all these matters. The party committee must move from direct decisionmaking in production and operation to performing a supervisory role, handling the party's construction, ideological, and political work, and implementing party policies and programs. This change can be accomplished only with a plant-director responsibility system and with the party committee removing itself from everyday matters.

Fifth, implementing the plant-director responsibility system is necessary for constructing a modern socialist enterprise management system characteristic of China. One of the features of such a system is that it must have leadership authority and must ensure the position of staff and workers as masters—integrating leadership cadres, specialized personnel, and workers to establish a democratic and centralized enterprise leadership system. The plant-director responsibility system is different from the previous plant-director responsibility system under the leadership of the party committee. It is also inherently different from the one-director system of capitalist enterprises. It makes a clear division of labor among the party, the administration, and the masses within the enterprise. Each tends to its functions and bears its own responsibilities. This separation requires strengthening the plant director's control over production and operation as well as over the supervisory work of the party committee and the democratic management of staff and workers. The plant-director responsibility system and the coordination of the party, administration, and masses make it possible for the enterprise to be jointly run.

The trial implementation of the plant-director responsibility system has already produced some results. In May 1984, Premier Zhao Ziyang reported to the Second Session of the Sixth People's Congress that, in the State-owned enterprises, the plant-director (manager) responsibility system was being gradually implemented and that full authority over and responsibility for enterprise production command and administrative control would be entrusted by the state to the plant directors (managers). All regions and sectors in the country have selected key cities and state industrial enterprises to try out this reform. The introduction of the system has encouraged complementary reforms within enterprises in the areas of internal organizational structure, personnel matters, wages and bonuses, and so on. The system has also improved the various economic responsibility systems involving contracts, and it has made daring use of outstanding talent. Production and management are becoming more vital, and economic results have risen sharply. These results have given the enterprises a new lease on life. The trial implementation of the system has demonstrated that the people have accepted this reform.

One lesson learned from the trial implementation of this system is that the plant director must have authority commensurate with his title. In the plant, his authority must be firmly established, and he must clearly and fully understand his own functions and powers. He should be totally in charge, with full authority over the enterprise's production, operations, and administration. He must exercise centralized and overall command and have authority to make decisions or recommendations regarding the enterprise's operational principles and its annual, long-term, and major technical revamping plans. He must have the authority to create, revise, or eliminate rules and regulations. He must also be able to create, reorganize, or eliminate administrative units in the enterprise. He must have the power to propose a list of names for appointments and dismissals of administrative cadres within the plant, including the deputy plant director. He should also appoint and dismiss mid-level administrative cadres. No longer will he rely totally on the party committee for all matters, great or small. He must make decisions quickly and act efficiently to change the past situation in which no one was accountable.

The plant director of a state-owned industrial enterprise represents the corporate legal entity. He receives his commission from the state to provide overall leadership and to be fully responsible for the production, operations, and administration within the enterprise. Since the enterprise is a legal entity and the plant director is its representative, the efficiency of his work can play a key role in the prosperity or decline of an enterprise. The plant director must be responsible both to the state and to the staff and workers in the enterprise. Therefore, close attention must be paid to the cadre selection requirements of "revolutionization, youthization, intellectualization, and specialization." The plant director and his leadership team must first be selected properly: this is the key to reform of the enterprise leadership system.

A second lesson is that the plant-director must take full advantage of the enterprise's party committee. After the plant director has accepted responsibility for providing unified leadership in production control and administration and management, the party committee must fully perform its supervisory role, enthusiastically supporting the plant director's functions and duties in providing unified control of production and operations. It must supervise the implementation of all party and state programs and policies, strengthen the party ideologically, and provide organizational leadership for the enterprise's union and Communist Youth League. It must also make ideological and political work among staff and workers its own mission. This will make it possible to change the past situation in which all authority was concentrated in the party committee, with the committee intervening in and fully handling all administrative matters. The committee will then have ample time and energy to strengthen the party's own role as a battle fortress, with party members acting as models and vanguards.

A third lesson from the trial implementation of the plant-director responsibility system is that it must strengthen democratic management and fully realize the position of staff and workers as masters. Unified leadership in the areas of production, operation, and administration must be strengthened in combination with democratic management. Such unified leadership does not imply having one individual act arbitrarily. The greater the centralization, the more that democracy should come into play. A complete staff-and-worker assembly system, the enterprise's basic means of implementing democratic management, must be established. It must have the authority to deliberate on major decisions involving enterprise production and operation, to approve major rules and regulations, to make decisions regarding staff and worker welfare questions, and democratically to criticize and supervise the cadres in administrative leadership. In small enterprises where conditions are appropriate, it may democratically elect the plant director. The authority of the leaders of socialist enterprises is integrated with the labor force's position as masters, but the enthusiasm of the labor force must be effectively exploited. Therefore, as the plant-director responsibility system is being implemented, the problem of staff and worker participation in democratic management must be resolved in a way that ensures the right of workers to be the masters in their house.

A fourth lesson is that the plant-director responsibility system must provide the enterprises with a good framework for decisionmaking. As modern socialized production advances, modern science and technology become further integrated with production operations. The impact of operational management grows greater every day, and the task becomes more weighty. The state industrial enterprises, especially the large and mid-size enterprises, should not rely exclusively on the plant director's capacity to make decisions. Many large foreign enterprises now tend to make decisions collectively. They set up a general manager's office, an office of the chairman of the board, a management committee, or some other organization to replace the traditional approach of giving a chairman of the board or a general manager sole responsibility for decisionmaking. Some of the test-site enterprises are using a plant-affairs conference, others a joint party-administration worker assembly, and still others a management committee.

Many test-site enterprises claim that the management committee approach is best. The management committee is a deliberative structure; it is chaired by the plant director and includes persons from the administration, the party committee, the union, and the Communist Youth League. It meets at fixed intervals to discuss major production and operation matters and to assist the plant director in making decisions. This approach pools the wisdom of the masses and reduces decisionmaking errors to a minimum. It also does not hinder the plant director's decisionmaking. To avoid errors that an individual could make, many comrades now believe that authority over operations in such enterprises should be separated from authority over decisionmaking. It has therefore been suggested that major issues in the enterprise should be decided by the entire board. This would be similar to what foreigners call a system of "collective leadership by specialists."

In summary, the test-site enterprises showed that the plant-director responsibility system must put the relationships among the enterprise's administration, the party committee, and the assembly into proper order. The three should cooperate to strengthen production, to centralize operations, and to strengthen ideological work. These should be the starting and ending points of the plant-director responsibility system.

How should further implementation proceed? The state-owned industrial enterprises should be reformed as investigations are being conducted. The plant-director responsibility system is a major reform in the enterprise leadership system. It involves changes in ideological concepts, leadership methods, and work practices. The situation is complex, and our knowledge of certain major problems is not complete. As China rapidly develops its economic system, and as reforms proceed, many different types of economic associations will appear. Enterprises will continue to be reorganized according to the principles of specialized cooperation and economic rationality. Thus, new problems may arise, both in theory and in practice. These problems should be ironed out during the trial period so that the enterprise leadership system will continue to be perfected.

There is, for example, the question of the status of the plant director of a state industrial enterprise. In the test-site enterprises, the state commissions the plant director, who is considered the state's representative in the enterprise as well as the representative of the enterprise's administration and management. State industrial enterprises, vary, however, in size and administrative form. In many enterprises the plant director is democratically elected or hired. In some cases, the plant director works under an administrative contract, reporting to those who hired or selected him. But the enterprise's operating authority may be separated from the ownership system, and this may raise the question of who represents the interests of the state. Whoever does represent these interests may not be responsible for administering and managing the enterprise. In the long run, the state's interests and the enterprise's interests are the same. But in the short run, there may be some conflicts. The administration and management of some enterprises is poor. Too many bonuses are being given out. Who should supervise this? How should it be controlled? Should a representative of the government's interests also be appointed? These questions must be further studied and investigated, both in theory and in practice.

The reform of the urban economic system has helped to strengthen the horizontal relationships among enterprises. At the same time, diverse forms of economic associations are appearing. Some of them are interregional and intersectoral. Joint operations may be loose or tight; investment sources may also be sectoral, local, or from other provinces or enterprises. Who represents the separate interests of these parties? What type of enterprise leadership system is best for such economic associations? Is the plant director a decisionmaker as well as a direct controller? We fear this will not work. There should also be a board of directors to represent the interests of the various parties in making overall decisions. The board would appoint or hire the plant director. And what type of leadership system is best for Sino-foreign joint ventures? These questions must also be further studied and investigated, and regulations must be set and followed.

As we establish a completely new system of enterprise leadership, new problems will inevitably arise. These problems must be dealt with continually, and improvements must be made along the way. We must work for reform. Reform will be beneficial in strengthening a centralized, unified command adapted to the demands of modern production. It will also promote the building of a socialist democracy, ensure continued improvements in the economic benefits of enterprises, and invigorate the operation of enterprises.

Note

1. "A Decision of the Central Committee of the Communist Party of China on Reform of the Economic Structure," published in English in *China Daily*, October 23, 1984.

PART FOUR

State Enterprise Management in Other Countries

People differ (as conference participants did) on the lessons of international experience for China, but the contrasting approaches to similar problems provide a useful perspective on the issues in China. Janos Kornai, director of the Institute of Economics of the Hungarian Academy of Sciences and professor of economics at Harvard University, analyzes the Hungarian enterprise management system in chapter 13. After long debate over alternative partial and gradual modes of reform, Hungary completely abolished mandatory planning on January 1, 1968. Kornai argues that the change was highly successful for industrial output and productivity growth. Yet the reforms fell far short of creating a market socialist economy in Hungary, as has been suggested by some observers. Instead, the state enterprise has a dual dependence: on the market and on the government. The first is a horizontal dependence on other enterprises in their role as buyers and sellers. The second is a vertical dependence on the government authority to which the firm is subordinate, even though it no longer receives plan targets or supply allocations.

For the market to regulate enterprises efficiently, four conditions are necessary: a price system that gives the right signals, enterprise responsiveness to prices, prevailing buyers' markets, and a competitive market structure. Kornai argues that none of these conditions is fully met in Hungary. Prices are still arbitrary and inconsistent with a complex tangle of taxes and subsidies designed to attain social goals. Enterprises are responsive to prices on the output side but are relatively insensitive to the price of inputs. Buyers' markets prevail in only a few consumer and export industries; elsewhere, Hungary is still a "shortage economy." And Hungarian industry is highly concentrated, with official monopolies for many products and with restrictions on import competition.

The failure of markets to work effectively stems from continued bureaucratic intervention in microeconomic decisions. Taxes and subsidies are constantly changed by the numerous agencies that administer them. Although taxes and subsidies are ostensibly designed to adjust distorted market prices for social costs and benefits, in practice their institution is often motivated by a desire to redistribute income among firms—to compensate losers and to capture excess profits from gainers. Kornai shows that there is a very low correlation between the profitability before and after redistribution. (Interestingly, the correlation in the sample of Chinese enterprises is higher even though relative market prices in China are probably further out of line with production costs and world prices than in Hungary.) Redistribution and the underlying bargaining create a "soft budget constraint," which weakens enterprise incentives to improve efficiency and reduces price responsiveness. Rather than try to change irrational prices, firms bargain for additional subsidies or tax remissions. Thus, incorrect prices remain and lose prestige as reliable signals for adjustment. Profit-sharing incentives reinforce the soft budget constraint, since both managerial bonuses and workers' wages are linked to profits after redistribution.

Kornai shows that profitability has little correlation with either investment or the entry and exit of firms. (Again, it is interesting to note that profitability had a greater effect on investment activity among the sample of Chinese enterprises.) Thus, vertical dependence on bureaucratic decisions continues to play a stronger role than the market in determining the allocation of capital. A corollary is that firms bear little of the risk and capture few of the gains of investment decisions. This situation contributes to a hunger for investment, which, in turn, helps perpetuate sellers' markets.

Kornai concludes that Hungary's reform, despite considerable successes, has come only halfway. Needed are additional measures to reduce vertical dependence and increase enterprise dependence on market forces. Such measures include a shift in emphasis of government policy from microregulation to macroregulation; a social policy that softens the adverse effects of market outcomes through redistributive measures for individuals and households rather than enterprises; and new forms of managerial appointments and ownership structures. The parallels with many of the proposals in other chapters in this volume for further reform in China are striking.

In chapter 14 Martin Schrenk analyzes the implications of Yugoslav enterprise organization and procedures for microeconomic and macroeconomic management. Although Yugoslavia's institutions are unique, Schrenk's analysis suggests some features that may hold lessons for China.

The main institutional and policy characteristics of the Yugoslav economy are well known. Enterprises are self-managed. There is no mandatory central planning or price control. And socialist commodity production and the law of value are accepted as the principles of enterprise operations and relations between socialist firms (that is, enterprises are linked through markets). The broad outline of macroeconomic performance is also well known. From 1959 to 1979 Yugoslavia had a very high rate of output growth. Since 1979, output has stagnated and labor productivity has fallen. Employment has grown steadily but unemployment has remained substantial, and throughout the period capital productivity has been low and the inflation rate high.

Schrenk provides an overview of the institutional structure of the Yugoslav firm, the relations among firms, and the relations between the firm and the state. Firms comprise smaller Basic Organizations of Associated Labor (BOs) bound together by self-management agreements that prescribe how production, pricing, and income distributions are to be coordinated. The essential principles governing relations among BOs constituting the firm are "pooling labor and resources" and "sharing income and risks." Relations between firms are also governed by a series of interlocking self-management agreements. Thus, while exchange of goods and services is based on the market, prices are often set by long-term contracts rather than short-term market clearing. Relations between firms and the state are nonhierarchical in the sense that no orders are handed down. But the government and party influence enterprise decisions through involvement in selection of managers, in approval of investment, and in numerous other ways. Schrenk argues that enterprise decisions satisfy the interests of a coalition of actors (workers, managers, the party, and various levels of government) rather than optimizing a one-dimensional objective function. As in China, any tendency to restrict employment is offset by rules and pressures from other members of the coalition. In addition, Schrenk argues, there is no unified workers' interest on most issues.

Two features of the Yugoslav system have important implications for macroeconomic performance and hold possible lessons for China. First, as in China, there are barriers to interregional trade, and factor markets are fragmented. There is no labor market in the traditional sense; workers receive a share of residual income rather than a wage and they cannot be laid off. Nor is there a real capital market. Although there is no longer a budget allocation for investment, banks do not act as true financial intermediaries but as agents of enterprises—and a high share of investment is self-financed. BOs may also pool resources within or among firms on either a debt or equity basis. As with joint ventures in China, however, the motive for pooling is usually to obtain access to markets or scarce inputs rather than to obtain a higher rate of return. The second feature, to which Schrenk pays particular attention, is the system of price setting within and among enterprises. Prices are often based on shares of total income realized through final sales. This system has a strong equity appeal, but Schrenk argues that it creates little incentive to use inputs efficiently or to resist input price increases.

These features of the Yugoslav system, and the underlying principles of pooling resources and sharing income and risks, partly explain Yugoslavia's poor investment efficiency and high inflation. Investors bear no risk because losses are socialized or shared. The emphasis on consensus makes investment decisions political. Yugoslav banks are inefficient financial intermediaries and subject to political pressure. In addition, interest rates have been negative in real terms. Finally, the high degree of self-finance and the obstacles to capital flows across regions channel funds to firms that have been profitable in the past regardless of future potential. All these factors not only lower the overall rate of return on investment but create a hunger for investment that generates inflationary pressure. The system of price setting and the emphasis on an equitable income distribution reduces resistance to price increases. Because incomes are effectively inflation indexed and there is no "wage drag," the system is especially conducive to maintaining inflationary momentum. Finally, macroeconomic control is thwarted by the financial indiscipline of firms' extending "involuntary" credit to each other.

Although Schrenk is optimistic about the possibility of solving these problems in an economy which, until recent years, has generated rapid growth and secure employment, conference participants felt that Yugoslavia provides several (negative) lessons for China. Chief among these are the needs to create an effective financial market, to establish either a market or an administrative mechanism to control wages, and to reduce risk sharing in order to improve financial discipline.

13

The Dual Dependence of the State-Owned Firm in Hungary

János Kornai

In 1957 Hungary departed from the traditional socialist economy by abolishing the obligatory delivery of agricultural products to the state. Since then, reform has reached virtually all segments of the economy. This chapter focuses on Hungary's state-owned industrial firms, which were responsible for 93 percent of the country's industrial production from 1970 to 1983. (The remaining share was produced by cooperatives and private producers.)[1] Without question, the state-owned firm dominates Hungarian industry and has been a focal point for economic reforms. In this chapter I analyze the reform benefits and shortcomings in Hungary's state-owned sector to determine what lessons may be drawn by Chinese reformers.

The literature on Hungarian reform is rich.[2] Yet, many issues still need to be resolved. One of the virtues of present-day Hungary is the vigor of economic debates. This chapter reflects one author's views, not a generally accepted Hungarian opinion. The appraisal and suggestions, however, are shared by many of my colleagues.

The Abolition of Mandatory Plan Indicators

The prereform socialist system is often called a command economy. The state-owned firm in Hungary received commands annually in all sectors, quarterly in some sectors and in some periods, as a mandatory production plan prepared by a high-level government agency. Each plan contained hundreds or thousands of figures. It would include total output targets, for example, gross output of the firm at constant prices, and many disaggregated output targets as well. In most cases plans would specify quantities in physical units and delivery obligations to assigned users, such as the amount of export goods to be delivered to foreign trade companies. Plans also set constraints, such as the upper limits on the materials and semifinished products that can be acquired by the firm, the number of employees according to skills and jobs, and the ceiling on wages. Certain activities, such as the introduction of new commodities or investment within the firm, were prescribed. Finally, the plans contained financial targets for costs and profitability.

In principle the goals were obligatory, but in practice some were enforced more rigidly than others through a system of reward and penalty. The priority goals were the total output targets, the employment and wage quotas, and in some cases the export targets.

The shortcomings of the command system are well known. Firm managers disguised their capabilities to avoid more ambitious targets. They were driven to use any means to fulfill the targets, even at the expense of quality, the neglect of equipment maintenance, and an increase in production costs. The pace of production pulsated according to the calendar, lagging at the beginning and accelerating toward the end of the plan period. As a defense against late or unreliable delivery, firms hoarded input stocks. Nevertheless, production disruptions and material shortages appeared time and again, leading to wasteful improvised adjustments and underutilized capacity. Tight planning caused rigidities. The adaptation of production to ever-changing demand and technological possibilities was slow and conservative.

There were debates in Hungary about how much of the command system to abandon and when. Some of the suggestions for partial and gradual change follow.

- Decrease the number of plan indicators from around 100 to a dozen or less.
- Prescribe only aggregate figures and abolish disaggregated indicators.
- Prescribe only a part of the production and let the firm decide when and by how much to exceed the mandatory level.
- Introduce the changes in a few firms, or in some sectors, then gradually expand to other firms and sectors.

In the end, these ultracautious proposals were rejected because they would have led to intolerable inconsistencies. After careful preparation, the command system was abolished for all state-owned firms in one stroke on January 1, 1968. In the eighteen years since, it has been demonstrated that the dramatic change was feasible and effective. Firms now have the autonomy to set their own output targets. There is no administrative "material allocation" (rationing) of producer goods. State-owned firms sell and buy from each other without quotas or rations granted by administrators. State-owned wholesale companies also act as intermediaries between the producers and users of some goods. These changes significantly diminished

Table 13-1. *Volume, Employment, and Productivity of Hungarian State-Owned Industry*

	Indexes (1970 = 110)		
Year	*Gross output*	*Employment*	*Productivity*
1971	106.6	99.6	107.0
1972	111.9	99.1	112.9
1973	119.5	100.3	119.1
1974	129.6	101.1	128.2
1975	135.5	100.9	134.3
1976	141.6	99.9	141.7
1977	150.8	99.5	151.6
1978	158.0	99.5	158.8
1979	163.0	98.0	166.3
1980	159.5	95.4	167.2
1981	163.5	93.3	175.2
1982	167.4	91.5	183.0
1983	168.7	89.9	187.7

Source: Központi Statisztikai Hivatal 1984, pp. 92–93.

the role of the government bureaucracy as a dispatcher, urging deliveries and arranging purchases in minute detail.

The spectacular change was highly successful. Table 13-1 presents some data on the performance of the state-owned sector in industry. Hungary reached the intensive growth phase in the early 1970s. Unemployment had been absorbed, even disguised underemployment in agriculture disappeared, and there was chronic labor shortage. A decrease in employment as a result of a permanent increase in labor productivity is not a failure but a success. The workers released from industry were immediately employed by the service sector. The impressive rise of productivity is one of the great achievements of the reform.

Dual Dependence

After a superficial observation of the Hungarian economy, some foreign analysts assert that it has become a socialist market economy, or at least is close to being one. In my view, that is not true. For better or worse, the Hungarian state-owned firm has a dual dependence. It depends on the market to buy and sell products, but it also depends on the government authorities. The first is a horizontal relationship: buyers and sellers have the same legal rank. The second is a vertical relationship: the firm is legally subordinate to government authorities. The government agencies have the right to issue binding resolutions, which the state-owned firms must follow.[3]

There is nothing objectionable in the state-owned firm's dual dependence on the market and the authorities. An important objective of the 1968 reform was to strive for a regulated market, with a symbiosis of central control and market forces. What many Hungarian economists, myself among them, object to is the way the principle has been applied. Bureaucratic interventions in the market process are too frequent and excessively detailed. Instead of general guidelines and an effective macroeconomic policy, with a few specific microeconomic interventions as exceptions, millions of detailed interventions have become the rule. The market forces are endangered by the hyperactivity of the bureaucracy.

Horizontal Dependence: Strength and Weakness of Competition

Solemn declarations encouraging a stronger role for market forces are not sufficient. The market will have a beneficial effect only under certain conditions. Four of these mutually interdependent conditions are:

- A price system that gives the right signals to the firm in its role as a producer and as a buyer of inputs. Relative prices should reflect scarcities and play an important role in the adjustment to supply and demand.
- Strong incentives for the state-owned firm to respond to prices for its output and for its inputs.
- A prevailing buyers' market where the producer of goods and services has strong incentives to adjust to buyers' demands, such as those of other firms and nonbusiness institutions in their role as purchasers and those of households as customers.
- Competitive market structure. The more competition that exists between sellers, the more firms will adapt to demand and sell better goods at lower prices.

I have no illusions about the perfection of competitive markets. The market fails regularly to solve some important allocative and distributive problems. Corrective government measures are certainly needed. The market is a regulating mechanism that has simultaneously beneficial and harmful effects. The conditions listed above are necessary to obtain the benefits even without excluding adverse side effects. Now the question arises, to what extent are these four conditions met in the state-owned industrial sector of Hungary?

A Rational Price System

There have been repeated partial price reforms. Prices of raw materials and energy have drawn closer to world market prices. The exchange rate was made more reasonable. Some links were created between the domestic and world market prices of tradable goods. Buyer and seller firms are now frequently allowed to agree to prices on a contractual basis. In addition, many but not all consumer goods and services have market-equilibrating prices.

Despite some progress, the price system is still inconsistent, a peculiar blend of arbitrary and rational relative prices. Because all prices are strongly interdependent, the arbitrariness of some prices affects the others. There is a high variance of taxation, both as a reflection and a partial cause of arbitrariness. The state-owned sector as a whole is a net taxpayer. The revenue from the state-owned sector—that is, taxes levied on firms plus the state's share of profits—is the largest contribution to the government budget. The net taxes are highly differentiated over the firms, with dozens, if not hundreds, of income-flow channels, taxes, and subsidies. A firm must pay many different taxes but may receive various subsidies at the same time. As a consequence, the price ratio of two substitute inputs does not reflect the ratio of their true marginal costs. Even if a firm tried to find a cost-minimizing technology, carefully considering the best input combination, it would not necessarily ensure the most beneficial use of resources from a social point of view.

Price Responsiveness

Similar inconsistencies exist in the price responsiveness of the state-owned sector. In some branches of industry, price responsiveness is a bit stronger, in many others weaker, but nowhere is there a quick and forceful response to price changes. Because chronic shortages prevail in many segments of the economy, responsiveness to relative prices is stronger for outputs. In a sellers' market, the producer is in the stronger position. A multiproduct firm is able to select between alternative outputs by considering their relative prices and relative profits. The same firm, however, has less choice in its role as a buyer. The less reliable the delivery of materials, semifinished goods, and parts, the more the bottlenecks and shortage-caused disruptions in production—and the less sensitive the firm to the relative price of inputs. This proposition was evident in industry's sluggish reaction to the oil-shock and to the sudden changes of energy prices on the demand side.

A Buyers' Market

Before the reform, the state-owned sector worked under constant shortages in a prevailing sellers' market. Reform changed the situation by shifting subsectors or single firms to a buyers' market. This shift occurred, for example, in many branches of the food industry. In other sectors, firms that specialized in export production for market economies now face serious difficulties in sales. Some construction firms that specialize in industrial and transport projects have difficulty utilizing their capacity, since investment

Table 13-2. *Ratio of Input Stocks per Output Stocks in Industry*

Country	*Period*	*Ratio of input stocks to output stocks*
Buyers' market economies		
Austria	1972–77	1.50–1.50
Sweden	1968–72	0.70–0.74
United States	1960–77	0.94–1.16
Sellers' market economies		
Hungary	1971–80	7.26–8.52
Poland	1975	10.30
Soviet Union	1960–77	9.20–12.30

Source: Hungarian data from Fábri 1982, p. 134; other data from Chikán 1984, p. 50.

demand has been severely restricted in recent years. The shift toward a buyers' market leads to improved quality, wider assortment, and quicker delivery. Households can observe such improvements in the food supplied by the state-owned food industry. Foreign buyers saw similar improvements in exported Hungarian goods.

These favorable changes are not sufficiently widespread or stable. Selling difficulties in some parts of the economy coexist with buying difficulties in other parts. There are recurrent shortages of some materials, semifinished goods, parts, and equipment along with intensive shortages of labor and imported goods.

A useful way to determine whether the economy is a buyers' or sellers' market is to study firms' inventories. In a buyers' market, a firm accumulates inventories of output. It has difficulty selling or wants to be able to respond quickly to the buyers' demands. Usually, the firm is reluctant to accumulate large stocks of inputs, becaue it expects quick and reliable delivery of inputs. In a sellers' market, the situation is the reverse. Inventories of output are small, because the buyers absorb production quickly, often after a long wait. For inputs, the firms hoard large inventories, because delivery is unreliable or late. Some producer goods disappear from the production line altogether.

An apt aggregate measure is the ratio of input stocks to output stocks. Table 13-2 presents an international comparison. The difference is striking. The table shows that Hungarian industry did not change from being a shortage economy. Even if shortages have been eliminated in some segments of the economy, firms still lack the confidence that a buyers' market will prevail. Their conduct still reflects the conditions of chronic shortage.

Competitive Market Structure

The dichotomy of a buyers' market versus a sellers' market is more crucial than the number of firms. Whether a certain good or service is sold by a few firms or by only one, the sellers may still be in the weaker position if the total capacity is significantly larger than demand at prevailing prices. Sellers might face indirect competition with the producers of substitute products and services.

Although not the primary issue, the number of rival sellers of a certain good is of some consequence. In the Hungarian economy, two contradictory tendencies can be observed. The first, favored by reformers, is to strengthen competition between producers. Stronger competition can be achieved in several ways. A huge firm that monopolizes an entire branch of production can be divided into smaller, independent firms. Such a breakdown occurred in segments of light industry and of the food industry. Large firms are encouraged to establish new, small subsidiaries, which may become semiautonomous and compete with other firms. In some parts of the economy cooperatives and private business are given greater freedom to compete with state-owned firms, breaking their monopolistic position. In other cases, goods are imported to compete with domestic products.

A strong countertendency exists, however. For a long time, certain state-owned firms have been officially declared as solely "responsible for the supply of certain goods." A firm could be reprimanded if its good of exclusive "responsibility" were in short supply. In such cases, the firm is expected to take action, for example, to expand production. In return for this responsibility, the firm attains monopolistic privileges.

A further problem is the high degree of concentration in Hungarian industry. Despite counterefforts, the number of economic units is permanently decreasing, as shown in table 13-3. To illustrate the overconcentration, the distribution of firms by size in Hungarian and Danish industry is compared in figure 13-1 (excerpted from a book by Iván Schweitzer, who calls the Danish distribution a pyramid and the Hungarian a reversed pyramid).

Competition between domestic production and imports is stifled by Hungary's macroeconomic difficulties—its foreign debt and its austerity program. This situation leads to frequent and drastic import cuts, which reinforce the monopolistic position of domestic industries.

Vertical Dependence: Financial Ties

The profitability of a genuinely autonomous firm depends on its success in the market. The firm's profit increases if it adjusts quickly to changes in demand, introduces new products successfully, or cuts production costs through better organization or the use of new technologies. Of course, profit depends also on random external conditions. Bad luck in the market for inputs or outputs could lead to losses. Bad external conditions can be counterbalanced, however, by the firm's adjustment measures. In a genuine market economy, there is a strong interdependence between efficient performance and profitability.

The hope of Hungarian reformers to achieve a similar interdependence has not been fulfilled. The link between firms' performance and profitability has

Table 13-3. *Number of Firms in Industry*

Year	*State-owned firms*	*Cooperatives*	*Total*
1962	1,286	1,089	2,375
1963	894	993	1,887
1964	863	882	1,745
1965	840	811	1,651
1966	827	799	1,626
1967	807	784	1,591
1968	811	792	1,603
1969	803	813	1,616
1970	812	821	1,633
1971	818	833	1,651
1972	812	829	1,641
1973	806	825	1,631
1974	794	816	1,610
1975	779	793	1,572
1976	737	737	1,474
1977	712	701	1,413
1978	700	685	1,385
1979	702	670	1,372
1980	669	661	1,360
1981	714	664	1,378
1982	724	635	1,359
1983	715	623	1,338

Source: Laki 1984.

Figure 13-1. *Distribution of Firms*

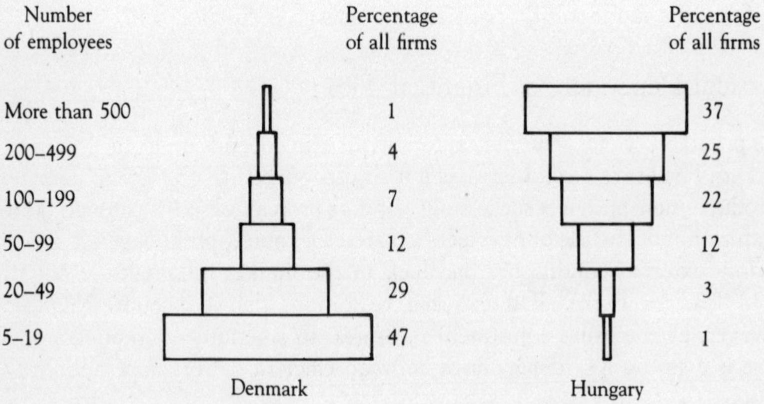

Source: Schweitzer 1982, p. 130.

been severely weakened by excessive government intervention. Hungary has a complex system of taxation and subsidization. Each tax or subsidy serves a specific purpose, such as stimulating exports, discouraging imports, motivating innovation, supporting priorities, or redistributing in terms of social policy. The hundreds of different tax or subsidy channels are controlled by state agencies; one in charge of foreign trade, another supervising production, a third overseeing customs, and so on. Some taxes and subsidies are permanent, others are implemented as needed. Most tax formulas are modified repeatedly. As a consequence, the fiscal system is a puzzling cobweb of regulations.

The deep fiscal redistribution is, to some extent, subject to bargaining.[4] If a firm enjoys high profits, it keeps silent so that a supervising agency will be less likely to skim away the extra earnings. If too many funds accumulate in the firms' bank account, the financial administrator becomes nervous and will find ways to tax away at least part. On the other hand, if a firm has financial troubles, laments will be heard by the authorities. Because fiscal redistribution is not strictly centralized, it is possible to play one agency against another. When bargaining with central authority number 1 fails, there is still a chance to get help from authority number 2 or 3. Political pressure can be exerted, and help from the party or trade union can be requested. Sometimes the struggle is not a lonely one. Firms in a sector or region sharing financial troubles may collaborate in bargaining, led perhaps by a team of senior officials from that sector or region. Despite their formal obligation, the heads of sectors or regions do not represent the government in their areas. Instead, they represent the views of the sector, region, or firm under their control in bargaining with the government.

I called this situation the "softening of the budget constraint" in my book *Economics of Shortage* (Kornai 1980a). In theory, a firm's expenditure should be limited by what it earns from sales. In practice, its budget may expand or contract at the will of authorities, who can add or subtract from the pretax, presubsidy profit as much as they want.

Together with Á. Matits, I head a research team that studies fiscal redistribution of profits in the state-owned sector. Our analysis is based on the balance sheets of all state-owned Hungarian firms over an eight-year period.[5] Profits before redistribution, before taxes and subsidies, are contrasted with profits after redistribution. Table 13-4 shows the magnitude of redistribution: financial authorities are moving back and forth an amount of income more than twice as large as the total original profit. The last rows of the table reveal that fiscal redistribution and the softening of the budget constraint cut practically any link between the profits before and after redistribution.

An important characteristic of the soft budget constraint is leveling, which depresses the profitability of the successful firms, at the same time helping out the losers. Leveling is demonstrated by the shift in the distribution of

Table 13-4. *Size and General Impact of Fiscal Redistribution*

Item	*1978*	*1980*	*1982*
Total state-owned sector			
Total subsidy per total original profit	n.a.	1.09	n.a.
Total tax per total original profit	n.a.	1.28	n.a.
Correlation coefficient between profitability before and after redistribution	0.23	0.22	0.14
State-owned industry			
Correlation coefficient between profitability before and after redistribution	0.12	0.01	0.05

n.a. = not available.

Source: Kornai and Matits 1984 and unpublished research reports prepared by Matits in 1984–85.

profitability. Figure 13-2 shows the density function of this distribution. Before fiscal redistribution, profitability ranges from great losses to ample profits. After fiscal redistribution, the extremes are eliminated and the distribution moves closer to the median, concentrating around low profits.

Figure 13-2. *Distribution of Profitability in State-Owned Industry*

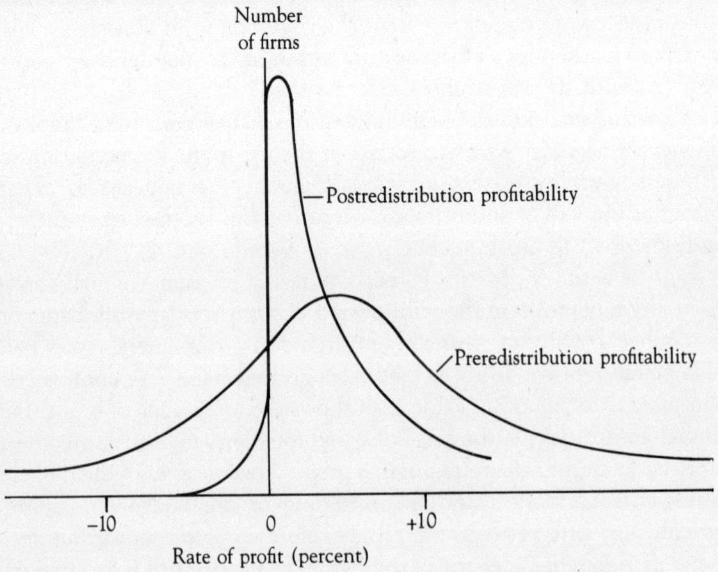

Source: Kornai and Matits 1984 and unpublished research reports prepared by Matits in 1984–85.

Table 13-5. *Leveling of Profitability in State-Owned Industry*

Indicator	1980 *Before redistribution*	1980 *After redistribution*	1982 *Before redistribution*	1982 *After redistribution*
Variation coefficient (standard deviation per mean)	2.72	1.57	4.55	1.29
Share of firms with more than 30% profitability (as a percentage of total number of firms)	3.60	0	4.80	2.20
Share of firms making loss (as a percentage of total number of firms)	24.02	0.18	17.32	8.38

Source: Same as table 13-4.

The same effect is shown in table 13-5. It exhibits a peculiar egalitarian tendency in contradiction to a profit incentive. Under such circumstances, the dual dependence of profit appears. It will be determined in part horizontally—by success or failure in the market—and in part vertically—by the generosity of financial authorities or the firm's ability to bargain with them.

The problem is closely related to the shortcomings of the price system. In the bargaining process, both sides—the firms and the authorities—refer frequently to the fact that an extra tax or an extra subsidy is needed because the original profitability does not express a social gain. This argument is legitimate in many cases. Yet it leads to a vicious circle of causality. Because the price system is arbitrary, fiscal redistribution is needed for compensation; because fiscal redistribution is arbitrary, so are prices. Cause and effect are practically indistinguishable. As a result of redistributive interventions, the budget constraint is too soft to provoke more than a weak response to prices. The fight for a correct price is not very forceful. Firms may try to influence the price, but if they do not succeed, fiscal redistribution will compensate for losses due to incorrect pricing. This possibility detracts from efforts to correct false, unreasonable, and arbitrary prices. Because incorrect prices remain, without being reliable signals for adjustment, this element of the causal chain is reinforced.

Parallel measures of a far-reaching price reform, and the hardening of the budget constraint through tough financial discipline, profit incentives, and accountability would help. Here again, experience differs from the original blueprint for reform. Reformers had suggested that both managers and employees must have a direct financial motive to increase profits. Some measures were taken to fulfill this requirement, but they were unsatisfactory. The managers' bonus was linked to profitability after redistribution, not

Table 13-6. *Relationship between Profitability before Redistribution and Wages in 1982*

Profitability before redistribution	*Probability of change in wages (percent)*			
	Decrease	*Small change*	*Large increase*	*Total change*
Decrease	6	86	8	100
Small change	4	92	4	100
Large increase	1	86	13	100

Source: Same as table 13-4.

before. In other words, they have a strong incentive to fight for tax exemptions and subsidies.

Profit sharing (so called) was introduced to ensure that employees at all levels had a personal interest in profits. Unfortunately, this profit sharing has little to do with original profits, for it is subject to a leveling that extends even beyond the equalization of profits. Most firms that operate at a loss still distribute profit sharing money among their employees. The highly profitable firms do not distribute higher shares than the less profitable ones. In other words, profit sharing is more or less proportional to wages, a regular complement of wage. It does not give the employee a sense of ownership.

It is not enough to look at the part of income that is called profit sharing. Wages must depend to some extent on profitability, according to the original blueprint for reform. There must be some link between the dynamic changes in wage differences and those in profitability. Again, the data in table 13-6 show this link to be very weak. There are changes in profitability before distribution: an index of change smaller than −0.95 is regarded as a decrease; between −0.95 and +1.1, as a small change; more than +1.1, as a large increase. What is the probability that these changes in profitability before redistribution could lead to different degrees of changes in wages? Again, the leveling tendency is observed. Improved profitability does not increase significantly the chance of wage increases within a firm. Nor does deteriorated profitability diminish the chance of wage increases.

Vertical Dependence: Allocation of Investment, Entry and Exit

Before the reform, investment decisionmaking and financing were highly centralized in Hungary. Now state-owned firms are allowed to retain a part of their profits and establish a development fund to be used for investment. The partial decentralization has proven useful by helping production adjust to technical developments, to the elimination of some bottlenecks, and to

Table 13-7. *Correlation between Profitability and Investment Activity*

Profitability indicator	Correlation coefficient with the indicator of investment activity 1976	1977	1978	1979	1980
Profitability before redistribution					
1975	−0.03	−0.03	−0.04	−0.04	−0.02
1976		−0.03	−0.07	−0.04	−0.08
1977			−0.04	−0.01	−0.07
1978				−0.03	−0.11
1979					−0.08
Profitability after redistribution					
1975	−0.07	−0.07	0.04	0.02	0.06
1976		−0.04	0.26	0.23	0.13
1977			0.30	0.27	0.14
1978				0.12	0.13
1979					0.09

Note: The indicator of investment activity is the ratio of investment expenditure in a given year to the value of real assets at the beginning of the same year.
Source: Same as table 13-4.

changes in domestic and foreign demand. The use of retained profit for investment created new capacity for export production. Nevertheless, many Hungarian economists feel that decentralization in this sphere did not go far enough.

As in other areas, the impact of excessive fiscal redistributive interventions can be felt in the firms' development funds. Due to an uneven levying of taxes and subsidies, the skimming away of large profits, and compensation for losses, the internal funds for investment depend very little on the pre-redistribution profits of the firm. In many cases, firms that did not earn much profit are in a better position to finance investment internally than other firms whose high profits were taxed away.

This is only part of the story. Internal financial sources from retained profits can cover only small investment projects. For medium-size or large projects, the firm must use either credit from the central bank or investment subsidies drawn from the central government budget. But the allocation of external financing is not related to the profitability of the firm. As a result, the investment carried out by the firm does not depend on profitability either before or after redistribution. Table 13-7 also shows that there is almost no correlation between profitability and the investment activity one or more years later. A correlation close to 1 between past profitability and investment activity is not suggested as normative. It may be reasonable to invest in a firm which is not profitable at the present but which could become profitable in the future because investment will help with innovations or a new product line. New firms can be established, and in that case, no comparison with past profitability is made. But many of the most solid, creditworthy firms that have been profitable would be expected to get the lion's share of total investment. Unfortunately, table 13-7 demonstrates that investment allocation and past profitability have been unrelated to an extreme.

Other criteria are seriously considered when investment funds are allocated to firms from central financial sources. Larger firms have a demonstrated priority. The share of external sources in total investment financing was 9 percent for small state-owned firms in 1982, 43 percent for medium-size firms, and 68 percent for large firms.[6] The large share of external financing makes central intervention in the investment process relatively easy. Not only is macroregulation determining the total credit supply for investment, but there is detailed, project-by-project microregulation as well. The firm's manager must receive approval from the supervising agencies to get the project started. Approval is usually not needed for minor actions, particularly for small firms, but all medium-size and large projects are started either by central initiative or after agreement is reached between the authorities and the firm. In other words, there remains a strong vertical dependence for the firm's investment.

Until the last few years each firm was allowed to use its development fund to reinvest within the firm, but a direct horizontal flow of capital was not permitted. In an important development a few financial intermediaries have been established to help transfer the accumulated savings of one firm to investment in another firm.[7] For the first time state-owned firms are allowed to issue bonds, which are sold to other firms and to individuals. The yield on bonds is significantly higher than the interest rate on bank deposits. The purchase of bonds became immediately popular with individuals, and thus a new way of financing investment in the state-owned sector was opened. Yet state-owned firms are reluctant to buy bonds. At present they strongly prefer to invest in their own expansion rather than to contribute voluntarily to the expansion of another firm, even if the second alternative promises significantly higher returns.

Apart from these new and underused opportunities in Hungary, profit retention and the chance to reinvest are necessary but not sufficient conditions for a more far-reaching partial decentralization of investment decisionmaking. The root of the problem lies in the peculiar sharing of risks between firm and state. Shared risks are an important aspect of the soft budget constraint discussed earlier. Hungarian literature speaks about investment hunger. Managers of the state-owned firm are always ready to invest if they can receive investment credit or subsidies. The demand for credit and applications for subsidies almost always exceed supply. There is no deterrent against investment hunger because decisionmakers are not afraid of the financial failure of investment projects. There are not even serious calculations afterward to determine whether the project paid off. If a firm is in financial trouble, due to an unwise investment, the usual instruments for softening the budget constraint are available: subsidies, tax exemptions, postponements of debt service, and adjustments of the selling price to the cost overrun of the investment project. Because managers are sure that they will be bailed out, they feel no compulsion to moderate their demands for investment resources.

Investment subsidies are gifts to the firm, which understandably want as many as possible. Interest must be paid on credit, but the real rate of interest (the nominal rate minus the inflation rate) is low. Even if the budget constraint were hard and firms were price-responsive, the low interest rate would still stimulate excess demand for the investment credit.

Under such conditions, the only way to control investment is by administrative means—intervening in the decision process of all medium-size and large projects. This is both a consequence and a cause of the soft constraints. It is a consequence because investment hunger makes administrative intervention and credit rationing inevitable. And it is a cause because the central agencies share the responsibility for the decisions and therefore prefer to cover up if something goes wrong. They can do this by making the firm profitable through redistributive interventions.

As for the control and microregulation of the investment process, the targets of the central planners vary over time. Firms exhibit investment hunger and an expansion drive starts, but officials at a higher level of administration show the same propensities, sometimes more intensely than their subordinates in the firms. There is a persistent drive for faster growth, even if the overambitious plans are not feasible and their forced fulfillment would lead to heavy losses and inefficiency. The spirit of great leaps diminishes only after the economy hits limits that cannot be exceeded.

The history of industrial investment in the last fifteen years is instructive (table 13-8). Long after the first oil shock, when the capitalist world's investment activity slowed dramatically, the investment boom in Hungary continued unimpeded. The driving force was overoptimistic central policy, but firms gladly joined in. External financing was drawn in, and credits were easily available on international financial markets. A drastic halt came several years later, when the central economic policymakers recognized the dangers of excessive foreign debt.[8] That was a great blow to the reform process, since the sudden stop was accomplished almost exclusively by direct intervention.

The problems of investment are closely related to the entry into and exit from state-owned industry. Hungary is seeking new ways to open the capital managed by the state-owned sector to individual initiative. Although this was an aim of the reform, an inventor or innovative individual still faces great obstacles in establishing a new firm with capital owned or lent by the state. Other organizations—local governments and nonprofit institutions—are subject to long procedures if they wish to establish a new firm.

Table 13-8. *Index of Industrial Investment*

Year	*Index (1970 = 100)*
1971	111.3
1972	112.1
1973	111.8
1974	122.2
1975	135.3
1976	146.1
1977	179.9
1978	185.6
1979	182.0
1980	161.3
1981	148.6
1982	149.1
1983	145.4

Source: Same as table 13-4.

A recurrent theme in Hungarian literature is the problem of exit and the desirability of allowing some natural selection by the market. The firm would survive as long as it were profitable or (if suffering losses) still creditworthy. Firms that have a persistent deficit or are insolvent and have lost their creditworthiness should go out of business in an orderly legal process, such as bankruptcy or absorption by a viable firm. This natural selection does not occur in the Hungarian state-owned sector. There are long struggles for survival, during which delegations approach various central organs and use any connections to get financial help. The soft budget constraint usually prevails, and the firm survives with external aid. There are liquidations, but the decision of the authorities usually is not guided by profitability and commercial creditworthiness. There are mergers, but the firm absorbed is often more profitable than the one taking over. In most cases, profit falls after the merger. These observations are presented in tables 13-9, 13-10, and 13-11. To sum up, entry and exit are rarely determined horizontally by market forces. In most cases, the administrative authorities decide on entry and exit, which makes vertical dependence stronger.

Conclusion

In retrospect the question arises whether the original idea of combining planning and the market economy was right or wrong. I am convinced that this combination was the right goal. The problem lies in the implementation, which has been only partly successful. The results of the Hungarian reform are superior to those of the old, overcentralized command system. The changes in the state-owned sector, the development of the cooperative and private sector, and the great success in agriculture distinguish Hungary from

Table 13-9. *Profitability and Liquidation in State-Owned Firms*

Industrial subsector	*Profitability before redistribution in 1978 in firms*	
	Surviving in 1979	*Liquidated or absorbed in 1978*
Mining	18.10	12.92
Electric energy	7.26	8.12
Engineering industry	17.43	30.50
Building industry	8.20	16.42
Chemical industry	13.02	18.52
Light industry	8.76	21.47
Food industry	1.26	4.82

Source: Same as table 13-4.

Table 13-10. *Profitability of Engineering Firms before and after Merger*
(number of cases)

Profitability after redistribution	*Year preceding the merger*	*Average of three years preceding the merger*
Higher in the absorber firm	20	16
Higher in the absorbed firm	30	27
Inappreciable	5	12

Source: Laki 1982, p. 101.

Table 13-11. *Change of Profitability of Engineering Firms after Merger*
(number of cases)

Year	*Profit compared with the year preceding the merger*		
	Smaller	*Larger*	*Inappreciable*
Year of merger	31	18	6
First year after merger	34	15	6
Second year after merger	32	14	9
Third year after merger	28	12	15

Source: Laki 1982, p. 103.

the rest of Eastern Europe. The supply of food, other consumer goods, and services is much better. And there is more room for initiative at all levels of decisionmaking.

Despite important improvements, the combination of centralization and decentralization, of planning and market mechanisms, is not a fortunate one. Decisionmakers at the firm get distorted signals from an arbitrary price system and from millions of bureaucratic interventions. Besides being given incorrect signals, they lack the proper incentives, because extra profits are usually taxed away and losses compensated. Vertical dependence remains strong, horizontal dependence weak.

Direct microregulation, through the many government interventions in daily business, was considered to be an inevitable but temporary arrangement following the brave one-stroke abolition of the command system. But what was meant to be temporary has lasted many years, since 1968, and still continues. It has become ingrained in the system, making it difficult to get rid of thousands of bureaucratic measures and institutions intended to be temporary.

Bureaucratic controls and market mechanisms cannot be blended in any arbitrary proportion, say 1:9 or 5:5 or 9:1 at will. The vigor of the market, the liveliness of initiative, and the feeling of full responsibility require a minimum of stable autonomy. If that is lost as the frequency and intensity of bureaucratic interventions surpass a critical threshold, the vigor and liveliness of the market give way to passivity or vertical activity, such as bargaining for special aid. One of the great virtues of a market is the motivation to search for new opportunities. That virtue cannot develop if the bulk of decisionmaking power remains with the administrative authorities. The loss appears in a lack of initiative, less innovation in flexibility, inefficient input-output combinations, lower utilization of equipment and manpower, slower technical progress, and fewer quick adjustments to the demands of buyers.

Many Hungarian economists believe that the present combination of planning and market mechanisms could be improved. Here only general requirements are stressed:

• Emphasis should be shifted from microregulation to macropolicy. After a thorough price reform and the hardening of the budget constraint, the government could rely more effectively on macroeconomic instruments such as constraints on the supply of credit, the interest rate, and the exchange rate.

• A carefully elaborated social policy is needed for the sake of implementing the ethical-political goals of a socialist society: equal opportunity, fairness, and security. The main instruments are redistributive measures for households and individual citizens, negative and positive transfer payments, taxes on income and wealth, and financial contributions complementing wages, salaries, and other earnings. After thoughtful deliberations, certain services offered free of charge, or subsidized, can be maintained. In any case, measures for the sake of social policy must be kept separate from the operation of the market of goods, capital, and labor. The market can work well only if price signals are not distorted by unnecessary interventions, and if producers are motivated to respond.

• The bureaucratic way of selecting production managers is probably not the last word in organizing a socialist system.[9] There is an international dispute about this problem. Here I want to point out only what is happening in Hungary. Many ideas have emerged from discussions, and some proposals were accepted for partial introduction or experiments. One inspiring idea is to appoint managers through an electoral process, as in Yugoslavia. This would bring the state-owned firm closer to a cooperative enterprise or partnership. Another proposal by M. Tardos and others is to establish a board of directors representing the state as the owner. The board would be independent of both sectoral and regional bureaucracy. It would supervise the activity of one or several state-owned firms, hiring and firing managers with profitability as the main criterion. The idea behind the proposal is a strict separation of ownership from management. A third alternative is renting: capital remains state-owned, but firms would be rented to manager-entrepreneurs, who would have full charge of the operation and pay a rent agreed upon by contract. The prime advocate of this form of renting is Tibor Liska. These and other suggestions are accompanied by proposals for policies that create more opportunities for the cooperative sector and the private sector. In my opinion, it would be a mistake to choose between these and other alternatives based on ideological prejudices. They are not mutually exclusive. They can work side-by-side, one in some sectors or some firms, a second in others. Only experience can show all the pros and cons of each alternative.

• It would be desirable for planning to become an overall exploration and coordination of society's activity. The senior government official immersed in minute details of production, prices, and investment projects is a caricature of the true planner. The planner should deal with the larger sectoral and regional goals, the leading indicators of production, investment, and consumption. In other words, the planner must elaborate the strategy for economic progress, then let the people at the lower levels of decisionmaking determine how best to execute the plan.

Hungary is halfway there. Although I am critical of the present system, I would not suggest returning to the command economy. On the contrary, my suggestion is to move ahead with more consistent reform toward a healthier combination of planning, central control, and market forces.

Notes

1. Központi Statisztikai Hivatal 1984, p. 104.

2. In addition to studies referred to in this chapter, the reference list offers a selected list of readings in accessible English publications.

3. There is a third kind of dependence: the conduct of the firm as a whole depends on the employees of the firm and, in particular, on the relationship between managers and employees. However important this third dependence might be, it is outside the scope of this chapter.

4. In this chapter I analyze the redistribution of gross profits over *firms* and not over *households*. The latter is extremely important, however, both in Hungary and China, and closely related to the dilemma of efficiency and equality.

5. More detailed explanation of the data base and of the definition of indicators used in the analysis can be found in Kornai and Matits 1984.

6. For the source of the data, see note 5.

7. In recent discussions on the Hungarian reform, M. Tardos, A. K. Soós, and others criticized the existing system because of the lack of a well-functioning capital market and came forward with various suggestions.

8. Table 13-9 shows the pulsating of investment. There was a stop in 1971–73, then acceleration until 1980, and then a contraction. There is a remarkable literature on investment cycles in Hungary and in other Eastern European countries. See information about the Hungarian cycle in T. Bauer 1978, A. K. Soós 1975–76, M. Lackó 1980, and M. Maresse 1981.

9. At the time I wrote the present chapter, new legal rules started to be applied in Hungary. They stipulate that the head of the enterprise (the managing director) be appointed through a special electoral process in the majority of enterprises. Long years of experience with the new rules are yet needed to enable evaluation of the electoral process.

References and Selected Readings

Antal, László. 1979. "Development with Some Digression: The Hungarian Economic Mechanism in the Seventies." *Acta Oeconomica* 23, no. 3–4:257–73.

Balassa, Bela. 1983. "Reforming the New Economic Mechanism in Hungary." *Journal of Comparative Economics* 7, no. 3 (September):253–76.

Bauer, Tamás. 1978. "Investment Cycles in Planned Economies." *Acta Oeconomica* 21, no. 3 (May):184–94.

———. 1983. "The Hungarian Alternative to Soviet-Type Planning." *Journal of Comparative Economics* 7, no. 3 (September):304–16.

Brus, Wlodzimierz. 1980. "Political System and Economic Efficiency: The East European Context." *Journal of Comparative Economics* 4, no. 1 (March):40–55.

Chikán, Attilo. 1984. *A vállalati készletezési politika* (Firm's inventory policy). Budapest: Közgazdasági és Jogi Könyvkiadó.

Csikós-Nagy, Béla. 1984. "Further Development of the Hungarian Price System." *Acta Oeconomica* 32, no. 1–2:21–38.

Ellman, Michael. 1983. "Changing Views on Central Economic Planning: 1958–83." *ACES Bulletin*, no. 5 (Spring).

Fábri, Ervin. 1982. "Superficial Changes and Deep Tendencies in Inventory Processes in Hungary." *Acta Oeconomica* 28, no. 1–2:133–46.

Hare, Paul G. 1983. "The Beginnings of Institutional Reform in Hungary." *Soviet Studies* 35, no. 3 (July):313–30.

Hare, Paul G., Hugo Radice, and Nigel Swain, eds. 1981. *Hungary: A Decade of Economic Reform*. London: Allen & Unwin.

Hare, Paul G., and P. Wanless. 1981. "Polish and Hungarian Economic Reforms: A Comparison." *Soviet Studies* 33, no. 4 (October): 491–517.

Hewett, Edward A. 1981. "The Hungarian Economy: Lessons of the 1970s and Prospects for the 1980s." In *East European Economic Assessment, Part 1, Country Studies, 1980. A Compendium of Papers Submitted to the Joint Economic Committee, Congress of the United States, 1981*. Washington, D.C.: Government Printing Office.

Knight, Peter T. 1983. *Economic Reforms in Socialist Countries: The Experiences of China, Hungary, Romania and Yugoslavia*. World Bank Staff Working Paper 579. Washington, D.C.

Kornai, János. 1972. *Rush versus Harmonic Growth: Meditation on the Theory and on the Politics of Economic Growth*. Amsterdam: North-Holland.

———. 1979. "Resource-Constrained versus Demand-Constrained Systems." *Econometrica* 47, no. 4 (July):801–08.

———. 1980a. *Economics of Shortage*. 2 vols. Amsterdam: North-Holland.

———. 1980b. "The Dilemmas of a Socialist Economy: The Hungarian Experience." *Cambridge Journal of Economics* 4, no. 2 (June):147–57.

———. 1980c. "'Hard' and 'Soft' Budget Constraint." *Acta Oeconomica* 25, no. 3–4:231–46.

———. 1981. "Some Properties of the Eastern European Growth Pattern." *World Development* 9, no. 9–10 (September–October):965–70.

———. 1982. "Adjustment to Price and Quantity Signals." *Economie Appliquée* 35, no. 3 (Autumn):503–24.

———. 1983. "Comments on the Present State and the Prospects of the Hungarian Economic Reform." *Journal of Comparative Economics* 7, no. 3 (September):225–52.

Kornai, János, and Ágnes Matits. 1984. "Softness of the Budget Constraint—An Analysis Relying on Data of Firms." *Acta Oeconomica* 32, no. 3–4:223–50.

Központi Statisztikai Hivatal (Central Statistical Office). 1984. *Statisztikai Évkönyv 1983* (Statistical yearbook 1983). Budapest: Statisztikai Kiadó Vállalat.

Lackó, Mária. 1975. "Consumer Savings and the Supply Situation," *Acta Oeconomica* 15, no. 3–4:365–84.

———. 1980. "Cumulating and Easing of Tensions: A Simple Model of the Cyclical Development of Investments in Hungary." *Acta Oeconomica* 24, no. 3–4:357–77.

Laki, Mihály. 1982. "Liquidation and Merger in the Hungarian Industry." *Acta Oeconomica* 28, no. 1–2:87–108.

———. 1984. "The Enterprise Crisis." *Acta Oeconomica* 32, no. 1–2:113–24.

Laky, Teréz. 1980. "The Hidden Mechanisms of Recentralization in Hungary." *Acta Oeconomica* 24, no. 1–2:95–109.

———. 1984. "Small Enterprise in Hungary—Myth and Reality." *Acta Oeconomica* 32, no. 1–2:39–64.

Maresse, Michael. 1981. "The Bureaucratic Response to Economic Fluctuation: An Econometric Investigation of Hungarian Investment Policies." *Journal of Policy Modeling* 3, no. 3 (Autumn):221–43.

Nove, Alec. 1983. *The Economics of Feasible Socialism*. London: Allen and Unwin.

Nyers, Rezsö, and Márton Tardos. 1978. "Enterprises in Hungary before and after the Economic Reform." *Acta Oeconomica* 20, no. 1–2:21–44.

———. 1984. "The Necessity for Consolidation of the Economy and the Possibility of Development in Hungary." *Acta Oeconomica* 32, no. 1–2:1–20.

Schweitzer, Iván. 1982. A *vállalatnagyság* (Firm size). Budapest: Közgazdasági és Jogi Könyvkiadó.

Soós, Attila K. 1975–76. "Causes of Investment Fluctuations." *Eastern European Economics* 14, no. 2 (Winter):75–6.

Szamuely, László. 1982. "The First Wave of the Mechanism Debate in Hungary: 1954–57." *Acta Oeconomica* 29, no. 1–2:1–24.

Tardos, Márton. 1982. "Development Program for Economic Control and Organization in Hungary." *Acta Oeconomica* 28, no. 3–4:295–316.

Tyson, Laura D'Andrea. 1983. "Investment Allocation: A Comparison of the Reform Experiences of Hungary and Yugoslavia." *Journal of Comparative Economics* 7, no. 3 (September):288–303.

Vissi, Ferenc. 1983. "Major Questions of the Improvement of Economic Control and Management in Hungary in the Mid-Eighties." *Acta Oeconomica* 30, no. 3–4:325–40.

14

The Self-Managed Firm in Yugoslavia

Martin Schrenk

In this chapter I describe the system that socialist Yugoslav firms use for computing and distributing income and analyze some of the consequences for microeconomic and macroeconomic management. The vast differences between China and Yugoslavia in size, political traditions, and state of development rule out any attempt to compare their economic systems. But the observer of China's moves toward greater economic decentralization will probably discover certain commonalities. Since Yugoslavia started down the path of reform three decades before China, these commonalities may suggest options for China. In this sense, Yugoslavia is almost a laboratory for observing how certain institutions work in reality. Only the Chinese reader can judge which Yugoslav experiences—which successes or failures—hold relevant lessons for the reform of the system in China.

The Origins of the Self-Management System

The present Yugoslav perception of socialist ownership and control and of the role of the state are molded by Yugoslavia's historical background, which could hardly be more different from China's. First, Yugoslavia has existed as a country only since 1919, when it was created from parts that for centuries were held by major powers and that shared little historical or cultural heritage beyond an affinity for the Slavic languages. From this legacy of foreign domination the state traditionally was seen as an alien bureaucratic power, sometimes benevolent, often oppressive. Second, the regions that made up Yugoslavia each developed a strong internal ethnic identity under foreign domination. Although ethnic diversity has now lost its centrifugal force, the internal coherence of the "nations" that constitute the republics and autonomous provinces of the Yugoslav Federation remains a strong political factor. This accounts for many of Yugoslavia's peculiar institutional arrangements and economic problems.

Yugoslavia subscribes to Marxism-Leninism, with the party (League of Communists) as the guiding political force. After the break from close allegiance to the U.S.S.R. in 1948, the ideas of "self-governing association of producers," described in Marx's writings on the Paris Commune, became the guiding political model. In contrast to state-centered socialism, this model emphasizes a socialist order at the microeconomic level, with decisionmaking powers assigned to those directly affected by the decisions.

The traditional distrust of the central state, the strong ethnic identification of parts of the country, and the emphasis on direct democracy in basic social units were brought together in the concept of self-management. This concept emphasizes the devolution of power and control to the lowest effective level. Decentralization became a guiding principle for the political evolution of the system in two ways: state power was to be organized in the smallest unit feasible, in the order of community, republic, and federation; and state power at any level was to the degree feasible to be replaced by direct arrangements between individuals or organizations.

In the economic sphere, workers' self-management separated ownership and control. Society is the owner of the means of production, but control rests with the workers using them. The workers acquire the right to use these assets for the generation of personal income and common consumption, in exchange for the obligation to maintain and to further the value of assets entrusted to them by society.

The institutional developments during the last forty years can be summarized as follows:[1]

1945–48 Yugoslavia adopted a system of economic management, including mandatory planning, patterned after that of the U.S.S.R.

1948–51 After the break with the U.S.S.R., workers' self-management was introduced as the guiding principle of Yugoslavia's route to socialism. Socialist commodity production and the law of value were accepted as the principles for socialist firms.

1951–55 The practice of macroeconomic and microeconomic management was gradually adjusted to these two principles. Mandatory annual plans for outputs and inputs, along with central price setting, were phased out.

1955–65 Accumulation and allocation of investment resources were gradually separated from the budget and became the responsibility of enterprises and banks. State planning was restricted to medium-term macroeconomic proportions, and it became largely indicative for enterprises.

1965–71 A series of economic reforms established almost unrestricted autonomy for manufacturing enterprises, trading firms, and banks. Managers were given almost complete independence in decision-making on investment, acquisition and mergers, and in areas of internal control. Yugoslavia's economic system was designated as market socialism.

1971–76 The economic system that had developed was criticized by the party leadership as technocratic under managerial power and dominated by group-ownership tendencies. Critics said socialist legitimacy had eroded, turning workers' self-management into an empty formalism. This led to reforms that brought about a fundamental rearrangement of power and control in and between enterprises and other social organs.

1976–86 No major changes have been made in the system.

The Firm

The Yugoslav firm is internally decentralized into Basic Organizations of Associated Labor (BOS), the smallest technically identifiable units producing a commodity or service.[2] This was done because workers' self-management can be most effective in units small enough for individual members to have direct contact with each other and for operational efficiency to be boosted through peer pressure. Large units were made to depend on the decisions of small ones under the direct control of workers to prevent professional managers from usurping power.

Several rules were introduced to ensure that BOS retain vitality within larger firms. First, BOS are legal entities, and income statements and balance sheets are drawn for each BO, not for the firm. In the Chinese phrase, the firm is no longer "one big pot" from which everybody receives a share. The financial autonomy of BOS is balanced by the socialist concept of solidarity, however, which means that BOS within the firm are expected to support each other during temporary difficulties. Second, each BO has to prepare an annual plan, as does the firm, but the plan of the firm requires consent by all BOS before it is valid. Third, BOS also have the right to split off to become an independent firm or to join an existing one.

The first two rules are particularly important. If income is computed and distributed independently for each BO, the valuation of the transactions among the BOS in the firm becomes critical for each BO. Their joint plan, apart from the coordination of deliveries and investment from pooled resources, is a plan for the internal distribution of earned income. In vertically organized firms, income is generated at the last stage of the internal production chain.

To ensure coherence among the BOs and to permit specialization of professional staff, certain management functions must be handled by the firm, rather than by each BO. Planning, analysis, accounting, financial management, and, frequently, such other services as product development and social services are centralized voluntarily. These services are provided to the BOs in the firm for the reimbursement of costs.

The Management Structure

The Yugoslav firm is not a homogenous entity but a complex internal structure of decisionmaking, management, and control.[3] The Associated Labor Act (ALA) of 1976—sometimes referred to in Yugoslavia as "the constitution for the economy"—is the basis for all specific legislation on microeconomic matters.

The workers' council is the most important organ of the self-management structure. Comprising delegates that the workers elected by secret ballot, it is the "organ responsible for managing the work and business of the BO" (ALA, art. 490). Its rights, exercised either directly or through special committees elected by the council, include arranging for self-management agreements (SMAs) with other BOs in or outside the firm, determining the annual plan of the BO and the firm, setting business policy and income scales, preparing income statements and balance sheets, recruiting and dismissing workers, handling all disciplinary matters, appointing and taking part in the dismissal of business managers, and issuing guidelines to business managers and supervising their implementation (ALA, art. 495). With minor modifications, the same rights are given to the workers' councils of firms.

Firms and BOs have professional business managers. They are proposed by a commission representing the BO or the firm, trade union, and local community. They are appointed by the workers' council for a term of four years (no limit to reelection). Business managers may be recalled before their term expires on the initiative of either of the three parties that nominated the manager (ALA, arts. 520–22). Their authority is as follows: they "manage the business of the BO, organize and coordinate the labor process, propose business policy and measures for its implementation, execute decisions . . . adopted by the workers' council, . . . consider the draft plan . . . and give opinions and proposals thereon"; they "independently decide on how to run the business of the BO, the execution of individual tasks or performance" and organize and coordinate "the labor process"; and they "have the right and duty to issue orders to individual workers or groups of workers concerning the performance of individual affairs and tasks" (ALA, arts. 513–15).

The same provisions apply in general to business managers of firms, who also supervise the common service organizations (ALA, art. 544), which gives them control over the information base of the firm. Business managers have no right to hire and fire workers or to reward or penalize with promotions, demotions, or income differences. Business managers also have oversight functions over the workers' council. If the council makes decisions that conflict with the law or existing agreements, the business manager must warn it against them. If the warning is not heeded, the business manager must stop the action and report to the supervisory organ of the state (ALA, arts. 518–19).

Each level of organization, from the working group (normally ten to twenty workers) up to the firm, has its trade union organization, which is intimately linked with the self-management organs. The trade union nominates the candidates for election to the workers' councils and can institute proceedings for their recall (ALA, arts. 494, 558). It participates as one of the three parties in nominating and recalling business managers. It has the right to propose self-management agreements affecting work relations, computation, and distribution of income among the BOs of the firm or among groups of firms (ALA, art. 590) and among workers within BOs. Trade union representatives are not professional cadres but are elected for a limited term by their work unit.

The party—the League of Communists of Yugoslavia (LCY)—has an organization at each BO, which also corresponds to the local community organization. Formally, the LCY does not participate in the decisionmaking of the BO or the firm. Its delegates are not professional cadres. The role of the LCY is indirect; almost all elected self-management delegates, trade unionists in the firm, and most business managers are members of the LCY.[4] The influence of the LCY on these active members of the workers' community is established through the principle of democratic centralism, which obliges members to implement the formal decisions made by the LCY.

The absence of career cadres in the self-management organs, the trade unions, or the LCY raises the question of whether they can match the professional competence and control over information of the business managers and their qualified administrative and technical staff. But overlapping membership in the LCY, frequently at 20–30 percent of the work force, is normal—as are rotations between the three organizations. Thus, the same group of active members is likely to be extensively, if not permanently, involved in the management of the firm in a variety of functions (Lydall 1984, pp. 112–14). This situation would also explain the insight, competence, and self-confidence shown by many members of self-management organs (Schrenk 1981, p. 38).

One way that business managers and the elected leadership of the three organizations meet informally on equal ground is in the Political Active, which discusses matters of management and development of the firm (Granick 1975, p. 367, and Lydall 1984, pp. 118–19). A more formal forum is the Collegium, usually including the business managers of all units, the chairman of the workers' council, and frequently the trade union of the firm

(Lydall 1984, p. 120, and Schrenk 1981, p. 40). Policy options are extensively explored in these forums, and the consensus reached is proposed to the full workers' councils.

The Real Model of the Yugoslav Firm

From these elements, the real model of the Yugoslav firm emerges. In the Yugoslav system the firm is not clearly defined in legal terms. The lines of authority are hazy, and there is no sharply defined locus for decisionmaking. Even so, the firm does have elements of internal cohesiveness that strengthen long-term stability over short-run profitability. Firms are held together by interlocking self-management agreements. These agreements regulate medium- to long-term links between BOs (ALA, art. 586), establishing a relationship between BOs to pool labor and resources, and to share income and risks.[5] The agreements are distinct from conventional business contracts, which regulate short-term transactions and have no sharing of income or risk (ALA, arts. 71, 586).

Among the features regulated by internal SMAs are the following: First, the units in the firm normally assume mutual and joint liability for debts, improving the creditworthiness of each unit. Second, units pool liquid resources to help meet their obligations to other firms and banks, reducing their need for working capital and investment funds. Third, financial claims among units in the firm are always met, while claims outside are frequently in arrears and can cause serious collection problems. Fourth, risks are pooled, and the principle of solidarity is taken very seriously in the firm. If a BO is in difficulty, other member units normally provide almost unlimited support, apart from accepting formal liability. Fifth, the principle of solidarity includes also a strong commitment for a coordinated if not integrated policy of remuneration, and when BOs suffer from a redundancy of workers, the firm tries to ensure their employment at the same wages either by expanding other BOs or by diversifying. Sixth, if BOs are vertically linked, fluctuations in demand and supply are reduced for internal transactions. The same is true for pricing internal transactions. All these elements are subject to joint planning. The internal cohesiveness of firms reduces transaction costs. It also reduces the uncertainties from strategic and tactical opportunism between firms, since the joint accounting services, daily collaboration, and physical proximity leave almost no room for secrets or deception in the firm, and internal SMAs are usually sacrosanct.[6]

A diverse coalition with multiple checks and balances normally guides Yugoslav firms. As any coalition, it works by compromise and persuasion, with some form of moral persuasion from the outside when internal compromises are difficult. These outside pressures come from the residual, but powerful, informal role of the state.[7]

Relations with the State

In the Yugoslav system, the state is in three layers: the federation, the republics and autonomous provinces, and the local communities, all referred to as sociopolitical communities.[8] In the system of workers' self-management, the role of the state is decentralized to the lowest feasible level. The three layers of sociopolitical communities assign the residual functions of the state to the most suitable layer, rather than have the same function handled at three levels of authority, with instructions being sent down and information being sent up between levels. The relationship between firms and the state has two qualitatively distinct channels: as administrative link to the bureaucratic apparatus and as a political link to the assemblies and political leadership. Although the separation is not always clear, rejection of the role of the state is directed primarily against the bureaucracy's sending down orders. The political link is, in practice, symbiotic rather than hierarchical.

Although the state does not own the means of production, there is a multitude of control links between firms and sociopolitical communities. First, the sociopolitical community has the right to "determine, consider and assess the results of . . . business organizations" (ALA, art. 144). Second, "if self-management relations are substantially disrupted or social interests seriously damaged . . . the assembly of the sociopolitical community may . . . dissolve the workers' council . . . or take other measures" (ALA, art. 35). Third, business managers are obliged to report unlawful decisions of the workers' council to the sociopolitical community. Fourth, the sociopolitical community is one of the three parties nominating the candidates for business managers, and it can initiate their recall. Fifth, if an organization gets into financial difficulties, "the competent organ of the sociopolitical community shall be bound . . . to extend to such organizations economic and other kinds of assistance and to take measures for its financial rehabilitation" (ALA, art. 38). Sixth, local communities are "normally required to guarantee loans to organizations on their territory" (Lydall 1984, p. 99). Other provisions of law, however, leave no doubt that the obligation to assist firms in difficulty is not an unconditional bailout. It can be combined with far-reaching rights to interfere in such a firm, including liquidating it if the unit is not viable (ALA, arts. 152–55, and 622–35).

In most instances, the sociopolitical community involved is the local community. The dominating role of the local community was summarized by *Borba*, the LCY daily, as follows: "The commune is so much involved in economic affairs that without its approval it is not possible to appoint a director, to build a new factory, or to pool labor and resources. . . . We constantly build new factories, often without justification, on the orders of the commune, because only in that way can the commune solve its local problems—from employment to the building of flats, schools and roads"

(Lydall 1984, p. 282). On the other hand, the link to the federation is almost nonexistent, whereas the republic is somewhere in between.

Since political links dominate over administrative links, generalizations about the relationship of power and control between the firms and the state are impossible. Most Yugoslav and foreign observers assume, on the basis of anecdotal evidence, substantial informal influence from political organs on firms and banks. Whether this influence constitutes any dilution of the principle of self-management is another question. Yugoslav political leaders suggest publicly that the role of the LCY is to act as the guiding force of society in shaping economic and social development. This self-perception, together with the party principle of democratic centralism, would go a long way to support the suggestion of a strong, informal political guidance on all major decisions of firms.

Political guidance may affect economic decisions, but that fact alone does not indicate whether it leads to an improvement or a loss of welfare. Most Western economic analysts axiomatically assume that every political influence on economic decisions leads automatically to undesirable consequences, and in Yugoslavia political factories are frequently cited as prime examples of economically disastrous interventions. On the other hand, where the public needs protection from gross market power, from the reckless disregard of the negative side effects of decisions, or from incompetence, political intervention can be beneficial. Political guidance does not simply imply giving instructions. As Lydall has pointed out, the Political Actives of firms not only transmit political instructions but also act as a lobby for the specific concerns of the firm (1984, p. 118). Two-way communication can bridge the gap between social, political, and purely microeconomic interests.

Political guidance can flow in both directions. The assembly of local communities is composed of delegates nominated by the workers' councils of local firms (ALA, arts. 239, 461, 487). Control by the local community, thus, automatically has an element of peer control. And given this link between the local community and local firms, guidance could be reversed where a single firm dominates the local economy. Since republican assemblies are composed of delegates from the communities, large firms can have direct influence on the republic as well. This may explain the survival of some technically bankrupt political factories.

Sociopolitical communities and in many instances "economic chambers" of republics, or associations of industries and trade unions (comprising all firms within a branch), sign social compacts. These unique legal instruments of self-management have something in common with SMAS, contracts, executive orders of the government, and laws (ALA, arts. 17 and 573–85). Social compacts regulate "socioeconomic and other relations . . . in the spheres of planning, prices, distribution of income and allocation of resources for personal income and workers' collective consumption, external trade, and the policy of employment" (ALA, art. 579). While SMAS can be renegotiated or abrogated and—if they are violated—can trigger financial compensation for losses, no such provisions are part of social compacts, and the ALA is silent on the effects of violating them. Given the importance of the issues that social compacts regulate, this omission seems curious; the probable explanation is that social compacts are enforced by moral suasion supported by the party. This may be the most obvious case of an economic instrument that rests entirely on the authority of the LCY over its members.

Relations between Firms: Self-Management and the Market

Self-management finds its strongest expression in the concept of pooling labor and resources in the firm, through self-management agreements among BOS. Such agreements, however, also shape relations between organizations that are not part of the firm. This situation seems to raise a possible conflict between the market in the conventional sense of survival of the fittest and the idea of self-management as the nonconfrontational approach to economic problem solving with a high social value assigned to consensus and long-term solidarity among the participants. To many outside observers, the two concepts are contradictory, and an uncomfortable compromise has been struck between them.

For labor, a market does not exist in the neoclassical sense, with wages as a market-clearing price and labor viewed as a productive input. Wages and salaries have been abolished, not just from the official terminology but as concepts. Workers do not receive financial remuneration per unit of labor time specified beforehand. Instead, they acquire the right to some share of the residual income of the BO after it has honored all other obligations. Workers' remuneration in the Yugoslav system is, from the perspective of classical economics, an inseparable amalgam of reward for labor services, of part of the profit, and of economic rents. The rent component results from access to socially owned land and capital free of charge and from an oligopolistic or monopolistic position of the firm. Firms do not purchase labor time as a current input in a quantity adjusted to short-term output projections. Since the association of labor in the BO, rather than its balance sheet, constitutes its very essence, workers cannot be laid off, only expelled by their peers for gross violation of internal rules, or released through liquidation of the BO in the wake of bankruptcy.[9] For these reasons, remuneration would differ greatly among firms for any given level of qualification, in the absence of intervention or market forces. Therefore, although some subtle features of a labor market persist (such as fringe benefits to workers of scarce and critical skill), most analysts agree that the traditional labor market does not operate.

For capital, a market in the neoclassical sense does not exist either. Although investment resources are no longer allocated through state budgets or state-owned banks as in centrally planned socialist economies, autonomous financial intermediation does not exist despite the large number of banks. Banks are not independent profit-making and risk-bearing financial organizations, which collect and allocate money at borrowing and lending rates that reflect the risk and capital's scarcity price at the market. Yugoslav banks are service organizations for their founding members—the BOs that deposit and borrow money. They manage the financial transactions associated with pooling of resources among members in accord with the concluded self-management agreements. Banks do not have the right to accumulate resources from their income, except some moderate liquidity reserve, and they have to distribute among their members any surplus that remains after paying expenses and remunerations to the staff (ALA, art. 89). The BOs keep financial assets under their control and in their balance sheets.[10] The only bank resources without such restrictions are household deposits, some share of the primary emission from the National Bank system, and (before the arrival of the external debt crisis) loans from foreign banks. Decisions over the allocation of resources available to a bank is the prerogative of its members, and the members as a group are liable for the bank's debts. It is widely believed, however, that most of these decisions are effectively influenced by the leadership of local communities and the republics who support the expansion—and often the financial survival—of large existing firms among the members.

This limited, quasi-capital market is supplemented by direct arrangements between BOs. The organization that makes financial resources available is entitled to participate in the net income of the capital user—that is, after deduction of material inputs and depreciation from its gross income. The reward for the capital supplier can take several forms. Either the user has to repay the principal and some freely negotiated interest, similar to debt servicing to a bank, or the two organizations agree on the payment of a share of the user's net income to the supplier over a period of time. In this case, profits and risks are shared between the organizations in an arrangement comparable to a joint venture over a limited time. While repeated investment in this form is possible, permanent income sharing and control on the basis of equity is considered incompatible with socialism and is illegal (ALA, arts. 81–88).

Either form of pooling of investment resources is normally part of an SMA on long-run cooperation that also regulates other conditions, such as joint planning, price formation, and marketing. Therefore, there is no direct way to assess financial cost or return for users or suppliers, or of the cost and benefit of any other element of the self-management agreement. Return on investment is rarely the primary motive for suppliers. Pooling of resources within the firm can be regarded as an extended form of self-financing, and in such instances the primary motive for pooling of resources outside the firm is some other tangible benefit, such as priority access to scarce inputs or the creation of captive markets.

For goods and services, the market is explicitly given the determining role. There is no administrative intervention in the firms' decisions about the size, composition, and destination of outputs. And with the new law on prices in 1984, there is no longer any control of prices, with few exceptions. This law, however, leaves little doubt that the term "market" refers primarily to long-term balancing of capacity and demand without state intervention, rather than to short-run market clearing through the price mechanism. Irregular transactions are by contract, and prices are set by the parties involved. Transactions are frequently regulated, and must be regulated for trading firms, by self-management agreements on transfer prices or income sharing. Agreements on pooling labor and resources for medium- to long-term duration tend to regulate other matters as well. Evidence from interviews with firms suggests that price setting can cover a wide spectrum. For example, in some firms BOs agree to use international prices, with or without some smoothing for short-term market distortions. In other firms BOs agree to cost-plus prices, computed from technical standards and evidence supplied by the producer. In still others BOs agree to assure comparable levels of personal incomes to the participating organizations. Price formation through self-management agreements on pooling labor and resources and sharing income and risks among BOs in a firm is favored politically for internal relations and for intermediary goods in general.

Income Distribution, Price Formation, and Microeconomic Planning

In gross simplification, the income of BOs is, according to Yugoslav accounting conventions, computed as:

Revenues from sales + share of joint income = gross income
Gross income − material cost − depreciation = income
Income − taxes and contributions − interest payments = net income

Most of the items are self-explanatory. The BO receives revenues from sales to other BOs in the firm or to outside customers at transfer or market prices. Alternatively, it can receive a share of joint income that the firm earns at the final stage of the production as its reward for internal deliveries to other vertically linked BOs. The sum of these items is the gross income. After costs for material inputs and depreciation are deducted, the remainder is the income. After deducting taxes on the BO's income and contributions to financing of social and communal services, interest payments are deducted to derive the net income.

Two points are worth noting. First, the computation contains no provision for wages and bonus. Second, there is no profit or loss. Net income, therefore, is the residual available for distribution between the community of workers of the BO and society as the owner of the means of production. The workers receive personal incomes and some other benefits from allocations to the collective consumption fund; society receives its portion of net income as allocations to the business fund and reserve funds. Since both parts come out of the residual income of the BO, the income of workers and the income appropriated by society depend on the business's success. Without a labor market, wages do not exist in this system, nor are labor costs part of production cost in accounting. Workers receive monthly payment advances according to the plan and its realization. Final remuneration is computed only after the end of the business year and may result either in additional payments or in reduced advances paid during the subsequent year. The absence of profit or loss is primarily semantic. Apart from an undefined profit component distributed to the workers as part of their personal income, the BO's funds are equivalent to undistributed profits under common accounting conventions.

The transformation of personal income into payments is carried out in three steps. Each worker is assigned a certain number of work points according to the self-management agreement of the BO. The value per work point is computed by dividing the aggregate personal income by the total number of work points earned by all workers. Finally, individual incomes are computed by multiplying the individual number of work points with the value per point. The remainder of the net income is allocated to the business fund.

In principle, the BO workers' councils have the right to determine the distribution of net income into its components. In practice, social compacts (normally on the level of the republic) and self-management agreements (normally of the industry branch within the republic and firm) establish rules, frequently a complex formula that limits the net income that can be distributed as personal income. Into the early 1980s, they usually stipulated that when productivity (net income per worker) was above the branch average, the firm could pay a worker above the average of the branch.[11] If the productivity was below the branch average, average personal income per worker would fall below the branch average. In either direction, however, the differences in personal income per worker were not proportional to the productivity differences. For BOs above the average, the share of accumulation in net income would rise with increasing margins of excess productivity; in the obverse case, it would fall—that is, both workers and society share the difference, but society's share is higher the larger the deviation. This formula gave special rewards to workers in capital-intensive units. Since practical difficulties arose with a formula based on absolute value figures under inflationary conditions, the approach was gradually changed to link growth rates of average personal income to growth rates in productivity. This did not change, however, the favored position of capital-intensive firms.

The federal social compact on incomes for 1985 shifts the standard for computing the maximum share of personal income from productivity to profitability, defined as the ratio of the business fund allocation to the sum of the adjusted value of fixed assets and working capital. The functional relationship between average personal income and profitability will be similar to that for productivity in the past—rising shares of income accumulation with rising profitability, and vice versa. This changeover signifies a major change in the Yugoslav system.

If net income was high enough, capital-intensity determined how much the BO could distribute to workers under the previous rules, turning accumulation into forced savings. This did not exclude cases of higher voluntary savings if major investment programs required self-financing. Nor did this mean that such residual forced savings were irrelevant for BOs: because they constituted financial assets under their permanent control, they improved the future ability to earn income. Under the new rule, accumulation is turning from a residual into the determinant for the personal income. This change is likely to create a stronger motivation to maximize net income. And by linking accumulation to the value of employed assets, regardless of the source of financing (permanent funds or credits), the rent for using socially owned capital is appropriated by society rather than by the workers in the privileged position of having the monopoly on access to the capital. Furthermore, excessive assets change from a desirable insurance against future uncertainties to an acute burden as they reduce profitability and, ultimately, personal income. This incentive under the new rules should minimize the use of assets at a given level of business activity, inducing rational overall use of capital.

While social compacts and self-management agreements deal with issues related to organizations' and personal incomes, they do not seem to be designed for explicit macroeconomic income policy. For example, they do not aim to establish particular macroeconomic proportions, such as the share of aggregate personal income or accumulation in gross domestic product (GDP). Nor do they explicitly aim at growth rates of income as a means of inflation control.

Internal Prices

If BOs in a firm are vertically integrated to deliver parts, components, and services to one another in the stages of production, the valuation of those internal deliveries has to adhere to certain rules. The income computation scheme shows that the net income of BOs depends predominantly on gross income, the way these internal transactions are valued. This raises the issue of transfer prices, which can be linked directly or indirectly to observed market prices or to planned income relations.

It is evident from the income computation scheme that there are two ways to generate a level of gross income in each BO which satisfies the conditions of having comparable levels of personal income per worker and preagreed shares in total accumulation. Income can be computed either as the algebraic product of the appropriate transfer price per unit and the number of transferred units or as a percentage of the total income of the firm from final sales. Once an agreement is reached on the average personal income per worker, on the respective portions of total accumulation, on the value of material inputs, and on each unit's depreciation, one can compute the shares of total generated income which have to be applied to total income to compute the income of each participating BO. The absolute amount can be converted to equivalent transfer prices by dividing the absolutes by physical volumes of internally transferred deliveries. Whether transfer prices or income shares are being used is entirely a matter of convenience.

The method of using shares of total income has four additional advantages. First, under inflationary conditions the respective shares of each BO require only minor adjustment for differences of rates of price increase for different inputs and outputs. Second, the principle of sharing income and risk, which underlies the notion of pooling labor and resources, is automatically met. If sales prices or quantities change, the resulting gains and losses are automatically shared backward in fair proportions. Third, basing income distribution among BOs on the sharing of incomes lends itself to easy planning. The shares can be determined in advance and applied after the fact. If BOs achieve their outputs with lower material or labor inputs per unit than planned, they achieve a higher net income per worker and thus higher personal income per worker and higher profitability. And fourth, if the BOs agree to redistribute net income among themselves, either for reasons of solidarity with a distressed BO or to channel more accumulation to a BO that needs major investment, it can be done easily by changing the shares in gross income.

Two possible drawbacks are immediately evident. First, the BOs participating in this distribution rule have little interest in searching for the cheapest source of outside inputs. Because costs are deducted from the income computation, such savings would have to be split among all associated units, and the impact on each one's net income would be marginal. Second, drastic improvement in efficiency through either reduced input or labor coefficients would be discouraged. Since equalizing personal incomes among participating BOs is an underlying principle of the collaboration, any major and permanent gains in personal income would tend to enter next year's planning assumptions in order to contain internal income inequalities among BOs. This internal income distribution model thus tends to produce its own version of the ratchet effect, normally associated with centrally planned economies.

Microeconomic Planning

All BOs and firms are obliged by law to prepare their own internal plan. Given the technical links between the BOs in the firm, their plans tend to be a derivative of the firm's. This hierarchical link is strengthened by two organizational factors. First, as mentioned earlier, the planning staff is a separate unit under the supervision of the firm's business manager (ALA, arts. 543–44). Second, the distribution of jointly generated income through the self-management agreement on pooling labor and resources establishes the cohesion of the firm. Planning of income, therefore, is as important as coordinating inputs and outputs in a consolidated plan of action. The two are, in fact, the same process.

Income planning starts from the bottom up. Each worker is assigned a certain number of work points per unit of time worked, which to a large extent reflect educational background, and the same standard is used in all BOs of the firm as part of its internal self-management agreement on pooling labor and resources.[12] On that basis the number of work points can be computed for each BO and for the firm. Market forecasts provide estimates of outputs, which are converted into material inputs though technical coefficients. Required depreciation is computed from data on fixed assets. From recent experience, or from social compacts and industry branch self-management agreements, estimates are provided on productivity development. After making an assumption on the amounts to be allocated to business funds, the remainder—total planned personal income—is divided by the total work points of the firm. On that basis, what each BO needs to receive to meet these planned components, either directly or through equivalent transfer prices, is computed from the total income shares.

Thus, the plan establishes simultaneously the distribution of planned net income among the BOs and the planned distribution of personal income among all workers. This plan has to be ratified by all BOs in order to come into force. The actual income per work point may, of course, differ on average and among BOs, as some BOs are more successful in meeting their output targets or containing their inputs.

The same principle of planning shares in joint income is applied in SMAs on pooling of labor and resources among firms. The common denominator of all these internal income-sharing agreements can hardly be overemphasized: the participating organizations jointly share market opportunities as well as risks.

The method of setting inflation-neutral profit-sharing and risk-sharing transfer prices through income sharing is logically elegant. In practice, however, it can lead to considerable conflicts, which have to be resolved through tedious negotiations. One cause of conflict is the fact that the labor force of the participating BOs normally is not optimal in size or composition. At the planning stage, there is no incentive for the BOs to contain the labor force since the sum of personal incomes is generated on the basis of actual employment. Conflicts arising from this problem are apparently more severe among firms, where direct evidence of overstaffing can be more easily disguised, than among BOs in a firm. Another problem arises in the case of a single BO that generates consistently higher personal income per worker than the others.

Link to Macroeconomic Planning

Microeconomic planning is a step toward macroeconomic planning. In Yugoslavia this takes the form of five-year plans for the federation, each republic, and each local community. The general concept of plan preparation is straightforward. The planning process starts simultaneously at the top, in the planning offices of the sociopolitical communities, and at the bottom, with the firms. While the planning offices start with macroeconomic projections, the firms are to draft their own five-year plans with their expectations and intentions. These microeconomic draft plans are then to be exchanged and discussed with suppliers and customer firms and with firms in the same industry branch. The purpose of these consultations is to induce all participants to arrive at firmer, more realistic, and more consistent expectations and intentions. At the same time, the sociopolitical communities gradually refine their draft plans by filling in more details and coordinating with other communities. These two sets of iterative processes, referred to as harmonization, are to converge eventually. When they do, the plans of sociopolitical communities are finalized for publication as the social plans, with social compacts as integral parts. Firms are expected to conclude self-management agreements that are consistent with the social plans and the financial plans of the banks they belong to—and that are, in addition, as consistent as possible with the development plans of other firms.

The principal ideas are similar to those of the theory of indicative planning (Meade 1970). The convergence of expectations and plans of action should reduce uncertainty and its associated financial and social costs. While the social plans bind the organs of the state, at least as long as reality does not deviate too much from the basic assumptions, self-management agreements merely obligate firms that conclude them in the context of planning. Since violations of these agreements rarely cause direct harm to other firms and seem to be practiced whenever expectations and reality start to diverge, the commitment of firms to these plans is minimal. The firms' own microeconomic plans cover a shorter period, one for which income distribution is a key issue—usually one year or, in cases of joint investment, for the expected life span of the assets rather than for a fixed five-year period. Thus, firms seem no more interested in the overall planning exercise than is required by the law. Nor do they seem to take the result very seriously without a central authority to enforce action in accord with plans. What is important, however, is that major projects of firms are in the social plans, since without such recognition the chances for bank credit are almost nil.[13]

The Objective Function

The objective function of the firm is not only of academic interest but also of great practical relevance. How the firm should behave, its reasoning for operational decisions, depends on what its purpose is. Traditional objective functions—like maximization of profit, market value of assets, or stream of residual income accruing to the individual owner-manager—obviously are not relevant in Yugoslavia. The owner (society) is not controlling decisions, nor is there another manager who has the sole decisionmaking power. Other models—such as an owner-manager coalition which strikes a compromise, according to the relative bargaining power, to satisfy all parties—come closer to the Yugoslav reality. To understand the motivation of the Yugoslav firm, one has to drop the convenient assumption of the firm's behaving like an individual owner-manager and look at the motives of the groups belonging to the coalition that affect the firm's decisions.[14]

Formally, the collective will of the workers is to guide the firm. Presumably, personal income in various forms, job security, and the quality of the work environment are most important. But individual factors—such as the position in the firm, education, skill, age, sex, family status, mobility, and so forth—determine the individual preferences for courses of action in the firm. The formal representative of the work force, the elected workers' council under the leadership of the trade union, has an almost impossible task in finding a consensus among conflicting interests of many individuals.

The same ambiguity prevails for business managers. As individuals, they are—as managers everywhere—motivated by financial considerations, by making the firm grow, and by career ambitions.[15] But career success depends as much on rapport with organizations and individuals responsible for nominating, electing, and recalling managers as on professional qualification or the success of the business. This emphasis on cooperative behavior is encouraged by the Yugoslav system of rotating cadres between various areas of leadership, between management positions in industry, banks, the sociopolitical communities, trade unions, and the LCY. Career ambitions are thus best served by responsiveness to expectations in the firm and in the local community, the LCY, and the political leadership of the republic.

External parties influence the decisions of firms through the power of moral suasion that they exert on workers' councils and business managers. The LCY, which also affects decisions of trade unions, local communities, and higher political levels, obviously determines its own decisions on the principles and the directions of social and economic development. The local communities pursue various goals, such as promoting local employment; financing housing and the physical and social infrastructure from the firm's taxes and contributions; and maintaining a semblance of income equality among various firms in its territory. Similarly, the republican governments try to reduce the economic and social disparities among the local communities, using investment and economic growth as instruments.

This complex network of direct and indirect powers, with social compacts and self-management agreements as additional constraints on firms, suggests that the influence of the workers' community on the firm's actions is fictitious. But there is evidence to the contrary. First, Yugoslav managers refer too frequently and too articulately to shop-floor sentiments—and the limits these sentiments pose to accumulation or changes in work rules or discipline—to be dismissed as lip service. Second, Yugoslavia's open political style allows the expression of dissatisfaction with economic events. Third, the frequent incidence of work stoppages, often caused by decisions supported by self-management organs, demonstrates that the formal workers' representation and the collective feelings of the community of workers are not automatically identical.[16] Since such conflicts contradict the cherished vision of social harmony, firms take the likely shop-floor response into consideration. Fourth, Yugoslav managers and administrators hint that the spirit of laws, regulations, social compacts, and self-management agreements must sometimes bend in order to maintain internal peace. This bending is one of the problems underlying many of the macroeconomic problems of Yugoslavia.[17]

Given so many influences, decisions tend to be compromises of the coalition of decisionmakers acting on unwritten rules and the perceptions of power. Since such compromises elude an analytical framework for evaluation, personalities and particular circumstances further muddle the mode of reaching decisions. This is not to say that decisions of Yugoslav firms are irrational but to indicate that Yugoslav firms are rarely optimizing according to a one-dimensional objective function. They rather tend to satisfy the interest of the coalition. In the process, the loss of analytical rigor may in part be replaced by a comprehensive input of information and by a stronger commitment resulting from the participation of all affected parties in the jointly agreed course of action.

The literature about the formal theory of the Yugoslav firm, based on normative or behavioral premises, is extensive. If the model of decisionmaking presented before is a valid approximation, there is limited value in reviewing the formal theory. The most common assumption is that the Yugoslav firm behaves like a producer cooperative and maximizes average personal income per worker. This line of analysis goes back to the seminal work of Ward on the Illyrian firm, a line that most of his successors maintained.[18] The model derived from this approach generates some perverse features. On the microeconomic level, it predicts a tendency toward a backward-sloping supply curve—that is, a reduction of output and employment in response to a rising price of the product, resulting in unstable markets.[19] In addition, the Illyrian firm exhibits the tendency toward ever-growing capital intensity, and it reaches its optimum if capital intensity, financed from credits, approaches infinity and all workers but the last are dismissed.

Finally, the Illyrian firm has a chronic tendency to distribute all income to workers. Since society appropriates net income that the firm retains as accumulation, the workers earn a part of the additional income from the investment-financed accumulation but have no ownership of the financial assets or any other rights or personal claims from appreciation of assets. If, on the other hand, workers distributed all income to themselves, they could invest a corresponding portion in private savings accounts, earn income from interest, and retain unrestricted ownership over the principal. Therefore, workers would voluntarily choose the former alternative only if the discounted value of the additional personal income exceeds cumulative interest, plus the value of principal, of private savings.[20] Since the financial planning period for households is usually short, and since there is less risk involved in private savings, workers would be willing to sacrifice present income only in cases of exceedingly profitable investment choices. Normally they would distribute all current income to themselves and prefer to finance investment from credits or to invest up to the limit of outside credits.

The main weakness of the Illyrian model is that its key assumptions are inconsistent with the present Yugoslav reality.[21] Due to the institutional environment, firms do not automatically identify with the personal income interests of the workers' community. They are not autonomous in their decisions on the distribution of net income because of the social compacts, self-management agreements, and political suasion. Firms cannot lay off workers to increase the productivity and personal incomes of the remaining ones (except through attrition). A choice between financing investment from credits or from retained earnings does not exist because the rules for bank credit require that firms provide some of the required investment resources themselves. Finally, the macroeconomic statistics do not support the predictions from this microeconomic theory (Horvat 1982, p. 342). The Illyrian model of a producer cooperative is a theoretical construct, apart from the inconsistency of its assumptions and predictions with the Yugoslav reality. The best-known model of industrial producer cooperatives, the highly successful Mondragon cooperative system in Spain, has demonstrated that the assumptions of the Illyrian model are by no means inherent to the cooperative (Thomas and Logan 1982).

Although the maximization of personal income per worker is the most common hypothesis, it is not the only one. The Yugoslav economist Branko Horvat, who apparently bases his hypothesis on direct observation, has made a particularly interesting case (1982, pp. 542–44). Firms start the planning process with an aspiration level of personal income per worker, according to the previous year's incomes, sales expectations, incomes in other firms, taxation, inflationary expectation, and so forth. Once the expected income level is figured into the plan, the Yugoslav firm behaves like a capitalist firm by striving to maximize profit (accumulation). The only difference is that real personal income may deviate from the planned level. Finally, other objectives—such as maximizing growth of employment, sales, or assets, with constraints on personal income growth and financial ratios—would be as plausible under the Yugoslav system as they are in a capitalist firm with dispersed and powerless shareholder ownership. Maximizing the growth of sales would be a logical choice as long as business managers, the local community, and the LCY all agree, even for different reasons, that growth is a desirable end. Priority for growth would be a realistic assumption if the workers' council is either coopted or meek, and if the workers' community is docile due to local unemployment.

If a social compact on income prescribes a link between average personal income per worker and productivity of the firm, if all parties in the coalition agree that maximizing average personal income per worker is the goal, and if the firm is reasonably healthy, the most likely pattern would be the following. The firm would probably, in the short run, choose the output level (or price level, according to its market position) that would maximize net income. This would permit the firm to distribute as much personal income as permitted under the prevailing rule while maximizing the residual accumulation, to be plowed back into the firm. The pattern of investment is likely to maximize the growth potential for average personal income by increasing and modernizing the capital stock as much as possible with the available resources and increasing labor productivity while stabilizing employment.

If the link to profitability becomes the rule and is applied without additional criteria that effectively neutralize it under the same assumptions made above, the firm would still behave the same way in the short run. The thrust of the growth strategy, however, is likely to be different. For any given level of output and prices, a technological change increasing capital intensity will reduce total net income, owing to higher depreciation, unless it also drastically reduces the coefficients of material inputs (an improbable and at best accidental side effect of rising capital intensity). At the same time, the share of accumulation that needs to be set aside from the reduced net income would also have to rise to meet the profitability condition for higher personal income payments. This, in turn, would reduce even further the portion of net income available for distribution as personal income to the workers. In addition, the reduction of the labor coefficient in production, without the right to dismiss redundant workers, would only be possible if output could increase drastically to keep the labor force at the same level without serious repercussions on the price. In short, although a continuing preference for capital intensity for the purpose of increasing income cannot be ruled out, it should become less likely than under the present rule.

Some Macroeconomic Implications

As an agenda for further inquiry, rather than as an attempt to draw definitive conclusions, a few observations can be made here on the parts of economic performance that the microeconomic rules of self-management seem to affect. I refrain here from speculating on which of the effects are genuinely systemic and which can be remedied by more efficient procedures and policies.

Until Yugoslavia was hit by the second wave of oil-price rises, the simultaneous rise of international interest rates, the economic slack in major export markets, and an acute debt crisis, its economic development was clearly a success. During the two decades from 1959 to 1979, the gross national product (GNP) grew by an average annual rate of more than 6 percent. Combined with an average annual population growth of about 1 percent, the result was a high growth of the standard of living. After 1979, however, the growth of output came to a near standstill. Employment generation in the social sector—often considered by outside observers as one of the failures of the Yugoslav system—proceeded at an impressive average rate of more than 3 percent during the twenty years of uninterrupted growth, and it continued to grow by 2.6 percent thereafter. This growth reflects the rapid transformation of the country, which led to a massive transfer of the labor force from peasant agriculture, where underemployment was endemic, to the modern sector.[22] Nevertheless, underemployment and unemployment are still sizable but increasingly localized, with emerging labor shortages in the more developed regions and persistent rural overpopulation and labor surpluses in the less developed ones. The comparison of the growth rates of GNP and employment also suggests that until 1979 productivity grew on average by an impressive rate of around 3 percent a year but declined in the crisis after 1979.

Investment in fixed assets grew slightly faster than GNP between 1959 and 1979 but dropped by a total of 20 percent thereafter. The investment rate during the 1970s, the decade of fastest growth, averaged 32 percent of GNP but was increasingly financed by foreign borrowing. The average incremental capital-output ratio (ICOR) during the decade of rapid growth came close to 6.0. Yugoslavia had a high share of investments in the nonproductive sectors (housing and social infrastructure) and in heavy infrastructure (roads), for which the partial ICORs tend to be high. Although the aggregate ICOR is a less-than-perfect yardstick for the efficiency of investment allocation even during periods of sustained rapid growth, there can hardly be any doubt that by international standards Yugoslavia was using its investment resources inefficiently. Regardless of country or economic system, the efficiency of investment allocation is believed to decline if the investment rate exceeds the 30 percent limit.

Yugoslavia's poorest record is in prices and the balance of payments. During the 1970s the average rate of inflation (wholesale price index) increased continuously at an average of about 14 percent per year. Between 1980 and 1984 it accelerated to an average of 45 percent a year, and it has accelerated further since. The current account deficits rose to about 6.5 percent of GNP in 1979, and the foreign debt reached 25 percent of GNP. As a result of the adjustment measures introduced, the current account changed to a small surplus in 1984, but foreign debt had grown by about a third in the intervening years.

Investment

Several interrelated reasons are frequently cited for the inefficiency in allocating investment resources. First, considerations of risk barely affect potential investors. Experience has taught them that, in cases of failure, relief will always be available, with bankruptcy and liquidation unlikely. Furthermore, the loss of financial assets in the case of failure is by itself no deterrent to risky or questionable ventures, since it is assumed by society, rather than by individuals or groups, regardless of their contribution to the outcome. The socialization of risks or of losses are terms frequently used in Yugoslavia to describe the absence of restraints on investment.

Second, decisionmaking by consensus and compromise within a coalition keeps investment choices from being based on an objective assessment of costs and benefits. Instead, those choices tend to be subject to the results of negotiations among parties, which can have different perceptions about their specific costs and benefits in the project. Under such circumstances, and if main proponents or opponents of a project are powerful, an unbiased assessment may not be possible, given the pressures on the staff of the bank and the bureaucracy.

Third, Yugoslav banks are not efficient intermediaries in channeling savings (from households or firms) to uses where the rate of return is highest. They are unable to do so because they are formally a service institution of their members; their autonomy to accept or reject credit requests on the economic merits of the project is very narrow. In addition, banks are bound to give priority to projects that have been included in the five-year plans. And they are subject to informal pressures by the governments of the republic and the local communes to give priority to their favored projects. Moreover, until very recently, bank credits were extended at highly negative real interest rates. This added a subsidy to borrowing and contributed to an excess credit demand over available resources, which made a careful screening of all project applications exceedingly difficult given the analytical limitations of banks.

Fourth, a firm's accumulation of funds remains under the control of the BOs that generated it and allocated it to their business fund. This leads to a built-in tendency for self-financing, either directly in the BO or firm or through self-management agreements on pooling of resources in an associated firm. Self-financing, particularly as a condition for additional credits, channels investment resources to recipients who were financially successful in the past but not to those who have economically promising projects for the future.

A related problem is the choice of technology. There is evidence that most Yugoslav firms tend to choose the most advanced technology available, which is often the most expensive one. The drive to maximize productivity—a response to the past income-distribution rule linking the upper limit of personal income to productivity—is further supported by the belief that without the most modern technology the country has no chance to compete internationally with low-wage countries.

A second problem is the restricted entry of new firms that would increase competition by offering better or cheaper products—and the restricted exit, through bankruptcy and liquidation or through merger, of firms that have a poor record of product quality and efficiency. Unrestricted entry and exit are crucial for effective competition and for the vitality of the economic system. But in this area the Yugoslav record is very poor. Established firms tend to have a strong support for their claims to resources, due to their connections; their major projects are also included in the social plans, assuring them credit priority. Potential new firms normally have no support. As a result, they cannot receive start-up credit or find partners willing to risk direct financing through pooling resources. On the exit side, a firm in trouble normally is able to marshall support for social reasons. This means debts are written off or extended; additional credits are made available; relief from taxes is granted; solidarity contributions come from other firms; joint reserve funds are tapped; and payment of supplier bills is delayed. These features—which characterize the soft budget constraint of the firm and which are as endemic in Yugoslavia as in most other socialist countries—provide almost unlimited protection against failure (Kornai 1980, chap. 13). Another reason they survive is that all major decisions are taken not by individuals who can be held accountable but by a coalition. That coalition, if the project is a major one, involves almost everyone with political leverage in the local community, if not the republic. Under such circumstances liquidation would expose an embarrassing collective error and is therefore to be avoided at almost any cost.

A common factor is the lack of mobility of capital and of the technical and managerial know-how associated with capital. Profitable self-managed firms have little interest in investing in other firms, except when such investments assure them of access to scarce raw materials or intermediary goods. Under the system of social ownership, investment in other firms transfers at least partial control over financial assets, and firms tend to prefer low-return internal investment under their own permanent control. This is also one of the reasons why there is almost no voluntary transfer of investment resources between republics, perpetuating the interregional income disparities.

The Labor Market

The absence of a labor market in which marginal productivity determines wage rates for each category of workers is another serious impediment to efficiency. Since workers do not receive a contractual wage—equalized by government fiat, collective bargaining, or the mobility of workers—the levels of personal income can vary greatly between firms even in the same industry. Much of this difference is the result of rents from free use of the firm's inherited social resources for which no compensation has to be paid to the society as the owner and of a monopolistic position in the small and regionally fractured Yugoslav market. So workers tend to stay with firms where personal incomes are higher—with the rent element growing with the age of the firm—rather than to move to jobs where the social marginal product is higher.

Commodity Markets

From an orthodox vantage point, the institutional model of price setting for producer goods by mutual agreement is bound to lead to inefficiency because of the suppression or exclusion of short-term market forces. It has frequently been observed that set input prices can reduce price responsiveness if firms are vertically linked. Similar links are standard practice, however, in many efficient industries in other countries. Evidently, industries producing a complex output, such as an automobile, require close collaboration with suppliers in areas ranging from product development to investment programming and quality control, collaboration that cannot function without some durable agreements on cooperation and the sharing of benefits.[23]

Perhaps more serious is the concern about collusion between vertically linked firms. Similarly, the limited size of the Yugoslav market and the difficulty of entry for new suppliers create opportunities for monopolistic practices. Horizontal contacts that exist formally through industry associations invite collusion among competitors. None of these distortions has been proved, but references to these problems by Yugoslav sources are too pointed to be easily dismissed as conjectures.

Inflation

There is no generally accepted theory of the causes of inflation in Yugoslavia, although most analysts suspect that at least some causes are systemic. Among the reasons for inflationary pressures is a persistent tendency of aggregate demand to exceed aggregate supply. The reason for this tendency is that firms have an almost insatiable investment hunger, driven by the illusion of shortages in the market, the lack of risk in the absence of financial penalties for failure (the soft budget constraint), and the moral value associated with growth. At the same time, firms want to satisfy the work force by raising personal income through increasing productivity. The result is that they often initiate ambitious investment projects with insufficient funds. To maintain liquidity and complete their projects, the firms then try to mobilize funds through higher prices. A second reason for inflationary pressure is that BOs or firms sharing income from the final stage of production have little concern about the rising of input prices. The reason is that the transfer price arrangement under a self-management agreement does not provide an incentive to hold material costs down at any stage of production. Monopolistic or oligopolistic practices may also play a part.

Another factor in inflation is the income inequality between firms. Income distribution is fairly egalitarian in each firm, due to a scale of work points ratified by the workers' councils. But the value per work point can differ greatly between firms, owing to their specific income situation and the contributions of profit and rent to personal incomes. In a socialist society committed strongly to the idea of equal pay for equal work, these differences propel a constant drive for higher incomes in firms that cannot really afford them and that raise their prices as a result.

The Yugoslav system may also be conducive to perpetuating the inflationary momentum once it has started. Since workers do not receive contractual nominal wages that are changed only from time to time, price increases for wage goods spill over into higher personal incomes almost instantaneously, feeding back into output prices. The absence of a wage drag keeps the vicious spiral in motion. It also explains why devaluations and increases in interest rates have fed the inflationary momentum rather than improved the balance of payments, reduced aggregate demand, or induced a more efficient pattern of investment (Lydall 1984, chap. 12).

Yugoslavia's antiinflationary policies have not been very successful so far. Until the second half of 1984, emphasis was given to various forms of price control that were, as is now acknowledged, ineffective in the short run and structurally distortive in the long run. These controls were abandoned. The scope for fiscal policies is limited, because the federal structure of the country reduces the federal share in revenues and expenditures and leaves much of fiscal autonomy to the republics and local communities without effective coordination. The Yugoslav fiscal system also has many specific earmarked taxes and quasi-taxes (mostly in the form of "contributions") for nonproductive services. The National Bank tries to pursue a restrictive monetary policy, but firms and banks resort to financial indiscipline. They default on payments or collections of debt service or on payments to suppliers. The effect is an involuntary creation of credit outside the regular monetary system. Furthermore, there are limits to the rigor with which monetary policy can be pursued when there is a danger of massive financial defaults with unacceptable political and economic costs. Systematic income policy, for which the instruments of social compacts seem suitable, has been used merely to affect the distribution of net income, not to reduce the pressures of income on prices.

Operational Efficiency

There has been much debate about the operational efficiency (X-efficiency) to be expected in the Yugoslav firm—that is, about the intensity of effort and the motivation of workers. Perfect X-efficiency would eliminate all institutional slack in the work process, raising output to what is technically attainable with the given productive assets, material inputs, and work force (Leibenstein 1978). Discipline, diligence, conscientiousness, and a sense of responsibility of the workers are the attitudes that lead to high X-efficiency.

Some people believe that X-efficiency in Yugoslavia can be attained only through coercion by hierarchical authority. They hold the view that X-efficiency tends to be low under the conditions prevailing in the Yugoslav firm: supervisors have no power to reward or punish workers, and the workers' collectives are too strongly affected by misplaced solidarity to bring social pressure to bear on shirkers (Lydall 1984, chap. 11). Other observers believe that self-management creates a heightened spirit of workers' responsibility that cannot be emulated effectively by coercion, particularly if high X-efficiency makes part of the labor force redundant. Under such circumstances, the supervision cost of effective coercion can become excessively high. Tyson (1979) argues that peer control can lead to more effective coercion than hierarchical coercion, and that the combination of profit-related personal incomes and self-management in relatively small BOs would create excellent conditions for high X-efficiency. But because X-efficiency eludes systematic measurement, it is not possible to assess the validity of these mutually exclusive assertions.

In comparison with a centralized, hierarchical institution of management, self-management may have an economic cost that may exceed its compensating economic benefits. For example, Horvat lists the following real problems that must be carefully examined: waste of time in discussions; confusion between guidance by the workers' council and day-to-day administration by the business managers, with the resulting conflicts and blurring of responsibility; divorce of decisionmaking and responsibility; popularity-based or inconsistent decisions; misconceived justice and misplaced solidarity; impossibility of separating political and administrative work; power based on control over information; fragmentation due to decentralization of decisionmaking and management in the firm; multiplication of conflicts in the absence of conflict-resolution through hierarchical authority; misuse of democratic procedures by individuals and groups in furthering their particular interests; and dangers of inefficiencies from indecision, and of regression into statism as the solution (Horvat 1982, p. 250). Since this catalog comes from an insider and a staunch proponent of self-management, these managerial problems have to be taken seriously.

Adjustment Behavior

Key features of the Yugoslav system—notably the dependence of personal incomes and accumulation on business success of the firm after covering all costs to the outside and the prohibition against laying off redundant workers—result in a specific adjustment pattern. Business fluctuations do not result in fluctuations of employment as in capitalist economies. The fluctuations, rather, affect the intensity of work and the levels of personal incomes and accumulation earned.[24] Under these rules, all workers in the firm or branch, or all members of society, share equally in the effects of economic booms and slumps. The burden of adjustment is not shifted to a minority.

In principle, the same mechanism should also permit a greater flexibility in price policy. If workers cannot be laid off, firms should be more willing to reduce prices (rather than output and input) than they would tend to do if employment were variable in the short run. A consistent application of the Yugoslav income accounting rules should lead to greater social and economic stability than exhibited by a system based on rigid wage contracts, unless other rules neutralize this potential.[25] It seems that the absence of a neoclassical labor market, considered elsewhere as an efficiency drawback, can be turned into an advantage.

Notes

1. Milenkovitch (1971) gives a detailed description of the ideological and institutional evolution for the transition period from traditional central planning (1948) to a socialist market economy (1965–70).

2. The enterprise as a legal concept has been replaced in Yugoslavia by a variety of other concepts, such as the Work Organization of Associated Labor and the Composite Organization of Associated Labor. In this chapter, they will be called by the generic term, "firm."

3. This chapter uses the official translation of the ALA, prepared by the Secretariat for Information of the Federal Assembly of Yugoslavia (Ljubljana, 1977), extensively as a source.

4. There are no formal requirements for membership. To elect members of the LCY as business managers is rather a matter of prudence, because cordial relations with the local community and the leadership in the republic can be as important for success or failure of the firm as professional competence. See Lydall 1984, p. 119.

5. Self-management agreements can also be concluded among firms or among BOs in different firms.

6. Sacks (1983, pp. 61–73) has elucidated these cohesive forces binding Yugoslav firms together.

7. Lydall (1984, pp. 112–15) arrives at the same assessment of a number of distinct formal and informal participant individuals, groups, or organizations forming jointly the "will" of the firm.

8. The federation consists of six republics and two autonomous provinces; for simplicity, and because in the economic sphere the differences are immaterial, this chapter uses the term "republic" for both republics and autonomous provinces. The country is organized into 527 local communities, with an average size of 41,300 inhabitants.

9. There is no unconditional job guarantee, however. Workers can be fired if they refuse to accept retraining for new jobs and reassignment to another comparable job in the same or another BO (ALA, arts. 211–19).

10. Before 1972, banks were managing repayments of earlier credits provided by the state and were permitted to generate accumulation of their own. This practice, however, was considered an alienation of surplus value from the producers and was replaced by the present framework.

11. The work force of the firm is, for the purpose of these computations, standardized by converting the distribution by skill categories into normalized "accounting workers."

12. This description is somewhat oversimplified. It seems to be a widespread practice to provide a moderate premium, in the order of up to 10 percent, to the value of work points of effective workers on the basis of suggestions by direct supervisors to a special committee of the workers' council. For a detailed description of the work-point system, see Schrenk (1981, pp. 51–54). There is also a bonus for seniority as a reward for past labor (that is, allocations to the business fund during all previous years of employment).

13. This chapter is not the place to analyze the methods and the record of Yugoslav planning. But one could add that the process of self-management planning, particularly its harmonization, has remained a puzzle to outside observers. Most of them tend to agree that no efficient approach to decentralized macroeconomic planning has yet emerged to match the decentralization of the economic system. See, for example, Lydall 1984, pp. 107 and 137–49, and Sacks 1983, p. 15.

14. Lydall (1984, pp. 112–15) arrives at the same assessment of a number of distinct formal and informal participant individuals, groups, or organizations forming jointly the will of the firm.

15. The relative spread of salary, however, is only moderate in comparison with capitalist firms and, according to some recent observations, rarely exceeds the range of four-to-one between the highest and lowest income in a firm. In addition, the salary scale of firms is determined by a fixed number of work points laid down in internal documents, and the reward to the business manager rises and falls by the same percentage as that of all other workers, depending on the position and success of the firm.

16. In 1980, 245 work stoppages occurred according to the Yugoslav press (Lydall 1984, p. 122). The drastic decline in real personal incomes thereafter is likely to have increased the frequency of spontaneous expressions of discontent.

17. Financial indiscipline resulting from inconsistent application of regulations at the microeconomic level, motivated by concern about economic discontent resulting from rigorous application, has been a common phenomenon in Yugoslavia for many years. In connection with discretionary support actions by state authorities, it makes for the pervasive efficiency losses of the system due to what Kornai (1980, chap. 13) calls the soft budget constraint.

18. See Ward 1958, Vanek 1970, and Meade 1974. An excellent summary of this traditional theory of the Yugoslav firm can be found in Estrin 1983, chap. 2. One cannot overemphasize, however, that Ward (1958) located his model in a mythical Illyria rather than in Yugoslavia, indicating merely a faint association. And Vanek (1970) speaks consistently about the labor-managed market economy rather than a self-managing one. Much of the subsequent literature ignored these important qualifications.

19. But Vanek (1970, pp. 53–56), following a similar argument by Domar (1966), has shown that a change in the model from the single-input and single-output case to the more realistic one of multiple inputs and joint outputs changes the supply response back to the normal type, though the elasticity of the supply response to price changes may be fairly low. And Lydall (1984, p. 39) demonstrated that the backward-sloping supply curve can occur only under conditions of perfect competition, hardly a realistic assumption about the prevailing market structure in Yugoslavia.

20. Workers would retain rather than distribute profits per dinar only if $(1 + r)^t - 1 > (1 + s)^t$, where r is the rate of return of the investment from accumulation, s the interest rate on savings, and t the time horizon in years. If, for example $s = 5$ percent, for $t = 5$, r would have to be in excess of 18 percent, and for $t = 3$, in excess of 27 percent; in both cases the uncertainty for income from investment would require an additional risk premium.

21. They may not always have been as unrealistic as at present. During the late 1960s, firms did have much more autonomy in distributing their net income, which led to an extensive political campaign against what was then termed "group-ownership behavior," denounced as inconsistent with the tenets of socialism.

22. The agricultural population declined from around 67 percent in 1948 to less than 20 percent by 1981.

23. It is widely believed that this cooperation is one of the reasons for the efficiency of Japan's automobile industry.

24. The year-to-year fluctuations of personal incomes and their determination by firm-specific business cycles—which would be predictable under the rules of Yugoslav income accounting—was shown in the income data for four Slovenian firms over a period of ten years. In all cases the work force grew by rather constant rates, whereas real output growth fluctuated considerably. As a result, both productivity (net income of the firm per worker) and personal income per worker fluctuated by astounding annual margins. While the average annual change of average personal incomes differed between the firms between −0.1 and +3.2 percent, annual changes within firms in sixteen out of thirty-six observations exceeded 10 percent per year, ranging from −23 percent and +41 percent from one year to another. See Schrenk 1981, p. 98.

25. This particular flexibility of a system based on a mixture of payment of contractual basic wages and success-dependent profit shares to workers—pointing to

Japan and South Korea as model cases—has been suggested recently in the theoretical literature. See Weitzman 1985.

References and Selected Readings

Assembly of the Socialist Federal Republic of Yugoslavia. 1977. *The Associated Labor Act of 1976*. English edition prepared by the Secretariat for Information. Ljubljana: Dopisna Delawska Univerza.

Bergson, Abram. 1982. "Entrepreneurship under Labor Participation: The Yugoslav Case." In Ronen Joshua, ed., *Entrepreneurship*. Lexington, Mass.: D. C. Heath.

Brus, Wlodzimierz. 1975. *Socialist Ownership and Political Systems*. London: Routledge and Kegan Paul.

Camisso, Ellen T. 1980. "Yugoslavia in the 1970s: Self-Management and Bargaining." *Journal of Comparative Economics* 4:192–208.

Domar, Evsey. 1966. "The Soviet Collective Farm as a Producer Cooperative." *American Economic Review* 56:734–57.

Estrin, Saul. 1983. *Self-Management: Economic Theory and Practice*. Cambridge: Cambridge University Press.

Furobotn, Eirik. 1976. "The Long-Run Analysis of the Labor-Managed Firm: An Alternative Interpretation." *American Economic Review* 66, no. 1 (March):104–23.

———. 1980. "The Socialist Labor-Managed Firm and Bank-Financed Investment: Some Theoretical Issues." *Journal of Comparative Economics* 4, no. 2 (June):184–91.

Furobotn, E., and S. Pejovich. 1970. "Property Rights and the Behavior of the Firm in a Socialist State: The Example of Yugoslavia." *Zeitschrift fuer Nationaloekonomie* 30:431–54.

Granick, David. 1975. *Enterprise Guidance in Eastern Europe*. Princeton, N.J.: Princeton University Press.

Horvat, Branko. 1982. *The Political Economy of Socialism*. Oxford: Martin Robertson.

Kornai, Janos. 1980. *Economics of Shortage*. 2 vols. Amsterdam: North-Holland.

Leibenstein, Harvey. 1978. *General X-Efficiency Theory and Economic Development*. New York: Oxford University Press.

Lydall, Harold. 1984. *Yugoslav Socialism: Theory and Practice*. Oxford: Clarendon Press.

Meade, James. 1970. *The Theory of Indicative Planning*. Manchester: Manchester University Press.

———. 1974. "The Theory of Labor-Managed Firms and Profit Sharing." *Economic Journal* 82, no. 1 (supplement, March):402–28.

Milenkovitch, Deborah D. 1971. *Plan and Market in Yugoslav Economic Thought*. New Haven, Conn.: Yale University Press.

———. 1977. "The Case of Yugoslavia." *American Economic Review, Proceedings* 67, no. 1 (February):55–60.

Nove, Alec. 1983. *The Economic Theory of Feasible Socialism*. London: Allen and Unwin.

Nuti, Mario. 1981. "Socialism on Earth." *Cambridge Journal of Economics* 5:391–403.

Prasnikar, Janos. 1985. "Observing Behavior of Yugoslav Self-Managing Firms and Present Yugoslav Economic Reforms." *Journal of Comparative Economics.*

———. 1983. "Case Study of Brewery Union, Ljubljana." Unpublished draft.

Sacks, Stephen R. 1983. *Self-Management and Efficiency: Large Corporations in Yugoslavia.* London: Allen and Unwin.

Schrenk, Martin. 1981. *Managerial Structures and Practices in Manufacturing Enterprises: A Yugoslav Case Study.* World Bank Staff Working Paper 455. Washington, D.C.

Schrenk, Martin, Cyrus Ardalan, and Nawal El Tatawy. 1979. *Yugoslavia.* Baltimore, Md.: Johns Hopkins University Press.

Selucky, Radoslav. 1974. "Marxism on Self-Management." *Critique,* no. 3 (Autumn):49–63.

Thomas, Henk, and Chris Logan. 1982. *Mondragon: An Economic Analysis.* Winchester, Mass.: Allen and Unwin.

Tyson, Laura D'A. 1979. "Incentives, Income Sharing, and Institutional Innovation in the Yugoslav Self-Managed Firm." *Journal of Comparative Economics* 3, no. 3 (September):285–301.

Vanek, Jaroslav. 1970. *The General Theory of Labor-Managed Market Economies.* Ithaca, N.Y.: Cornell University Press.

———. 1977. *The Labor-Managed Economy.* Ithaca, N.Y.: Cornell University Press.

Ward, Benjamin M. 1958. "The Firm in Illyria: Market Syndicalism." *American Economic Review* 48, no. 1 (March):566–89.

Weitzman, Martin L. 1985. "Profit Sharing as Macroeconomic Policy." *American Economic Review, Proceedings* 75, no. 2 (March):41–45.

World Bank. 1975. *Yugoslavia: Development with Decentralization.* Baltimore, Md.: Johns Hopkins University Press.

INDEX

Administrative barriers to flow of producer goods, 222–25; circumventing, 225–28
Administrative solutions, 51, 202–03, 204
Administrative structure, 49–50; authority and, 62, 278, 309; decisionmaking and, 81, 216–30; factor allocation and, 98–99; segmented authority of, 278
Allocation of materials, 5, 42, 108; commodity trading and, 234; gaps between requirements and, 216–22; output plans and, 105, 121, 145; system of, 229–30
Anshan Iron and Steel Corporation, 214, 285–86; collectives of, 71–72
Association of Chongqing Clock and Watch Company, 290. *See also* Chongqing Clock and Watch Company
Associations, 92–97, 277, 289–92; restrictive labor quotas and, 72. *See also* Corporations
Automobiles, 212, 233–34
Autonomy, 19, 39; capability for, 44–50; conditions needed for, 55–59, 204; expansion of, 172, 297; factor allocation and, 98; financial, 4–5; over investment, 9, 83–84; in lower levels of government, 181; need for, 133; restricted, 66

Banking system, 91–92; financial controls through, 83; loans and, 85, 89, 90; in Yugoslavia, 348, 355. *See also* Loans
Baoji Nitrogen Fertilizer Plant, 212
Bargaining, 198–99, 203; with authorities, 62, 183; between enterprises, 170. *See also* Barter
Barriers to flow of goods, 222–25; circumventing, 225–28; transport, 220–21
Barter: to circumvent administrative barriers, 225–26; between enterprises, 107, 108; lifting of ban against, 226; to obtain above-plan supplies, 193. *See also* Bargaining
Basic Organizations of Associated Labor (BOS), 341–44, 349–52
Bonuses, 17, 114, 115; incentive system and, 182; for managers, 62, 73; minimum level of, 184; plan fulfillment and, 184; productivity and, 73–74; profits and, 184; taxes and, 52, 73; for workers, 3, 4, 17, 73
Budget constraints, 53–55
Businesses. *See* Enterprises
Buyers' markets, 147, 201; for commodities, 238; competition and, 240; creation of, 9; economic performance and, 204, 268–70; enterprise responses to, 243–44; government responses to, 254–56; in Hungary, 321–22; for investment goods, 267; prices and, 192, 241; production plans and, 178; reversing, 257; sustaining, 265–68; variety targets and, 192

Capital: Chinese markets for, 91; cost of, 4, 5, 90–91; foreign, 305; per worker, 14; in Yugoslavia, 347–48, 361–62. *See also* Investment; Investment finance
Capital goods. *See* Investment goods
Centralization, 123–24, 133
Central planning. *See* Planning
Chengdu Locomotive and Rolling Stock Factory, 219–20

China Petrochemical Industrial Corporation, 285
Chongqing Clock and Watch Company, 52, 55, 192, 290–92
Cities, economic network of, 166–67
CMEA. *See* Council for Mutual Economic Assistance
Collectives, 7, 70–72
Commodities: distribution of, 211; marketing plans for, 164; reforms of process of, 137–38; relation to currency, 154, 155; scarcity of, 161; prices of, 140, 142; trading of, 234–35; Yugoslavia markets for, 362
Communication, inadequacy of, 228–31
Communist Youth League, 309
Companies. *See* Corporations; Enterprises
Compensation trade, 6, 93, 194–95
Competition, 49, 56–57, 66–67, 108, 238–41, 255; in Hungary, 320–23; obstacle to development of, 259; patterns of, 257–62
Consumer goods: distribution of, 154; market adjustments and, 262–64; supply and marketing of, 210; wholesale markets for industrial, 238
Contracts: for goods, 164, 211; for workers, 116
Corporations: administrative, 50, 293; advantages of, 281–82; development of, 282–84; enterprise-type, 293, 294–95; examples of, 284–92; formation of, 277, 281; industrial, 92, 94, 281–95; integrated industrial, 285–86; nationwide readjustments of, 282–84; organizing of, 278, 292; plants and enterprises not participating in, 292; specialized national, 211, 283. *See also* Associations
Cost reduction, 239; lack of pressure for, 269
Council for Mutual Economic Assistance, (CMEA), 103–04
Cultural Revolution, 300
Current operations, regulation of, 117–23

Data. *See* Information
Decisionmaking authority: compartmentalization of, 81; economic, 47; of enterprises, 47–49, 286, 288; information for, 228–31; of management committee, 310; of state, 47
Delivery problems, 220–21, 222
Demand: meeting popular, 46–47; and supply relationship, 49, 133, 216–22, 234
Dependents: employment of, 62, 63, 70–72; of state workers, 7
Depreciation funds, 85, 89–90
Distribution: of industrial products, 237; market mechanism for, 107–09, 237; of producer goods, 103–09
Dongfeng Automobile Corporation, 289–90, 292

Economy: adjustment and reform program for, 1, 2–3; diversity of market conditions in, 238; in Hungary, 317–18, 322; methods for managing China's, 155–57; planned commodity, 134, 234; socialist, 149–50, 154–55, 268–70; weakness of Chinese, 1, 146; in Yugoslavia, 314–16, 365
Education: job transfers and, 116; of workers, 164. *See also* Training
Egalitarianism, 4; pressures for, 73, 74; rewards for performance and, 114
Electricity: allocation of, 190; shortage of, 105, 189–90
Employment. *See* Labor; Workers
Enterprises: acquisition by other, 94; assessing performance of, 169–70; associations of, 19, 72, 92–97; autonomy of, 4–5, 9, 19, 39, 44–50, 55–59, 66, 83–84, 98, 133, 172; behavior of, 170–74; benefits and, 52–53; central and regional control over, 125; differences between Soviet and Chinese state-owned, 103, 105, 107, 109, 110, 111, 113, 117, 119–20, 121, 122, 123, 124–25, 126; driving force of, 51–55; expansion of, 61, 63–64; experimental, 16; government and, 150–52, 345–47; in Hungary, 323–30, 332; jurisdiction over, 49–50; large, 58; leadership in, 180–82, 278–80, 297–312; lifelong attachment of workers to, 98; market forces and, 153–54,

241–53, 313; motivations of, 3, 62–67; objectives of, 45–47, 61–67; ownership and operation of, 9, 158–59, 287; pilot reform, 16; planning for, 117–23, 168, 171, 172; relationships among, 42, 92–98, 103, 107, 170–71, 311, 318, 347–49; relocation of, 79; self-management of Yugoslavian, 339–41, 347, 364; special treatment of, 57; status of state industrial, 149–52; in study sample, 11, 13–19; trade among, 42, 103, 170–71; vitality of, 39, 44–50, 136, 139; in Yugoslavia, 341–44, 355–59, 361–62

Equipment: imports of, 265; needs, 163; replacing, 224

Exit: difficulty with, 259; forced, 258; as response to buyers' market, 243–44; as response to deterioration in quality, 203–04; sellers' markets and, 243

Exports, 250–51

Factor allocation: interenterprise relations and, 97–98; system of, 99; weak market mechanism for, 98

Family motive, 40, 41, 62–63, 66, 67

Financial controls, 82–83

Financing. *See* Investment finance

Firms. *See* Enterprises

Fixed assets: fee, 90–91; taxes on, 4, 90

Foreign exchange: corporate retention of, 196, 286; for imports, 226–27

Gang of Four, 283, 303

Goals. *See* Objectives of enterprises; Targets

Government: benefits of enterprises, 52; decisionmaking authority of, 47; enterprise and, 150; financial help from, 54; lower levels of, 198; policies of, 53; response to market conditions, 147, 253–57; in Yugoslavia, 345

Grants, 85, 89

Great Leap Forward, 299

Hiring. *See* Recruitment

Horvat, Branko, 357–58, 364

Hungary: buyers' market in, 321–22; competition in, 320–23; economy of, 317–18, 322; financial ties of enterprises in, 323–28; firms' development funds in, 328–30; interenterprise sellers' market in, 107, 318; investment in, 328–30, 331; mandatory plan indicators in, 317–19; market economy in, 319–23, 332–34; price system in, 320–21, 327; profit of firms in, 324–25, 328; reform in, 314; survival of firms in, 332; wage-profit relation in, 328

Incentives, 3, 4; bonuses and, 182; enterprise, 7; innovation and, 224; for investment, 88–91; market, 125; multiple objectives and, 66; new system of, 179–80; performance and, 126–27; planning and, 197–98; pricing of agricultural products and, 139; response to, 7; Soviet payments for, 112. *See also* Motivation

Incomes: enterprise performance and, 126–27; inequality of, 115; of peasants, 139; personal, 350–51, 352; seniority and, 114; as workers' motive, 62

Industrial organization, 6–7. *See also* Corporations; Enterprises

Industrial products: marketing of, 5, 232–35; distribution of, 237; supply of, 231–32. *See also* Consumer goods; Producer goods

Information: availability of, 166; from enterprise to state, 172; inadequacy of, 228–31; on international market, 58; need for economic, 137; prices as, 58; technological advances in, 161; use of market, 155

Innovation: lack of incentive for, 224; technological, 239

Integrated economic entities. *See* Associations

Integration, regional, 292–93

Interenterprise relations, 42, 92–98, 103, 107, 170–71, 311, 318, 347–49; achievements and problems of, 96–97; factor allocation and, 97–98; kinds and examples of, 92–97

Interenterprise trade, 42, 103, 170–71

Interregional trade, 258–60

Inventory problems, 221–22
Investment, 39; ceilings on, 81; demand for, 88–89; enterprise authority over, 48; foreign, 6; funding of, 81–83, 84–85, 88, 124; government-mandated increases in, 257; in Hungary, 328–30, 331; incentives for, 88–91; mechanisms for control of, 80–84; prime constraint on, 92; of profits, 290, 291; state control of, 48; in Yugoslavia, 360
Investment finance, 4–5, 81–83, 84, 124; cost of, 88–89, 90–91; implications of, 91–92; new methods for; 85, 88; profit retention for, 85; self-, 85; sources of, 89–90
Investment goods: buyers' market for, 267; market adjustments and, 264–65. *See also* Producer goods

Jinling Petrochemical General Corporation, 220, 285–86
Jobs. *See* Recruitment
Joint ventures, 6, 79–80, 93, 96; failures of, 97; Sino-foreign, 305

Labor: allocation of, 67–69, 74–76; costs, 350; excess, 72; factor markets for, 109–17; hiring of, 69–72; incentives for, 73–74; mobility of, 42, 56, 74, 122; productivity of, 69; quotas, 68, 69, 70, 72; recruitment of, 121, 122. *See also* Workers
Labor force: allocation of, 121; output plans and, 122; plans for distribution of, 164; sex ratio in, 164
Labor-managed firms, 61
Labor markets, 42, 56, 103, 113–17; obstacles to creation of, 115; Soviet, 109–13, 117; in Yugoslavia, 347, 362, 365
Land: allocation of, 76–77; 79–80, 98; compensation for, 76; means of obtaining, 78–79; price of, 77, 80; shortage of, 77; use of, 77, 78–79, 80; waste of, 80
Leadership system: abuses of, 303–06; basic principles of, 303; historical review of, 297–302; multiple, 65, 162–64, 166, 302, 303; new developments in, 303, 305; plant directors and, 299, 302, 306–12; research on, 11; Soviet, 299; staff and worker participation in, 298, 299, 302, 305, 310; in state enterprises, 278–80. *See also* Management
Loans, 4, 5; bank, 85, 89; between individuals, 56; repayment of, 90, 91
Localism, 42, 124–25
Losses: risk and, 54; subsidies to offset, 55

Machinery: imports of, 265; marketing of, 237
Management: award for, 16; by committee, 310; decisions of, 126; democratic, 301, 305, 309–10; excessive reliance on, 133; of plants, 298; reforms in, 3–7; by revolutionary committees, 300; by the state, 50; in Yugoslavia, 364–65. *See also* Leadership system
Management system, 11, 278, 293–94; in Yugoslavia, 342–44. *See also* Leadership system
Managers: appointment of, 279; authority of, 62; compliance and, 65; concerns of, 125; engineers as, 64; factory, 7; plan targets and rewards for, 61; salaries of, 62. *See also* Plant directors
Market forces: and allocation of materials, 55, 228, 240; constraints on enterprise objectives and, 66–67; cost reduction and, 239; enterprises' responses to, 241–53; government responses to, 253–57; in Hungary, 319–23, 332–34. *See also* Competition
Marketing: direct, 247, 249–51; of industrial products, 5–6, 146, 232–33, 287; removal from government control of, 235. *See also* Self-marketing
Market mechanism: benefits from, 239; for distribution of products, 107–09, 237; for factor allocation, 98
Markets, 238–41; associations and position in, 95; bureaucratic intervention and, 314, 320; commodity, 362; for inputs and outputs, 251–53; for means of production, 237–38; opening and guidance of, 57;

planning and, 152–57; regulatory role of, 125; segmentation of, 42, 107–08; steel, 233; socialist, 268–70; use of, 107–09, 177; in Yugoslavia, 349. *See also* Buyers' markets; Labor markets; Sellers' markets
Materials: distribution of, 105–06, 222–28; supply of, 163. *See also* Allocation of materials; Producer goods; Raw materials
Mergers, 94, 96, 292; failures of, 97; to increase land, 79–80; to overcome supply problems, 185, 195–96; restrictive labor quotas and, 72; into specialized industrial corporations, 283, 284
Mindong Electrical Machinery Corporation, 94–95, 286–88, 293
Monopolies, 57; regional, 107
Motivation, 40, 41, 62–67; for associating by enterprises, 95–96; income and, 62, 126. *See also* Incentives

Nanning Textile Mill, 92–93
Negotiation. *See* Bargaining; Barter
New products, 288, 290
No. 2 Automobile Plant, 212, 233–34, 292

Objectives of enterprises, 45–47, 61–67
Operations, authority over, 144, 310
Ordering conferences, 211, 219, 238
Output: allocation of industrial, 175; constraints on, 189; sale of, 125; targets for, 45–46, 105, 121, 145, 182; per worker, 14. *See also* Production
Overstaffing, 68–69, 72, 74
Ownership of enterprises, 9, 158–59, 287

Party committees in plant management, 299, 300, 302, 304, 309
Performance: assessments of, 169–70; incentives and, 126–27; prizes for, 288
Piece-rate system, 73, 74, 114–15
Planning, 5–6; central, 81, 144, 175, 176–77, 267; changes in theory of, 148–49; focus for, 166–67; forecasting and, 137; forms of, 157–62, 167; fragmented, 185; macro- and micro-, 148; mandatory, 8; markets and, 152–57; multiple leadership in, 162–64; responsibility in, 133; time frames for, 167–69; in Yugoslavia, 353–55, 358
Planning system, 162–67; defects of, 42–43, 133; evaluation of, 196–202; flexibility of, 135; main features of, 175–84; model for, 132; needed changes in, 172; reforms of, 133–34, 136–37; scope of, 132
Plans, 144; allocation of materials and, 121, 145; annual, 117, 137, 167, 171; for enterprises, 119–23; five-year, 167; formal, 42; fulfillment of, 119–20, 184; guidance of, 134, 136, 159–60, 179; irrelevancy of, 120; land-use, 80; long-range, 137; mandatory, 134, 157, 158, 160, 161–67, 168; multiyear, 123; output, 105, 121, 145; overfulfillment of, 182; production, 219; revision of, 183; Soviet enterprise, 117–19
Plant directors, 304–05; authority of, 308–09; election of, 310; reports to staff-and-worker assembly, 298; responsibilities of, 299, 302, 306–12; as state's representative, 311. *See also* Managers
Power: of lower levels of government, 198; political abuse of, 165
Prices, 5–6; adjustments of, 260–62; of agricultural products, 139; buyers' and sellers' markets and, 192, 260–62, 268, 270; commodity, 138, 140, 142; competition and, 257–62; control of, 48–49, 194; differences in, 57–58, 106, 108, 145; dual, 140; government responses in, 256; in Hungary, 320–21, 327; in interenterprise trade, 103; lags in changes of, 270; marginal, 103; market, 140; of means of production, 235; multiple, 106, 108, 177, 199–201; policies for, 106; of raw materials, 286; reform of, 8, 43, 108, 127, 137–42, 145, 204–05; in Yugoslavia, 349, 351–52
Producer goods: categories of, 175–76; competition for, 223; delivery problems of, 220–21; distribution of, 103–09; gaps between allocations of and requirements for, 216–22; obtaining (by enterprises),

Producer goods (*continued*)
210–16; state management of, 210. *See also* Investment goods
Product design, 224, 290
Production: allocation of, 144; ceilings on, 256; departures from plans for, 125; dependence on supplies, 218; plans for, 121, 122; responsibility for targets of, 181; subcontracting of, 79; system to regulate, 52–53. *See also* Output; Socialist production
Productivity: bonuses and, 73–74; labor, 69; total factor, 14, 60, 74
Product mix: altering of, 247; determination of, 126; enterprises' right to choose, 204; profitability and, 126, 260; supply constraints and, 191–97
Product use value, 46–47
Profit: bonuses and, 4, 184; as a goal or motive, 46, 65; in Hungary, 324–25, 328; as incentive, 3, 180; rate of, 14, 251; responsibility for, 54; remittance of, 3, 52, 261; retention of, 3–4, 17, 62, 90; sharing of, 290; targets, 52; tax on, 91; use of retained, 62, 65, 85, 88; in Yugoslavia, 350
Profitability: in buyers' market, 251; as determinant of product mix, 126; expansionist enterprises and, 63–64; influence on investment, 83; product mix and, 126, 260; promotions and wages and, 18
Project approval, 80–81
Promotions, 18, 62
Protectionism: internal, 256–57; regional, 107, 144

Quality of products, 64, 203
Qingdao Forging Machinery Plant, 53, 212–13
Qinghe Woolen Textile Mill, 219
Quotas, 126, 132; labor, 68, 69, 70, 72

Ratchet effect, 46, 144, 182, 352
Raw materials: agricultural, 210; internal prices for, 286; sources of, 251–52; supplies of, 190
Recruitment, 18, 69–72, 121–22
Reforms: by Central Committee in 1978, 300; Chinese debate over, 39; direction of, 134–35; in Hungary, 314; future, 7, 42, 306–08; needed, 99, 133–34, 172–73; in 1984, 300; objectives of, 1–5, 146; price controls during, 49; of pricing, 8, 43, 108, 127, 137–42, 145, 204–05; principles of, 8–9, 134, 202–05; progress in, 231–35; trial, 54
Regions: authorities in, 103, 123–25; development of backward, 55; evaluating success of, 132; integration of, 292–93; markets of, 107–08; movement of funds and materials between, 55; movement of labor between, 56; protectionism in, 107, 144
Regulation: through planning and markets, 153–54; price as means of, 139; of socialist economic development, 155
Research: institute for, 291; and production, 287
Resources: barriers to flow of, 222–28; sharing of, 286. *See also* Producer goods; Raw materials
Retail outlets, 238, 267

Sales promotion, 238
Self-marketing, 5, 19, 177, 178–79, 266, 286
Sellers' markets, 147, 240; causes of, 104; in centrally planned economies, 238; competition and, 204; enterprise responses to, 241–42; in Hungary, 107, 318; government responses to, 147, 254; prices and, 192
Shanghai No. 17 Cotton Mill, 93, 97
Shenyang Smelting, 215
Shortages: chronic, 99, 240; demand for investment goods and, 268; of electricity, 105, 189–90
Socialist countries: buyers' markets in, 270; China and, 143; economic functions in, 151–52; economy in, 149–50, 165; market forces in, 228; planning organization in, 165; production goals in, 46

Soviet labor market, 109–13, 117
Soviet management and leadership system, 299
Special Economic Zones, 6
Staff-and-worker assembly, 298, 299, 302, 305, 310
State. *See* Government
State industrial enterprises. *See* Enterprises
State Material Supply Bureau, 210
State Planning Commission, 210
Steel market, 233
Supplies: allocation of, 178, 181; arrangements for, 211–16; importing, 196; mechanisms for obtaining, 145; obtaining above-quota, 192–96; ordering problems, 218–20; from outside the plan, 187–88; production dependent on, 218; stockpiling of, 222; underallocation of, 186–88. *See also* Investment goods; Producer goods
Supply: access to, 95; constraints on, 188–92; and demand relationship, 49, 133, 216–22, 234; flexibility of, 201; of materials, 163; multiple channels of, 175, 184–86, 199
Supply system: constraints in, 188–92; evaluation of, 196–202; fragmentation of, 185

Targets: allocation of supplies and output and, 145; annual rise in, 46; assignment of, 132; of enterprises, 170, 177–80; evaluating success in meeting, 132; managerial rewards and fulfillment of, 61; output, 45–46, 105, 121, 145, 182; policy, 166; production, 181, 182; profit, 52; revision of, 183; set by state, 45. *See also* Goals
Taxes: on bonuses, 52, 73; on fixed assets, 4, 90; product, 288; sales, 124; profit retention and, 3–4, 16–17; value added, 288
Technology: batch production, 246; continuous process, 246; and forecasting, 161; foreign, 6; incentives and, 64, 224; profits and, 290; in Yugoslavia, 361
Textile enterprises, 213–14
Tianjin Color Textile Corporation, 288–89
Trade: compensatory, 106–07; inter-enterprise, 42, 103, 170–71; inter-regional, 258–60; in producer goods, 103
Training: of new state employees, 121; of technicians and managers, 290, 291. *See also* Education
Transport: inadequate capacity of, 220–21; restrictions on, 227

Unions, 309

Value, law of, 134, 137, 153
Vitality of enterprises, 39, 44–50, 136, 139

Wages, 4, 17–18; bonus payments and, 73, 184; differentiation of, 42; funds for, 111, 114, 122; in Hungary, 328; reforms of, 74; rigidity of, 73; seniority and, 114; in Yugoslavia, 347, 350
Wholesale networks and outlets, 211
Workers: appointment of managers and, 62–63; assignment of incapacitated or aged, 164; benefits to, 52, 63; bonuses for, 3, 4, 17, 73; contract, 69–70; contracts for, 116; demands for higher income, 126; dismissal of, 18, 42, 68, 72, 114, 116; education and, 164; employment of dependents of, 62, 63, 70–72; female, 69; hiring of, 18, 69–72; incentives for, 3, 4, 73; managers and interests of, 63; number in collective industrial enterprises, 6; participation in management, 298, 299, 302, 305, 310; production responsibilities of, 171; promotion of, 115; recruitment and training of, 121–22; relation to enterprise, 62, 98; unemployment of young, 62. *See also* Labor; Staff-and-worker assembly
"Work Regulations for State-Owned Industrial Enterprises" (Central Committee, 1961), 302–03

Xiangxiang Cement Plant, 215

Yugoslavia: banks in, 348, 355; Basic Organizations of Associated Labor (BOS)

Yugoslavia (*continued*)
in, 341–44, 349–52; capital in, 347–48, 361–62; characteristics of economy in, 314–16; choice of technology in, 361; commodity markets in, 362; economic adjustment in, 365; firms in, 341–44, 355–59, 361–62; inflation in, 362–64; investment in, 360; labor costs in, 350; labor-managed firms in, 61; labor market in, 347, 362, 365; layers of government in, 345; macroeconomic implications of self-management in, 359–65; management structure in, 342–44; managerial problems in, 364–65; market for goods and services in, 349; operational efficiency in, 364–65; party role in, 343; personal incomes in, 350–51, 352; planning in, 353–55, 358; prices in, 349, 351–52; profit and loss in, 350; ratchet effect in, 352; relations between firms in, 347–49; relation of firms to state in, 345–47; self-management in, 339–41, 347, 364; sharing of income and of risk in, 352; wages and salaries in, 347, 350